*C*YBERSPACE:
THE HUMAN DIMENSION

CYBERSPACE:
THE HUMAN DIMENSION

David B. Whittle

W. H. FREEMAN AND COMPANY

NEW YORK

COVER DESIGNER: Michael Minchillio / Victoria Tomaselli

TEXT DESIGNER: Victoria Tomaselli

Library of Congress Cataloging-in-Publication Data
Whittle, David B.
      Cyberspace : the human dimension / David B. Whittle
      p.   cm.
      Includes bibliographical references and index.
      ISBN 0-7167-8311-8 (hardcover).
      1. Information superhighway—Social aspects. I. Title
HE 7568.W47   1996
302.23—dc20   96-18801
                                                CIP

Printed in the United States of America
First printing 1997, RRD(H)

W. H. Freeman and Company
41 Madison Avenue, New York, NY 10010
Houndmills, Basingstoke RG21 6XS, England

*T*o my family—Serena, Jared, Nicia, Michael, Andrew, and Ashley—
with high hopes that their eternally treasured lives will be
richer and fuller for knowing cyberspace.

CONTENTS

Preface

PREFACE

Are you new to cyberspace? Or have you spent time on the Internet or online services like CompuServe, Prodigy, or America Online but found it a less enjoyable experience than you expected? Perhaps you have decided to postpone your entrance into this controversial new virtual world or minimize your participation there, basing your decision on things you've heard or read in the press about abusive behavior, privacy, or pornography. Or do you recognize the enormous potential of cyberspace but believe its culture to be in some ways ethically immature? If so, this book was written for you. I hope it will attract even more caring, decent people to cyberspace than are already there. I hope it will help provide a perspective on the electronic frontier that will help you understand the importance of participating not only in cyberspace but also in the national debate on the information superhighway.

This book was conceived during a lunch with my friend Jim Seymour, on his deck overlooking beautiful Wren Valley in the hill country outside Austin, Texas. As we discussed technology and trends in cyberspace that spring day in 1994, I bemoaned the lack of attention in the ongoing discussions and debates on cyberspace to qualitative human issues such as culture, language, morality, and ethics, attention that would lead to positive experiences online. Without hesitation or equivocation, Jim said, "You need to write a book." Within weeks, I was once again having lunch at Jim's—this time with Burt Gabriel, at the time an editor for W. H. Freeman and Company. He shared my view for a serious but popular book that would bring together in a readable and comprehensive manner the numerous issues that surround cyberspace.

Although this project has been through the inevitable pains of birth, it remains true, I hope, to the original vision. There are hundreds of books that will tell you *how* to get wired. This book will help you understand *why* you should be connected. It is meant for anyone—novice or experienced user—who wants to understand the human issues, opportunities, and challenges surrounding the cyberspace phenomenon. It introduces many of the key issues that must be addressed in our national debate and are being discussed daily in the press. It offers food for thought to help make your experiences in cyberspace more rewarding. It particularly benefits those who may not have the time or inclination to research each topic in depth but nonetheless want to see how the various issues concerning cyberspace fit together. Much has been written on advances in technology and its exploitation via the information superhighway and on legislation regulation and organizations related to cyberspace. Discerning how all this fits together and why it is relevant to you and your family—the human dimension of cyberspace—proves extremely difficult.

The success of books like Stephen Covey's *Seven Habits of Highly Effective People* and M. Scott Peck's *The Road Less Traveled* confirms my belief that large numbers of readers want to discuss personal and social issues in a context that is both culturally grounded and spiritually rewarding. As we face the prospect of spending more of our lives than ever in the mental realm we've named cyberspace, I hope this book not only offers novice readers an introduction to cyberspace but also provides insight and meaning to the many changes being wrought by cyberspace and the related communications technologies in society, the economy, business, and politics and in our personal and family lives.

You may encounter on these pages many things that surprise you. You will find discussion of most of the issues that constitute the national debate: free speech and censorship, the nature of the public and private realms, government regulation and private sector initiative. Discussions of values, argumentation, logic, anonymity, and the role of the individual may not appear immediately relevant to cyberspace. If cyberspace were merely a technology, I would agree; but it is also a society and a culture. We have to approach our discussion using the same parameters we would in a study of any other culture. Wouldn't you be disappointed if you bought a guide to Italy that told you only how to get there, how the trains work, and what time stores and offices are open? Wouldn't you look for the discussions on the people, the language, the culture, and the history? Cyberspace has a history, a short but dynamic one. I lived through it, and on these pages I share personal experiences with the reader in the hope that the roots of cyberspace will be exposed in meaningful and provocative ways. I hope that by describing the impact of the online culture and the debates surrounding OS/2, Windows, IBM, and Microsoft, readers will see how cyberspace cultures have been influenced by certain beliefs and assumptions and will understand the implications for them, their communities, their companies, and their political perspectives.

Since my first online experience in 1978, I estimate that I have spent, conservatively, almost 15,000 hours in cyberspace—roughly the equivalent of seven full-time work years. I asked Serena, my partner in life, what she has seen of the results and impact of those many hours on me and her and our family and on others. She said, "There is good and evil in the world and there are those who embrace good with hope to enrich humanity and there are those who are insecure who indulge in evil that harms themselves and others. I have encountered some caring people in cyber-space who see it as a way to benefit humanity, and I consider them friends who have inspired me and helped me become a better person. There are also people out there who degrade, demoralize, and harm others—often unaware of the impact they're having." Remember that technology is neu-tral. I hope my experiences, including those I'm ashamed of and those I'm proud of, help illuminate the human dimension of cyberspace.

The book bridges generations, the generations within cyberspace and the generations within families. My aunt says that after reading the manuscript, she was able to have an intelligent discussion with her wired, computer-savvy son for the first time. That's gratifying: I can think of no higher value for my efforts than helping to bridge the gaps between people in positive ways, especially between those who are already wired and those who are yet to be. My fondest dream for this book would be for it to be read by families and in neighborhood, civic, and church groups as part of their discussion on the role cyberspace will play in their activities and how they will interact with it.

If you're like me, you don't necessarily read every book cover to cover, and I organized this book with that tendency in mind. Let me offer a few suggestions. The book is divided into two parts. If you are new to cyberspace, you'll want to read or peruse Part One, Cyberspace, for the necessary grounding in concepts and terms before continuing onto the heart of the book in Part Two, The Human Dimension. Those already familiar with cyberspace can profitably skip the first three chapters and dive right into Part Two (Chapters Four through Eight), then return to Part One for tips, tools, reference, and perspectives.

Part Two is structured thematically. Four concentric circles of dis-cussion start with the individual and move outward through issues of soci-ety, business, and government. This organization places the individual at the heart of the book. If cyberspace is to be a meaningful experience, if the vir-tual communities are to constitute a true society, if business, as well as poli-tics, is to be conducted responsibly online, then all of us must define our own roles in cyberspace just as we do in our neighborhoods and in our economic and political communities in real space. I'll also tell you up front that I'm biased: in my view of life, the good guys always win in the long run. So since this isn't a mystery novel, you can, of course, just jump to Chapter Eight and start at the end. You see the cyberspace I envision if we as a nation, society, and culture bring to the Net the best we have to offer.

I probably don't need to tell you that the world is changing and that our lives are changing at a pace that is at once cause for exhilaration and cause for pause. And yet, for all the progress and technical sophistication, many people are arguably less happy and more uneasy than previous generations would have imagined possible, given the relative freedom from hunger, discomfort, and danger that most of us in the developed nations now enjoy. There must be more to life than the magic of technology and the constant flow of information. I hope that this book gives you a firm foundation for making positive choices that will make a real difference in the lives you will touch and be touched by in cyberspace.

ACKNOWLEDGMENTS

This book would have probably remained a hope and a dream had it not been for Jim Seymour. Like more and more of my friends in life, Jim was a cyberspace acquaintance long before I ever met him in person. Jim is one of those rare individuals with a grace of spirit that blesses anyone fortunate enough to know him. May cyberspace continue to be enriched by the presence of noble souls like Jim!

With Jim, Burt Gabriel deserves much credit for seeing the vision of this book and convincing me to take it seriously. I also appreciate the support provided me by IBM in the early stages. My editor, Richard Bonacci, deserves thanks for his refusal to accept anything less than my best, his many insights and suggestions, and his willingness to keep the project alive through thick and thin. Although we disagreed often, the disagreements were almost always fruitful and evidence of the value of reconciling differing perspectives. To the technical and copy editors and anonymous reviewers, I also offer my thanks for many ideas and a great deal of helpful advice and criticism. I greatly appreciate the professionalism and support of Bob Biewen, Marian Brown, Maia Holden, Cary Holcomb, Penny Hull, Stacey Landowne, Sloan Lederer, Philip McCaffrey, Debbie Siegel, Tim Solomon, Laura Spagnoli, and others at W.H. Freeman and Company.

I have been especially blessed by the outpouring of support, information, encouragement, kindness, and friendship that is the essence of cyberspace—including some of the best communications this life has to offer. I would like to thank my mother, Arlene Bascom; my aunt, Darla Isackson; and Stephen Covey, John Dvorak, Jim Engebretsen, Jim Fallows, Britt Hagen, Victoria Laney, Howard Rheingold, Jim Seymour, and Chip Smith for their reading or proofreading of inadequate early drafts and their valuable feedback; Will Zachmann and his free-wheeling CANOPUS forum on CompuServe which has been—idealists, cynics, sharks, sleaze and all—like a graduate school in the ways of the world of cyberspace for me; those who provided the software and services I used in the production of this book, including Corel (WordPerfect Suite and CorelDraw), Caere (OmniPage Pro), Microsoft (Windows 95 and Office 95), Netscape (Navigator), PowerQuest (Partition Magic), IBM (OS/2 Warp), and CompuServe.

I'd like to express my gratitude to the following for their assistance, ideas, wisdom, contributions, support, and/or generous willingness to share, inspire, and help me discover and explore cyberspace, which time and again has made such an enormous difference: Linda Anderson, Bob Angell, Calvin Arnason, Alan Ashton, Doug Azzarito, Lucy Baney, Stephen Banker, Gene Barlow, John Perry Barlow, Joe Barr, Joshua Beall, Bill Bennett, Jeff Beamsley, Bruce Bierman, Dale Bills, Edwin Black, Richard Blalock, David Blair, Gloria Brame, Scott Brooks, Charlie Brown, Judy Brown, Kim Cameron, Cathy Cantwell, Orson Scott Card, Wayne Caswell, Mark Chapman, Lloyd Christensen, Ward Christensen, Dave Chess, Roland Cole, Dick Conklin, Vicci Conway, Bill Cook, Gordon Cook, Norris Couch, Mike Cowlishaw, Scott Cress, Dave Crockett, Bob Cronin, Alan Crudden, Bob Daines, Monte Davis, Rick DeLott, Sam Detweiller, Mark Dixon, John Dvorak, Esther Dyson, Max Eidswick, Jim Engebretsen, Mike Engleberg, Jim Fallows, David Ferrel, Larry and Donna Finklestein, Davis Foulger, Tom Francese, Orville Fudpucker, Sam Gerber, George Gilder, Paul Gillin, Greg Girard, Brett Glass, James Gleick, Janet Gobeille, David Goldman, Dick Goran, Britt Hagen, Bruce Hallberg, Mel Hallerman, David Hart, Mercer Harz, Gabriel Hatcher, Pete Hayes, Rich Heimlich, Ned Hill, Bill Hinkle, Dave Hughes, Jeff Jones, David Kenison, Peter Kennedy, Joe Kessler, Bill Kleinebecker, Serge Khripoun, Koji Kodama, Dan Kruse, Avery Lackner, Victoria Laney, Graham Lea, John Lederer, Ken Lerner, Peter Lewis, Don Loflin, Jim Louderback, R. C. Love, Bill Machrone, Phil Mandato, Bruce McCausland, Dave McManigal, Wes Merchant, Roger Merrill, Mike Miller, David Moskowitz, Walt Mossberg, Nicholas Negroponte, Todd Nielson, LeRoy and Janice Nisson, Rik Noring, Pete Norloff, David Norton, Louren Nowlin, John Patrick, Kerry Patterson, M. Scott Peck, Tony Pereira, Nick Petreley, Lisa Petruchi, Paul Pignatelli, Robert Pirsig, Jerry Pournelle, Brian Proffit, Katherine Prouty, Mike and Peggy Pulsipher, Bill Purtill, Wayne Rash, Dave Reich, Lee Reiswig, Howard Rheingold, Jack Rickard, Wendy Goldman Rohm, Lance Rose, Rob Rose, Neil Rubenking, Eric Ruff, Rich Running, Marly Rusoff, Ted Salamone, Gene Schaerr, Rick Segal, Larry Seltzer, Jerry Schneider, Strat Sherman, David Singer, Tim Sipples, Larry Solomon, John Soyring, Allen Stalvey, Mary and Bob Stanley, Bruce Sterling, Dee Stevenson, Adam Strack, Bob Sztybel, Karen Thomas, John Tiede, Brad Wardell, Terry Warner, Ellen Williams, Ora Williamsen, Dean Williamsen,

Keith Wood, and Alan Zeichik. I also thank supportive, loving relatives too numerous to list and the IBMPC virtual community. I'm amazed that the list of those who have touched my life because of cyberspace is so long— credit cyberspace with extending the scope of our relationships. To anyone I've forgotten, please accept my apologies, and send me e-mail. I'd love to hear from you again

Above all, I cannot in good conscience neglect to acknowledge the source of all good. The flaws in this work are mine alone; anything good comes from a higher power.

PART ONE

CYBERSPACE

CHAPTER ONE

CYBERSPACE, AN INTRODUCTION

A Virtual State of Mind

Cyberspace. A consensual hallucination experienced daily by billions of legitimate operators, in every nation, by children being taught mathematical concepts. . . . A graphic representation of data abstracted from the banks of every computer in the human system. Unthinkable complexity. Lines of light ranged in the nonspace of the mind, clusters and constellations of data. Like city lights, receding . . .

—William Gibson

Cyberspace! A word born from the dark visions of a science-fiction genius, now often used to describe a world brilliant with promise and fraught with peril. Uncharted; yet as familiar as the phone in your ear, the radio in your car, or the television that hypnotizes young children and weary adults. Unparalleled potential. Dark and foreboding to some; yet sparkling in the bright hopes of a new generation. Like stars in the vastness of the universe, rising . . .

Close your eyes and say the word aloud. Cyberspace! What do you see? A black hole sucking you into a vortex of the unknown, or a galaxy of sparking stars that beckons you to explore? A utopia of goodwill, or a wasteland of corruption? To me, cyberspace is a state of possibilities—a place where space and time lose meaning as barriers, where the timeless, timely, and obsolete unite.

Perhaps if William Gibson knew in 1981 what he knows now about the use of the term he coined for a new virtual world and what is happening in that world, he might have described it differently. He might even have chosen a less intimidating word. Yet for now, cyberspace is the word that best fits the phenomenon. We are witnesses to an extraordinary era that will no doubt be remembered in history as an appropriately revolutionary development to accompany a new millennium. I hope, by the time you finish this book, that that last sentence will be regarded as mild understatement rather than wild, wide-eyed hyperbole. Even the struggle surrounding the semantics of cyberspace is simply evidence that we are on to something bigger than we can grasp. Although some have dismissed cyberspace as nothing more than "CB radio for the nineties," few who are participants believe it to be a fad. In fact, our greatest challenge is facing a fear that forces beyond anyone's power to control have been unleashed. Will individuals enjoy increased freedom, or will they simply face increased temptations and threats to their well-being, character, and traditional values? Will unimagined evils be empowered beyond anyone's capacity to challenge? Will our identities as families, tribes, cultures, and nations be lost as some variety of cyberspace culture predominates? Will the free-spirited cyberspace norms become a new world of anything-goes license? Will we face an unprecedented explosion of economic activity only to see a similarly unprecedented gaping gulf form between haves and have-nots? Will traditional government survive the waves of technological change we face?

Nobody knows cyberspace well enough to answer all of the many questions facing us today or even to describe cyberspace in totality, but that needn't stop us from the exploration of this "electronic frontier"—another term describing the phenomenon coined by cyberspace visionary John Perry Barlow, lyricist for the Grateful Dead. In that exploration rests the hope that each of us can shape the raw materials of cyberspace into a powerful force for good—for ourselves, our children, and our posterity.

ORIGINS

Although the science-fiction writer William Gibson is credited with coining the word "cyberspace" in one of his first science fiction stories and later in his book *Neuromancer* (1984), Gibson himself reportedly credits the concept to John Brunner, author of *Shockwave Rider* (1975). Brunner in turn credits its origin to futurist Alvin Toffler in *Future Shock* (1970). In this landmark, visionary work, Toffler devotes several pages to a section entitled "The Cyborgs Among Us," in which he discusses, with almost eerie prescience, the possibilities of human/machine integration and even of human brains functioning independent of their bodies. By the early eighties,

California State San Diego mathematics teacher Verner Vengie's book *True Names* (1984) was often cited as having had a seminal influence on many in their understanding of the possibilities of networked communications. In an ironic twist of fate, Orwell's vision of an invasive cyberspace presence called "Big Brother" in *1984* was repudiated by 1984, the year in which Gibson's novel introducing cyberspace appeared.

MEANINGS

Whatever the origin of the concept, Gibson's term is a stroke of Shakespearean genius. *Cyber* connotes automation, artificial control, and computerization. *Space*, of course, means a multidimensional place. The word is as futuristic as the concept—and although it regularly draws criticism from an old guard as being a fad, "too techie," and "only for nerds," the word "cyberspace" continues to increase in popular usage and meaning. The fact that even its critics cannot answer the question of which word should be used to replace "cyberspace" tells me that this already commonly accepted word has become a necessary permanent fixture in our language.

The purists also complain that "cyberspace" (pronounced "sī-bûr-spās" in general use today) is derived from "cybernetics," which in turn was derived from the Greek "kubernetes," and thus should be pronounced "kī-bûr-spās" I'm not a purist and prefer the corrupted but widely accepted "sī-bûr-spās" pronunciation. There is little question that the purists have lost this battle.

In Gibson's *Neuromancer*, the word was introduced in poetic prose with echoes of the possible influence of Japan's Matsuo Bashō, seventeenth-century master of hokku: "A year here and he still dreamed of cyberspace, hope fading nightly." That line is found on page 6—yet one must wait until page 51 before cyberspace is finally described in any detail. The now famous description of cyberspace that Gibson offered, while revolutionary in concept and creativity, might be a worthy description of the still fictional cyberspace, but it is, nonetheless, not quite adequate as a definition or description of the existing cyberspace.

Gibson has said, speaking of those who work on computers or play video games: "They develop a belief that there's some kind of actual space behind the screen, some place that you can't see but you know is there." Such an assumption, often made unconsciously by those who spend so much time absorbed beyond the physical plane of a computer or television screen, is perhaps so pervasive now that it is quite surprising to see Gibson disassociate himself, however subtly through use of the third person, from the illusion—since that illusion is the best (perhaps only) evidence available of the actual existence of cyberspace itself. Given the somewhat dark nature of Gibson's vision for cyberspace in *Neuromancer,* it is perhaps understandable that he would see it as someone else's world; nonetheless, the term cyberspace has, in the past few years, been commandeered for everyday use to represent concepts and applications that the visionary Gibson himself could not have completely foreseen or predicted.

John Perry Barlow, lyricist for the Grateful Dead and one of the founders of the Electronic Frontier Foundation, has described cyberspace simply but symbolically as "that place you are in when you are talking on the telephone." In other words, when our focus shifts to a place other than our immediate surroundings via the use of technology, we enter cyberspace. Most of us, as a matter of fact, are more familiar with cyberspace than we may have realized—the only thing new about cyberspace is the name we apply to a familiar phenomenon we have previously taken for granted.

One of the best descriptions of cyberspace is found in Howard Rheingold's *Virtual Communities:* "Cyberspace . . . is the name some people use for the conceptual space where words, human relationships, data, wealth, and power are manifested by people using computer-mediated communications." This is the best description yet—but it doesn't quite jive with Barlow's notion that you are in cyberspace when speaking on the telephone, unless we can stretch the popular understanding a bit and view a phone conversation as "computer-mediated communications." Although it is tempting to limit cyberspace to computer-mediated communications, I believe that the concept begs for a broader definition and a wider view. In attempting to define "cyberspace," I found that few have dared attempt a definition—yet the word is commonly seen in a wide variety of national publications. Nevertheless, the word "cyberspace" is missing not only from traditional dictionaries, but also from *The IBM Dictionary of Computing Terms* and *Microsoft's Dictionary of Computing Terms*. Even *The Cyberspace Lexicon* uses Gibson's description, adding "Cyberspace is the virtual space of computer memory and networks" and another more cryptic Barlow description, "Cyberspace is where your money is."

It would seem that "cyberspace" either defies definition or is one of those intuitive words that is understood without a definition. Nonetheless, I believe that a definition is in order, however informal. A good definition should convey the following key characteristics of cyberspace.

■ It is a virtual space, i.e., a state of mind, a place simultaneously real and artificial; it is not a physical location. It is often a trancelike state we enter when we are absorbed in visual or even verbal communication, such as reading, writing, observing and examining pictures or video or art, or listening carefully to music or speech. Cyberspace, in many ways, is a digital complement (but not a mirror or inverse image) of our atomic world.

■ It can be entered only by means of some sort of physical access device that incorporates an artificial processing mechanism, such as digital computing power and/or software, and that is joined with other access devices on a network of physical connections. Whether the physical access device is a computer screen, a telephone, a personal digital assistant, a terminal, or even two cans and a wire or some other such device, without an access device, there is no distinguishing between cyberspace and communications in the real world. Whatever tool we use, it defines the nature of our experience in cyberspace and may be considered the border of cyberspace or our window into cyberspace.

■ It enables and facilitates interaction and communication between individuals and groups of individuals and their creative output, largely independent of time and space. Cyberspace seems somehow incomplete without interaction. This interaction is different from interaction in the typical sense in that it may often be somewhat indirect—delayed in time or separated by distance. The sense of immediacy that comes from interactions in cyberspace is artificial at best, since our communications almost always lack concurrency in place and usually lack concurrency in time as well. Ironically, it is this characteristic of cyberspace that also reduces the importance of time and space as barriers to communication.

It seemed natural to try to use cyberspace itself as a resource in defining cyberspace. Therefore, I initially started with a working definition that I submitted for review to peers in a CompuServe forum:

> Cyberspace: the imaginary or virtual zone just beyond any group of related physical access devices which may connect to facilitate interactive communications or exchange of information which transcend the limitations of time or space through artificial representations of reality.

As you might guess, my forum-following peers who expressed an opinion asked me to try again using understandable words commonly considered part of the English language by reasonably educated readers. Many of the discussions centered around the manifestations and instances of cyberspace and the similarities that could be drawn from them. More often than not, the computer screen acts as a window into this new world of today, where physical networks and connections (both human and hardware) are coupled with the focused state of mind of participants to create an alternate reality or, in other words, a virtual space. Most of the connections today center around the spoken and written word, which are most easily represented artificially and transmitted technologically, given the state of the art of existing technology and its ever-present limits. The explosive growth of the World Wide Web (WWW), however, is rapidly ushering in connections that add pictures, sound, and even video to the cyberspace experience. In the future, the connections will become more and more realistic, more like "being there," more like "virtual reality," and more like the futuristic fantasies that today exist only in the imaginations of visionaries.

Thus, there are numerous manifestations of cyberspace, and although they have much in common, each is distinguished by the nuances of the connections and their purpose and origin. Examples:

- telephone conversations
- electronic mail
- telephone mail and answering machines
- newsgroups and forums
- mailing lists
- chat rooms
- Telnet destinations
- Web sites
- electronic libraries, such as FTP sites
- electronic conferencing
- conference calls
- MUDs (Multi-User Domains)
- virtual reality
- interactive TV of all forms, including visual telephones

From these examples, you might be surprised to learn that you have lived more of your life in cyberspace than you imagined, even if you have never touched a computer. Most of us have actually lived a healthy share of our life in cyberspace without knowing we were there. Most of us can probably say that we have indeed entered cyberspace on numerous occasions and have an intuitive understanding of what it is. Other examples of cyberspace experiences with which many people are already familiar might thus include

■ watching a movie "on demand" obtained by ordering from a pay-per-view cable set-top box
■ submitting an order for merchandise via a toll-free number
■ using an automated teller machine (ATM)

After much give and take of ideas (more take than give in my case—call it author's prerogative), I chose the following definition:

> **cy•ber•space** (sī-bûr-spās) *n*. 1 A fictional, psychic space where minds fuse in a trancelike "consensual hallucination." [Gibson, 1984] 2 The conceptual world of networked interactions between individuals and their intellectual creations and everything associated with such networks and interactions. 3 the state of mind shared by people communicating using digital representations of language and sensory experience who are separated by time and space but connected by networks of physical access devices.

MISUNDERSTANDING

With any new concept that is understood more easily in the specific than in the abstract, that which something is is more easily understood and distinguished by comparing it with that which it is not. Thus, it should be useful to take a look at some of the common misunderstandings concerning what cyberspace might be, but is not.

Improper Metaphors

Any time new phenomena develop that must be experienced to be understood, writers and teachers understandably develop a plethora of metaphors and analogies to help the uninitiated understand what is happening. Metaphors are perhaps one of the most powerful ways to convey new ideas. They convey the sense of the familiar to the unfamiliar and render our minds able to grasp new concepts by building on the foundation of familiar concepts. However, we must be careful about which metaphors we use to present new ideas, lest the metaphors limit our thinking and distort our perceptions.

For example, the "Information Superhighway" metaphor is a good one when applied to the infrastructure of the backbone of a network, but it quickly fails when used to describe cyberspace itself. Although initially valuable as an aid to understanding cyberspace, the "Information Super-highway" is truly an abused metaphor.

According to a John Heilemann article in *Wired Magazine,* Vice President Al Gore claims to have coined the term the "Information Super-highway" at a meeting with computer industry technologists in 1978.[1] Gore's father played a significant but often overlooked role in the development of the national network of interstate superhighways—thus, Gore's use of the metaphor is quite understandable and even makes a great deal of sense to describe the physical infrastructure that constitutes the standards and bandwidth of the networks and connections upon which cyberspace is being built. "Information Superhighway" is arguably adequate to describe the legitimate role of government in subsidizing the building of the infrastructure and in ensuring that public rather than exclusive private purposes are best served as that infrastructure is built. However, it is entirely inappropriate to describe the entire set of online phenomena. "Information Superhighway" raises a variety of images that don't apply well to the reality of what is happening in cyberspace:

- travel along wide, well-paved paths funded and owned and controlled by the federal government (cyberspace is more like a network of highways, avenues, streets, and roads covering the world, funded by governments and private enterprise and owned and controlled by no one)
- travel from a known beginning to a known end for a known purpose (in cyberspace, the journey is represented by seconds of delay and is pointless; destination is everything, and often the destination is unknown before arriving. "Trips" are usually unplanned.)
- a finite number of broad and spacious, high-traffic connections between only the most important cities (in cyberspace, there is every size of connection and every size of node)

Fortunately, the use of the more accurate and more descriptive "cyberspace" is increasing dramatically in the popular press while the use of "Information Superhighway" seems to be decreasing in popularity. Derivative metaphors—digital fast lane, on-ramp to the Information Superhighway, speed kills on the Information Superhighway, road kill on the Information Superhighway, potholes on the Information Superhighway—convey mistaken impressions and illusions along with valuable comparisons. To use one rather extreme example, one might draw the conclusion that "speed kills" on the Information Superhighway just as it does on the Interstate Superhighway system. Yet in actuality, speed is hardly a problem at all on the Information Superhighway—just the opposite in fact. An inferior technological foundation, i.e., an inadequate architecture, might just make the Information Superhighway seem more like a dirt road before all is said and done. And there is little chance a novice will be crushed or even much humiliated for being on the Net, no matter how inexperienced—so a metaphor that suggests a brutal fate awaits novices is simply misleading.

Even the electronic frontier, which is my favorite metaphor, won't be appropriate forever. Alaska may now seem like the next-to-last frontier in the face of the electronic one, but the electronic frontier will probably be tamed long before Alaska. Many of us "pioneers" already feel as if the frontier has given way to hordes of ranchers, miners, merchants, bankers, bandits, harlots, sheriffs, bartenders, and gunfighters, and we feel it won't be long before the prairie, mountains, forests, railroads, shacks, mines, and cabins give way to ribbons of pavement, parking lots, logging ventures, jets, skyscrapers, and suburbs. And what will it be then—an electronic nation? Somehow the metaphorical imagery is lost. When the frontier is no longer a frontier, other derivative metaphors such as "silicone snake oil" also lose relevance.

The most serious dangers, however, come in straining metaphors or in extending the metaphorical implications to make short-sighted decisions. For example, to set usage limits and ration Internet access "because, after all, there are speed limits on a real superhighway" would be foolish and misguided. This might not be evident, however, to someone who only understood the Net as an "Information Superhighway." More to the point, some legislators might assume that the Net, being an Information Superhighway, should be subject to the same laws as the airwaves or other public communications channels. John C. Dvorak wrote a masterful column in the April 1, 1994, issue of *PC Magazine*, in which he described in brilliant detail legislation that would ban "driving drunk on the Information Superhighway." It sounded so realistic that many didn't realize it was an April Fool's joke until they read the last sentence, which only shows just how powerful metaphors can be and just how carefully they should be used. Cyberspace itself is real—it must be understood on its own merits and should not be confused with any metaphor.

Improper Projections

My personal opinion is that the dark and disturbing visions of cyberspace originally painted by William Gibson may be of interest and may have contributed to the initial views of cyberspace as a haven for cyberpunks, criminals, anarchists, politicians, and of course greedy businessmen and capitalist pigs; but the fictional cyberspace as portrayed by Gibson and other writers no more depicts the real cyberspace than did Dante's *Inferno* paint a picture of the real world in which he lived.

Such movies as *The Net* or *Johnny Mnemonic* paint an essentially inaccurate and misleading picture of cyberspace and therefore represent an improper projection of reality. The idea that our identity can be easily stolen by hackers, while otherwise raising valuable red flags concerning security and privacy, is so strained in the movie that the enjoyment of seeing a movie that acknowledges the power of cyberspace is strained. Obviously, we are indebted to Gibson for the word and to numerous science fiction writers for the conceptual foundation. There is a great deal of value in understanding the views and visions of those who first identified cyberspace as they imagined it might be—but there is little value in accepting any of those views as a *fait accompli* or in trying to understand the fictional cyberspace as a harbinger for cyberspace.

Improper Comparisons

Some people confuse cyberspace with the mental state and visual images of virtual reality. Virtual reality is the simulation of actuality through the manipulation of sensory feedback using electronic and digital technologies. Although the worlds created by virtual reality overlap cyberspace, cyberspace itself extends beyond "virtual reality" to encompass a much broader range of human communications and interactions. Certainly, virtual reality will be found in cyberspace—but the two concepts are as dissimilar as the spoken word is to radio.

COMPOSITION

Cyberspace is not only difficult to define, it is difficult to dissect and describe. Nevertheless, I have found it helpful to think of cyberspace as a place, with differing states, i.e., locations and destinations, and at the same time as a thing, composed of both physical and abstract elements.

States

Just as our world contains many sovereign states and nations, cyberspace can be subdivided into differing "states"—each with its own laws, cultures, and resources. The secondary meaning of "state" as a condition of mind or temperament is a serendipitous parallel to the meaning of cyberspace; hence, I believe it is the appropriate name for the distinctions between places in cyberspace. However, just as we should avoid stretching metaphors, we should avoid drawing too much from the parallels between a state with geographical boundaries (a political state) and a state in cyberspace.

Citizens of political states are relatively more permanent by virtue of residence; cyberspace citizens (cyberzens, to coin a word) are more temporary by virtue of subscription, accessibility, or membership. Political states have elected governments, whereas cyberspace states are generally governed through cooperation of various blends of corporate entities, volunteers, sysops, webmasters, moderators, committees, and outspoken participants. Citizenship in a political state is often a function of birth rather than choice; membership in a cyberspace state is usually due to active selection and choice. Our success in cyberspace partly depends on our ability to understand the differences and to proactively select the state of cyberspace that is the best fit for us and our objectives, just as selecting a city and state of residence might affect our careers and family life. Many who have moved from state to state in the United States or have lived in multiple countries have come to realize just what a difference differences in laws and cultures and resources can make in their quality of life; similarly, changing Internet Service Providers (ISPs) or online services can make a big difference in the quality of ones time online.

Just as the United States expanded from a beginning of thirteen original core states, cyberspace currently has a number of states that have proven to be attractive to many participants and subscribers and may survive and expand over the years. Specifically, these states include the Internet (including the graphical "World Wide Web," or WWW), online services (such as CompuServe, America Online, and Prodigy), computer bulletin boards, and "telestates" (such as television and telephone).

Internet

The Internet was born in the sixties. Cold War fears dictated that this important government network should be decentralized, without a single point of control, in order to provide relative immunity from the threat of nuclear attack. A Rand Corporation think tank laid the groundwork for the Internet by devising a scheme for just such a centerless network of computers. The Internet began life as a government network named ARPAnet, which was designed to enable communications between researchers, government contractors, and the government itself (including the military). A protocol named TCP/IP, or "Telecommunications Protocol/Internet Protocol," was designed by a relatively small team for the Defense Department to meet the requirements and fit the assumptions upon which this decentralized network was built.

The Internet is based on the idea that all computers in the network work together as peers. The links between these computers allow packets of information to be transferred over the network using any convenient route rather than the shortest, the most convenient, or the fastest. These packets, much like hitchhikers, each carry an envelope (like a hitchhiker's sign), attached by the computer originating the packet, that designates its final destination. The packet travels along the links, or "highways," between computers completely at the mercy of the computers in the network, each of which looks at the attached envelope and forwards the packet along an available link likely to move the packet towards its destination. No computer on the network is concerned about how or when the packet reaches its final destination. That depends on the paths, or "rides," available from one computer to another. Eventually, the packet is passed from one computer to another until it reaches the destination computer, which discards the envelope and processes the packet. The analogy of packet as hitchhiker breaks down because a packet can travel around the world almost at the speed of light and thus it is not terribly important for the packet to travel the shortest distance between two points. Nonetheless, practical realities such as high traffic, bandwidth limitations, and technological barriers combine to create the nondeterministic "hurry-up-and-wait" character of the Internet as it exists today.

Because of this decentralized design, the Internet possesses outstanding flexibility and resiliency in terms of routing information. This has given it a robust appeal as a medium "for the people and by the people." The Internet is the collective achievement of many thousands who have contributed to the Internet technically, culturally, and theoretically. The early culture of the Internet and its participants was one of creative sharing and interactivity. Software was often created by individual users who shared it freely with others on the Internet itself to simplify or enable various tasks. In the process, de facto standards were created that provide in usefulness what they lack in elegance or marketing sophistication. Many of these standards live with us today in the form of quaint names like *gopher, archie, veronica, telnet, ftp, usenet,* and so on. No one has the right to complain, however, because few profited from these contributions to the Internet. Until recently.

In the mid-1980s, the National Science Foundation (NSF) began to fund foundations and universities in order to link researchers, faculty, and students to the Internet and its large computers and resources. The Internet grew rapidly from hundreds of computer networks to thousands. "Knowbies," or old-timers on the Internet, complained about "newbies," or newcomers, and justifiably bemoaned the loss of community spirit as new-bies came to view the Internet less as a valuable shared resource and more as an exploitable public service. The NSF established an acceptable-use pol-icy that stated:

> NSFNET backbone services are provided to support open research and education in and among U.S. research and instructional institutions, plus research arms of for-profit firms when engaged in open scholarly communication and research. Use for other purposes is not acceptable.

However, the NSF soon learned that its ability to enforce this policy was limited to its own backbone; by 1991, with the establishment of the Commercial Internet Exchange Association (CIX), the inevitable extension of the use of the Internet to business began. Companies such as IBM, MCI, Sprint, PSI, Merit, General Atomics, and UUNET Technlgies were instru-mental in making the Internet a universal network serving a multitude of interests.

There is little doubt that the Internet, for all its faults, is perhaps the most fascinating and explosive technological and social development of the twentieth century. Most nonparticipants see the Internet as unapproachably arcane and technical—and for now, they're right. Only recently, with the advent of the World Wide Web (WWW) and relatively easy to install "Web browsers" has the Internet been even approachable without the availability of serious technical expertise. As the access mechanisms become more read-ily available and more easily installed, the Internet promises to become an increasingly important part of our lives

The addition of the World Wide Web (WWW) has had a significant impact on the perceptions of others regarding the value of the Internet—there seems to be little doubt now that the Internet, in spite of its arcane complexity and often inadequate performance, will be the foundation and common denominator of the "Information Superhighway." Consumers of technology are notorious for favoring speed to market, simplicity, and flex-ibility over reliability, security, and superior technology. Therefore, those who assert that the WWW and its underlying Internet technology founda-tion aren't secure enough or robust enough to become the national infor-mation infrastructure are almost certainly ignoring the lessons of the past. The impetus and investment in Internet solutions, including those that directly address the security, reliability, and performance weaknesses of the Internet, will almost certainly guarantee its continued success and viability, even though better, less expensive, and technologically superior alternatives might be available. Internet and WWW protocols and standards will simply

ELEMENTS OF THE INTERNET

The Internet is a constantly evolving, eclectic mix of servers, clients, connections, protocols (TCP/IP, SLIP, PPP, HTML, etc.), languages (Java, CGI, PERL, etc.), and software written by users and vendors to accomplish certain specific tasks. Examples include the following.

Mailing lists Mailing lists allow Internet users to self-subscribe to messages relating to topics of common interest. Subscription requests are e-mail messages containing the word "subscribe" sent to a **list server**. Software at the list server maintains a file containing all of the addresses of the subscribers. Then, each time anyone sends a message to the designated service address, or **majordomo**, the message is broadcast to each address contained in the file.

Newsgroups Newsgroups are to mailing lists what bulletin boards are to newsletters. Rather than clutter your mailbox with messages from mailing lists, you can opt to follow certain topics at your convenience. The messages are kept in files that can be read using a newsreader program. The names of newsgroups follow a specific protocol that serves to identify each newsgroup by name and category. The primary categories are COMP (computers), MISC (miscellaneous), REC (recreation), SCI (science), SOC (social), TALK (conversation), NEWS (news), and ALT (alternative, anything-goes topics).

FTP (File Transfer Protocol) FTP allows you to upload or download files from an FTP client to an FTP server. FTP sites are libraries of files that may be downloaded, or "FTP'd," by any other Internet user.

Archie Archie helps you search for and find files on the Internet. If you provide a keyword, Archie will access a database of lists of

be altered or enhanced to handle the ever-increasing demands for security, bandwidth, and performance.

It is easy to envision increasingly universal access because the WWW is so flexible, open, and relatively easy to access and use (either as a server or as a client), but also because of ongoing technological advances and changing telecommunications laws. Advances in technology allow Personal Digital Assistants (PDAs) to access the WWW, without wiring, from devices smaller and lighter than this book. Advances in display technology coupled with the ability to make secure monetary transactions in cyberspace enable online catalogs with easy searching and instant ordering. Linked networks of online files and then list the locations that contain files that match your key word.

Telnet Telnet allows a user to actually log on to another computer elsewhere on the network and run a program or use that computer as if it "belonged to" that user. In technical terms, Telnet allows you to make your computer a terminal on any other Telnet-compatible computer on the Internet.

Gopher Gopher was created by students at the University of Minnesota and named after their "Golden Gophers" mascot, complementing a "go fer this, go fer that" functional description. Actually, gopher provides a nested menu system that allows a user to find specific information by exploring predefined links.

Veronica Veronica allows users to search Gopher menus by key word.

World Wide Web (WWW) The WWW is revolutionizing the Internet simply because it's easy to learn and use. You install a browser such as Mosaic, Netscape, or Microsoft's Internet Explorer on your computer, connect to the Internet, and then point and click your way around the various "home pages" of the Internet. Each page (or screenful of information) is connected by means of hypertext links. Thus, the IBM home page might have the highlighted word "News" as part of its offering. When you click on "News," you get another page offering a variety of headlines. When you select the headline you're interested in reading, the text is displayed for you to read. Of course, any description of the WWW is inadequate. Its flexibility means that no two WWW experiences will ever be exactly the same.

databases and improved search capabilities will surely change the face of research and education. Changes in the telecommunications laws are enabling the increased exploitation of existing wires as well as wireless technologies in such a way that access to the WWW anywhere and anytime by anyone is rapidly becoming real, providing unparalleled convenience and mobility.

The Internet dominates the scene for relatively universal, utilitarian public connectivity while commercial, proprietary services continue to offer more expensive, specialized, differentiated information and services. Already, an Internet e-mail ID is considered the standard for nearly universal connectivity. Hence, even those with a primary ID on one of the commercial services generally use the Internet form on their business cards. The commercial interests of those who are already lining up to use the WWW for advertising, publicity, feedback, and order taking are keeping access costs low and enabling ever easier access. Simply put, doing business on the Internet enables enormous savings in distribution, clerical, communications, and transaction costs, which will continue to motivate businesses to divert budgets for marketing and distribution through traditional means to cyberspace technologies that will enable their customers to find and do business with them in cyberspace. These forces will continue to unfold on the Internet to fundamentally alter the face of commerce and society for decades to come.

Online Services

Commercial information services constitute another group of cyberspace states. These services have been created and have evolved over the past 15 years and share much in common. Most online services provide access to the Internet and WWW as well as to a wide variety of information and files, such as forums, reference, electronic mail, news, weather, sports, software, shopping and ordering centers, and entertainment. Access has evolved from text-based systems driven by menus and commands entered from a command line to the easy-to-use, graphically oriented systems of today. Most online services are available for a monthly subscription fee that covers certain basic services such as news and electronic mail, while charging for other more specific services using various metering or per-use schemes.

CompuServe is the oldest and, in many ways, the best of the online services. It has excellent file libraries, an extensive and mature set of forums and services, and many of the most influential customers to be found online. Unfortunately, it was designed around character-based software, which was state of the art in the early 1980s when CompuServe became the established standard for online services and served as a model for later efforts, but which has since become a liability. Efforts to increase its ease of use and accessibility without compromising its compatibility with large numbers of user-developed "offline readers" and forum following tools have been fairly successful. CompuServe Information Managers for DOS, Windows, OS/2, and the Mac have made the service more accessible to beginners without forcing established users to adopt new access mechanisms. Pricing has traditionally been a bit higher than alternatives, consistent with the quality of the information and services available. It is also the favorite of computer companies offering online technical support for customers, boasting the widest variety of support available. By offering WOW, a graphical, family-oriented service based on the WWW, CompuServe has also been able to diversify to compete effectively with America Online and Prodigy and other Internet Service Providers.

CompuServe seems to have been involved in fewer controversies than its two largest rivals, Prodigy and America Online, but it has certainly not been immune to criticism. The most visible controversy occurred when CompuServe restricted access to various Internet forums offering explicit sexual content after the German government complained. Otherwise, CompuServe has been a careful leader in the nascent online services arena.

Prodigy began as a joint venture between Sears and IBM, and it is, not surprisingly, the most family-oriented and conservative of the services. Prodigy pioneered the "advertising on every screen" approach to keeping costs low, as well as the "all-you-can-use" approach to pricing. Prodigy is based on a graphically oriented, easy to use, visually appealing interface that nonetheless preserves the transfer speed of text. Prodigy has been a pioneer in marketing online access as a product for the masses and has attracted a notable reputation with investors, movie buffs, genealogists, and others for whom accessibility and critical mass are key ingredients of a successful online experience.

Prodigy has attempted to control user-contributed content to a greater degree than any of the other services in an effort to stay family-safe, which has incurred the ire of some customers and seems, ironically, to have now exposed Prodigy to a greater measure of legal risk than its competitors who take a much less active (or nonexistent) stance toward governing content. Prodigy seems to be between a rock and a hard place. When anti-Semetic slurs appeared on one forum, Prodigy was heavily criticized on the one hand for not acting more aggressively to eliminate the offensive material and on the other hand for attempting to censor its users at all. In one closely watched legal case, Prodigy had its hand slapped by a judge who, in a controversial ruling, stated that because Prodigy had advertised itself as a family service, it had incurred a higher standard of responsibility and could thus be included in a libel suit brought by a company after one Prodigy user accused them of fraud online.

America Online (AOL) is the new kid on the block made good and is now the largest of the commercial services. Perhaps more than any of the other services, AOL has been designed for ease of use, flexibility, and visual appeal. Although sharing with Prodigy the ease-of-use goal, AOL takes a contrasting position on controlling content. America Online encourages pseudonyms and is thus well known for its almost anything-goes chat groups and file libraries and the quality of its content.

Led by Steve Case, America Online has also been the most controversial of the services. It has blanketed America with free sign-up diskettes to the point that ownership of multiple AOL sign-up disks has become a standing industry joke. In spite of the ease with which one could sign up for AOL, early in its history AOL required users to cancel their service online or in writing. Millions of users who had signed up using the free diskettes then felt trapped by the difficulties in canceling their membership, and AOL was forced to respond with simplified handling of cancellations. AOL has suffered significant rates of customer turnover. That turnover, coupled with a controversial accounting practice, since abandoned, wherein AOL amortized marketing and sign-up expenses over time under the theory that loyal customers were an asset, has attracted the attention of the *Wall Street Journal* and other publications. As recently as August of 1996, AOL suffered an embarrassing 10-hour outage.

Genie was, in its early days, apparently a way for GE Information Services to derive revenue from the sale of unused, after-hours time on its time-share computers. Many subscribed to Genie in the mid-1980s because the per-hour cost was low and no monthly service charge was required. It offers good to excellent file libraries and access to news and investment services; but, like CompuServe, it is based on an outdated character-based, menu-driven interface and, unlike CompuServe, has never really developed a widely accepted, easy-to-use front to the character-mode command-line interface.

This category (online services) also includes such specialized services as Lexis (a favorite of lawyers and journalists for its comprehensive offerings of publication archives), Dow Jones (widely used by investors and businesses), Dialog (a favorite of researchers), and The Well (the prototype "virtual community").

Computer Bulletin Boards

In 1974, Ward Christensen, an IBM systems engineer, attended an IBM technical session at which he first saw an Intel microprocessor and learned from the instructor that an individual, without extensive engineering knowledge, could build a computer around that single chip. That was enough for Christensen, one of those rare individuals who creates and invents for the love of doing it. Within a few months, he was deep into the issues of research and design of a small computer and software based on an Intel 8008.

Although that early research and development effort was to be upstaged by Ed Robert's Altair and Bill Gates's Microsoft BASIC and garnered what amounted to little more than a yawn from IBM, it was foundational to a creation that may eventually overshadow in importance any other development of the 1970s. During a snowstorm on January 16, 1978, Ward Christensen called his friend Randy Seuss and proposed setting up a dial-in computer for the local Chicago Area Computer and Hobbyists Exchange (CACHE) club in order to keep members up to date about club events. Over the next few weeks, Randy worked on the hardware (an Altair with an S-100 bus), and Ward developed the software. Thus was born the Computer Bulletin Board System, or CBBS. By late January, the pieces were in place. Dennis Hayes had developed the MicroModem 100, a modem for S100 systems such as the Altair, and Christensen himself had released into the public domain, in September of 1977, the details of a file transfer protocol now known as XMODEM, which was gaining popularity as a means of transferring files between systems with differing file storage formats. The software was written in 8080 Assembler, offering a menu of such capabilities as (E)nter (message), (R)ead (message(s)), (S)ummary, and (Q)uick Headers.

According to Christensen, the first call to the new CBBS was received in early February; however, when he was pressed in later years to name the date, he designated the official birthday as February 16, 1978 (one month after his fateful—and documented—conversation with Seuss). As an aside, Ward claims that the computerized bulletin board system couldn't have been invented in California, since without the Chicago snowstorms, he might not have called Seuss that fateful day, and club members wouldn't have been quite so motivated to have and use a bulletin board that didn't require a trip outdoors to read.

CBBS was up and running for over 16 years before it quietly "died in its sleep." Unlike some industry pioneers who went on to found their own companies, Ward Christensen still works in Chicago as a systems engineer for IBM—his pioneering effort reaped little monetary reward. Thankfully, Ward's contributions have not gone unrecognized, however. At the first ONE BBS CON convention for system operators (sysops) held in Denver in 1992, the modest Christensen was honored with standing ovations, adulation, and the first Dvorak Lifetime Achievement Award. When offered his choice of any of the available prizes on hand that had been donated to be given away by lottery, Christensen passed up all of the expensive hardware and software and selected instead *Dvorak's Guide to Telecommunications*, bringing gales of appreciative laughter from the crowd and the masters of ceremony, John Dvorak and Nick Anis—coauthors of the selected book. As a friend, I can attest that he still lives the unselfish qualities of integrity and generosity that have characterized so much of the early bulletin board community.

Since 1978, there has been a grass-roots explosion of interest in bulletin boards. Jack Rickard of *Boardwatch Magazine* estimates that there are over 100,000 bulletin boards in the United States alone. ONE BBS CON, a trade show specifically for bulletin board systems operators (sysops), seemed to double in size and sophistication every year until 1995, when it plateaued in size as the World Wide Web began to offer bulletin boards a new, more graphical home with access to a far larger audience. Although most of the bulletin boards are owned and operated by hobbyists and are free to callers, dozens of sysops have left corporate jobs and are making very healthy incomes treating their respective bulletin boards as a business and living off the income from the voluntary subscriptions. A worldwide network of self-selecting sysops and their bulletin boards are linked in an amazing system called "FidoNet." With over 25,000 participating bulletin boards, it is the largest grassroots network in the world. Every night, between 0900 and 1000 Universal Coordinated Time (4:00 A.M. Eastern Standard Time), these 25,000 bulletin boards call each other and exchange message packets—thereby enabling what is probably the lowest-cost online computer conferencing service available. With the overwhelming rush to the WWW, many sysops have leveraged their skills and knowledge and have become local Internet Service Providers (ISPs). More and more of these boards are finding an amazing number of creative ways to connect to the Internet, making their content available to the millions who have access to the Internet or the World Wide Web.

Boardwatch Magazine regularly publishes lists of the bulletin boards and the respective phone numbers, and most recently, an extensive list of ISPs. Over the past few years, issues have trumpeted lists such as

- 167 Milwaukee BBSs (March, 1995)
- 287 Medical Bulletin Boards (January, 1995)
- The Top 100 BBSs in the U.S. (September, 1994)
- 252 BBS Run by Women (August, 1994)
- 707 New Jersey BBSs (January, 1994)
- 358 Product Support Bulletin Boards (May, 1993)
- 322 Russian/CIS Bulletin Boards (February, 1993)
- 100 OS/2 Bulletin Boards (July, 1992)

The variety and surprising number of BBSs represented in the list only hint at the incredible diversity of bulletin boards found worldwide. *Boardwatch Magazine* lists include general bulletin boards as well as specific, hobbyist bulletin boards that span a wealth of human interests, including poetry, pets, genealogy, programming and every other aspect of computer life, photography, human sexuality, gardening, games, sports, science, weather, teaching, government, legal issues, ham radio, and reading. You name it and you can probably find it somewhere in the world on a bulletin board system maintained as a labor of love.

Bulletin boards are generally accessed by calling the phone number of the BBS, waiting a moment for the modems to negotiate the connection (usually identifiable as a series of raspy, screeching sounds), and then navigating a series of menu choices. Although fairly simple to learn with instructions, accessing a BBS is nonetheless still a rather arcane process that is more difficult than programming a VCR. Yet, as evidenced by the tens of millions of modems in the marketplace, the bulletin board community was thriving and growing in the late 1980s and early 1990s in ways and at a rate strikingly similar to the PC boom of the early 1980s.

The significance of these bulletin boards should not be overshadowed by the emergence of the World Wide Web. In the 1980s, bulletin boards connected worldwide via FidoNet represented an astounding development: for the first time, communications between geographically dispersed, grassroots "communities" were possible at little or no cost.

Telestates

For years, many of us have lived much of our lives in the primitive visual and auditory states of cyberspace—television and telephone. These are the aging states of cyberspace that only barely share the characteristics that make cyberspace a distinctive new place. Television is only marginally interactive, requiring little more of us than adjusting volume and changing channels from time to time—and hence it is probably a stretch to include traditional television as part of cyberspace. Telephone, while more interactive, is so familiar that we sometimes forget how revolutionary and relatively new it really is. Telephone has been the harbinger of cyberspace. Conference calls, toll-free numbers, phonemail, and point-of-terminal credit checking are preparing us all to be far more accepting of forums, cybershopping, e-mail, and cybercash. The twin telestates of television and telephone will no doubt undergo significant transformation in years to come but will remain important foundation states in our experience with and understanding of cyberspace.

Elements

The various states we have discussed constitute the invisible boundaries of cyberspace, but cyberspace is also composed of various physical and abstract elements that bind cyberspace to the real world. Just as our world is composed of physical elements such as air, water, and earth and abstract elements such as culture, language, and information, so cyberspace is composed of a subset of similar physical and abstract elements.

Physical Elements

Software and hardware are the primary physical elements of cyberspace. They technically enable communications (exchange of information) between systems and people who use those systems.

The hardware of cyberspace is composed of the physical access devices and networks by which connections are made and information exchanged. This hardware, in turn, includes a wide variety of inventions that make such connections possible. Software, to be precise, is not completely physical, but for our purposes it may be considered a physically necessary enabling mechanism for cyberspace.

The hardware required to facilitate the exchange of information has progressed rapidly since the days when exchanging text between machines located across the country was considered a technological coup. Now, we are rapidly approaching the day when a face-to-face conversation with someone halfway around the world will no longer seem like a miracle. Over the years, layers of hardware and software have been added to facilitate and simplify the process of communicating between more and more systems running differing software, until today the advanced technologies in place make things seem much simpler than they once were. Where once connecting computers meant leased lines, mainframes serving as time-sharing systems, and sophisticated terminals designed for specific tasks, now ordinary people from all walks of life have learned how to use personal computers, modems, and telephone lines to link to cyberspace. And it's bound to be get much easier over time.

There is such a wide variety of hardware and software used today to make cyberspace possible that it would be impossible to describe it in detail, and such a description is beyond the scope of our inquiry. However, let's take a brief look at some of the more common ways to get connected to cyberspace.

Briefly, you need a physical access device (client), a connecting device, a network providing bandwidth, software, and a target connection (server). Physical access devices include any device that facilitates input, output, or processing of the information you exchange in cyberspace. They include computers, displays, televisions, telephones, microphones, speakers, keyboards, touch pads, mice, sound cards, video boards, and so on. The connecting device might be a network adapter, a modem, a router, a telephone, an NT-1 (a network terminator used by ISDN), a set-top box, an infrared link, a cellular phone, a PDA, or some other means of linking to another system in order to interactively exchange information. The network bandwidth is used by the connecting device to link to another connecting device for the target, or server, system(s). It might be a phone line, optical fiber, local area network wiring (twisted pair or thin coax), or a coaxial cable. It should be noted that as technology has advanced, network bandwidth has become more abstract, such that it is often no longer classified as hardware or software or even physical. Now, network connections are often made using the airwaves, spread spectrum, microwave transmissions, or an infrared link. Thus, in describing the physical elements of cyberspace, we must necessarily include some of those abstract elements that blend almost seamlessly with the physical elements of hardware and software. One such abstract element is bandwidth.

Technologists use the term bandwidth quite specifically to mean not only the "pipeline" through which information is exchanged but also the size of that pipeline. The greater the bandwidth, the greater the throughput. Thus, "high bandwidth" is desirable because more information can be exchanged. The highest bandwidth medium available is optical cable, with a modem and telephone wire being somewhere nearer the bottom of the bandwidth scale. In general, the higher the bandwidth, the more expensive the medium—but that is more of a rule of thumb than a law.

In any connection, there is some combination of hardware and software that enables one computer to share information and resources with another. The software is composed of microcode, operating systems, utilities, and applications. The microcode is a computer program written to control the hardware in a language the hardware understands. An example of microcode is the BIOS of an IBM-compatible system or the programming that allows the set-top box of a TV connected to a cable system to change channels or turn on or off automatically. The operating system is software that provides an interface for people and other computer programs to work with the hardware through microcode and other hardware drivers. The operating system performs the valuable function of a middleman, negotiating between user and hardware to facilitate understanding and efficiency. DOS Windows, OS/2, System 7, and UNIX are examples of some common operating systems. Finally, the application software allows users to do what they need to do in cyberspace. Examples of applications include web browsers, commercial service access software, an e-mail manager, an offline reader, a bulletin board system, a communications package, a real-time stock quotation program, and network management software.

Inherent in both the hardware and software design are architectures and protocols, which ensure that the hardware and software and connections each speak the same language in order to facilitate communications and avoid interface problems. Because companies in free markets fight for competitive advantage by differentiating their offerings to customers, the process whereby companies agree to use the same architectures and protocols to make life easier for users is anything but quick and efficient. Sometimes it doesn't happen at all, e.g., the lack of any clear standards for file exchange on personal computers. Sometimes it happens only because a dominant company establishes the standard by default or fiat, such as when IBM chose Microsoft to supply the operating system (DOS) and Intel to supply the microprocessor (8088) for the IBM PC.

Even when agreement is reached through open industry alliances, it is likely that the agreed-upon protocol will be a lowest-common denominator solution that doesn't benefit any single company any more than any other rather than the most elegant or best choice technologically. For example, the Sierra standard for CD-ROM formats was developed through just such a process. The arcane technical arguments used to explain and justify the varying advantages of and reasons for each of the architectures or protocols are often confusing to the layman but do, nonetheless, have important consequences to end users. For example, in the choice between BetaMax and VHS, the best technology lost. Consequently, users now have inferior picture quality and larger video cassettes. The market made a rational decision, because Sony was charging more for BetaMax and essentially had a monopoly on the technology, but consumers lost in the end because an inferior technology was adopted as the video tape standard. Other examples of technological decisions and standards that have impacted our daily lives include LP records and CDs, leaded and unleaded gasoline, RJ-11 modular telephone jacks, VHF/UHF and cable-ready televisions, cable TV wiring in homes, home stereo speaker wiring, and AM vs. FM radio. Although we as consumers may not have had an opportunity to participate in the debate surrounding those standards, we live with them daily. In other words, even the esoteric debates of engineers, technologists, and marketing mavens eventually make a difference to us, and the winners of those debates don't always have our best interests in mind.

For example, the Internet was initially designed to enable highly decentralized networked communications that could not be thwarted by an enemy taking out single or even multiple nodes. This has enabled the explosive growth of the Internet, it has also encouraged a network infrastructure that can often be as arcane and unreliable as it is free and uncontrollable. Anyone who has "surfed the net" has probably experienced delays, inconsistent ability to access other destinations, and even, on rare occasions, lost e-mail. In large measure, this is because the Internet has significantly outgrown its originally intended design. As challenging as such problems may be, the already widespread popularity of the Net practically ensures that solutions will be found as necessary—although it is also likely that consumers of the Internet will continue to suffer from such problems from time to time, just as Windows users suffer from the legacies of DOS and the originally rather short-sighted design of the IBM PC because IBM expected to sell only 250,000 PCs over its life.

In the world of technology, standards play an interesting role. We can't live without them, and almost can't live with them, because they're usually too static and inflexible. But we use them nonetheless, usually debating them every step of the way. Thus, like many political decisions, our understanding of the issues and participation in the process can often make a significant difference. The sooner we can gain familiarity with the issues and voice our desires, the better able we will be to influence the process. Ultimately, our best weapon is to vote carefully with the dollars we spend on technology.

The following list describes some of the widely-used protocols in cyberspace, many of which are still being debated and discussed, with the fortunes of several companies at stake. Whether we know it or not, our future will no doubt be shaped by the outcome of some of the debates currently occurring within companies and board rooms worldwide.

■ **ActiveX** A recent Microsoft protocol consisting of a superset of OLE controls (See OLE) named OCX controls (similar to OpenDOC) and scripting to support interactive objects embedded in Web pages (similar to Java).

■ **ATM** Asynchronous Transfer Mode is a digital transport protocol for voice and date transmission developed in order to balance the competing interests of Europe and the United States. Based on packet, or cellular, technology, it is enjoying rapid acceptance and could eventually be the standard for local area networks and backbones, replacing Ethernet, Token Ring, and Fiber Distributed Data Interface (FDDI).[2]

■ **ADSL/HDSL** Asymmetrical Digital Subscriber Line and High Speed Digital Subscriber Line were designed by Bellcore Labs as a way to use existing phone lines to deliver inexpensive video, audio, and data information to homes, including plain old telephone service (POTS) and ISDN.

■ **Ethernet** The most common local area networking (LAN) standard. It is not yet two decades old but has the principle advantage of being relatively simple and inexpensive. In its original form, it's bandwidth is 10 MBps. Current implementations are 10 times that fast at 100 MBps.

■ **HTML** Hypertext Markup Language is the language of Web pages on the World Wide Web, and was developed and released by Tim Berners-Lee as recently as 1990. HTML was based on SGML, or Standardized General Markup Language—a mature, sophisticated text-processing language developed jointly by IBM and world standards bodies. As a new standard, HTML is maturing. There is a typical struggle underway between extensions to the HTML standard and newer versions of HTML undergoing review by multivendor committees.

■ **IPX/ODI** Common PC networking protocols used by Novell networks. IPX is the current form; ODI is no longer current.

■ **ISDN** Integrated Services Digital Network is a digital transport protocol now being offered for residential use by most of the local phone companies in the United States. It offers high speed connections that are close to the physical limits of PC serial ports, as well as two phone numbers on one line, i.e., one twisted pair.

■ **Java** is a language developed by Sun Microsystems for programming WWW applications. It is close to being a universal standard, having been widely endorsed by many companies, including IBM, NetScape, HP, and Microsoft.

■ **NetBIOS** A common PC networking protocol originally developed by Microsoft and IBM.

■ **OLE** Object Linking and Embedding architecture (OLE) provides a means for industry software applications to work together and share objects, allowing Microsoft to control interoperability between applications. Microsoft claims that their Object Linking and Embedding architecture, which predates JAVA, is their answer to JAVA—although even Microsoft has licensed Java. ActiveX extends OLE to complement (and perhaps eventually compete with) Java.

■ **OpenDoc** An elegant object-oriented programming standard that could significantly reduce programming effort and maintenance required for PC applications, including "weblications," or WWW applications, OpenDoc is an effort by IBM and Apple to unseat Microsoft's OLE.

■ **SNA** IBM's System Network Architecture, a robust and secure, but proprietary, networking architecture widely adopted in the corporate environment worldwide. For many years, SNA was the world's leading protocol for defining how systems could talk to one another.

- ■ **TCP/IP** The networking protocol of the Internet, characterized by impartiality in the distribution of data, relatively little security, and decentralization of control.
- ■ **Token-Ring** IBM's choice of a LAN standard that has the advantage of being deterministic and thus more reliable and less subject to failure than Ethernet, but it is more expensive.

The physical elements of cyberspace, including the abstract standards and protocols, may be thought of as the infrastructure upon which cyberspace is built, just as the buildings and streets of New York make up that city's infrastructure. Yet just as the heart of the city itself is the people, so is the heart of cyberspace the people and the human interactions that occur there. All of the media and connections and nodes must cooperate using compatible architectures and protocols, or else communications will not occur—and without those communications, there is no cyberspace. Thus, the standards play a critical role in the building of cyberspace

One of the primary purposes of the Telecommunications Bill of 1996 was to enable free markets to determine standards, allowing more competition between local telephone companies, cable TV companies, long distance companies, and anyone else who wants to go into the business of providing a communications infrastructure leading to your door. This places more responsibility on us the consumers—to understand what we want, to ask for it, and to purchase wisely for the long term, remembering that we vote with our dollars for those technologies we would like to see as standards. And the technical elegance of the protocols that are chosen will, to a large degree, determine the nature of our experiences in cyberspace in the future.

Abstract Elements

An examination of the elements of cyberspace would not be complete without a view of its abstract parts, which are essentially what is most valuable about cyberspace. Abstract elements include data and information, culture and values, and interfaces and language.

Data is factual information used as the basis for reasoning, discussion, or calculation and must often be processed to be meaningful.[3] Data therefore denotes facts and representations as contained in images, sounds, text, and files. The format of data is of critical importance. For example, "raw" data, such as unfiltered noise, is often useless until patterns of order are discerned and interpreted. Generally, once data has been ordered and interpreted such that it contributes to understanding and knowledge, it is called information. Nonetheless, data is usually also considered to be information—the assumption being that all data, ordered or not, contains value, discovered or not. I have found, however, that it is useful to think of data as the cellular structure and information as the lifeblood of knowledge and intelligence. If knowledge is the possession and grasp of data, then intelligence is the ability to gain and apply information. Subject to ones culture and values, knowledge and intelligence are rightfully highly prized. There should be no doubt concerning the value of knowledge and intelligence in our culture. Knowledge is indeed power—power that can be used for good or evil. Intelligence is arguably even more important than knowledge if we accept its connotation as the capacity to set and attain realistic goals, create, persuade, understand, accept, and to progress and achieve.

The phrase "Information at Your Fingertips," reportedly originated by Fred Gibbons and borrowed by Bill Gates of Microsoft, describes a compelling vision of the future. Imagine having the body of knowledge of a subject that interests you available on demand just beyond the virtual window of your computer screen or, alternatively, calling up specific details from the universe of knowledge by isolating a few key search words.

By browsing, we discover incidental new facts and truths as we pursue known interests. By searching by key word, we directly address our areas of ignorance. Whether browsing or searching, our ventures in cyberspace can increase our knowledge and understanding in both predictable and unpredictable ways.

As the embryonic embodiment of that vision, even now cyberspace represents one of the most significant advances the world has ever witnessed in providing humankind with a vehicle to access data and information in unprecedented quantity and disseminate it to unprecedented numbers of people with unprecedented rapidity. That is not a statement I make lightly. The development of language, the invention of the printing press, the creation of libraries, the advent of a mass media—all have played pivotal roles in advancing civilization; but none has had the explosive impact and potential of cyberspace.

As cyberspace becomes the repository of huge volumes of knowledge, it becomes possible to imagine that humankind might at last solve problems such as hunger, famine, pestilence, war, and disease that have plagued humankind throughout history. As this information becomes more available to increasing numbers of people, the realization of such imaginings will be far more a matter of moral will than of mere technological prowess. Although the amount of information in cyberspace is astonishing, the lion's share must still be gathered and indexed. The tools to make it real are here or will be available shortly, but the economic motivation to do so is lagging. The ramifications are enormous. Is the world ready for such a revolution? Can we use cyberspace as a global tool of enlightenment and enrichment, or will it be a captive of more narrow economic interests?

The answer, I believe, lies in culture and values. I remember that one of my MBA professors, Kerry Patterson, defined culture as "a set of shared assumptions." I have found this definition to be of enormous value in understanding many of the dynamics of human behavior and interaction. Individuals, families, and nations often disagree because they make different assumptions. Often, we make assumptions about the assumptions of others without questioning our own assumptions. If we learn about the cultures of others—their values and assumptions—and allow them as different rather than wrong, we can begin to think of a global community in which everyone's lot in life might be improved. The alternative is ongoing factionalism, strife, and a scarcity mentality that keeps us in a feudal state of win/lose and lose/lose thinking. If our shared assumptions and values are rooted in primitive notions of dominance and submission (winners and losers), then it should be no surprise if our assumptions are played out in our lives and society. Assumptions and values are a more important part of cyberspace than modems and wires—and yet receive far less attention.

Values are those assumptions we accept as important. They are those assumptions that relate to beliefs and behavior. Closely related to culture, values are the lens through which we view the world. While we are often not even consciously aware of most of the assumptions we make that comprise our culture, we are far more often keenly aware of the choices we make regarding values, because they often demand of us thought, behavior, and communication in dealing with others who do not share our values.

An example of a cultural assumption is the American ideal of individualism. American film heroes are often loners who defy the establishment and the bad guys. Yet in Japan, with its differing cultural assumptions regarding teamwork, loyalty, and harmony, such an individual might be considered an outcast. The cultural assumptions are simply different—one is not superior to the other. An individual steeped in the traditions of American culture might value individuality more highly than teamwork.

An individual in the United States might, in the absence of mitigating tolerance, view with disdain a Japanese colleague who values loyalty to his superiors more highly than the independence to defy them. Such disdain in the absence of an appreciation of the underlying cultural differences, however, is harmful. Seeking the advantages of mutual understanding is a far better response. Such tolerance can, however, be carried to an extreme. If someone is a drug dealer or a wife beater, for example, then we would rightfully resist accepting their values or respecting the differences in underlying assumptions. The assumptions we accept and the cultural values we choose largely determine the quality of our lives. Rarely, do we have the opportunity to shape an emerging culture—and yet that is precisely the opportunity we face in cyberspace. The choices are ours.

In dealing with differences in culture, we must remember that all cultures and all human beings usually have much more in common than not. An essential respect for our mutual humanity yields the necessary respect for the differences in culture. This respect is a critical element in building a cyberspace that will prove more constructive than destructive as individuals interact in cyberspace. Special attention must therefore be paid to the interfaces through which this interaction occurs.

Interfaces are those points at which differing and often unrelated systems meet and interact. Thus, when you wish to access cyberspace, you interface first with the physical access device(s), then with the software that will enable your connection or access, and finally, through their connections and devices, with the other human beings who are also cyberspace citizens.

The interface with the physical access device is often limited and constrained. Touch typists, for example, will have a distinct advantage over nontypists for as long as the keyboard remains the primary input device for computers. The physical access device itself is often limited by design or reliability considerations. The software interface ranges from the sublime (World Wide Web browsers or graphical online service providers) to the ridiculous (the command line interface of UNIX or DOS).

Although we need not be as concerned about the many defined interfaces between the access devices used by those who communicate in cyberspace, we should nonetheless be aware that they exist, however invisibly, and influence our experiences in cyberspace. For example, if an important e-mail were to be lost in transit, you may not be aware that an interface has failed you. Instead, you might silently assume that the person never actually sent it.

The human interface necessarily involves language, in all its rich and subtle beauty. I probably learned more about language in my first "semester" online than I did during my entire college freshman English class. The nuances of the written word, rhetoric, and logic are extensive, even when used to communicate with others even within one's native language, and are proving to have a significant impact on cyberspace culture and the nature of the experience there.

These abstract elements are the most important in cyberspace and will be the primary focus of this book. They involve human history in the making, human nature, human language, human interaction, human communication, human values, human culture, and most important, the human spirit. In our rhapsodic contemplations regarding the future as influenced by cyberspace, we must not neglect the challenges and concerns that currently stand in stark contrast to the enormous opportunities posed. There is cause for concern regarding the effects of cyberspace life on individual liberty and morality. There is cause for concern regarding the future of family values. There is cause for concern that cyberspace will trigger an economic boondoggle for some and disaster for others—thus widening the chasm between the haves and the have-nots. There is cause for concern regarding the accountability of those who create and define the interfaces we will use. There is cause for concern that government and society will be seriously weakened by cyberspace rebellions. There is cause for concern that cyberspace will be a refuge for criminals where law enforcement officials will be the parties who are handcuffed and helpless. There are many causes for concern—there always have been—but there will be those who rise to the occasion, as always, and we can emerge from the crisis with a renewed sense of purpose and hope for the future. So it will be, I trust, with the crises we will surely encounter in cyberspace. The possibilities outweigh the challenges—but only if we are clear and unmuddled as we acknowledge our values and purpose in order to build on what we share rather than attempting to tear down that which we don't understand.

BENEFITS AND PURPOSES

In the early days of black-and-white television, just after World War II, those who foresaw and forecast the international ubiquity of television and its impact on families and nations might have been easily ignored. Economically, it seemed impossible to believe that expensive technology such as television would become so pervasive, even in third-world countries.

I believe we are today facing the same situation with cyberspace. It may seem difficult if not impossible to believe that in less than two decades, perhaps within one decade, almost one billion people worldwide will have access to cyberspace—yet such is my prediction, which I believe to be a conservative one. The primary existing barriers to the access of cyberspace, technical and economic, are falling rapidly. Technology is making such access easier and less forbidding on an accelerating schedule. The world economy is being energized by what Alvin Toffler named the "Third Wave"—the shift from the Agrarian Age to the Industrial Age to the Information Age, where many of the most valuable products and services are composed primarily of knowledge. For example, the heart of any computer (the microprocessor) is created from silicon—one of the most abundant elements on earth—and a few chemicals. The bulk of its value is derived from intelligent engineering, programming, and design, not from scarcity. The wealth of nations has often been viewed as a function of natural resource, but it seems that every country shares equally in the natural resource of the intelligence of its people—in an era where knowledge and intelligence is valued so highly and the exchange of those "commodities" is as easy and inexpensive as a local phone call to access "the Net," most countries worldwide could conceivably prosper if access to cyberspace could be provided as an important part of an individual's education. The promise of that prosperity alone could trigger a significant shift away from the zero-sum assumptions regarding the limited "wealth of nations," i.e., that wealth must be guarded zealously lest other nations prosper at the expense of another. Those assumptions, which have often led to costly tariffs and restricted trade, have arguably hindered international growth in the past. New assumptions that take into account the new dynamics of the value of intellectual resource as a raw material and thus advance those policies that are designed to unlock the intelligence and thus the labor and even the natural resources of every country worldwide could fundamentally enhance the standard of living for everyone in the entire world. It will require visionaries and forward-thinking politicians and statesmen, though, by any measure. Without them, cyberspace could remain a wedge separating the wealthy from the poor, ensuring that class structure plays an indelible role in enriching the rich and impoverishing the poor.

Personally, I trust that the positive potential of cyberspace can and shall overpower those forces and private agendas that threaten the many possibilities for good and the barriers that exist that divide good people from increased participation in cyberspace. As those barriers fall, we will witness the maturation of the use of cyberspace to accomplish the purposes of communication, education, convenience, commerce, and entertainment.

Communications

Notes and letters between friends and family and coworkers are flying through cyberspace daily at not quite the speed of light but close enough—as are resumes, birth announcements, support group discussions, jokes, proposals, chitchat, genealogies, deep political and philosophical discussions, child care recommendations, satire, frank carnal exchanges, creative writings, critiques of all kinds, news and commentaries, product details, problem solving discussions, want ads, legal advice, information about business opportunities, press releases, cartoons, technical support, medical opinions, gardening tips, and so on and on and on. It is truly a wonder to behold. Communication is the principal driver behind the emergence of cyberspace as the most important development of the personal computer (PC) revolution. Never mind the early promise that personal computers (PCs) would help you do your work faster: the revolutionary difference that PCs have made, are making, and will make is to provide individuals with a means of communicating with family, friends, associates, and strangers alike.

Communication is and will remain the primary purpose of participants in cyberspace. The goal of communication is to transmit knowledge from one sentient being to another. Our desire to communicate is closely tied to our yearning for knowledge and is an inherent part of our humanity. Now the human family seems to be discovering new ways to communicate—including the new modes of communications that distinguish cyberspace.

There are a number of forms of communication with which we are familiar, most falling under the categories of speech, written communications, and visual communications. The traditional forms of communication include:

- conversation
- mail
- magazines
- books
- oratory
- music
- art
- messages and messengers
- meetings

In the twentieth century, we have added new forms of communication, most of which can be categorized as cyberspace communications:

- television
- radio
- electronic mail (e-mail)
- forums and newsgroups
- bulletin boards and Web pages
- chat rooms

Our knowledge of cyberspace adds new means of communications to our arsenal. In the last decade, cyberspace has enabled more informal, responsive group communications, even between strangers. It has expedited and simplified personal communications without regard to distance and with much less regard to time—no longer is it critical that we be in the same place at the same time.

We examine communications in depth in Chapter 2, since it is such a key ingredient in the human dimension of cyberspace.

Education

Much has been made of the "education crisis" in America. One wonders how much of this crisis is simply the rest of the world catching up with or exceeding us in the levels of discipline and expectation imposed on their students as compared to ours—yet far less is made of the crossroad education is at. The old model (Take one teacher and 30 students, expose each student to lecture, exercises, tests, and correction, and repeat once a day for each subject for nine months per year) hasn't changed in generations. Perhaps it's time it did—cyberspace makes that possible. Whether or not change is desirable remains to be decided, but at least we have more choices than ever before.

While I recognize that it would be unrealistic to expect overnight changes, I also recognize that the schools will have no choice but to change. The rapid changes in society and in children's homes will mandate responsiveness in schools nationwide. A grass-roots effort named NetDay 96 to wire most of California's primary schools was so successful that President Clinton and Vice President Gore showed up in work clothes to show their support, referring to the event as a modern equivalent of a "good old-fashioned barn raising." Children will interact with other children online, exchanging information about whatever interests them freely over the phone lines. I've already found faxes from my 12-year-old son's friends among my own incoming faxes, and once I showed him how to access the World Wide Web, America Online, and Prodigy, he is spending more of his time exploring then watching TV. Already, his school is experimenting with a dial-in "Homework Hotline" so parents can check their children's homework schedule. Can e-mail, forums, and Web pages for students, parents, and teachers be far behind? The only obstacle is lack of equipment and knowledge of how to use it—but now that homes are buying more computers than television sets, it would be unwise to be too short-sighted in naysaying the significant possibilities for education. Technologies that serve real human needs have a way of finding their way into the mainstream, even if they require a fair degree of adaptation on the part of users.

As children, parents, and educators begin to realize the power and opportunity that is inherent in broadening the awareness of children by extending their education to cyberspace, the children of this generation will have increasing opportunities to interact with American heroes and outstanding role models. Imagine a cyberconference where Steve Young and Jerry Rice, or Karl Malone and Jeff Stockton, explain to children (on screen) the value of education and hard work and answer questions in real time from children who are one at a time shown on screen as well. Who wouldn't want such an experience for their children? I believe it is inevitable. At least some of our modern heroes will choose not to shun their opportunity to be role models. As they learn that their influence in cyberspace can be extended far beyond the traditional "physical presence" exercises at hospitals and camps, bypassing the often-biased (or at least constrained) media, they will choose to work directly with thousands of children at a time in cyberspace teaching moments.

What's more, the changes coming in cyberspace education don't stop with formal education. Over the years, I've learned far more online about how things really work than I learned about how things should work in theory in six years of higher education as an undergraduate and graduate student. Even more important, my education has proceeded based on my own interests according to my timetable—it has seemed more like entertainment than education. Thus, the word "edutainment" is often being used with increasing effectiveness to denote the brand of learning that is both educational and enjoyable. Cyberspace offers the promise of education that is often indistinguishable from entertainment.

Entertainment

According to an August 1995 *Business Week* editorial, "Entertainment is the No. 1 American export (bigger than aircraft), new-job generator (bigger than health care), and technology driver (the hottest software is developed for *Jurassic Park,* not Star Wars missile defense)." Entertainment is something almost everyone seeks. Even as entertainment increases steadily in importance, various new forms of entertainment are enjoying even more stratospheric growth. According to some estimates, Americans have spent more money in recent years on computer games and video games than on movie tickets. In spite of (or perhaps because of) the push to work harder for longer hours, selling ways to spend leisure time is a booming business. "We work hard and play hard" seems to be a common refrain, especially among ambitious young workers. Entertainment may be an escape to those who consume it; but it is increasingly big business to those who provide it. Economically, socially, and culturally, entertainment will be a key factor triggering the acceptance and exploitation of cyberspace.

Let's face it: cyberspace is entertainment. It is novel, new, and exciting. It allows us to communicate and share experiences vicariously and anonymously in ways never before possible. It not only provides entertainment directly by means of online, computerized games but also enables new forms of entertainment, including interactive role playing games, multiplayer simulations, the exploration of a variety of fantasies and adventures, and, of course, the entertainment of simply "surfing the net" and interacting with others in discussions of favorite topics. In the future, cyberspace will offer even more entertainment. Video on demand, increasingly sophisticated simulations, virtual reality, browsing art of all kinds, exploring the hyperspace links of cyberspace, and amusements we haven't yet conceived are certain to be real within most of our lifetimes.

One of the most promising new varieties of online entertainment is interactive role-playing, where groups of individuals in cyberspace working interdependently and over long periods of time, create entire universes defined by participants and populated with creatures of their creation—avatars that embody the alter egos of the participants. Whether such role-playing games are more education or entertainment is moot—those who have participated in such entertainments call them "addicting" and point to the tremendous sense of liberation available in exploring the challenge of interacting in these new self-contained worlds, whether they choose to be themselves or to represent a person or creature of their own creation. The world thus created can become extraordinarily complex, complete with political systems, governments, legal systems, economies, and so on—all created interactively by participants and "the administering gods." Called MUDs and MOOs for now, these forms of entertainment are growing in popularity, even though they are still largely constrained by their text-based heritage.

The forces that are at work to exploit cyberspace as a means of delivering traditional entertainment are also compelling. Although the most widely touted benefits of interactive TV is "movies on demand," that is only a small piece of the puzzle. Imagine being able to "order" this week's episode of your favorite program for viewing at your convenience. Push a button, get a menu, choose a program, and presto: you are watching the program you want to watch when you want to watch it. No more need scour the *TV Guide* looking for programs to record that week. Instead, you can either order what you want for immediate viewing, or alternatively, you might be using a computer and inexpensive disks to store your favorite shows— "recording" (downloading) them in minutes or seconds, instead of hours, with the assurance that they will theoretically last forever in near-perfect digital form. No more scratches, no more hiss, no more snow—no matter how long you wait. Recording and watching home movies will certainly become more popular as our means to manipulate and edit the images improve dramatically. Imagine quiz shows where the contestants aren't in the studio, but rather are participants all over the country who compete not against two others at any given time but against hundreds or thousands or even millions at a time. Already, most computers are sold as appliances with the means for you to connect your camcorder to your computer and your phone lines so that you can participate in real-time video interactions of your choice—including Saturday night card or board games between family members and friends even when the players are in four different time zones.

The meaning of fame will also gradually change: Andy Warhol may not have been far off when he spoke of the 15 minutes of fame we would each enjoy. In the past, the economics of creation and production have vested enormous power in a select few (relatively speaking) in Hollywood and New York to select and bring to market the movies and books we could each choose from. While this served to ensure a relatively high level of artistic and market merit in the works that survived the process, it also concentrated the power to shape our culture in the hands of those same few. Now, anyone with access to cyberspace is exposed to a much greater variety as authors increasingly self-publish in cyberspace. New movie-making talents will almost certainly vie for attention via cyberspace when cyberspace video technologies mature. Just as local Little Leagues prepare talent for the Major Leagues, so might local cyberspace venues become an increasingly important element in providing practice and opportunity for writers, musicians, filmmakers, and artists. We may not expect the same level of play in a Little League game as we in a World Series game, but then again, we often enjoy the Little League game even more because it is a work in progress by people we know. Expect the same forces to shape the entertainment we choose when new possibilities are enabled by the dramatic new technologies of cyberspace.

Convenience

Because cyberspace is as near as an access device, it can simplify our lives through, to name a few conveniences, telecommuting, cybershopping, research, correspondence, and handling transactions.

Many of the naysayers of cyberspace point out that no screen or other access device will replace books; that people still want and need physical contact; that libraries won't disappear because they can't be digitized easily; and that if everyone doesn't have access to cyberspace, then there will still be a need for physical world equivalents of cyberspace conveniences. Of course, they are right. That doesn't negate for a minute, however, the stunning potential of cyberspace or our relentless pursuit of convenience and efficiency, with the resultant "trickle-down" effect that ultimately benefits all as economies of scale make such conveniences less expensive and available to all. The stimulating and even sensory experience of browsing in a bookstore or lounging with a compelling book or the simple pleasures of a conversation with a friend will not disappear just because we can do those things more conveniently. However, the less pleasant tasks, such as standing in line at a bank or trying to find an ATM, could easily vanish as access to cyberspace means become more available.

Of course, most of us have learned that newly adopted time-saving conveniences do not necessarily make our lives more leisurely. Surprisingly, most of us have probably found that conveniences serve instead to increase the pace of life as they enable us to do more in less time. The competitive assumptions that are ingrained into our culture play a significant role in ensuring that most of the time saved by increasing convenience will be spent competitively trying to get ahead or stay ahead of some imaginary enemy intent on getting our share of the supposed "zero-sum pie."[4] We can only hope that cyberspace might be one of those cultural triggers that forces us to examine our assumptions about life such that we begin to learn that time is not an infinite resource.

A Doonesbury cartoon hits the nail on the head. When the boss notices that employees have been working around the clock to meet a production deadline, he calls for their attention and comments, "No product launch is worth that kind of sacrifice. Highly stressed, chronically fatigued employees can't give their best, and I need your best!" He announces that he will be shutting off the power at 5:00 P.M., urging employees to "go home, lead lives, rest." He further explains, "We can't build a future by trashing the present." The stunned employees are silent for a moment before they begin to talk among themselves. "He's gone mad." "The company'll crash! We'll be the next Apple!" "We better take this to the board."[5]

It only hurts when we laugh, but something has gone wrong. Something has happened to our values when the frenetic round-the-clock pace of many executives becomes the ideal rather than the aberration and sixty-hour work weeks become the norm instead of a deviation. In a society possessed of such a value system, convenience is paradoxically mandatory. Cyberspace offers conveniences once found only in science-fiction in so many aspects of life that its adoption by the hurried and harried as well as those seeking leisure is a virtual certainty.

Commerce

Although still in its infancy, commerce in cyberspace is maturing rapidly as a place for business transactions and will soon be of even more significance to consumers, merchants, employees, news makers, advertisers, bankers, reporters, executives, investment analysts, consultants, writers, and anyone else interested in making or spending money—including politicians. According to a study by the information technology market intelligence company, INPUT, worldwide spending on goods and services traded over the Internet will grow from $70 million in 1995 to over $255 billion in the year 2000. INPUT forecasts that user spending for information services alone in the retail and wholesale trade market sectors will reach $14.8 billion by 2000. In a February 1996 study, International Data Corporation (IDC) pegged the 1995 electronic commerce services market at $1.5 billion in revenues. Jupiter Communications forecast in January 1996 that cyberspace ad revenues would exceed $4.5 billion by the year 2000, eclipsing radio advertising revenues. It would appear that the forecasters are either exaggerating in a concerted enthusiasm reminiscent of Dutch tulip-bulb buying, or we're on the brink of a fundamental change in business and commerce. I hope to convince you in Chapter 6 that the forecasts are justified.

Cyberspace has many key advantages for sales, public relations, advertising, news gathering, opinion making, research, communications, publishing, trade, and investing. From that fateful time in the early 1990s when the Internet was opened to commerce, much has changed dramatically; business will never be quite the same again. The opportunities for the alert are enormous, residing in the dramatic changes that are underway which are already having a major impact on:

- transaction costs
- awareness of and timely access to critical information
- international boundaries and barriers to trade
- language and culture
- the nature of money

Some have likened the Electronic Frontier to the California and Alaskan gold rushes. As then, it is likely that more money will be made by those who provide the supportive infrastructure of hardware, software, and intellectual property—the picks and shovels of cyberspace—but nonetheless, there will almost certainly be a dramatic impact on our economy. Cyberspace will likely be a significant means whereby almost everyone on the planet benefits directly and indirectly from the increased efficiencies and knowledge possible in the information age.

NETTING IT OUT

The world of cyberspace is real. It is not science fiction. You could be in cyberspace tomorrow if you have either a friend who can show you the way or a computer and a modem and one of the many step-by-step "how-to" books available. It is not my purpose with this book to teach you the hows of cyberspace but rather to build a foundation of more timeless principles that will enable you to make sense of what you might find there and to exploit the opportunities you are sure to encounter in positive ways.

The benefits of connecting with others via cyberspace are immeasurable—the lives of those who discover this world are almost invariably changed as they become involved in one online community after another and find information, dialogue, convenience, kindred spirits, and like minds. I can still remember the thrill of receiving dozens of thank-you notes from individuals who had benefitted from the first technical tip I offered on IBM's internal IBMPC disk. Later, I created a few technical tables of specifications for IBM's PS/2 product line and made them available online. Soon, suggestions began to pour in from users. As I read and implemented the suggested changes, the tables improved. Then one day, I received a rather long and fairly critical e-mail note from Ward Christensen—the father of the bulletin board. I was rather awe-struck to think that Ward himself was using my tables and cared enough to take the time to help me improve them, so I worked hard to improve them to please Ward and the many other IBMers who were using them. Since that day, I have crossed paths with many who helped me with those tables, including Ward—and I doubt any of it would have happened were it not for the "connections," in various forms, that we had forged in cyberspace. After a year of "casting my bread upon the waters" in the form of maintaining, in a labor of love, the extensive technical details of my tables, IBM awarded me a large Suggestion Award—those tables had reached tens of thousands of people and saved IBM $22 million. Needless to say, the tables would never have progressed beyond their initially feeble form had it not been for the feedback I received from cyberspace. I learned that cyberspace represented possibilities I hadn't previously imagined. That award brought many good things to my family, including a new home; my life was irrevocably changed once I knew that I could reach, help, and be helped by so many so easily.

Over the years, my unabashed enthusiasm for cyberspace—born based on my participation on moderated internal IBM conferences—has been mitigated by seeing an entirely different side of cyberspace outside IBM during my years as IBM's "Online Advocate." Although my enthusiasm remains, as you will see, it has been tempered by serious concerns over the potential for abuse and even the simple possibility that cyberspace might be, as television has arguably been, dehumanizing for many and highly beneficial only for a disciplined minority who use it carefully and sparingly.

From many angles, cyberspace has a dual nature not unlike that of the larger world (or "meatspace," in the cyberspace vernacular). Cyberspace will change the way most of us view the real world in ways we can only now begin to predict. In my personal experience, and in the experience of many of those I have observed, cyberspace brings increased awareness, understanding, and cooperation; but it also encourages cynicism, a decline in civility, and a squandering of time.

Clifford Stoll, in his outstanding book of warning, *Silicon Snake Oil,* articulates those concerns well:

> I do want people to think about the decisions they're making. It'd be fun to write about the wonderful times I've had online and the terrific people I've met through my modem, but here I'm waving a flag. A yellow flag that says, "You're entering a nonexistent universe. Consider the consequences."

> It's an unreal universe, a soluble tissue of nothingness. While the Internet beckons brightly, seductively flashing an icon of knowledge-as-power, this nonplace lures us to surrender our time on earth. A poor substitute it is, this virtual reality where frustration is legion and where—in the holy names of Education and Progress—important aspects of human interactions are relentlessly devalued.[6]

Stoll's work accurately describes the downside of cyberspace; however, I don't believe he fully acknowledges the forces at work that will both attract the most eager or drag the most reluctant into cyberspace. Whether ones view of society is cooperative or competitive (or both), cyberspace offers compelling grounds for involvement. Idealists and visionaries are already at work forming virtual communities, as described so brilliantly in Howard Rheingold's seminal work, *The Virtual Community* (1993). Simultaneously, businessmen and opportunists are rushing to find competitive advantage to exploit the once-in-a-generation opportunities for profit and power available in cyberspace. In any case, the greatest challenge facing our generation may well indeed be the laying of the foundation of a new society—the free state of cyberspace.

In cyberspace, most of us will be less able to stereotype or judge our fellow beings on the basis of appearance or race; yet we will be even more subject to the vagaries and distinctions of more subtle differences, including those arising from written communications. The genius of language is often exalted at the expense of common sense—rhetoric, more often than not, becomes more important than reality.

This dual nature of the medium demands of us choices—choices that must be made if cyberspace is to be a pleasant place for those ever-increasing numbers who drop in for a visit to see what it's like. This book will help you understand those choices *offline* in order to make your *online* experience more positive.

Although I value freedom highly and admit to an unabashed faith in human potential and the difference we can make, I also believe that law is the rightful and fundamental means whereby societal values are formed and enforced as necessary to protect citizens from the harm we can so easily and thoughtlessly do one another. Thus, I often find myself engaged in discussions with online libertarians who believe that almost any law is bad law and almost any control is unnecessary. So long as there are those willing to selfishly do wrong to others, I can't accept arguments for anarchy, even when posed as defense of freedom; because without law and government to enforce law, freedom is impossible. Although I don't wish to see our core freedoms diminished and am opposed to oppressive government interference, I *will* ask that we consider the impact and consequences of the various choices we all face in cyberspace and must make. That is, after all, the foundation of society—the acknowledgment that choices *do* have consequences and that a civilized person not only takes responsibility for his or her own choices and actions, but also accepts responsibility for the broader societal consequences of the choices he or she makes. In cyberspace, it is unfortunately easy, if one so chooses, to hide behind a facade and thus apparently escape personal responsibility for consequences. Yet the consequences are nonetheless real, even in the nonspace of cyberspace.

Some contend that it's all "just a game" without serious consequence—that cyberspace is nothing but entertainment. They see it narrowly as a passing fad, much like CB radio. Others see it as a competitive frontier where the strong will thrive. Still others believe, as I do, that cyberspace is a revolutionary extension of our ability to communicate, cooperate, learn, and share, but that it is neither a panacea nor a miraculous new tool that will automatically usher in a utopia of civic freedom and enlightenment. All of the extensive resources of cyberspace are probably inadequate to eliminate greed and lust, alleviate suffering and pain, end world hunger, or usher in world peace. But they can bring us nearer those goals if we agree that they are worth pursuing, however unlikely it is that we will reach them.

What one chooses to believe about cyberspace no doubt colors one's interactions with others in cyberspace. If one sees it all as a game, one is more likely to toy with the emotions and minds of others in win/lose games. If one sees it as a fad, one might simply dismiss it or discount and ignore much of its value. If one sees it as a frontier, one might become con-frontational—adopting in unconscious imitation the online posture of ones choice of bandit, sheriff, settler, bartender, harlot, or perhaps even posse member. If one sees it as a revolutionary extension of life, then the likeli-hood increases that it will be exactly that. There is no escaping, however, that cyberspace is not only whatever we choose to believe about it but also what we will make it.

My hope for this book is that it will provide a firm foundation for explorations and choices. I hope to examine the human dimension of cyberspace from the perspectives of the individual, society, commerce, and government; with special attention to the human issues of freedom, com-munications, principles, and values. I especially hope that we can find together, in cyberspace, the means whereby the "hopes and fears of all the years" can be realized and overcome, respectively.

CHAPTER TWO

CYBERSPACE COMMUNICATIONS

New Reasons for Reasoned Exchange

Freedom from something is not enough. It should also be freedom for something. Freedom is not safety but opportunity. Freedom ought to be a means to enable the press to serve the proper functions of communication in a free society.

—Zechariah Chafee, Jr.

One of our most valued freedoms is freedom to communicate. Communication is the *raison d'être* of cyberspace. In the preceeding quotation, Zechariah Chafee could just as well have been speaking of cyberspace, where new technologies have enabled new paths of communication and have granted the power and reach of the press to individuals. But what are the proper functions of communications in a free society, and how do the new paths of communication enabled by cyberspace interface with these functions? In this chapter, I try to answer these questions, not from the perspective of an academic, but as a reflective and practical guide to improving cyberspace communications.

Freedom of speech serves the proper functions of communication in a free society with even greater power than freedom of the press. Thus, as one of the rights preserved by the Founding Fathers, free speech is still defended with passion. Deprive a person of the freedom or ability to communicate and you rob that life so deprived of almost everything that truly matters. Solitary confinement is a punishment so harsh that it is often viewed as a form of torture. The courage and nobility of soul of Helen Keller was evident in her ability to overcome the challenges she faced in communicating through visual and auditory means. The pursuit of happiness, knowledge, and relationships are wholly dependent on the ability to communicate—in whatever forms those communications occur.

The basic forms of communication are speech, writing, and visual or sensory forms such as body language or intuition. The functions of communication are as numerous as the stories we have to tell and the information we have to relate. The function of the communication often determines the form it takes. For example, an engagement announcement might take the form of an informal speech before a group of friends, while a wedding announcement takes the form of a precise written communication. Form, in these cases, is mediated by a variety of characteristics of the function of the communication. Tradition and social etiquette guide us, in most cases, to understand the form communications should take, even if we are unconscious of the underlying characteristics that have determined the forms in the past.

The paths of communication in the preceding examples are, respectively, voice and ink on paper. Other functions call for different forms or paths as dictated by a variety of characteristics of the communication. Time, place, and technology also mediate communications. For example, in a medical emergency, you would dial 911 rather than send an e-mail message to your doctor. If you were stranded on the freeway or in high water, you might seek help via your cellular phone, or you might flag down a passing motorist. In each of these examples, the communication would also be mediated by its character, or personality.

Because cyberspace offers so many new forms of communication with few precedents that offer the comforting guidance of tradition, I have chosen to offer my own perspectives on the nature and character of these communications rather than rely on communications or academic theory. I offer a general overview of some of the key characteristics of communications, which will help us better understand how cyberspace can increase our opportunities to communicate effectively. Then I offer my thoughts on the foundations of valuable communications—reason and rhetoric, particularly as applied to cyberspace discussion—which will help us to enhance the overall quality of those communications.

CHARACTERISTICS OF COMMUNICATIONS

Communications have a number of characteristics that render them more or less suitable to differing circumstances. These characteristics include a variety of elements such as familiarity and formality, audience, purpose, timeliness, method, language, and style. In choosing the method of communication that will best accomplish our purpose, we often unconsciously take these factors into account. Understanding the characteristics of communications helps us use the many forms of communication available to us, both within cyberspace and without.

Some of the more important factors that make up the character of any given form of communications are introduced in the following comparative list:

Directed
Broadcast with no expectation of response.

Examples: press release, TV broadcast, announcement, hand gesture

Interactive
Involve others where give-and-take responsiveness is expected and appropriate.

Examples: survey, question posed via e-mail or at a meeting, sign language

Formal
Ceremonial, highly structured, and/or standardized in format and expectations of quality and outcome.
Examples: application or registration, resume, speech

Informal
Casual, unstructured, and without expectations regarding form or outcome.
Examples: conversation with a friend, chat room, e-mail to a pen pal

Pushed (Supply-Driven)
Intrusive, i.e., enter the awareness of a recipient who did not request the communication.
Examples: advertisements, telephone solicitations, broadcast e-mail

Pulled (Demand-Driven)
Sought or requested by the recipient who welcomes the communication.

Examples: downloading a text file, calling an 800 number for information, lurking in a forum

Time-critical
Linked with some other event in time and commands a response, usually urgent.
Examples: contractual deadlines for a response, formal meeting, 911 phone call

Casual
Occurs independent of other events in time and does not require a response; not urgent.
Examples: chance meeting and exchange, fan mail, junk mail

One-time
Directed communications which are not repeated and are often urgent.
Examples: time-critical meeting, pink slip, 911 call

Recurring
Occur repeatedly, usually at regular intervals.
Examples: newspapers, weekly meeting, daily talk show

Private
Intended to be limited in distribution to a clearly defined target audience.

Examples: confidential note, discussions with doctor, lawyer, or accountant, personnel jacket, payroll stub

Public
Intended for indiscriminate widespread distribution with no restrictions on receipt. Note that this is not the same as "public domain."
Examples: news articles, radio and TV broadcasts, newsgroup postings

1:1 (One-to-One)
1:1 or 1:N (one-to-one or one-to-many); synchronous; originate with a single source with a targeted destination of one or many recipients.

Examples: sharing a secret with a friend, e-mail, memos, mail

N:N (Many-to-Many)
N:N or N:1 (many-to-many or many to one); have an audience consisting of multiple participants who may contribute to or receive the communications.
Examples: newsgroups or forums, jury verdict, mob action, meetings, conference calls

Reactive
Made in response to the demands of a previous communication.

Examples: reply to a customer complaint, answer to a question, flaming on a forum

Proactive
Initiatedby the sender, independent of the demands of any previous communication.
Examples: first posting in a forum thread, whistle-blowing phone call to a reporter, unsolicited resume

Personal
Consciously customized by the sender for the recipient.

Examples: handwritten correspondence, birthday card, e-mail message to a friend

Impersonal
Originate from a source without the individual awareness of the recipient.
Examples: broadcast news, junk mail, renewal notices

Most communications reflect each of the characteristics, or personality traits, to one degree or another, usually falling somewhere between the two characterizing extremes in the list. For example, a memorable conversation with a friend is likely to be informal but could also be formal or somewhere in between. Depending on the circumstance of the conversation, it might reflect varying degrees of each of the other characteristics as well. A Form 1040A sent to the IRS, for example, is highly directed, very formal, pulled, time-critical only as April 15 nears, annually recurring, generally private, 1:1 or 1:N, wholly reactive, and somewhat impersonal. All communications possess what might be called a personality that reflects the multifaceted characteristics of the communication.

Cyberspace has increased the number of technological paths of communication available to us, thus changing the character and personality of the communications options available to us. Now we have communications choices that are more interactive, informal, pulled, casual, public, many-to-many, and personal than we have traditionally had. Communications with these characteristics are triggered not so much by the need for any particular bit of information as by a general desire to learn about and understand what is going on around us. Before the advent of computer-mediated communications, communications were usually oral and took place in such places as coffee shops or around water coolers. Now, in cyberspace, these communications are written, can be preserved, and no longer require those communicating to be in the same place at the same time.

As cyberspace technology progresses to support quality video and sound in addition to text and graphics, the variety of communications options available to us in cyberspace will exceed those available to us outside cyberspace. In cyberspace, we can meet and converse with friends and strangers alike, at once, without regard to physical presence. We can browse catalogues, obtain product information, discuss products with current owners, and place an order without leaving home or speaking to anyone else. We can find information without visiting a library or consulting a librarian or expert. We can write, create art, or perform for potentially large audiences without finding an agent or publisher. There is little doubt that cyberspace communications will become a key part of our lives.

FORMS OF CYBERSPACE COMMUNICATIONS

Let's examine each of the most common types of cyberspace communication in greater detail to understand their character and personality, including their function.

E-Mail

Electronic mail, or e-mail, is perhaps the easiest to understand and the most widely used computer-mediated communication. It is like traditional mail, except that an e-mail message carries a computer-defined address rather than a geographically defined one and is routed and delivered electronically by computers over networks in minutes rather than physically by postal workers through rain or sleet or snow in days. E-mail communications are typically written interactive, informal, casual, private, one-to-one or one-to-many, and personal. E-mail is appropriate for correspondence, inquiries, providing information to others, and even, to a degree, personal solicitation. Even random solicitations such as junk mail—once considered an unacceptable breach of cyberspace norms—are beginning to increase in frequency and acceptability.

The format of an e-mail message may vary from one system to another, just as the format of a traditional letter varies according to individual preference. The parts of an e-mail letter are essentially the same as those of a traditional letter and its envelope—sender's name and address, recipient's name and address, salutation, body, closing, and signature. Some of the elements of an e-mail message are assigned by the computer, including the date and time, routing information, message number, and a closing line or lines from a user-customized "signature file." Typically, when you initiate a letter to someone, you need enter only the recipient's address (which occupies a single line instead of two or three in a traditional letter), the subject, and the body of your text. Your computer can usually be set up to automatically take care of everything else. When replying to an e-mail message received from someone else, you need only enter the text of your reply. Most software designed to handle e-mail can automatically find and use all of the other elements of an e-mail message. Additionally, you might also be able to "attach" a file, to be sent in binary, or computerized, form for downloading by the recipient. An e-mail message typically looks like this:

```
MSG FROM:    Jonathan Jones,        johnj@noname.net
      TO:    Dave Whittle,          whittle@newbie.net
    DATE:    11/07/94  09:35:41
 SUBJECT:    Comdex

Good to hear from you, Dave. Hope all is well. Please let me know if you
will be at Comdex so we can arrange lunch

Regards,

Jon
```

```
Chief Executive Officer, NoName Corp.
2823 Main Street, Washington, D.C.
Phone: (888)555-1212, Fax: (888)555-2121
```

Note that its format resembles a memo rather than a formal letter.

E-mail addresses vary in form from one online service to another; but the addressing scheme used on the Internet has become the standard, and online services route e-mail via the Internet. The Internet format consists of the user's alias, or name, followed by his or her domain, separated by an ampersand or an "at" symbol (@). For example, the following are valid e-mail addresses with their Internet equivalents:

ONLINE SERVICE	E-MAIL ADDRESS	INTERNET EQUIVALENT
CompuServe	76711,1061	76711.1061@compuserve.com
Prodigy	JKFV64A	JKFV64A@prodigy.com
America Online	teamos2dw	teamos2dw@aol.com

Note that the online service e-mail addresses do not include the domain. These addresses are valid for use internally, within the service, i.e., domain. If, however, a nonsubscriber to the online service sends you e-mail, it is usually routed through the Internet and therefore must include the full Internet form of the address. This follows the same principal as traditional business mail. If you send a memo to a coworker, you insert it in an interoffice routing envelope on which you write the recipient's name. If, however, you are sending it to someone outside the company, you insert it in an envelope that includes not only the recipient's name but also his or her complete address.

Just as real-world addresses convey messages about culture or status to those who might be concerned about such things, so do e-mail addresses carry connotations, as the following list of fictitious Internet addresses suggests.

- john@doe.com
- moron@harvard.edu
- billg@vnet.ibm.com
- redneck@whitehouse.gov
- goodguy@alcatraz.pri
- rush@very.liberal.org

Some long-time Internet denizens look askance at addresses that end with the domain name of one of the commercial online services, such as @aol.com or @prodigy.com, assuming that the address holder is an intruder who is computer or Internet illiterate. Conversely, anyone with a domain name that is part of his or her actual name, such as john@doe.com, is presumed to be an important person who is Internet savvy, has command of net resource, and has clout. Those whose addresses include the name of their school or business (@vnet.ibm.com, @microsoft.com, @mit.edu, @byu.edu, etc.) is often associated with the image of that organization, for better or worse. One of the challenges we face is resisting the temptation to judge our cyberspace compatriots by their e-mail addresses.

E-mail's greatest advantage is rapid delivery You usually receive your mail within minutes of the time it was sent, which beats even the quickest of overnight couriers. As with traditional mail, once you receive an e-mail message, it is up to you to open and respond to it within an appropriate length of time. You may read each message as it comes in (if your computer is switched on and your e-mail software is active), or you may choose to "collect" it only once or twice a day. Even if you check for and respond to your e-mail only once a day, turnaround time (from the moment it was sent to the moment you respond) is less than 24 hours. If you check and respond twice a day—say, first thing in the morning and at the end of the day— turnaround time generally does not exceed 16 hours. It would take two days for an overnight mail service to accomplish an equivalent turnaround, and with e-mail you don't have to leave your desk, fill out a form, waste paper, or incur a postal or courier fee. Certainly, the telephone is a more rapid path of communication, but it does not provide you with a printed record of the communication and the net cost of communicating by telephone is greater. Perhaps more important is that the ring of a telephone can be intrusive—"pushed" communication—whereas e-mail can be "pulled" at your convenience.

The rapid communication, convenience, and economy of e-mail promotes efficiency, a significant factor in today's economy. If we choose to participate in that economy, we embrace e-mail. If, on the other hand, we are mired in the familiar, we might respond to e-mail in the same way a nineteenth-century British gentleman responded to his mail when he learned that it was routed from one city to another by train rather than horse: "I shall open my mail in three days' time, when it should have arrived."

Although net culture is fairly flexible about e-mail turnaround time, the nature of the communication should factor in your decision of when and how to respond, if at all. If everyone felt obliged to respond to every e-mail received, we would probably soon be buried in trivial or obligatory messages of little value. Fortunately, not responding to an e-mail message is only rarely considered a serious breach of good manners. A distinction is usually made, however, between professional and casual use of e-mail. If you use an e-mail address in your profession, you are expected to respond to your e-mail fairly quickly—within a few days, unless you are vacationing or traveling, in which case an explanation of any delay is usually in order. Some e-mail systems even allow you to set an automatic response to be sent explaining your circumstances. Casual e-mail, on the other hand, isn't terribly time-sensitive and can be read and answered at your convenience or not at all.

E-mail within a company or between companies is usually considered an informal means of communication. You would not, for example, typically send your supervisor a letter of resignation or your customer a contract via e-mail. Protocol still dictates a more formal means of communication. Neither would you communicate an emergency or urgent matter via e-mail. Timeliness would dictate the type of immediate communication offered by a telephone with a "live" person at the other end to either answer the call or respond to a pager. In most urgent situations you cannot afford to guess whether the recipient of the communication is at his or her computer to receive the message. Further, sensitive communications are usually best handled in person or on the phone, where nuances of tone or body language contribute to effective communication. In brief, e-mail increasingly is becoming the most efficient means of informal communication among individuals, in spite of the relative complexity of establishing and maintaining the one-to-one and one-to-many direct lines of communication of e-mail within workgroups, as illustrated by the accompanying figure.

In the figure, the circles represent the members of the workgroup. The lines connecting the circles represent the lines of communication among the members. Each of the eight members is connected to every other member of the workgroup by different lines, for a total of 48 lines, and the complexity of the network increases as the number of members increases. For example, if we were to add one more person to this workgroup, we would have to add another eight lines to establish communications among all members. The implication, of course, is that communications within large workgroups and organizations become progressively more difficult to manage and support than those within smaller groups. Thus, workgroups quickly reach the point where more efficient means of many-to-many communication become important. Conferencing, or computer-mediated collaborative communications, is that means.

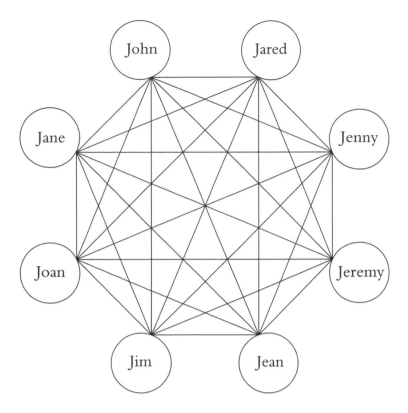

Direct workgroup communications

Conferencing

Although e-mail is probably the most common type of cyberspace communication, conferencing is arguably the most important. This many-to-many type of open, global communication is known not only as conferencing but also as collaborative computing, interpersonal computing, networked communications, computer-mediated communications, and computer-based communications. Instances of conferencing are also known by a number of names, including forums, round-table discussions, groupware, and even virtual communities.

At its simplest, conferencing is an electronic bulletin board system whose principle is the same as that of a traditional cork bulletin board message center. Each "bulletin board" includes a title describing a topic of interest to participants. For example, one bulletin board might be labeled "Buying and Selling," another "Politics," and still another "Windows 95 Problems and Support." On each of these boards you would find a series of notes from various people. Each posted note would include a posting number, a "to" line, a "from" line, a date and time line, and a subject line, which describes a specific subject that is related to the bulletin board topic. For example, on a "Classifieds" board, you might see the following note posted:

```
POST #:   1212
  FROM:   Davey Jones
    TO:   ALL
  DATE:   March 25, 1996 - 12:05 PM
    RE:   Treasure Chest for Sale
```

I have a used Treasure Chest several hundred years old, in rather poor condition--the lock is broken and it won't open. I'll take $100 or best offer.

Most notes also include a line that refers to another note. The various notes that discuss a particular subject, or at least display the related subject-line title, are referred to as a "thread," as in "thread of conversation." For example, we might find below our sample note, which begins the "thread," the following post, which in referencing the first note continues the thread:

```
POST #:   1217
  FROM:   Bluebeard Hook
    TO:   Davey Jones
  DATE:   March 25, 1996 - 17:10 PM
    RE:   Treasure Chest for Sale
   REF:   POST #1212
```

Would you take $50 for it if I wired you cash today?

Bluebeard Hook may be a stranger to Davey Jones. That's part of what makes conferencing fun, interesting, and valuable. Not only do you reach more people than you would if you were to post your note on the supermarket or office cork bulletin board, but you also encounter people you would not otherwise communicate with.

Conferencing holds many surprises—you never really know who will respond or how. For example, someone might then respond to Bluebeard Hook as follows:

```
POST #:   12 87
  FROM:   Roger Hammerstein
    TO:   Bluebeard Hook
  DATE:   March 26, 1996 - 11:43 PM
    RE:   Treasure Chest for Sale
   REF:   POST #1217

Bluebeard Hook said:
>> Would you take $50 for it if I brought you cash today? <<
Come on, Bluebeard--spare us all and either make a reasonable offer or
none at all, OK?
```

You can never fully predict whether the thread will weave a coherent fabric of communication or a crazy quilt. This variability of experience is the result of a singular feature of conferencing: anyone with access to the bulletin board may, at any time, "walk up to" and interact with it in a variety of ways. You might

- read all notes on an existing bulletin board.
- read only those notes with subjects of interest to you.
- respond to a previously posted note with a new note, using the same or a new title. This would be like posting a new note immediately below an existing note on a cork bulletin board message center.
- start a new thread by posting a new note on a new subject. This is like adding a new note at the top of a cork bulletin board message center, thus introducing a whole new topic of exchange.
- introduce a new topic of discussion. This would be like hanging a new bulletin board next to the old one.

Conferencing represents a breakthrough in our ability to communicate. The character of conferencing is unique in our modern experience: it is the first form of communications to be simultaneously public, many-to-many, personal, pulled, interactive, and informal. Compare the accompanying diagram representing conferencing connections to the earlier figure representing e-mail connections. The figure representing shared workgroup communications diagrams the structure of conferencing. The space labeled "Computer-mediated conferencing" represents the forums of interest to participants. Once the connections are established, members can conference at their convenience. This many-to-many communication can and

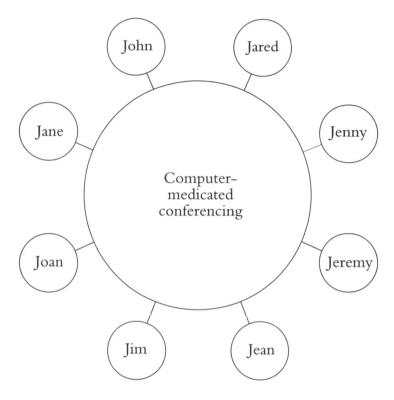

Shared workgroup communications

often does replace more inconvenient means of communicating, such as status meetings, informational meetings, and conference calls. Also, conferencing requires fewer lines of communication than does e-mail, which requires of participants a knowledge and awareness of the names and e-mail address of all intended recipients. Conferencing requires only one connection—between the member and the conferencing forum, thus providing an audience that is both larger and more focused than is likely with e-mail. When combined with e-mail, this significantly simplifies communications within workgroups. Topics of interest are individually selected by participants, who can find not only the information they need but also the qualified target audiences that could, outside cyberspace, be difficult to bring together.

In a business, these forums can be internal, on a Notes server, for example, or external, such as a CompuServe forum or an Internet newsgroup. Realistically, no one in the group is privy to each communication of anyone in the group; yet theoretically everyone in the group has access to all of the conferencing communications of everyone in the group, assuming none of the forums are private or restricted. In practical terms, however, for a workgroup to gain full advantage from conferencing, each participant must agree to frequent an appropriate forum and interact there. This often necessitates practical training and cultural convincing. Many individuals simply communicate better orally than they do in writing. Thus, they are reluctant to use a form of communication that puts them at a disadvantage. In my experience, those individuals who excel in oral communications are likely to be managers or executives, which explains why companies don't embrace conferencing as readily as one might expect, given the significant advantages it offers.

Conferencing evolved concurrent with computer networks. Early efforts derived from timesharing and networking concepts included ARPANET, Usenet, computer bulletin boards, BIX, CIX, CompuServe, timesharing, The Source, BITNET, and a number of internal corporate communications systems. At IBM, these conferences were established in the late seventies and early eighties by enterprising systems support personnel using IBM's enormous worldwide network (the largest in the world at the time), mainframe communications programs, and Mike Cowlishaw's TOOLS mechanism. The most popular conference, IBMPC, was supported and developed by groups in Yorktown and Kingston, New York, and grew quickly from a few thousand participants in 1983 to perhaps a hundred thousand, almost half the company, by the early 1990s. As a moderated conference, development and growth was not without its problems—but what is most remarkable is that the norms developed early on sustained the system, allowing it to handle enormous increases in traffic without significant increases in human resource. Forums could be found covering every conceivable topic related to personal computers as well as many other business issues. The content was of remarkable quality because of the discipline imposed by the early efforts of the pioneer moderators to establish a disciplined forum culture appropriate to IBM's stated purpose for funding the forums: to assist employees acting in management-approved purposes, i.e., "doing their jobs." Flaming (a flame is a critical online diatribe), topic drift, personal attacks, profanity, and other such problems common to most conferencing systems were simply against the rules, and when they occurred, peer review and management sanctions were usually effective in preventing their recurrence. In spite of the success of this IBM example, such relatively strict moderation is not consistently appropriate or even possible because moderation is expensive and may be viewed as an infringement on free speech or as a form of censorship. Nonetheless, it should be noted that in spite of the fact that moderated conferences might indeed be viewed as censorship or a suppression of free speech, the rules and limits of a moderated conference can contribute significantly to the value of such a forum. After all, the underlying principle and the purposes of such a forum are the same as those of a moderated political debate or town meeting—to provide structure, focus, and fairness to the interactive dialogue.

Wherever it occurs, conferencing educes a wide range of participation, from experts to neophytes, from good writers to poor writers, from wise men to fools. Of course, one needn't participate—and my experience has been that most do not. Those who choose to read the exchanges but not to participate are called "lurkers," since the fact that one is reading the exchanges is often easily hidden from the active participants. Participants rarely know who is actually reading their publicly posted notes unless the "lurker" becomes a participant. Naturally, participants in the exchange would prefer that others join in and contribute—thus the term lurker started as a pejorative but has been transformed over the years until now it has gained an affectionate quality not unlike the "dummy" in the best-selling series of books whose titles end in "for Dummies." Lurking can be an enormously valuable, risk-free way to learn a great deal about a variety of subjects.

The value and integrity of a conferencing forum is largely dependent on the quality of the thought that precedes the contributions of participants, so it is important for participants to think before they write. Participants should consider whether their messages are meaningful to the topic at hand, whether they are appropriately sensitive to the views and concerns of others, whether they are in adherence to the rules of the conference, and whether they are adding something new to the discussion or merely repeating observations made by other participants. If a message lacks meaning or clarity or is nothing more than an emotional outburst or attack on another participant, the communication is better left unposted. Much "bandwidth" (meaning attention and online time) is wasted on personal attacks, flaming, innuendo, disparagement, and other less valuable communications. Finding a conference that addresses a topic that excites your intellect and arouses your passions is like stumbling onto a mother lode; but those who do not respect its integrity will render it a river of shifting sands where seekers of information must pan the gravel of inappropriate posts to yield nuggets of valuable information.

Although the implementations of conferencing systems vary widely, this "bulletin board" metaphor applies to most, if not all, of the ways such communications are handled between the various online services and the Internet. For example, CompuServe has "forums," each with an area for messages. Message areas are subdivided by "section," with each section containing "threads." Each thread consists of an original message and subject line and all responses to that message and subsequent responses. The links between messages and responses form the treelike structure of the thread. Messages "scroll" regularly—meaning that they are deleted after a certain period of time. The structures employed by Prodigy and America Online are not much different, even though they use different names for the concepts, such as "bulletin board" and "topic" instead of "forum" and "section." The WELL uses a different approach, which structurally, through the use of its proprietary software, forces one to scroll through (and presumably read) all previous messages on a topic before contributing. Messages are never deleted. The WELL, then, seems to educe a sense that the discussions are important and deserve to be treated as history in the making. The online commercial conferencing has an altogether different culture, with more repetition and temporary and trivial discussions. The respective structures clearly contribute to the respective cultures. The Internet newsgroups are the most unstructured of all, creating the free-for-all character of most Internet discussions. Each newsgroup has a name, such as `alt.politics`, and within that newsgroup are dozens of simultaneous threads. Because the newsgroups are less structured than most conferencing communications, there is a great deal of quoting used to maintain continuity. Whatever the structure and form, computer-mediated conferencing represents a new form of communication that contributes significantly to making cyberspace what it is.

Subscription Lists

Many computer conferences, forums, and newsgroups are not only directly accessible online but are also available through subscription lists, or mailing lists. A subscription list permits those interested to subscribe to a forum by sending an e-mail message containing the word SUBSCRIBE to an e-mail address specifically designated to electronically handle the mundane chore of adding the subscriber's name and e-mail address to the electronic mailing list. Then, when anyone sends a post, or e-mail message, to a different address designated as the "mail list" address, it is redistributed to everyone who has subscribed and is on the current mailing list.

One must be careful about following forums in this manner. Some newsgroups generate so many posts that you could be quickly buried by the volume of mail, making it difficult to find your more valued e-mail. It is also quite common for individuals to confuse the subscription address with the mail list address—thus resulting in worthless messages in your e-mail which say nothing more than "SUBSCRIBE" or "UNSUBSCRIBE" or the flames that follow, telling the person what they've done and how to correct it.

Subscription lists are quite common, however, and can often be a valuable way to stay current on topics of particular interest. Subscription lists are also ideal for the distribution of news and other time-sensitive information.

Real-Time Chat

In computer lingo, "real time" means that interactivity occurs with no discernible time delay. Thus, a real-time chat is the computerized (typed) equivalent of a telephone conversation—a participant types message on a display and presses Enter to transmit the message, almost instantaneously, over the modem to the respective displays of the other participants. The following "dialogue" represents the format of a typical online exchange:

```
You are entering the Chat Room:
LYNN:  Hello, is anyone home?
CHUCK:  Are you kidding? It's TOO crowded already! But welcome
anyway . . .
JOE:  Hi, Lynn! M or F?
LYNN:  Thanks for the warm welcome, Chuck. Joe, I probably shouldn't
admit it, but yes, I'm a woman. But don't get any ideas! I may be
gorgeous, but I'm here to find someone who wants an intellectual
discussion.
JOE:  Sure, that's what they all say. I'm just more honest than
that . . .
```

Online services use real-time chat mode for interactive sessions with celebrities or experts in a variety of disciplines—advertising in advance the session's time and cyberplace. Individuals commonly use real-time chat mode for cybersex and other exchanges between strangers. Most of the few children who have been lured away from home by strangers they met in cyberspace first encountered the stranger in a real-time chat room; it is therefore a potentially dangerous mode of communications for teenagers and children.

Multimedia Exchange

Web pages and sites based on multimedia exchanges promise to be a ubiquitous form of communication in the future. Although these pages and sites currently present a curious mix of text, graphics, sound, video, menus, software programs, and forms, they are decidedly useful for a wide variety of communications. Imagine a television with a million channels. Each channel you activate presents a screen filled with information, options, or both. By pointing to graphics or words on the screen, you can instantly access another screen or hear sounds that correlate to the selected graphic or word. The path you take through the information, as well as the timing of the journey, is up to you—limited only by what's available on the Web and the hardware and software you're using to access that information. That, in theory at least, describes the World Wide Web.

Many types of communications exist and are evolving on the World Wide Web. Its applications are numerous, including billboards, catalogues, classes, conferences, contests, games, libraries, directories, and shopping malls. This novel arena of communication, not yet a decade old, is exploding with activity and opportunity. It is likely to become one of the predominant modes of communication within the next century, subsuming all other modes of cyberspace communication—including e-mail, conferencing, subscription lists, real-time chatting, and even telephone and videoconferencing.

Because these new communication technologies promise to become more affordable, easier to use, and increasingly more interactive, they will almost certainly have an enormous impact on each one of us and our ability to interact with others and gather and use information—and that covers just about everything we do in life.

CONVENTIONS

Every form of communication entails conventions that facilitate effective exchanges. In cyberspace, the limitations of the medium in its earliest forms have given rise to conventions that are peculiar to cyberspace communications. Limited bandwidth, the fact that the "meter is running," and the absence of body language have led to the widespread use of a variety of shorthand expressions and acronyms. For example, to avoid typing and save computer and human time, users frequently substitute acronyms for frequently used phrases. Since you can't use body language online, users have substituted a variety of clever punctuation pictures called *emoticons* (short for "emotive icons").

Acronyms

Entire dictionaries and online lookup mechanisms have been developed just to track acronyms; however, the most widely used and commonly encountered Ones are listed in the following table.

ACRONYM	SHORT FOR:	USAGE NOTES
<g>	Grin	Also seen as <G>
<bg>	Big grin	Also seen as <BG>
<s>	Smile	Also seen as <S>
<vbg>	Very Big Grin	Also seen as <VBG>
AAMOF	As a matter of fact	
BTW	By the way	
BYKT	But you knew that	
CMIIW	Correct me if I'm wrong	
EOL	End of lecture	
FAQ	Frequently asked questions	
FITB	Fill in the blank	
FYI	For your information	
FOAF	Friend of a friend for an unidentified source	Disclaimer of sorts
FWIW	For what it's worth	
IAC	In any case	
IANAL	I am not a lawyer	Usually prefaces a legal commentary offered anyway
IMHO	In my humble opinion	Ironically, the opinions are rarely offered in humility
IOW	In other words	
IRL	In real life	
ITRW	In the real world	

ACRONYM	SHORT FOR:	USAGE NOTES
LJATD	Let's just agree to disagree	Used to end a conversation going nowhere
LJBF	Let's just be friends	
LOL!	Laughing out loud!	
MorF?	Male or female?	Primarily used in chat rooms
OTOH	On the other hand	
ROTFL!	Rolling on the floor laughing!	Variations include RotF,L! and ROTF,L!
ROTFLMAO!	Rolling on the floor laughing my "head" off	"A" is commonly used in place of the "H.";-)
RTFM	Read the "fine" manual	Implies impatience
TANSTAAFL	There ain't no such thing as a free lunch	
TDNBW	This does not bode well	Often used ironically
TIA	Thanks in advance	Offered at the end of an open-ended request
TIC	Tongue in cheek	Also expressed using emoticon (:-Q).
TTFN	Ta-ta for now	Insouciant expression of Tigger (friend of Winnie the Pooh)
TYVM	Thank you very much	
WIBNI	Wouldn't it be nice if...	
WRT	With regard to	
XOXO	Hugs and kisses	The more XOs the stronger the sentiment
YMMV	Your mileage may vary	

Emoticons

I doubt even half of the different emoticons to be found in books have ever been used much online—but the following represent a healthy share of those I've actually seen used.

EMOTICON	MEANING
:-)	Smiley, smile, happy face
:)	Same as smiley
:-(	Frowney, frowning, sad face
: (	Same as frowney
;-)	Winking
:->	Sarcasm, but no offense, intended
:-D	Really big smile
:-o	Surprised or amazed
0:-)	Halo or bald head
:-)>	Beard
:-|	Indifferent, not sure how to react
:'-(	Crying
:'-)	Tears of joy
*	Kiss
{ }	Hug
{{**}}	Hugs and kisses

Expectations

There are a number of expectations for online communications that anyone attempting to communicate should know. Violation of the expectations of others can have undesirable consequences ranging from being ignored to being bombarded with mail. You are expected to understand the following communication conventions on most forums and services.

- ■ USE ALL CAPITAL LETTERS ONLY IF YOU WANT YOUR MESSAGE TO BE READ AS SHOUTING! If you have some form of antique terminal that has no lowercase letters, then explain and apologize as a preemptive measure to avoid being reminded of your bad manners.
- ■ Keep every message short and sweet. Consider the relative importance of every word and sentence and edit ruthlessly.
- ■ Don't dive into the middle of a discussion unless you are familiar with the territory already covered by the participants. Nobody appreciates someone who repeats points already made and asks questions that have already been answered.
- ■ Profanity and vulgarity are not only inconsiderate and rude but are also considered by many to be a crude attempt to strengthen the expression of weak ideas.
- ■ Don't contribute to the spread of baseless rumors, gossip, and innuendo. Always specify the source of information you pass along.
- ■ Use paragraphs properly and generously and leave space between each paragraph.
- ■ Make every effort to ensure that your post is formatted properly for those who will be reading it—especially if it involves information in tabular format. Remember to keep it simple and to understand the specific peculiarities of the target forum and service.
- ■ Be sure that the content of your post is meaningful and appropriate to the purpose of the forum and the topic of the thread.
- ■ Use descriptive, specific, and interesting subject or header lines.
- ■ Be sensitive to geographical and cultural boundaries and avoid overly specific posts. In other words, don't post in a national forum something of interest only to your neighborhood.
- ■ Target your audience carefully. Don't send e-mail to a large mailing list unless you are certain that it is appropriate and necessary. Don't indiscriminately "carbon copy" (cc) others.
- ■ To preserve context as you respond to a previous message (which may no longer be accessible to your intended audience or recipient), include the appropriate quote(s) from the original message in your response.

THE POWER OF WORDS AND REASON

Because cyberspace is first and foremost a place of concentrated communication, one is quickly likely to encounter a real-life course in the use and abuse of words and reason there. I've learned more about the limits and uses of language online than I did in 18 years of school. The ability to shape words into coherent sentences and support those sentences with reason and logic is the foundation of effective communication in cyberspace, which in turn is necessary for us to find fulfillment, develop relationships, and work with others there. Time spent learning about words and reason can pay big dividends. Although a complete tutorial in rhetoric and logic is beyond the scope of this book, a practical introduction can greatly enhance the effectiveness of your online communications.

Rhetoric

Rhetoric is a word of multiple meanings. It is defined most simply as the art of speaking or writing effectively, and yet it is also often used to imply the manipulation of words. *Rhetoric* carries the additional connotation of appealing to emotion as well as reason, so for our purposes, we will examine some of the rhetorical devices that might address our emotions before turning our attention to logic and fallacy. To simplify the presentation, I've divided this introduction to rhetoric into three uses: positive, neutral, and negative. I've seen enough of the effects of different types of rhetoric to be quite certain not only that certain approaches are better than others but also that some uses of rhetoric are seldom, if ever, justified.

Positive Uses

Rhetoric can be used in positive ways to increase knowledge, promote harmony, and communicate more effectively. Although rhetorical devices and linguistic technique are poor substitutes for character and sensitivity to others in any discussion, we can often learn from our own mistakes by comparing our problematic communications with certain rhetorical objectives and ideals. I believe that the nearer we can come to reflecting the golden rule in our communications, the more effective they will be.

In most of the following examples, I'm assuming exchanges in an open forum between two public participants and frequent adversaries named JaneD and RichM.

Affirmation Even in disagreeing, we can, with words, demonstrate our fundamental respect for the other person—in particular, their right to hold and express an opinion that differs from our own.
Examples:
▪ RichM states in his post to JaneD that he hopes she doesn't vote in a coming election. JaneD replies, quite appropriately, "I respect your

right to believe as you choose—can you respect my right to do the same?"

▪ When JaneD makes a point that soundly discredits a point that RichM has been vigorously trying to make in a discussion, RichM makes a comment questioning and attacking JaneD's intelligence and education. Rather than give credence to RichM's diversionary points by addressing them, JaneD's response is respectful but firm: "In the future, can you agree to direct your disparaging comments at my ideas and not at me personally? You have some good ideas that shouldn't be lost in distracting hostility. Thank you."

Sincerity Although a cynic would say that all sincerity is feigned, I believe that emotional honesty is indeed the best policy and is easily spotted and respected as evidence of character.

Examples:

▪ RichM admits that he was unaware of a fact offered by JaneD and concedes that he has changed his mind based on her contribution.

▪ JaneD answers a question with "I don't know the answer to that, but I suspect that if you were to ask that same question on the KNOWITALL web site, you could get an answer."

▪ In spite of their ongoing arguments, RichM offers his private condolences to JaneD when he learns that her mother has passed away.

Understanding A primary positive use of rhetoric is to communicate effectively enough to achieve understanding. This is incumbent on both writer and reader—but if both share the same goal and are willing to put themselves in the shoes of another, then breakthroughs can be easily achieved through the wise use of language.

Examples:

▪ JaneD has long maintained that OS/2 is the best operating system available. RichM is a fan of Microsoft. After much discussion, JaneD and RichM learn enough about the position of one another to reach agreement that OS/2 is the best operating system for knowledgeable, advanced users and Windows 95 is the best operating system for novices and home use.

▪ JaneD and RichM have argued long and vehemently over whose car is best. They finally agree that they should both test drive other cars on the market and share their findings. JaneD and RichM, surprisingly, reach agreement that a third brand is superior to either of their former autos.

Neutral and Dual-Edged Uses

Most rhetorical devices can be used positively to further worthy goals or negatively to pursue harmful selfish objectives. If we strive to understand the concerns and perspectives of other participants, we should also strive to reflect our understanding and sensitivity in the language we use in order to prevent misunderstandings and enhance communication. Until cyberspace technology permits visual and oral interaction, we are limited to written interaction—and must therefore use rhetoric wisely to help, rather than harm, others.

Ambiguity Ambiguity can result from faulty sentence structure, poor choice of words, lack of inflection, misunderstanding of connotation, or other causes stemming from a lack of clarity. In cyberspace, we lack many of the clues that we use in oral communication. We are forced to craft our words more carefully because we are deprived of the winks, smiles, nods, inflections, and other unspoken nuances of face-to-face communications. Emoticons, such as :-) (a sideways smile) or <g> (grin) can mitigate, if used wisely, some of the confusion. Nonetheless, ambiguity is ever present in conferencing communications and often leads to unnecessary dispute. Thus, ambiguity should usually be avoided, even though it is sometimes appropriate as a deliberate response to avoid embarrassing clarification while still making a point. It can also be used to bring a tiresome discussion to a close without renouncing principle. The obvious approach when faced with someone else's ambiguity is to resist drawing and/or attacking conclusions while seeking clarification, at least if the matter is important enough to pursue.

Examples:

■ JaneD writes, "RichM thinks women are simple." RichM responds, "Wrong, as usual. If women were easy, the world would be a better place." (Negative)

■ JaneD writes, "I'm sorry I can't personally give that response the attention it so richly deserves." RichM concludes the thread with a sincere "Thank you. I'm glad to see we finally agree on something." (Neutral)

■ JaneD responds to a rude and pointed question about her marital status from RichM, saying, "I'm sure my husband could answer that question for you, if I knew where he was right now." (Positive)

Broadening, Narrowing, and Diverting Any exchange can be broadened or narrowed, depending on whether a response focuses on only portions of the original post or offers new ideas or questions that build on the original post or combines the two in order to steer the conversation towards a different track. This rhetorical technique can be used to steer a discussion in either positive or negative directions.

Examples:

■ JaneD comments that abortion is wrong and gives three reasons to support her belief. RichM responds by rebutting each of the three reasons and offers four reasons why a woman's right to choose should take precedence over moral judgments about abortion in making law. (Broadening)

■ JaneD responds by pointing out that all four of RichM's reasons are based on the assumption that morality cannot be legislated, and she rebuts that assumption by pointing out that ALL legislation is based on morality—i.e., society's concept of right and wrong. (Narrowing)

■ Another participant jumps in and comments that the separation of church and state demands that all morality be kept out of all legislation. (Diverting)

Silence The "WIZOP" (a word often used for a CompuServe forum owner and head systems operator, or "sysop") of the Canopus forum, Will Zachmann, is fond of pointing out that "the appropriate response to a fool is silence." In my experience, ignoring those who make outrageous or patently false or volatile comments is usually the best policy. Unfortunately, most of us regularly succumb to the temptation to tweak the nose of any "fool" willing to expose his or her folly right under our collective nose. Such a response is rarely handled with the kind of good-natured grace required to leave the "fool" with a face-saving out, so such a response is almost always less appropriate than silence.

Sometimes one gets involved in a discussion with someone who is not necessarily a "fool" but simply unreasonable. In such a situation, letting the other person have the last word is, more often than not, the right thing to do. It is also one of the most difficult to learn of all online communications skills.

A negative use of silence is to drop out of a discussion without comment rather than face up to the weakness of one's position.

Examples:

■ Following a long and intelligent discussion concerning the theory of evolution involving JaneD, RichM, and BenG, FoolH jumps in to post a note stating that everyone involved is obviously a religious fanatic, stupid, ignorant, and misinformed. Everyone ignores the post except FoolU, who excoriates FoolH by stating the obvious from every possible angle. The thread quickly degenerates into the FoolH and FoolU show, and the more articulate FoolU is in exposing the foibles of FoolH, the more credence FoolU lends to FoolH with all of the attention. (Negative)

■ JaneD notices that RichM is repeating his arguments, apparently unable to understand her points. JaneD offers to agree to disagree and offers RichM the last word. (Positive)

■ Following a legitimate—but challenging—question in the middle of a discussion, RichM disappears and the question remains unanswered and an otherwise valuable discussion simply dies away. (Negative)

Humor Humor is one of the best tools in anyone's repertoire of rhetorical devices. Self-deprecating humor and the ability to laugh at oneself or even at jokes about oneself almost inevitably changes the tone of discussion. Often, the best humor satirizes ideas, events, policies, and news rather than people other than yourself or groups other than the ones to which you clearly belong and know well enough not to offend. Although targeted humor can be effective when both sides know each other well and understand the limits of good-natured teasing, it is generally best to avoid humor that targets individuals and groups and derives its humor from their foibles. In such instances, humor can easily offend and lead to serious but fruitless metadiscussions (discussion about the discussion itself).
Examples:

■ JaneD responds to a pointed barb in which RichM declares that she is recommending a product because she has friends at the company that makes the product. JaneD responds with good humor, thanking RichM for pointing out that she's happy to learn more about her motives so she can understand herself better. (Positive)

■ HalH posts a biting satire aimed at an unethical, wealthy businessman which triggers a flurry of both defensive and "ROTFL!" posts. (Neutral)

■ RichM tries to be funny and discredit the position of JaneD by asking if she knows that PMS stands for "primordial mental stupidity." (Negative)

Appeal to Authority When an answer lies outside the grasp of those discussing the question, it is often surprising how long the exchange can continue before either will quote an expert on the subject or suggest that the dispute could be settled by asking an independent expert. On the other hand, however, individuals might attempt to evade responsibility for their own statements or conclusions by hinting or implying that their position is consistent with the position of experts (who are wisely silent on the issue) or take statements of experts out of context to discredit opponents.

Examples:

- HalH settles an argument between RichM and JaneD over character development in *The Mote in God's Eye* by sending an e-mail message to the author, Jerry Pournelle, asking for a definitive answer.
- RichM, a liberal, quotes Thomas Jefferson at the drop of a hat. JaneD, a libertarian, quotes Thomas Jefferson in response to RichM's quote of Thomas Jefferson. HalH then quotes Rush Limbaugh to support Thomas Jefferson and refute Thomas Jefferson.

Negative Uses

Words and language can be used to manipulate, disparage, and deceive. These negative uses of rhetoric pollute the public dialogue and make cyberspace communications less valuable than they might otherwise be.

Personal Attacks Personal attacks take many forms, but the most common are name-calling, sarcasm, belittling, and presumption. Some personal attacks are obvious, but many are more subtle.

Examples:

- RichM says that JaneD is a "feminazi."
- JaneD responds and says that if RichM had graduated from fifth grade, then he would be able to find a more creative pejorative.
- RichM asks JaneD if it is typical for a Christian to be so rude.
- JaneD comments publicly to another participant in the thread that RichM isn't worth engaging in any discussion.
- RichM wonders "out loud" to yet another participant if JaneD wasn't perhaps abused as a child.

The Big Lie One of the most interesting dynamics in certain online exchanges is the willingness of some to engage in attempts to deceive with bold proclamations that would normally embarrass anyone making the same claim in person. This method of deception is based on the same human tendencies by which con artists can get whole cities to believe elaborately concocted schemes designed to separate fools from their money. It is human nature to "strain at a gnat and swallow a camel."

Examples:

- Company B announces that its latest software product (B!) will do everything ever envisioned by anyone and that it will be available in six months. Three years later it ships a barely competent product; but Company B is, by then, already talking about its NEW and IM-PROVED software product (C!), which will be even better and will ship in six months. Almost everyone buys product B! and waits eagerly for product C!

■ Company C spends three years and millions of dollars developing a new automobile (C!), which soon develops a relatively small but devoted following. Right up until the moment Company C announces that it is discontinuing the manufacture of C!, corporate representatives vehemently deny, in press releases and interactive forum discussions, the reports of industry analysts who note that profit pressures will force Company C to abandon the entire model line.

Logic

Much of the communication that occurs in cyberspace serves one of three purposes: to inform, to test and explore, or to convince. Often, we must convince in order to respond appropriately to the testing and exploring of someone else as they express opinions and fledgling beliefs not supported by facts, logic, or reason. Whatever the purpose of the communication, logic is a key element in the process of turning information into knowledge. Although a complete exploration of logic is beyond the scope of this book, an introduction to the basics of logic and fallacy can go a long way in helping us recognize some of the tactics that might be used or abused in any discussion. None of us is exempt from such abuse, since most errors of logic are not made deliberately. In my experience, most cyberspace discussions could use more logic and less posturing and rhetorical excess.

In communications, logic is the basis of rational discussion. Statements and assertions made and supported are called conclusions. The reasons given in support of any given conclusion are called premises. A deductive argument is one in which the conclusion *must necessarily follow* from the premises. An inductive argument is one in which the conclusion *probably follows* from the premises. "All Dachshunds are highly intelligent; Dax is a Dachshund; therefore Dax is highly intelligent" is an example of a deductive argument. "Most Dachshunds are very intelligent; Dax is a Dachshund; therefore, Dax is probably very intelligent" is an example of an inductive argument.

An argument is valid if it has been properly inferred from the premises, without regard to the truth of the premises. Premises are true if they are in accord with all known facts. An argument is sound if the premises are true and the conclusion has been validly derived from those premises. The following table describes the four types of argument.

PREMISES	VALIDITY	CONCLUSION	EXAMPLE
True	Valid	Sound	All Dachshunds are dogs. Dax is a Dachshund; therefore, Dax is a dog.
True	Invalid	Unsound	All Dachshunds are dogs. Dax is not a Dachshund; therefore, Dax is not a dog.
False	Valid	Unsound	All Dachshunds are cats. Dax is a Dachshund; therefore, Dax is a cat.
False	Invalid	Unsound	All Dachshunds are cats. Dax is not a Dachshund; therefore, Dax is not a cat.

Note that even when the conclusion is unsound, it might still be true, although it is true only by chance. Note also that only the first case creates an argument that is sound. This is obviously the most desirable case. Happily, it seems to be the most common case, as well, at least in discussions where the premises and conclusions are clearly stated. In many cases, the most difficult part of examining logic is determining the premises and conclusion by stripping away excess verbiage and irrelevant statements and imputing the unstated.

Fallacies

Anyone with a vested interest in protecting a position that may not be true or sound may, unconsciously or deliberately, obscure the truth using a multitude of illogical devices to confuse the issues and cloud or steer discussion. These devices are called fallacies, and their subtle use is often called sophistry. In discussions with others, one can often judge veracity and reliability of those discussing the issue by paying careful attention to the degree to which that persons uses or abuses logic. Individuals who consistently use a variety of logical errors and rhetorical devices more often than not are sporting hidden agendas. One should avoid, whenever possible, any discussion with such individuals just as one would avoid an obscene phone call. Little good is likely to come from it.

Many discussions in cyberspace seem to be mental gymnastics—exercises designed to sharpen the minds of the participants. Other discussions are actually working toward agreement and an action plan. In either case, logical fallacies are likely to be used to bolster arguments, especially those made to further a hidden agenda. Most of the examples that follow are drawn from personal experience in cyberspace. There is no shortage of fallacious reasoning and hidden agendas in cyberspace. Whether your purpose is convincing others reasonably or exposing flaws in the reasoning of opponents in a debate, an understanding of common fallacies to avoid and/or expose can make any discussion more effective and more likely to result in understanding and/or agreement than in unproductive endless argument.

In examining some of the most common informal fallacies, I have borrowed real examples from discussions I have seen, attempting to present these in order from the most common in my experience to the least common. Because some of these fallacies are common, it may not be obvious that their conclusions are unsound. Be careful not to get caught in the trap of overlooking the fallacy being demonstrated because you either agree or disagree with the conclusion. This is precisely why I have selected examples from real life—I hope to encourage a reexamination of the reasoning processes by which we are sometimes led away from the truth. It is *not* my intention to establish the truth or untruth of any particular conclusion in any example. Just because a fallacy is used in the examples doesn't mean that that conclusions drawn in the examples are untrue—only that the conclusion is unsound given the reasoning used in the example.

Composition (Generalization) Composition is the fallacy that what is true for the parts is true for the whole. Generalization is the process of drawing conclusions and making judgments about a group based on the observed characteristics of one or more (but not all) individual members of that group. A variety of other fallacies can also be included in this category. A sweeping generalization is the application of a generalization that is normally fair and acceptable to a single, isolated case without consideration of the exceptional characteristics of that case. A hasty generalization occurs when a conclusion is drawn based on too small a sample to be representative of the population. An unrepresentative sample occurs when conclusions are made about a population from a sample that is drawn from a biased segment of the population.

Examples:

- RichM asserts that the SF 49ers will win the Super Bowl because Jerry Rice is the most talented player in the NFL. (Hasty generalization)
- JaneD writes, "Typical. I would expect that kind of answer from a man." (composition)
- RichM questions the ethics of Company Z after Sales Rep Z mistakenly misrepresents Product Z. (Sweeping generalization)
- "Since DOS had a command line and was so successful, Microsoft's next operating system should also have a command line." (Generalization)
- "That New York man cheated me in business; New Yorkers are crooks." (Hasty generalization)
- "The exit polls in the New Hampshire primaries demonstrate that Steve Forbes will be our next President." (Unrepresentative sample)

Division (Stereotyping) Division is the fallacy that what is true for the whole is true for its parts. Stereotyping is drawing conclusions or making judgments about individual members of a group based on the characteristics of the group.

Examples:

- "Troy Aikman is the best quarterback in the NFL because he is the quarterback for the Super Bowl champion Dallas Cowboys."
- At their first meeting, JaneD accuses RichM of being just like all the other men—egotistical and arrogant.
- "Watch your back when you meet George—he's a New Yorker."
- RichM questions the ethics of a sales rep for Company Z, pointing to a long history of questionable practices by Company Z.

Confusing Cause and Effect Causal relationships are difficult to establish with precision. There are numerous ways to confuse cause and effect and thus draw inappropriate conclusions. If A occurs whenever B occurs, but generally does not occur whenever B does not occur, then a causal relationship can generally be inferred. By inferring a causal link between two such events or phenomena without supporting evidence, however, we can easily confuse cause and effect. Another form of this fallacy, called "joint effect," occurs when A is associated with B and is assumed to cause B, or vice versa, when in reality both are caused by C. A genuine but relatively insignificant cause can also be wrongly attributed for a given effect. Cause and effect can often be reversed as well. There are often many causes for a given effect, and we often single out one of those causes without justification.

Examples:

■ "The most populated cities have the most crime. Therefore, dense population causes crime."

■ "That garden has been growing very well for three months in the shade. Shade is obviously good for the tomatoes."

■ "The poverty in the United States is caused by a minimum wage that is just too low."

■ "Our cat ran away from home twice the day after we brought her home from the vet. She must not like the vet."

■ "The increased sex education is causing an increase in AIDS."

■ "Smoking is causing too much smog in Austin."

Hypostatization and Personification Hypostatization is when we treat abstract words as if they were concrete. Personification is when we attribute human features to nonhuman objects or animals. Although poetic, attributing concrete characteristics to abstract objects can often lead to false premises, erroneous conclusions, and confused logic.

Examples:

■ "The system robs men of their identity."

■ "Company Z is ruthless and will stop at nothing to dominate the industry."

■ "Science is responsible for all technological progress."

■ "Religion teaches men to kill in the name of God."

Straw Man Arguments A straw man argument is an artificial construct that can be easily refuted. It is generally created for the express purpose of refuting it easily, by restating or reconstructing the argument of an opponent.

Examples:

■ JaneD says, "Abortion is wrong because it does harm to the psyche of women who undergo the abortion." RichM responds, "If women who have undergone abortions are mentally ill, then why don't we hear more about the millions of women who have had abortions who are in sanitariums?"

■ RichM writes, "There are too many Americans from other countries, and therefore there is no American sense of identity any more." JaneD asks, "So America is no longer a melting pot but has instead gone to pot?

That's nonsense. The more citizens we gain from other countries, the more American America becomes and the stronger the country gets."

Begging the Question Begging the question is relying on a form of the conclusion as a premise, whether that premise is stated or not. The truth of the conclusion is assumed by the premise(s).
Examples:

■ JaneD proclaims, "O.J. couldn't have murdered his wife!" "How do you know?" asks RichM. "Because the evidence against him doesn't demonstrate that he's such a bad person." "What makes you think that?" "Because O.J. just isn't the kind of person to murder his wife like that."

■ RichM writes: "You should voice your displeasure with the manipulative, scheming plans of Congress regarding the Clipper chip because they're trying to pull a fast one over on you."

■ JaneD writes: "There's no question that the Cowboys are the best team in football. They're simply a great team, top to bottom." (Note the fine distinction between "There's no question" and "I believe.")

■ "God doesn't exist; he has played no role in human history."

■ JaneD says, "Clearly, RichM is an anarchist. He voted Libertarian, didn't he?"

■ "When did JaneD stop beating her husband?"

Bifurcation (False Dilemma) Bifurcation is distinguished by citing a nonexclusive set of possibilities as exclusive. In other words, if there are alternatives other than the alternatives cited which are being ignored in the argument, then a false dilemma has been created.
Examples:

■ "Anyone who is opposed to abortion must be either opposed to women's rights or insensitive to women's needs."

■ "If OS/2 doesn't sell 2 million copies next month, then we'll know that it is either dead or nearly dead."

Double Standard A double standard is evident when unjustified, unreasonable exceptions are made, usually on the basis of self-interest rather than reasonable cause.
Examples:

■ RichM states, "Just because I'm no virgin doesn't mean I don't deserve a wife who is."

■ Joan B writes, "To ensure that women gain parity and equality with men, government should fund abortions for any woman who wants one."

Irrelevant Thesis Dialogue often wrongly attempts to prove a thesis or conclusion that is not at issue in order to strengthen the case for the conclusion under discussion. In other words, it is a fallacy to bring irrelevant conclusions into an argument.

Examples:

■ JaneD states, "The advocates of relaxing copyright constraints believe that the new information-based economy will boom if we adopt their proposals. They are deluded, since everyone knows that copyright law protects the rights of writers, artists, and musicians."

■ RichM argues, "Pornography should be completely legalized since it hasn't been shown to cause additional crime on the Internet."

Ad Hominem Attacks Ad hominem describes a fallacy that "argues to the man;" that is, the person making the argument attacks the opponent instead of the argument. The person making this error of logic attempts to turn the argument away from reason and toward appeals to emotion and/or the nationality, character, religion, motives, or associations of the opponent.

Examples:

■ RichM writes, "It's obvious that you don't know your head from a hole in the ground if you actually believe what you say!"

■ JaneD writes, "Your argument is hypocritical. Does everyone in your church lie as you do?"

■ RichM writes, "We should disregard JaneD's argument against the flat tax because she's rich and stands to benefit most."

■ JaneD asks, "Have you lost all of your senses or just your mind?"

■ RichM says, "JaneD's opinion about abortion carries no weight—she's employed by a Right-to-Life group."

Genetic Fallacy When one focuses on the background or origin of an idea or conclusion rather than the idea itself or the supporting reasoning, one has committed a genetic fallacy. Note that this is not the same as attacking assumed premises.

Examples:

■ JaneD says, "Pornography contributes to rape." RichM responds "That can't be true—JaneD has no experience with pornography or rape."

■ "Company Z is full of dishonest people—just look at the lies of its founder."

Poisoning the Well When one attempts to preclude discussion by discrediting the opposition in the opening barrage, one "poisons the well" of legitimate discourse.

Examples:

- *"Anyone who says that JaneD is not a liar is obviously the friend of a liar."*
- "Only a liberal twit would believe that abortion is good."
- "The right-wing fanatics would have us believe that Christianity is the state religion."
- "Ignore him! He's proven again and again that he doesn't have a clue."

Exclusion Just as serious as introducing irrelevant information and arguments into a discussion is to ignore or downplay the relevant. The exclusion of important evidence from consideration undermines an inductive argument. Good judgment is always necessary to good logic and good discussion.
Examples:

- "The fact that I was convicted of perjury has nothing to do with the veracity of my assertions. Stop attacking the messenger."
- "My promise to you doesn't count because, at the time I made it, I didn't foresee these current circumstances."
- "Smith will win the nomination because he won three of the first four primaries." (They were Western states—Smith is a westerner and was expected to win by bigger margins.)

Bad Analogy An analogy is a comparison of two or more things that agree in enough particulars to imply that they also agree in others. A bad, or false, analogy infers agreement where none exists.
Examples:

- RichM writes, "The decision to wait to raid the compound at Waco was a bad one. If that had been a hijacked jet, would they have waited so long to attempt a rescue of the hostages?" JaneD replies, "First of all, no one hijacked the compound. Second, the residents were not held hostage. Third, hijackers normally don't hijack their own homes."
- "Alcohol and marijuana both make us feel good; therefore, marijuana should be legal, too."

Argument from Ignorance An argument from ignorance occurs when one assumes that, since a conclusion has not been proven false, it must be true; or, conversely, if something has not been proven true, it must be false. In other words, in this fallacy, the absence of proof is used as proof itself.
Examples:

- "You can't prove that UFOs don't exist—therefore, they must be real."
- "The theory of evolution has never been proven; therefore, man did not descend from apes."

- ■ "You can't prove that God created the world; therefore, creationism has no place in public schools."

Slippery Slope In order to argue that a given proposition is unacceptable, we may attempt to argue a sequence of increasingly undesirable consequences derived from the acceptance of the proposition. The illegitimate use of the "if-then" construct often identifies the "slippery slope" fallacy. Examples:

- ■ JaneD writes, "If we outlaw assault rifles and handguns, then it won't be long before the government takes all of our weapons and enslaves us all."
- ■ "If we allow any form of censorship on the Internet, then government will soon deprive us of other freedoms, and jack-booted thugs will soon be running rampant in America."
- ■ "If I make an exception for this admittedly worthy case, then everyone will clamor for the same. Permission denied."

Appeal to Motives An appeal to factors such as force, pity, emotion, conno tation, popularity, rhetoric, or consequences is fallacious when not accompanied by sound logic and reason. Examples:

- ■ RichM says, "If we accept the theory of human evolution as true, then we have no right to think ourselves any better than apes and monkeys."
- ■ "I hope you will accept these recommendations. Otherwise, my work for the past two months will be wasted."
- ■ "If you want to keep your job, you had better vote against the union."
- ■ "No right-thinking person could possibly vote for capital punishment."
- ■ "The bureaucrats should not be allowed to ram that proposal down our throats."
- ■ Everyone opposes school prayer except for a small minority of religious fanatics in our country.

Improper Appeal to Authority It is often appropriate to cite experts in order to strengthen an argument. However, such citations are often inappropriate when the authority cited is not qualified on the subject in question, when the authority is left unnamed, when equally expert authorities who disagree are not also cited, or when the cited remarks were made in jest or taken out of context. Examples:

- ■ RichM writes, "O.J. was innocent. F. Lee Bailey wouldn't have defended him otherwise."

- "*The New York Times* said that Powell would win the Presidency." (It actually quoted a poll asserting that Powell would win if the elections were held today.)

Slothful Induction Slothful induction occurs when, in spite of all evidence, the proper conclusion of an inductive argument is denied.
Examples:

- "The insurance company insists that each of the dozen things wrong with my two cars since they were in the flood is attributable to normal wear and tear."
- "In spite of losing by 35 percentage points in yesterday's election, I am delighted with the results, which put me in great shape to challenge the frontrunner in the next primary."

Non Sequitur In Latin, *non sequitur* means "it does not follow" and refers to the class of fallacies that occur as a result of invalid arguments.
Examples:

- "If I live in Austin, then I am a resident of Texas. If I am a resident of Texas, then I must live in Austin."
- "If this damage to the leather seats of your car were actually caused by the flood, then the appraiser would be able to state with 100% certainty that the flood caused the damage and the insurance company would be required to pay for the damage. Even though the car was underwater for several hours and the seats have been damaged by water, the appraiser cannot state with assurance that the damage was caused by the flood and therefore the insurance company is not obligated to pay for the damages."
- "Jared is older than Nicia, and Nicia is older than Michael. Michael is older than Jared."

NETTING IT OUT

The ability to communicate and communicate effectively is one of the keys to a fulfilling life. Cyberspace increases the communications options available to us but more significantly extends the range of individuals with whom we can easily communicate to include strangers, associates, friends, and family worldwide. No longer need we be limited in our ability to communicate by ignorance, delivery delays, distance, or isolation.

Because of the characteristics of cyberspace itself, we now have the choice of communicating more interactively, more publicly, more readily, more informally, and more proactively. We can carry on cyberspace discussions on carefully selected topics of interest with literally hundreds of well-informed strangers. We can learn from and take advantage of the experience and wisdom of others we have never met and share our own insights and experience with strangers (many of whom become friends). We can easily stay in touch with family and friends far away who are also connected to cyberspace without spending as much time and money on the communications, which previously were available only through post or telephone. We can find more information than ever before and can proactively choose which communications to consume and which to ignore. We can all cooperate to learn and choose wisely the forms our communications take in order to enhance the efficiency and effectiveness of those communications in which we choose to participate. By taking advantage of electronic mail, computer-mediated conferencing, real-time chatting, and multimedia exchange, we can enrich our own lives and the lives of others as we carefully use rhetoric and reason to maximize the effectiveness of our communications with others and minimize the difficulties and tragedies that often begin with poor communications.

These newfound possibilities for communications can also be ignored, abused, and misused. Conspirators can plot terrorism with advanced new encryption technologies with alarming freedom from detection or prosecution. Pedophiles can anonymously make friends with potential victims, selecting from among the thousands of youngsters communicating in otherwise harmless online chat rooms. Criminals and gangsters can organize with an increased effectiveness corresponding to their increased reach enabled by cyberspace. Everyone has easier access to pornography, gambling, gore, carnage, and other potentially destructive vices, temptations, and diversions.

On the brighter side, coming face to face with the new possibilities inherent in cyberspace communications gives us the opportunity to seriously renew and reexamine the exalted role of communications in a free society at the same time we reaffirm the importance of education and literacy, equality and fairness, work and leisure, freedom and responsibility, and all other values upon which our forefathers have built this great land of opportunity.

Ultimately, I trust that we will rise to the occasion. We will adjust to the new challenges by making the right choices and creating new solutions, but probably only after excessive hand-wringing, shouting, and venting and after much voting, debating, discussion, lobbying, buying, and deciding—i.e., after lots of (what else?) good old-fashioned communication. Even in cyberspace.

CHAPTER THREE

CYBERSPACE CULTURE, ETHICS, AND LAW

Quality in Progress

Every new generation is a fresh invasion of savages.

—Hervey Allen (1889-1949)

Society faces many challenges; however, its essential challenge is to equip its children—each "fresh invasion of savages"—with the means of effective participation in that society by teaching them the essential qualities of life in that society—its culture, ethics, and laws.

Webster's Third International Dictionary defines culture as the "body of customary beliefs, social forms, and material traits constituting a distinct complex of tradition of a racial, religious, or social group." More simply, I view culture as a set of shared assumptions and the manifestations of those assumptions. Ethics is defined by Webster as "a group of moral principles or set of values." Law is "a binding custom or practice of a community." Culture, ethics, and laws are not immutable. They shift to accommodate new and emerging patterns in society. Thus we can speak of those qualities of culture, ethics, and law which define the quality of culture, ethics, and law.

QUALITY OF CULTURE, ETHICS, AND LAW

Webster defines "quality," in one sense, as "a peculiar and essential character . . . a distinctive inherent feature . . . that makes it fundamentally unlike any other" and as "degree of excellence" in another sense. Thus, we might say that all things have qualities, or distinctive traits, that determine their quality, or degree of excellence. It is this latter meaning of quality that demands our attention in the moral choices we make.

In Robert M. Pirsig's twin treatises on modern philosophy, *Zen and the Art of Motorcycle Maintenance* and *Lila*, Pirsig expands our understanding of the importance and meaning of quality by describing Quality (with a capital "Q")—the highest degree of excellence. In these "culture-bearing"[1] works, Pirsig concludes that Quality has a dual nature—one that is static, immutable, and unchanging and one that is dynamic, infinite, and changeable. As Pirsig writes (using capitalization to communicate meaning we are left to discover for ourselves),

> Static quality patterns are dead when they are exclusive, when they demand blind obedience and suppress Dynamic change. But static patterns, nevertheless, provide a necessary stabilizing force to protect Dynamic progress from degeneration. Although Dynamic Quality, the Quality of freedom, creates this world in which we live, these patterns of static quality, the quality of order, preserve our world. Neither static nor Dynamic Quality can survive without the other.[2]

History is a story of progress based on this dual nature of Quality Dynamic quality is found in new ideas, freedom, emerging moral forces that compel us towards change and progress. Static quality provides the bedrock of society in the patterns of conformity, socialization, and value that provide civilization with stability and continuity. For example, at the time of the American Revolution, the static quality of loyalty to king and country finally gave way to the Dynamic Quality of self-determination, independence, and equality. So powerful was the static quality that bound the Americans as colonies of King George and the British empire that the first paragraph in the Declaration of Independence was devoted to a justification for "one people to dissolve the political bands which [had] connected them with another." The subsequent paragraph, of course, is one of the most powerful statements of dynamic quality ever articulated: "We hold these truths to be self-evident, that all men are created equal, that they are endowed by their Creator with certain unalienable rights, that among these are Life, Liberty, and the pursuit of Happiness."

At the time of the Civil War, slavery was a quality, a peculiar and essential characteristic, of southern culture in the United States in the mid-nineteenth century. Although it contributed to the quality of economic life for slaveholders, it was clearly lacking in quality, being unjust, repressive, exploitative, and simply evil. Dynamic Quality, as embodied by the dynamic application of moral precepts of equality and freedom espoused in the Declaration of Independence, and manifested in the technological and economic transformation of the northern states, triggered the overthrow of slavery and the adoption of new social standards. The base of static quality was, in effect, ratcheted upwards once slavery was prohibited by law—and yet it still lagged, as it always will, Dynamic Quality. The ideals of equality and brotherhood still beckon elusively, many years after the Civil War and the Civil Rights movement; nevertheless, static quality represents the general acceptance as "good" of the ideas that once represented Dynamic Quality in the past.

The primary lessons of the Revolutionary and Civil Wars are twofold. First, as Pirsig noted, "given a choice of two courses to follow and all other things being equal, that choice which is more Dynamic, that is, at a higher level of evolution, is more moral."[3] For example, Pirsig notes that given the choice between killing billions of germs to save a patient or allowing the germs to thrive at the expense of the patient, it is more moral to kill the germs because the patient "has precedence because he's at a higher level of evolution."[4] Pirsig asserts that there are "moral codes that established the supremacy of biological life over inanimate nature,"[5] social order over biological life, and intellectual order over the social order. The highest Dynamic morality isn't a code at all, but rather an essential "art" (such as love) that embodies Good—the highest good. Thus, the intellectual good articulated in the Declaration of Independence took precedence over the social good of loyalty to the king. The idea of "one nation under God, indivisible, with liberty and justice for all" took precedence over the economic and social stability of the South, and ultimately, the Good of love for one another was valued above the "good" of economic welfare through exploitation. Second, Dynamic Quality can never be effectively legislated or imposed from above. Notions and ideas must not only resonate as truth in the hearts and minds of individuals, but also must be experienced as truth through observation and experience. Thus, for example, one might intellectually accept the notion of "free love"—a quality of the 1960s culture—but if we observe that the free love disrupts families or leads to unwanted pregnancies or venereal disease, we might a return to the static quality of fidelity after marriage and chastity before marriage.

As in the above examples, technology, often a manifestation of Dynamic Quality, is usually one of the driving forces in change. During the Revolutionary War, technology had advanced to the point where the colonists could wage war in a nontraditional manner using muskets from behind trees and other obstacles, but not to the point where the British could respond in a timely manner with superior troops from across the sea. In the mid-nineteenth century, a northern dream of a government-subsidized transcontinental railroad that would link the Pacific and Atlantic oceans was continuously thwarted by southern congressmen and senators whose constituents had no need of an internal rail system, because cotton, the basis of the southern economy, was largely an export product that was transported by an extensive system of rivers and canals to oceangoing vessels. It was not until 1862, with the South out of the picture, that Congress chartered the venture. At the same time, the United States, particularly the northern states, had pioneered the mass production of interchangeable parts, whereby machines were designed to produce specific components of consumer goods. The components were fitted together to produce a gun, clock, sewing machine, or other item that previously had been hand-crafted. Machine-made items were less durable but more affordable and thus more widely available, which gave rise to a middle class that embraced not only the more democratic consumer economy but also the democratic political ideals. Moreover, economic prosperity engendered the leisure time for debating the issue of slavery and actively campaigning against it.

In the example of free love, medical technology in the form of drugs that could cure syphilis and gonorrhea had, for a couple of decades at least, relaxed fears of contagion of sexually transmitted diseases, while the birth-control pill had relaxed fears of unwanted pregnancies. Medical technology can relax fears of sexually transmitted diseases and unwanted pregnancy, but it cannot protect society from many of the other natural social, psychological, and scientific consequences of sexual promiscuity and ignorance. The technology can be used to increase the quality of life for those who use it responsibly and knowledgeably, or it can bring unhappiness and difficulty into the lives of those who ignore it or use it in ignorance of the bigger picture of culture, ethics, and law. Free love may have quality at a biological level, but at the higher levels of social and intellectual order, the wisdom and morality of the ages, as represented by family values, has a static quality that should rightfully be given precedence in society.

The lessons are clear—the emergence of new technologies in societies can force dynamic changes that culture, ethics, and law must accommodate—and that accommodation should be made without sacrificing static quality and good. Throughout history, the most common error may have been the suppression of Dynamic Quality; but in our day, we have perhaps overcompensated—rejecting much that is rich in Static Quality. Pirsig notes that "this has been a century of fantastic intellectual growth and fantastic social destruction."[6]

Thus, it is incumbent upon a society to adapt its culture, ethics, and laws such that in the process of embracing Dynamic Quality and discarding that which is low in quality, it does not also discard elements of the culture, ethics, and laws that are rich in static quality. We must teach our "fresh savages" not only to embrace new technology but also to embrace it responsibly with an adequate grasp of the larger, enduring issues surrounding the use of the technology. That instruction should occur as new technologies emerge, not ten or twenty years after the damage has been done.

We must be willing to create and enforce laws—but we must ever be mindful of their fallibility and their necessarily dynamic nature. We must harbor a healthy disdain for laws and limitations to individual freedom— but we must not abandon immutable principle or forget that some law is necessary to protect the weak and innocent against the strong and selfish. In examining culture, ethics, and law; it is important that we remember that Quality in culture, ethics and law is evidenced by two elements: the static quality of immutable principle and the dynamic quality of constant improvement. From the former is derived our safety and security, and from the latter is derived our progress and learning.

Interestingly, it can be said that the purer forms of love have this same duality of static and dynamic qualities. We should not be surprised: many see love as the ultimate Good. Viktor Frankl's epiphany was this: "The truth— that love is the ultimate and the highest goal to which man can aspire. Then I grasped the meaning of the greatest secret that human poetry and human thought and belief have to impart: *The salvation of man is through love and in love*."[7] In spite of the horrors of this world, which Frankl confronted intimately, the basis of society can still be said to be love; and love can be said to be rooted in the yearning for the Static Quality of security and the Dynamic Quality of stimulating fulfillment. Young children at a playground will frequently interrupt their play to verify that Mom or Dad is still there, often running back for the security of a brief hug or to tell a tale before resuming the stimulating excitement of play. The passion, excitement, and stimulation of young love is best tempered by the qualities of friendship, comfort, and mutual support. Most discussions in cyberspace seem to rock back and forth between stimulating discussion and argument and accord and good humor.

This dichotomy of quality seems to be rooted deep within the human experience. It rests quietly in the heart of our culture and the rules by which we live. We would be well-served to make it the heart of cyberspace as well—we have a sterling opportunity to return to fundamental principles

of fulfilling human interaction and progress by proactively and coopera-
tively choosing the culture, norms, ethics, and law of cyberspace.

The basis for all world views are shared values and beliefs—culture. If we
define culture in this context as a "set of shared assumptions," then culture
exists at any level values and beliefs are shared. Where there are shared values and beliefs, there is a culture or subculture.

There is a static quality to many traditional beliefs such as the importance of family and traditional values such as discipline, work, fairness,
decency, kindness, sharing, honesty, service, and love. These shared beliefs
have long been an important part of our American culture. Yet there are
emerging values, particularly noticeable in cyberspace and increasing in
cultural importance, which possess a dynamic quality that we cannot and
should not ignore: the importance of diversity, the demands for a shift of
power from big government and big business to the grass roots and individuals, a deeper respect for the dynamic quality of thought and rational dis-
sent, the reevaluation of the value of information and knowledge, and so on.

In this chapter, I address some of the cultural, ethical, and legal ramifications of existing and emerging cyberspace technology and attempt to share
my view of those larger issues which will ultimately define the essence and
quality of the cyberspace experience.

ELEMENTS OF CYBERSPACE CULTURE

Certain elements and issues of cyberspace culture influence not only the
ways we should participate in cyberspace but also its potential for each one
of us. The multicultural elements of cyberspace help us face the importance
of learning from others, and the abstract elements help us to place that
learning in the proper context to benefit our relationships with others as
we face the challenges born from opposition.

Multicultural

Cyberspace is a melting pot of cultures. It is a multicultural human dimension embraced by increasingly more individuals who bring with them to
cyberspace not only the perspectives of their respective national cultures
but also of their respective generations, professions, social classes, religions,
and other groups and communities to which they belong. The generation
gap, or youth culture—the "fresh invasion of savages," however, is common
not only to virtually all cultures but also to cyberspace.

John Perry Barlow is representative of the evolution of the "savage." As
a self-confessed acid-tripping hippie who wrote lyrics for the Grateful

Dead, he was probably considered a savage by many in the 1960s and 1970s; but by the mid-1980s, he was one of the stalwarts on The WELL— the community which served as the basis for Howard Rheingold's *Virtual Communities*. Finally, by the late 1980s, a more mature Barlow came face to face with "a fresh invasion of savages."

Harpers Magazine sponsored an online conference on The WELL to examine the issues surrounding cyberspace privacy and the electronic invasions of hackers and crackers—the savages of cyberspace. *Harpers* invited a number of articulate cyberspace figures, including Barlow, Rheingold, Dave Hughes (Old Colorado City's "Cursor-Cowboy"), Clifford Stoll (of Cuckoo's Egg fame), Stewart Brand (one of the founders of The WELL), and "a score of aging techno-hippies" to join the discussions with hackers using names like Acid Phreak and Phiber Optik. Barlow described the encounter in an online article entitled "Crime and Puzzlement":

These kids were fractious, vulgar, immature, amoral, insulting, and too damned good at their work.

Worse, they inducted a number of former kids like myself into Middle Age. The long feared day had finally come when some gunsel would yank my beard and call me, too accurately, an old fart . . .

The techno-hippies were of the unanimous opinion that, in Dylan's words, one "must be honest to live outside the law." But these young strangers apparently lived by no code save those with which they unlocked forbidden regions of the Net . . .

Presented with such a terrifying amalgam of raw youth and apparent power, we fluttered like a flock of indignant Babbitts around the Status Quo, defending it heartily.[8]

During the conference, Barlow invited Phiber Optik to call him, avoiding insult to Optik's skills by withholding his phone number. In the conversation that ensued, Barlow "encountered an intelligent, civilized, and surprisingly principled kid of 18 who sounded, and continues to sound, as though there's little harm in him to man or data."[9] Barlow attributes the flagrant online rhetoric of these Billy-the-Kid outlaws of the Electronic Frontier and their disrespect for cyberspace "property" and territorial rights to a few bad apples like Kevin Mitnick (one of the subjects of Katie Hafner's and John Markoff's seminal work, *Cyberpunk*[10]) and to what sociologists call self-fulfilling prophecy—the tendency of individuals to fulfill the ex-pectations of others, becoming what they are seen to be. The online persona created by these young men was not only an attention-getting device, but part of their exploration of this new world they not only lived in, but were also creating. Barlow raised some interesting questions:

> Can unauthorized electronic access be regarded as the ethical equivalent of old-fashioned trespass? Like open range, the property boundaries of Cyberspace are hard to stake and harder still to defend. Is transmission through an otherwise unused data channel really theft? Is the trackless passage of a mind through TRW's mainframe the same as the passage of a pickup through my Back 40? What is a place if Cyberspace is everywhere? What are data and what is free speech? How does one treat property which has no physical form and can be infinitely reproduced? Is a computer the same as a printing press? Can the history of my business affairs properly belong to someone else? Can anyone morally claim to own knowledge itself?[11]

Barlow puts his finger on a fascinating cultural and moral phenomenon represented by the advent of cyberspace. We are forging a new frontier that demands a reexamination of our dearly-held assumptions about rights and right—and the generation in power may just have something to learn from the younger "X-generation" before it will be willing to learn anything from the voices of maturity and experience. In Barlow, we see the successful evolution of the savage to a thoughtful individual addressing the challenges presented by cyberspace technology in the context of a multicultural world. As we learn to learn from others, we mature.

Abstract

Cyberspace is without geography or physical presence. It is almost wholly abstract. The digital words and images—the bits—that flow over telephone lines to be reconstructed by computer processors and software into intelligible images are all abstractions, because we are dealing with the realm of ideas. The role of physical things in our life, such as property, can be transformed for better or worse as we encounter these diverse ideas. Those encountering cyberspace can find themselves consumed by a newfound power to alter their reality, however virtual. The physical world can begin to seem less relevant and less rewarding. Molly O'Neill noted in a *New York Times* article on the addiction of life online that "initially, being online insulates people from their intimate setting while expanding their horizons electronically."[12]

Cyberspace can indeed easily represent a fundamental shift in how one views the world. It can become more difficult for some individuals to face the real world as they spend enormous amounts of time developing an on-line persona that is escapist and at odds with their essential personality. For others, facing the real world becomes easier as they learn more about the world and themselves from the information available in cyberspace. On the one hand, cyberspace can be seen as an addictive fantasy playground, on the other hand, as an empowering part of a balanced life. Balance, however, implies opposition; and opposition often leads to conflict.

DILEMMA OF CYBERSPACE CULTURE

Some issues in cyberspace, as in the real world, create conflict. Other issues find ready consensus. The challenge is to seek a resolution to all conflict, maintaining hope that dialogue might lead to understanding and either agreement or respectful disagreement.

Conflict

There often seems to be contention over even the simplest of problems. Why do the countless agreements that are reached daily get so relatively lit-tle press coverage? It might be because one of our cultural values is con-frontation and complaint. A strip from the late, great *Calvin and Hobbes* says it best. As they wander through forests and meadows, Calvin asks Hobbes, "Doesn't it seem like everybody just shouts at each other nowadays?" He observes that "conflict is drama" (which is marketable) and that "finding consensus and common ground is dull!" He continues, "Nobody wants to watch a civilized discussion that acknowledges ambiguity and complexity. We want to see fireworks! We want the sense of solidarity and identity that comes from having our interests narrowed and exploited by like-minded zealots!" Hobbes responds with a thoughtful "Hmm, you may be right," and in the last frame, after the two have walked together in silent contem-plation for awhile, Calvin remarks, "What a boring day this turned out to be!"[13]

It might also be that the mass media thrive on controversy and thus con-tinuously present us with pictures of dispute and contention by choosing representatives at the extremes of any position. As James Thurber said, "Discussion in America means dissent."[14] It might be that our two-party political system has distorted the democratic and republican processes as conceived by the framers of the Constitution. It might be charged to any number of cultural assumptions, involving such topics as competition, dis-sent, and individualism. In any case, consensus often arrives on the heels of conflict that is recognized and discussed reasonably. Thus, we must recognize and understand the diversity of culture and ideas of cyberspace before we can effectively address the challenges.

Consensus

Whatever the reason, any means whereby disagreement and divergence can be transformed into synergy and harmony should be a welcome addition to our toolkit. Just as musical notes in various scales and keys on the piano can blend in beautiful and inspiring music, our ideas and views need not be identical to produce harmonious results. The key is respect, tolerance, and understanding. If cyberspace can be built on a foundation where those assumptions are inculcated into the online culture, then the prospects for our wired future are bright indeed.

How can we better judge quality when we see it, whether it be dynamic or static? That, of course, is a question of the ages, similar to "What is truth?" I can offer my opinion that the answer lies not only within for each of us, but in consensus for all of us. My perspective is that we each have much to gain simply by recognizing that we may not have all the answers, and thus discussing the questions and possible answers with others in a search for harmony and consensus. Therein lies the promise of cyberspace. Never before have we been able to reach so many others for such stimulating interactive discussions. We can choose for ourselves what to believe—with more and better information available to us than ever before.

Most of us unconsciously share the assumptions that define our respective cultures. Individually, however, we can believe what we choose to believe about almost everything. This fact offers enormous power to choose our own happiness. Frankl, in *Man's Search for Meaning,* speaks of this power to choose in telling of the horror and heroism of the Death Camps:

> The experience of camp life show that man does have a choice of action. There were enough examples, often of a heroic nature, which proved that apathy could be overcome, irritability suppressed. Man *can* preserve a vestige of spiritual freedom, of independence of mind, even in such terrible conditions of psychic and physical stress.
>
> We who lived in concentration camps can remember the men who walked through the huts comforting others, giving away their last piece of bread. They may have been few in number, but they offer sufficient proof that everything can be taken from a man but one thing: the last of the human freedoms–to choose one's attitude in any given set of circumstances, to choose one's own way.[15]

When we consider how blessed and privileged we are, with or without cyberspace, we should perhaps be embarrassed that we are not more unabashedly joyous and grateful than we are. We are not only free to choose our attitudes and beliefs—our culture—but we probably have a greater range of choices than any other people in the history of the world. Now, as we stand on the edge of the new frontier of cyberspace, we should be fully aware that we are free to choose the norms and assumptions we will share there as well. How we choose will make as much difference for us in the plethora of choices we will have as it did for the victims of the concentration camps in the relatively few choices they had. Perhaps just as significantly, it will make an enormous difference for our children and descendants as well. Here again, the lesson is that we must value different cultures and individual beliefs to find consensus. Evil rests not in differences or variations, but in discrimination, intolerance, and hatred.

In making these choices, we must examine our assumptions—those beliefs we take for granted and rarely question until confronted with them. When we do so, we increase the range of our choice and thus increase our freedom. For example, I lived in Japan for two years. As I learned their language, I learned much about those things I take for granted as an American. I learned that subtlety in social interaction was often more important than the direct, blunt honesty I had been taught, at home and at school, to value. I realized that our often taunting social stereotypes of the Japanese said more about American cultural ignorance and arrogance than it did about the Japanese. Once my cultural bias was exposed to the vibrant reality of the life and culture of Japan, I became more sensitive to the importance of the assumptions we hold as a determiner of our values. From that awareness has come an increased appreciation for Japan and the Japanese that has enriched my life and increased my choices in life. I no longer view Japan as a country or people to be feared—but rather as representative of other opportunities available to me.

We can choose to view cyberspace in the same way. Although we may not understand much of what we encounter online, we should realize that it represents an entirely new culture and that through exploration, we can learn more about the world around us, as it was, as it is, and as it will be—truth. A deep understanding—the truth—of any matter is indeed liberating. As John says that Jesus said, "the truth will make you free."

Resolution

Forging a resolution between conflict and consensus depends on our ability to communicate differences so that we can break down the barriers between cultures and forge new understandings from which solutions emerge.

As we engage in exchange, we can increase the quality of exchange by examining the respective assumptions at work in the interchange of ideas. To offer a key example, our cultural assumptions about competition and "getting ahead" work against our ability to find resolution. It doesn't take long in any online discussion to realize that it can be difficult to find agreement or even to end the exchange gracefully without reaching agreement—probably because of our cultural assumptions about silence, failure to respond, or backing down from a fight. We simply view such responses as weakness and surrender.

There is a scene in *A Man for All Seasons* in which there is some debate over what may or may not be construed from silence. Sir Thomas More argues, in defense of his right to remain silent against an order to take an oath, that the law cannot punish his silence, since silence under the law implies consent.[16] That may be true legally, but culturally, I would argue that the assumption in cyberspace should be that nothing whatsoever may be construed from silence. I have seen those who attempt to attribute the silence of another to a "weak position," "consent," or even "cowardice," when in all probability that party was exercising extreme restraint, courage, and discipline in not responding to "flame bait"—an outrageous allegation made deliberately to insult or provoke an angry response, or flame, under the apparent assumption that the first person to "lose it" loses the debate. We can, with our silence and refusal to "take the bait," starve those who are ignorant or obnoxious and feed those whose comments we value with a considered response—in spite of all impulse to do exactly the opposite. If enough make such a choice, the cultural assumptions of cyberspace could very well change: refusal to respond to outrageousness, even in self-defense, might instead be seen as a response of dynamic quality more noble than responding line for line to outrageousness and absurdity.

Another example of a proactive choice that we can and probably should make in cyberspace relates to criticism and personal attacks, i.e. flaming. Opinions vary dramatically about the value of flaming—some claim that the United States was born in flames, i.e., that the Declaration of Independence was itself a flame. I'm confident that no flame I've seen in cyberspace was written with the discipline, quiet assurance, and dignity of the Declaration of Independence. Most cyberspace flames are more focused on individuals than ideas, more critical of people than assumptions. The Declaration of Independence, if we must call it a flame, is a courageous, if critical, expression of principle and an attack on the abuse of power, not on any single person except the King, who represented that power. To me, even a flame can be, from time to time, a matter of quality. The value of a flame is generally inversely proportional to its destructive intent. Flames that are intended to instruct and inspire change are in a different class in my mind from flames that attack, belittle, destroy, condemn, and bash without offering positive alternatives.

The implications for cyberspace are significant. We must carefully examine the assumptions we choose to share, lest we choose to share destructive ones unconsciously. If we do choose carefully and wisely, however, we stand to gain a great deal as we improve the quality of life for ourselves and our posterity.

Even in its infancy, cyberspace is developing a distinctive and recognizable culture, with numerous subcultures. Although I have deliberately avoided a presentation of the assumptions of various cyberspace subcultures, including the hackers, I believe that there is much value in studying and understanding their assumptions that have already developed in response to the unique opportunities and constraints of cyberspace. In making choices, we must be careful to consider the insight of youth and the dynamic quality it represents. For example, perhaps the hackers notion that trespassing doesn't apply in cyberspace as it does on land could trigger a reexamination of our assumptions surrounding what constitutes the boundaries of intellectual property. Perhaps finding ways to loosen copyright rules might improve the quality of life for everyone, including the copyright holders. Perhaps the hackers' attacks on the security of systems could prompt us to recognize that enhancing the security and privacy of cyberspace in many ways is not a luxury we can afford to postpone. Perhaps there is less virtue in leaving doors unlocked and trusting one another when technology might just as easily offer complete, trouble-free protection. Perhaps our privacy could be protected by laws that limit the ability of merchants to use data about us in our ignorance or without our permission. Perhaps we should reexamine the appropriate roles of online anonymity and accountability respectively in preserving privacy without compromising possibility.

As anyone who has lived in a foreign culture probably knows, there is much to be learned from carefully considering positions we may not at first understand or even be willing to consider. We should approach with hope and mutual respect the task of deciding which assumptions we should share in cyberspace. This process is underway in energetic debates carried on throughout cyberspace. There is much that is encouraging and much that is discouraging. It is, of course, often difficult to obtain agreement on which is which; but if we are conscious and aware of the assumptions and turn them into choices as we approach them, it may be easier to choose wisely.

CHALLENGES OF CYBERSPACE

Some of the areas that attract the most attention and discussion may very well be the areas where progress in our collective thinking about morality are to be made for the next generation. Although we must be careful to avoid embracing ideas that lack dynamic quality or rejecting traditions that posses static quality, we must consider the possibility that the only thing standing between us and an increase in quality of life and freedom is our own prejudice. Here are some areas in cyberspace that are frequently debated and remain essentially undecided and therefore offer the greatest opportunities for progress towards resolution.

Franchise

Perhaps the most important assumption we should share is whether cyberspace should be for everyone or just for those who can afford it and know how to use it. There are some who act as if all newbies are unwelcome intruders. Should the Net remain the exclusive playground of the technically gifted few and the dumping grounds of cynical existentialists? I think not—if we begin with the assumption that cyberspace should be an extension of the real world, then we can realize that it needs to be an all-embracing world, and the default assumptions need to be more inclusive than exclusive. This is actually one area in which there is a surprising consensus—even Vice President Al Gore and Speaker of the House Newt Gingrich agree on this objective.

This has important implications. Some means of providing service to the poor and otherwise disenfranchised must be found. Whether by targeted subsidies to the poor, or by some sort of universal service provision, or simply by ensuring that every public library and school in America has access to the World Wide Web, most observers agree that basic access should be as freely available as access to a public library.

What's more, if cyberspace is to be for children as well as adults, and if the commons of cyberspace are to serve an important role in education, then we need solutions that minimize offensiveness in the public places of the Internet, without impinging on legitimate exchange and our traditions of free speech. The answer lies not in misguided censorship laws and provisions or simple bans of indecency but more likely in voluntary standards forged by the cooperative efforts of individuals and the private sector, inculcated into the culture of cyberspace, and encouraged but not dictated by government.

Security and Privacy

Security and privacy issues in cyberspace are continually debated. How much security and privacy should citizens demand and receive in cyberspace? Should an individual's cyberspace activities be made available to government, business, or law enforcement agencies? If so, under what conditions? What power, if any, should a government possess to monitor private communications? Does it make any difference whether a government has evidence of criminal activity? Tax evasion? Terrorism? What expectations should consumers have about the use personal information they give online to vendors and companies?

These questions often elicit passionate responses, such as "Our e-mail should be protected against government snoops and jack-booted thugs." And "If we let government get a foot in the door, before you know it, we'll have no freedom remaining." While there is much discussion about keeping the government out of cyberspace, there doesn't seem to be as much concern about how to keep criminals and terrorists from exploiting cyberspace, which is equally threatening.

In 1991, Phil Zimmerman, a self-employed programmer, responded to a furor caused by reports on the Internet of forthcoming government attempts to restrict the use of encryption technologies by releasing an encryption program entitled "Pretty Good Privacy" (PGP). In its introduction, Zimmerman wrote:

> It's personal. It's private. And it's no one's business but yours. You may be planning a political campaign, discussing your taxes, or having an illicit affair. Or you may be doing something that you feel shouldn't be illegal, but is. Whatever it is, you don't want your private electronic mail (E-mail) or confidential documents read by anyone else. There's nothing wrong with asserting your privacy. Privacy is as apple-pie as the Constitution.[17]

When the United States government discovered that Zimmerman's program was widely used overseas, it launched an investigation of Zimmerman, alleging that he had exported the product in violation of a federal law ostensibly designed to protect national security. Zimmerman thus became an unwilling but representative victim of our national uncertainty surrounding this often esoteric debate. Before examining the implications of the Zimmerman case more closely, let's first examine the practical implications of the technological issues.

Encryption technology is used to place a shield around the electronically transmitted documents of those who use it, protecting the privacy of their cyberspace activities. This shield is created when a "key" is used to scramble (encrypt) a plain text or other file. This key is a series of random bits created by a computer. Depending on the translation scheme used to view the bits, it might appear as a series of ones and zeros ("10000001011100110011011001010000"), a single large number (2171811408), an ASCII sequence ("üs6P"), or some other digital form. That same key or a mathematically related key, then, is required by the computer to unscramble (decrypt) the file to its original, useable state. The strength of this shield depends on the size of the key, which is measured in bits. The more bits in the key, the stronger the shield. The example above represents a 32-bit key, which is considered easily breakable using today's technology. A key of at least 128 bits is considered virtually invincible with current technology.

Public key encryption is considered the strongest, most versatile encryption system available today. The problem with traditional encryption systems has been how to securely transmit the key itself. The public key system resolves this problem by using two keys for each individual—a public key and private key. These keys are generated for you by the computer, and can be stored and managed by computer as well. The public key is available for you to provide to people you'd like to exchange messages with, but the private key is yours alone. Any file encrypted with one of the two keys can be decrypted with the other. Thus, anyone who has your public key can use it to encrypt a file, but only you can then decipher it, using your private key. Similarly, anyone can encrypt a file with their private key, but it can only be decrypted by anyone who possesses their public key. For maximum protection, a communication you make to a given specific individual can be encrypted once using your private key and then again using their public key. This system provides powerful flexibility and security.

For example, if you want assurance that a message is from a certain person, all you need is that person's public key, and you are then assured that any communication which can be decrypted by his or her public key was originally encrypted using his or her private key. This provides a secure signature capability. If you wanted assurance that no one could counterfeit your communications, then you would simply encrypt communications with the outside world using your private key. Anyone able to decrypt your communication would be using your public key and would therefore know the communication was originally from you. Finally, if you wish to ensure that a communication is both secure from prying eyes and accomplished between two known and verified parties, then you first encrypt the file with your private key, and then again with the public key of the intended recipient. The recipient would then need to use his private key and your public key (in that order) to decrypt the file. This system can be used to protect financial transactions made in cyberspace, confidential communications concerning medical or financial histories, the exchange of proprietary files or trade secrets, or any other private or confidential exchange of information.

Public key encryption was patented in 1983 by a company named RSA (after the inventors, Ron Rivest, Adi Shamir, and Len Adleman), which holds most of the patents relating to civilian encryption standards. Zimmerman used public key cryptography and RSA's patent in PGP, and early copies of PGP which found their way onto the Internet were apparently in violation of this patent. Although Zimmerman claims he intended to secure a license before distributing the code commercially and obtained a licensing agreement later, when the program was uploaded to the Internet in June of 1991, no licensing agreement was in effect. The code is now available from a web site (http://web.mit.edu/network/pgp) sponsored by the Massachusetts Institute of Technology (M.I.T.) for non-commercial use within the United States. All in all, between the alleged violations of export restrictions and the possible patent infringement, it didn't look good for Zimmerman from the government's perspective in 1983, when the Department of Justice began an investigation (some call it a harassment) of Zimmerman. Because the strength of public key encryption was incorporated in PGP, U.S. government agencies alleged that PGP provided foreign governments, enemies, terrorists, and criminals with the ability to communicate without the U.S. government being able to intercept or eavesdrop the communications. It is possible, but not likely, that government cryptographers have discovered, or are well on their way to discovering, how to penetrate the shield of public key cryptography. Most experts believe, however, that national security agencies are unable to break such strong codes and are thus primarily concerned about the potential negative consequences of the widespread use of unbreakable encryption technology.

A Phil Zimmerman Defense Fund was raised not long after the federal investigation became known, and several lawyers contributed pro-bono defense. Jim Warren, a widely respected online activist, wrote a stirring article in March of 1995 entitled "The Persecution of Phil Zimmerman, American."[18] Ultimately, the investigation was dropped in early 1996 and the decision was made not to prosecute Zimmerman. Although it is easy to understand the government's desire to keep such extremely effective encryption algorithms out of the hands of terrorists and enemies to society, Zimmerman makes the point that serious criminals and drug dealers and terrorists are already using very effective cryptography anyway. PGP and other forms of effective and simple cryptography are simply the means whereby ordinary people can protect themselves and their privacy. Nonetheless, I think it is unfortunate that Zimmerman offers both unfaithfulness and defying the law as possible reasons and justifications for needing and using PGP. There are enough of legitimate uses and justifications for encryption, including securing commercial transactions and enabling e-money or cybercash, that to offer illegitimate reasons for encryption is self-defeating.

If we can get beyond the rhetoric and the paranoid fantasies—that the government might monitor all the private communications of citizens randomly on the one hand, or that terrorists and enemies will suddenly have a field day at our expense if encryption controls are relaxed on the other—I believe that progress toward a more secure and private state in cyberspace is critical to our future welfare. The Clipper chip proposals offered by the Clinton administration have been widely and rightfully criticized. Although much of the criticism has centered around the proposal for an escrowed key system, where the keys necessary to break encrypted exchanges are registered in secure escrow with a trusted third party, the real problem with the Clipper proposals is that they would be ineffective and would put America at a distinct disadvantage to the rest of the world. What many critics of the escrowed key system have overlooked is that many proponents of the public key system, including Zimmerman, have said that a trusted third party is actually necessary to the secure use of public key encryption. Zimmerman and others recognize that without a trusted third party, clever code crackers could substitute their public key for another, changing the name and then intercepting the encrypted communication intended for the victim.[19] A trusted third party could prevent such diversions, acting as a clearinghouse. Such a trusted third party, in the absence of legislation to the contrary, would probably be subject to due process of law under existing statutes. Thus, the answer to the problem rests not in the passage of any law mandating escrowed keys, but merely in the repeal of existing laws that restrict the export of completely secure encryption—legislation that is clearly hindering American firms such as NetScape, Sun, IBM, Hewlett-Packard, and others in the new world of global commerce. A policy of encouraging the use and sharing of the strongest encryption available worldwide actually strengthens those who wish to protect themselves and their privacy from the potential assaults of government, big business, and electronic criminals. That is a far more pressing concern in most everyday lives than the less imposing specter of terrorism, drug dealers, international criminals, and enemy governments.

Intellectual Property

Most people agree that artists, writers, producers, musicians, composers, inventors, programmers, and the creators of other types of "intellectual property" should control and be justly compensated for their artistic and cultural contributions. Questions arise, however, about what constitutes "fair use" and "just compensation." For example, if we order a pay-per-view movie, do we have the right to record it on a VCR for a repeat viewing? How about showing it later at a party to a dozen friends? Do we or should we have the right to make a tape of favorite songs from our CD collection as a gift for a friend? If we can loan a book to a friend, why not software— if we don't use the program while it's on loan? In cyberspace, should we be required to purchase access to certain information or sites? Under what circumstances? Or should sites be available under some sort of shareware system? How much compensation is due to those who participate in the creative process, such as authors and artists, editors, publishers, and producers? How much of the pie is a fair share to those who played little or no role in the actual creation of the intellectual property but rather offer ancillary services such as distribution, indexing, proofreading, marketing, maintenance, and distribution? Will cyberspace increase or decrease the importance of the respective players in the creation and marketing of intellectual property?

The Clinton administration responded to these types of questions in a 1996 report entitled "Intellectual Property and the National Information Infrastructure: A Preliminary Draft of the Report of the Working Group on Intellectual Property Rights."[20] It suggested a tightening of traditional copyright and intellectual property rights in cyberspace. According to Pamela Samuelson, a Fellow of the Electronic Frontier Foundation and a Cornell legal scholar, the report intends to "eliminate fair-use rights whenever a use might be licensed," increase the control copyright owners have over works in digital form by suggesting that even temporary copies made in computer memory constitute copyright infringement, force online service providers into the role of police and enforcers, and teach school children these rules and interpretations.[21]

Seemingly, the Clinton administration failed to figure into its equation the benefits that would accrue to individuals and education if certain copyright restrictions were *relaxed* in cyberspace. Fair use provisions, for example, might be expanded to allow the redistribution of entire copyrighted articles or stories so long as no fees are charged. Presumably, excellent articles would be redistributed widely and the reputation of the author would benefit accordingly, increasing the marketability of that author's work. Apparently, the Clinton administration did not learn the lesson of software sales. That is, when software vendors voluntarily relaxed copyprotection schemes, software companies didn't suffer at all, but rather continued to increase sales at an ever more dramatic pace—indicating that their respective products were reaching more individuals and thereby benefiting a larger percentage of the population, especially in the case of educational software.

Civility

Even many advocates of free speech tend to agree that cyberspace would be a safer, more pleasant environment if its citizens were to voluntarily agree not to access or store materials that others would probably consider offensive, inappropriate, or disrespectful. Most of the commercial online services include such standards as part of their service agreements with customers. For example, a member's binding Service Agreement with CompuServe includes the following:

> Member agrees not to publish on or over the Service any information, software or other content which violates or infringes upon the rights of any others or which would be abusive, profane or offensive to an average person.[22]

The adoption of such a norm would obviate many flame wars and even legal disputes—because such things as inflammatory language, profanity, defamation, and pornography would simply disappear from the Net. Clearly, though, this is not a challenge unique to cyberspace. Human-kind has tried to encourage an increase in civility throughout history in traditional societies, with only moderate success. Cyberspace, however, accentuates the problem by giving us such ready access to one another. Whereas before, we could more easily avoid physical encounter with bullies and those prone to be abusive or malicious, in cyberspace we cannot as easily avoid such individuals and the often poisonous consequences of their malevolence. A cyberspace with no restrictions on behavior represents an ideal stage for social misfits, malcontents, and miscreants. Unfortunately, there is a great deal of controversy surrounding the appropriate means for achieving the ends of decreasing harmful speech without harming stimulating civil discourse and the spread of provocative new ideas.

The Appropriate Role of Government

Related to many of these challenges is the question "What is the appropriate role of government?" Most people agree that government is established to protect the rights of its citizens and to promote the common welfare but disagree over the meaning of "rights" and "welfare." When does the protection of the rights of one group infringe on the rights of another? Which rights should be considered sacred and inviolate and which are simply manufactured?

Questions concerning rights and welfare address a number of issues in cyberspace. Are markets self-regulating, or do they tend to gravitate towards the lowest common denominator of money as a substitute for morality? Will deregulation of providers of high-bandwidth services result in mass confusion as they compete for access to our homes? Will excessive government interference subvert the natural processes by which cyberspace problems might eventually solve themselves? If competition, private investment and funding, and open and equal access for all are the goals, then what are the means and how quickly can government step aside from its current regulatory role? Who should be sovereign in cyberspace—businesses, governments, or the people? If the answer is businesses, then what is to prevent an elitist dominance in cyberspace? If we answer governments, then how will they establish jurisdiction over what is now an international space without national boundaries? Should cyberspace establish its own government? If we answer consumers, or the people, then what is to prevent mob rule in cyberspace? Nobody yet even knows all of the questions, much yet many of the answers.

NORMS OF CYBERSPACE BEHAVIOR

Norms are values and behaviors considered typical for a given group or culture. From the beginning of computer-mediated forms of communication, users have developed norms that facilitate efficient and effective communications and minimize the distractions that are caused by our inherent insensitivities—which are often painfully evident in cyberspace communications. Entire books have been written about these norms, popularly called "netiquette"; and rightfully so.[23] A key ingredient in making the cyberspace experience worthwhile for ourselves and for others is civility—and the more we can learn about how others would like to be treated, the more we can make that experience an enjoyable one for ourselves and for others. Let's examine the essentials of decency, sensitivity, and effectiveness in cyberspace communications.

At the heart of netiquette is concern for the well-being of others. If you are a kind and considerate person in real life, then it will be easier for you to be a kind and considerate person online. However, the challenge is often greater because of the increased likelihood that you will encounter unkind and inconsiderate people in cyberspace. One is quickly tempted to believe that the world is a nasty place after a visit to certain newsgroups where flaming and emotional, ad hominem abuse is all too common. Yet as cyberspace matures, such attacks and incivility can be forced out of the public square if they are widely seen, even in today's permissive and tolerant environment, as unproductive, annoying, rude, wrong, and indicative of bad manners.

This "anything goes" environment in certain parts of cyberspace has long been nurtured by hackers who seem to associate dominance over others online as a Darwinian struggle. Nonetheless, numerous principles of human interaction, which define cyberspace norms, are beginning to emerge.

Already, certain online norms have been accepted almost universally and are self-regulating. Although most seem like common sense, it is surprising how much excruciating online time and mental energy has been expended developing and discussing them. If some seem too obvious, it is probably because most cultural assumptions seem self-evident to any member of the culture. If some seem to contradict actual experience in cyberspace, it is probably because norms are much less likely to be enforced or enforceable than laws are. Here are some of the most prevalent rules of netiquette, or cyberspace cultural norms.

Be Respectful

Respect others as you would want them to respect you. This minor variation on the golden rule seems appropriate to a medium where respect is the fundamental principle of all positive interaction and where lack of respect is certain to result in contentious flaming and difficulty. One key ingredient of this norm is respecting the privacy of others. Another is to be tolerant and understanding of their mistakes but to point them out gently so they won't, in ignorance, make the same mistake twice.

Avoid personal attacks—focus instead, whenever possible, on the ideas, logic, and words of the discussion rather than the personalities. You may criticize ideas, but not individuals. This is not only good logic but common sense. Ideas can be encapsulated in a note and discussed reasonably—individuals are too complex to be judged so easily.

All participants in a discussion are accorded equal treatment and respect according to the respect they accord to others. Participants should seek to understand the specific norms and rules of whatever virtual community you join. Cyberspace is perhaps one of the most egalitarian places to be found. Although some participants are accorded more respect over time based on the consistency of their contributions, most come to discussions as relative equals. Most sysops attempt to be scrupulously fair in enforcing what rules there are without prejudice or favoritism, although disputes are inevitable. Most seem to agree, however, that the ideal is equal treatment for all, sometimes to seeming extremes of tolerance.

Be Generous

Sharing and giving are good. From the beginning of computer-mediated exchange, unselfish, open sharing has been viewed very positively. Everyone recognizes that without such sharing, there would be little purpose to the exchanges and perhaps even less benefit. The dynamics of sharing in cyberspace, however, are leveraged—which simply enhances the perceived value of sharing even more. The sharing of your tidbit of information, your tip, or your program increases dramatically in value when it benefits several hundred others. The enormous success of shareware and freeware is a model that clearly demonstrates the benefits of grass-roots sharing and reciprocity.

Ideas should be free. Although some say that "information should be free," those who produce information for a living rightfully point out that there is a great deal of value added to ideas and knowledge in their expression, and that those who add that value deserve compensation from those who benefit. There is, however, general agreement that ideas themselves are not intellectual property and should be freely shared.

Be Responsible

You own your own words. This widely accepted aphorism originated on The WELL and has come to represent the double meaning of acceptance of personal responsibility for what one says as well as the assignment of any intellectual property rights to the originator of the words. When you accept ownership for your words, you are concerned with the impact those words have and assume a responsibility to avoid harm to others. You accept the consequences, negative or positive, for your words. You deserve the right to enjoy any economic fruits derived from your original words that you share, but must also accept the negative consequences of such unwise choices as libel, copyright infringement, or fraud.

The destruction or theft of another's data is unconscionable. Most of the hacking that occurs leaves data untouched, or adds superfluous data of its own. For example, one programmer friend of mine jokingly displays on his wall two university diplomas he never earned. He is completely up-front about not earning the degrees, describing how he hacked into the school's systems and created a qualified transcript for himself, which led the school to send him the degree their records showed he earned. Although this hacker friend is an honest man who apparently justified the transgression against the university by saying that he would never use these falsified records to deceive anyone for personal gain, the point is that he draws the line of permissible hacking where someone else's data might be destroyed. Most hackers draw the same line. Very few hackers have maliciously destroyed data. Culturally, in the hacker community, it is simply viewed as an intolerant breach. Kevin Mitnick has served prison time for the malicious destruction and manipulation of others data, but few others have. The Kevin Mitnicks of the world are in a distinct minority, unappreciated and unsupported even by most of their fellow hackers.

Use only online services you have authorization to access. In other words, don't log on using someone else's account without their knowledge and permission. They'll pay for it—it's therefore stealing. Perhaps worse, it's a severe violation of their privacy, akin to finding their key and walking into their home and opening their mail.

Be Focused

Keep it as brief and simple as possible. Remember that others are often paying to read what you have to say, in time and bandwidth. In other words, ask yourself if *you* would pay to read what you have to say, even if it's only a cent or two. If your two cents worth isn't worth a lot more than two cents, then you'd be better off keeping it to yourself. The "cost" of your message can be calculated by adding the average value of the time it takes each reader to read your message plus the bandwidth cost to download and/or read it online. If your audience numbers in the hundreds, and it takes each person one minute to read your message, then the total cost of a given message can be at least $10, if we conservatively assume that most readers time is worth, on average, $6 an hour, or ten cents a minute. Try to make sure that each message posted is worth it. This principle also contributes to the frequent use of emoticons and acronyms online—they not only clarify intent, but reduce the amount of time required to read and digest a message

Avoid chain letters, "spamming," junk mail, indiscriminate carbon copying, and any other inconsiderate form of communication. One of the reasons e-mail has been such a valuable and productive form of communications is that it has generally enjoyed an extremely high signal to noise ratio. Chain letters, junk mail, spamming, and other such solicitations threaten that productivity. "Spamming" is sending an e-mail message or posting a note to an unrelated newsgroup or thread that is likely to be irrelevant to many (and thus unappreciated) in the hope that a few will respond. It is, in essence, asking hundreds or thousands of people to give you their attention for a moment or two on the off chance that one or two will be interested. It is widely viewed as one of the most offensive things one can do in cyberspace, where the goodwill of those who are willing to help others is threatened by those who exploit the community by selfishly forgetting that the community exists.

Be Disciplined

Heed the rules of the owner of the forum or web site. The moderators or owners of discussion groups, often called "sysops," are generally unpaid or underpaid, motivated by things other than greed. They usually also have the rarely exercised power to shut out individual participants at will. Thus, it is widely accepted that they have the right to make whatever rules they feel are appropriate for their forum or site. For example, the webmaster at www.newbie.net has a "no smut" policy, and if you click on "smut," you see his definition: "If the sysop says it's smut, then it's smut!"

In one example on CompuServe, a participant began to accuse others of racial attacks and threatened legal action against the sysops. No one could identify what racially motivated slurs had been made, and no one even knew the race of the accuser, so after repeated warnings, the participant repeated the offense and was locked out ("l-flagged") of the ordinarily very liberal and tolerant forum. Few, if any, complained about the loss of one undisciplined participant.

Feed the garden and starve the weeds. In an environment where a wide variety of individual behaviors are likely to be observed, it is important for those who interact there to reward desired behaviors and ignore undesirable behaviors. Thus, kudos are offered to those who make particularly worthwhile contributions. Those who contribute nothing, poison the well, flame, spam, curse, and abuse are often berated—which usually only serves to increase the level of contention and disharmony. The appropriate response, which requires discipline itself, is to completely ignore such behaviors in the public space unless you are the sysop or in a position to actually do something about them—such as speak with the person offline or forward their post to anyone in a position to impose disciplinary action.

ETHICS

Ethics, as stated earlier in this chapter, is a group of moral principles or set of values. Ethics can also be the rules of conduct and obligations of proper behaviors which apply to individuals, groups, or professions. For example, lawyers and doctors are bound by oath to adhere to specific, tailored codes of ethical conduct. The principles of ethical standards are surprisingly universal, including qualities such as propriety, fairness, honesty, and treating others as we would like to be treated.

Propriety

Propriety is the standard of what is socially acceptable in conduct, behavior, and speech. The online behavior of most individuals is indeed characterized by a sense of propriety, but there are always a few who refuse to abide by the standards and norms of society. Entrepreneurs know very well the importance of propriety in retaining and soliciting customers, and that same sense of responsibility will benefit anyone in cyberspace. If a participant does not voluntarily embrace standards of propriety, the likelihood increases that involuntary regulation of behavior will be enforced, whether imposed by other participants or by those with power to control the resources used by the participants. As a matter of policy, however, we must be careful in choosing the means of enforcement, since Dynamic Quality begins with individuals who act with courage and conviction to defy social norms.

On the net, although everyone seems anonymous and distanced by the lack of physical contact, it is nonetheless important to remember that there are likely to be hundreds or thousands of witnesses to all improprieties. Reputations can be easily stained, even perhaps unfairly through improper reactions to the improprieties of others. Even though cyberspace technologies may actually encourage unethical behavior through anonymity, lack of sanctions, or perceived obscurity, cyberspace technology is often used to address the problem of impropriety as well.

For example, most participants in cyberspace have better things to do than interact with "twits," as the rude and ridiculous are often called. Thus, some software is now available with "twit filters," or "UserID suppression," which users can enable to exclude communications from specific individuals. Nobody wants to be "twit-filtered," and thus the use of such filters has become one means of dealing with the obnoxious. Another means long used has been to "lock out" the offending users. Most forum software enables the sysops to exclude selected user IDs. Although some sysops are loathe to exercise any form of editorial control, many others have exercised their right to create the environment appropriate to their forum by locking out those who refuse to abide by the rules.

With twit filters and lockouts the ingenuity of cyberspace technologists has replicated a societal control in formats suitable for cyberspace. Just as traditional societies have ostracized and excluded those who behave improperly, so can cyberspace sysops and citizens decide for themselves to exclude others from their sphere of concern as appropriate.

The pillars of propriety are restraint and responsibility. It is often tempting to treat others as they treat us, thus justifying a flame for a flame, and a "dis" (current slang for "disrespect" or "disrespectful") for a "dis." Restraint, however, offers us an opportunity to take the high road. By responding to a flame with silence or a good-natured reply, we set an example by treating someone else ethically even though they have not extended to us the same level of respect. By taking the high road, we reinforce the norm that we are each responsible for our own actions, without regard to the actions of others. In other words, the old saw that two wrongs don't make a right is especially true online. The words of others need not be offensive unless they are true, in which case we should acknowledge that and apologize. If they are false, it is usually easy enough to demonstrate that they are. If a false allegation is made, it is almost always unsubstantiated. The appropriate response is to ask for substantiation and supporting evidence. If the other person engages in an ad hominem attack, it will be obvious to most onlookers with common sense that it is untrue if you simply reply with a good-natured refutation without attacking back. If someone twists our words, assume that they have been careless in reading and simply misunderstand. Give them the opportunity to understand by explaining without anger or bitterness. Always assume good faith until you have no choice but to believe otherwise—at which point simply refuse to engage that person further in any exchange. There is a great deal of wisdom in Thumper's Rule (Thumper was the rabbit in Disney's *Bambi*): "If you can't say anything nice, don't say anything at all." Naturally, there are times when we must be forthright and direct—nonetheless, we should seek to maximize the constructive good and minimize the harm that comes from such uncompromising revelations.

Although the ethical specifics of online behaviors are still in a nascent stage, we can examine and apply the same principles of static quality upon which most ethical standards are built to cyberspace situations as they unfold. Cyberspace clearly requires a new approach in many ways—particularly in relation to anonymity, an issue we will explore in considerable depth. However, the principles of static quality provide a clear sense of familiarity as we further explore the topic of ethics in cyberspace.

Representation

Whether in cyberspace or the real world, one must be clear about what and whom one represents in dealing with others if that representation is or might be relevant to your dealings. For example, on a bulletin board or forum, you will participate in a wide variety of conversations with others. In most of these conversations, you will be representing only yourself and perhaps your family name. In other conversations, however, you might *be perceived* as representing your company or some other organization.

This not only has ethical ramifications for you and your company, but it could easily have legal ramifications and might even affect your employment. Most companies have policies forbidding employees from representing themselves as anyone but themselves and from speaking for the company in any capacity outside their job. For example, if you assert the absolute safety of your company's product in a public post, then your company could be legally liable if someone relies on that representation to his or her harm. Thus, in discussions that involve your company, your business, or any organization to which you belong, you should have a clear understanding of the extent of your representation and, in each relevant post, clearly articulate, or disclaim, the extent of your representation.

For example, an employee of Company Z who has not been authorized by management to speak for that company might answer a question about product function on a forum. That employee should include a sentence that states he is an employee of Company Z, but that his statements and opinions are strictly his own and that he does not represent and has not been authorized to speak for Company Z. Similarly, an executive for Company A should be aware that everything he says in cyberspace can be construed as company policy.

In one real-life case study from personal experience[24] (none of the names are real for the individuals involved), an employee of Microsoft named Bob joined in discussions on a CompuServe forum about local area network (LAN) software. Bob praised Windows NT extensively—but when asked point blank by a respected systems analyst and writer named Bryce whether he or his company had any preferential ties to Microsoft that might be coloring his opinions of NT and his criticism of competitors, he replied that he worked as an independent consultant and denied having any preferential treatment from Microsoft.

Eventually, his identity was discovered by an astute sysop named Betty and he posted the following message:

This morning I was contacted by [Betty] advising me she planned to out me on this board as an employee of Microsoft Corporation.

I chose not to reveal my affiliation with Microsoft, as I do not represent Microsoft's interests as a spokesman. To publish my association with Microsoft means that any message I leave automatically defines this as an official position of Microsoft. Having read the rules, I see I am not in board guidelines for having not revealed my status. . . .

While I do not apologize for any of the messages I have left, I clearly have a crisis to resolve. Should I continue to be active on this forum—or, as I clearly am not politically correct in [sysop]'s book should I depart?

I'll take action based on your input.

Warmest regards,

[Bob]

What was perhaps the most revealing part of the incident was the reaction of many of the other participants and one of the other sysops. Their responses?

"By all means, be active!. . . We hold no grudge."

"No complaints from me. . . "

"I agree with Tim in that you should be as active as you wish to be. If you have a desire to help people with your knowledge, which is an attribute that I have experienced from all members of this forum thus far, then by all means contribute."

"Stick around, Bob."

In all fairness, it appears that few of those so willing to overlook this serious breach of good faith and ethical behavior had read his previous denials in detail. The person who had asked the question, however, responded appropriately by reminding Bob of his previous misrepresentations, adding:

[Bob],

This is a rather difficult message for me to write. But, being a direct person I won't beat around the bush. . . .

I am of the very strong opinion that your business ethics are reprehensible. In my opinion you, as an employee of a Fortune 500 corporation, directly and with intent lied to your company's customers (such as myself). I can see no possibility that your error was either inadvertent, or was "innocent." Most companies would fire you outright for lying to customers like this, no matter your motivation.

Also, the message to which I am replying attempts to put a positive spin on all this, but the fact is that you would have never come forward if [Betty] had not discovered your affiliation and called you on it. And so now you're in spin-control mode, perhaps concerned for your job.

It has been publicly posted on CIS that what you have done is expressly against MS policy, that everyone working for MS that has a CIS account knows that they need to disclose their affiliation, and that penalties for not doing so are harsh and severe. Further, it has been said that what you have done is not commonly done, even though there are many who believe that MS is into "dirty tricks" such as this. . . .

[Bryce]

Bob was increasingly apologetic and was apparently disciplined by Microsoft and has told me that he learned from the experience; but the tragedy is that Bob apparently didn't realize, from the beginning, the seriousness of his violation of ethical standards. The fact that so many of the other participants also failed to understand the magnitude or seriousness of the offense, perhaps because it occurred in the ethereality of cyberspace, is also cause for considerable concern. As an aside, it was soon after seeing this and other similar incidents that I decided to write a book on the human issues of cyberspace that seemed to be causing so many so much harm.

Bias

Bias is a certain bent or tendency which is skewed by unrecognized factors, such as a systematic error introduced into an analysis. Although few of us can eliminate our personal bias from our judgments, we can certainly recognize possible sources of bias and share that information with others whenever appropriate. Failure to notify others of information they need to be able to evaluate our potential bias concerning our statements or claims made in cyberspace should be considered an ethical breach.

For example, assume that you are an employee of the company that sells Product X and you are lurking while two strangers discuss the relative merits of Product X and Product Y. You know that you have something to contribute to the discussion, so you offer the information you have, which might be of interest to the two strangers. The probability is high that the information you offer would benefit Product X and that you would not voluntarily offer information damaging to Product X. To compensate for this probability, you should simply disclose that you are an employee of Company X at the same time that you offer your information. The strangers can then judge for themselves the relevance and possibly biased nature of your contribution.

Conversely, others might be biased by your disclosures. For example, if you were to state that you are a mother receiving welfare assistance in a discussion on welfare reform, some might be biased about the value of your contributions and miss the agreement that might have otherwise be reached and the insight that might otherwise have been gained.

Attempting to balance competing interests by splitting the differences can itself be grossly unfair and biased if one party has been the victim of a serious injustice. For example, in a hypothetical story concerning the business competition between a convicted felon out on parole and a model citizen, it would be unfair to the model citizen for an online analysis of the merits of the two businesses to take the position that the past has no bearing on which business is more trustworthy and thus fail to communicate those differences to readers.

Even the appearance of bias should be scrupulously avoided if possible. For example, avid supporters of OS/2 had, for years, a difficult time understanding why OS/2 was so often slighted and neglected by the trade press, in spite of its clear and often touted superiority to Windows. The trade press was often accused of bias and favoritism for Microsoft. *PC Magazine* once pulled a regular feature—a top ten listing of best-selling software—in order to leave more space to cover an emerging controversy. When a suspicious reader asked *PC Magazine*'s editor, Michael Miller, whether OS/2 hadn't topped the charts that week, he quickly posted the list, which showed that OS/2 was indeed in the #1 position. *PC Magazine* compounded the problem when they again failed to print the top ten listing the second week, with OS/2 Warp again in the #1 position. The subsequent protestations that the timing was a fluke, and the sincerity of the magazine's online and published attempts to correct the misperceptions and to tell the truth about the incident weren't enough to overcome the perception on the part of many individuals that the magazine was indeed biased, leading some to post messages that they were canceling their subscriptions as a result. It all might have been avoided if *PC Magazine* had only realized that perceptions of bias are often as important as the issue of whether the bias actually exists.

Conflict of Interest

A conflict of interest exists whenever a decision maker with multiple relationships involving responsibility to others faces a choice that involves conflicting loyalties between at least two of those relationships. An ethical breach occurs when one of the other parties in the conflicting relationships is either kept unaware of the conflict or the decision maker refuses to step down even though at least one of the parties to be affected by the decision reasonably believes that the conflicting loyalties might lead to a compromised decision. In general, one must simply avoid situations which involve such conflicting loyalties; or, if such a situation is unavoidable, one must ensure that all information regarding the potential conflicting loyalties is fully disclosed to all parties interested in the outcomes.

As the pace of cyberspace commerce increases, trust will become an increasingly important factor in economic exchange. Simultaneously, the opportunities for undisclosed conflicts of interest and other ethical breaches increases with the relative anonymity offered by cyberspace. As ever, "caveat emptor" (let the buyer beware) is a worthy motto—however, businesses with wise leaders will make the ethical choices and nurture trust as a source of distinct advantage.

On the other hand, however, we may need to reexamine some of the underlying assumptions that might make formerly unacceptable ties more acceptable in cyberspace. For example, it might be argued that the traditional publishing barrier between advertising and editorial could be eliminated in cyberspace without harming readers *if* the readers are offered information about how much revenue is derived by the publisher, or content provider, from each advertiser.

Although it is impossible to elaborate all possible conflicts of interest, it is possible to identify some situations where conflict of interest is most likely to occur. These situations include

■ accepting benefits secretly from any of the parties who could benefit from your decision.

■ selling your ability to gain access to friends and associates and hiding the facts surrounding your motives from those involved (influence peddling).

- using the resources made available to you by virtue of your position of responsibility to private advantage without approval. This can take numerous forms, including taking office supplies; steering business to a family member (nepotism); or using a company phone, fax, or copier without reimbursing the company if such use violates policy. Careful attention to the rules, limits, and perks surrounding each such position of responsibility is necessary to avoid this problem.
- using confidential information to private advantage. This can be a very serious matter. Purchasing stock, for example, based on confidential knowledge gained as a consultant or insider is not only unethical but illegal.
- moonlighting, even if your jobs seem unrelated. If the moonlighting is done with the approval of your company management, you may still find your loyalties torn between the time demands of the two jobs.

Identifying a conflict of interest on the part of a deceitful person is often impossible, but it is much easier to judge our own actions by this standard: would a reasonable person knowing the easily determined facts of the matter judge my decision as suspect because of my loyalties or hostility to any of the parties affected by the decision? When in doubt, careful discussion and disclosure of all relevant information with all parties that might be potentially affected is important.

There are numerous potentials for conflict of interest in cyberspace. A web site might urge visitors to adopt a certain browser or piece of software without revealing a significant interest in the success of that software, such as a significant holding of stock in the company making the browser. An employee of an online service provider might enter negotiations with a business partner at the same time he is exploring opportunities for employment with that business partner. An employee of an online service provider might give out free accounts or free "flags" (no-charge access permissions) to friends without an appropriate business case. Someone might serve as a webmaster for competing companies, thus raising the spectre of consciously or unconsciously borrowing ideas from each site for use in the other.

One of the surest signs that there is a potential conflict of interest is if you would feel shamed by another's discovery of the details of a business relationship. Examine carefully before proceeding.

Anonymity and Pseudonymity

The question of identity is a key cyberspace issue. In the traditional world, we rarely communicate with anyone in a truly anonymous fashion. Although we contact strangers regularly in the course of our daily business, they are almost always clearly associated with the business or organization they represent. We can usually ask for or track down a name or otherwise trace responsibility if we choose to or need to. Visually, we are accustomed to devices such as uniforms, signs, name tags, and labels to reduce levels of uncertainty when we deal with strangers.

In cyberspace, there are fewer signals or devices, and some long-time denizens of cyberspace are often reluctant to provide them, believing that individuals should be judged by the quality of their ideas and expression rather than by the more traditional trappings of appellation and association. They have a point: there are advantages to anonymous communications, and cyberspace is one primary means whereby such advantages can be easily realized. As with any new possibility, however, the potential for abuse is significant.

The Dangers of Anonymity

Let's examine both sides—dangers first. The reason anonymity can be considered dangerous is that it can be used to perpetuate deceptions and to escape the usual consequences of criminal activity and irresponsible behaviors. For those reasons, unrestricted general anonymity online should be considered a threat to serious cyberspace applications, especially discussion groups and electronic commerce.

Deception This is, unfortunately, probably one of the primary uses of anonymity online today. Whether the purpose is to pretend to be something one is not, or to defraud others, anonymity is often used as a means to deceive the unwary online. On some forums, I have seen the deceptions of others justified by noting that anonymity is so common in cyberspace that the deception should simply be expected whenever one is online. This is a classic non sequitur, because where anonymity is the rule and everyone understands that, deception is far more difficult to achieve. In many serious forums, however, anonymity and the use of pseudonyms is rightly discouraged or forbidden. In such a forum, deception of any form is simply not appropriate.

Expectations must be appropriately tuned to the environment. Deception is far more likely where it is expected that real names will be used. Thus, one must be sensitive to time and place to determine whether using a pseudonym is an appropriate means of protecting one's anonymity. In a MUD or a MOO, for example, you are *expected* to choose a pseudonym and adopt a persona that may or may not be consistent with your real self. Harmful deception is virtually impossible, because posturing is expected—it's the nature of the game. However, in a forum where the merits of two competing products are being discussed, the use of a pseudonym by an employee of the company marketing either of the products would be a wholly inappropriate form of deception—no matter how accurate that person's comments on either of the products. To put it simply, you would be expected to disguise your identity at a masked ball, but to don a mask at a conference table would be wholly inappropriate—*especially* if no one could tell you were wearing the mask.

Criminal Activity Obviously, anyone who seeks to avoid detection or prosecution and break the law is likely to try to use anonymity as a cloak. One of the most significant challenges we face in cyberspace is, as Speaker of the House Newt Gingrich puts it, to "codify a self-governing community on the Net." The potential for all kinds of deception and crime on the net, including new crimes we can't now imagine, is enormous. Crimes such as predation, tax evasion, terrorism, embezzlement, stalking, obscenity, and fraud have the potential to invade and thrive in cyberspace; thus, the possibility that such crimes will increase cannot be ignored. If the possibility of detection and apprehension is virtually non existent, the disincentives to commit the crime are seriously reduced. Thus, we must exercise caution before enabling and thus unleashing new means of irresponsible behavior. Anonymity (writing, speaking, or acting without being identified or identifiable) and pseudonymity (writing, speaking, or acting under a false or assumed identity) should be limited to those avenues where anonymity is clearly understood to be permissible.

Assuming that cyberspace consists of roughly as many citizens as New York City, the serious crime rate in cyberspace seems to be remarkably low—judging from the number of publicized crimes. To the best of my knowledge, no one has been murdered as a result of their cyberspace activity. Many physical crimes (such as rape, battery, burglary, and abuse) are simply impossible to commit in cyberspace, but other crimes certainly seem possible in cyberspace—including fraud, defamation, assault (plausible threats of bodily harm that cause a reasonable apprehension of such harm), stalking and other predatory crimes, and obscenity. Most victims, however, seem to be taking their lumps—since there have been so few published reports of criminal prosecutions of those committing crimes in cyberspace. I am assuming, of course, that crimes committed in cyberspace would have been reported by a mass media which seems to report regularly on almost every other aspect of cyberspace.

The reasons for this low crime rate probably vary. Criminals may be less technically inclined and therefore less likely to be in cyberspace in the first place; many victims may not even recognize the offense as a crime; others may be reluctant to admit they have been a victim. Some victims may have inadequate evidence; some may not even know how to identify the perpetrator; others may simply want to avoid the time and expense of pursuing justice. Whatever the reason, there seems to be less reported crime online than in the real world to date, although I have found no hard evidence to support the supposition—only an absence of evidence of an online crime problem that rivals the real-life crime problem.

It is perhaps only a matter of time, however, before the cyberspace crime rate increases. If cyberspace offers advantages to criminals, it is certain that those advantages will be exploited. We can and should prepare now to minimize the possibility that crime will be an inevitable growth industry in cyberspace. In its current state, cyberspace generally offers the protection of anonymity, and determined and savvy criminals can avoid detection with a minimum of effort. Even though the major online services require a name and credit card number for registration, the verification processes are inadequate—it is often difficult to prove the necessary link between registration and person. Eventually, I believe that the electronic services, including Internet Service Providers (ISPs), will increase the security and reliability of their registration procedures in order to enforce responsibility and secure a greater degree of accountability. I suspect, however, that such procedures will not be implemented until legal or economic forces necessitate such a move. In the meantime, wherever you travel in the electronic frontier, it is wise to be skeptical about all names encountered and to reserve trust to those confirmed as genuine through traditional "real world" means.

Irresponsibility Although online irresponsibility is by no means synonymous with anonymous irresponsibility, anonymity encourages a variety of forms of irresponsibility. These irresponsible pursuits are not identical to interacting anonymously with others who are also looking to engage in similar inconsequential or enjoyable pursuits and pretenses. While not necessarily illegal, certain online uses of anonymity or pseudonymity are ethically wrong. These include using a false name or the cloak of anonymity to

- knowingly provide flawed or false information as accurate.
- manipulate opinions using rumor, innuendo, and lies.
- toy with the emotions and trust of others.
- deceive others with gender role changes in serious discussions.
- unfairly manipulate the flow and content of discussions.
- create threads with titles that create false impressions.
- originate chain letters.
- "stuff" the "ballot box" in online surveys and polls.
- intimidate, harass, or threaten others.

Irresponsible behaviors surrounding anonymity and pseudonymity can have serious side-effects. In one incident that started as a petty prank and turned into a bizarre circus, someone using the name Steve Barkto logged onto CompuServe's CANOPUS FORUM in January 1994 and proceeded to bash IBM and complain about me and a few other IBMers. A columnist in an Austin, Texas, technical newspaper immediately recognized that Barkto's tone and style were eerily similar to those of a well-known forum regular—a Microsoft manager who often argued his company's policy there. Other keen-eyed CANOPUS regulars noticed other irregularities: that Barkto had logged on from a node far from "OKC," which he had mentioned in his messages; that his posts exhibited certain tics such as a double-dot ellipses and the occasional use of "then" in place of "than"—both of which were characteristic of the manager; and that his concerns mirrored those expressed by the manager in private e-mail. These stylistic similarities served as a "fingerprint." According to reliable sources, it appeared that the account used by "Steve Barkto" was registered in the name of and using the credit card of the manager. I confronted this manager, whom I considered a friend, asking if he was Barkto. He denied it, complaining about CompuServe's "breach of security." Many involved in the evolving discussions confessed that they saw nothing wrong with having an assumed public identity. I, on the other hand, did not want the issue to die. I didn't believe cyberspace could be an arena for serious conduct of business if participants could enter these discussions with pseudonyms. I went public with e-mail to me from the manager in which he had told me that Microsoft executives had once used pseudonyms regularly to "go online and have fun." The forum's sysop sent a letter to the Board of Directors of the publicly traded Microsoft, demanding an investigation. After a few weeks, the investigators concluded that, if anything, the manager was a "victim" of the fraud. I was not convinced, but when IBM ordered me not to discuss the incident or mention the manager online, I resigned my position as online advocate. This manager complained to IBM management and executives about my refusal to be completely silent on the issue. In the spring of 1995, an article in the *Wall Street Journal* reported that the manager's company had alleged that a competitor had been hiding behind pseudonyms to disparage his company online. Although I could not be personally vindicated, I felt that my position had been proved correct. Pseudonyms have no place in the serious conduct business.

Without minimizing my own foolishness in the incident, I have a keen sense of the dangers of irresponsible pseudonymity and anonymity and understand how little protection there can be against such dangers—especially when the surrealism of cyberspace collides with the realities of the real world.

The Advantages of Anonymity

There are also a few appropriate advantages and benefits of anonymity and pseudonymity, including protection against reprisal, the expression of unpopular ideas, venting, and the protection of privacy in certain circumstances. Even the benefits of anonymity, however, leave it a potentially threatening aspect of cyberspace if left unmanaged. In an environment where all communications are either anonymous or subject to spoofing, communications are less trustworthy than they should be. The avenues in which anonymity are appropriate should be identified and in all others the potential for anonymity and pseudonymity should be eliminated in order to secure the legitimate purposes of commerce without sacrificing the legitimate purposes of anonymity.

Protection of Political Ideas Against Reprisal The principle of free speech is firmly rooted in a healthy regard for individual capacity to choose well when faced with choices. Certainly, the principle of free speech was never meant to enable treason, illegal acts, or gross evil; but it *was* meant to protect individual conscience and freedom to believe and express belief without recrimination under law. Often, the ideas most likely to be suppressed by the political establishment are those most deserving of a hearing. Recrimination, however, may take more forms than can be prevented by law—such reprisals are often matters of life and death. Thus, there should be provisions for the anonymous or pseudonymous expression of political ideas, even radical ones, in selected locations online.

The Supreme Court has held, in *McIntyre* v. *Ohio Elections Commission*, that citizens have a core First Amendment right to distribute political speech anonymously, noting that the Federalist papers, which shaped many of the early political ideas imbedded in the U.S. Constitution, had been distributed anonymously.[25] Admittedly, that Constitution protects free speech to the point that anonymous political speech may not be necessary, and may even be considered craven—however, we must never take such civil liberties for granted. The more repressive the government and the less secure the rights of free speech may be, the more important anonymous speech becomes. In an international arena such as cyberspace, it is of critical importance that avenues for anonymous expression of free speech be provided universally. Imagine, for example, the impact anonymous messages from political dissidents in Iraq, China, Cuba, or other repressive regimes might have—although I'm confident that our utmost respect will always be reserved for those who put their reputations and lives on the line to espouse those principles they hold most dear.

The concept that anonymous political speech could have significant impact was explored at length in the works of Orson Scott Card, specifically in *Enders Game, Speaker for the Dead,* and *Xenocide.* A young girl, Valentine, takes the name of Demosthenes and challenges the political status quo with controversial essays and writings, which significantly influence those who read her writings, thus altering the balance of political power. Her anonymity protected her ideas both from reprisal but also from easy dismissal owing to prejudice.

On the flip side, as the means of mass destruction and murder have increased, there is the serious danger of providing advocates of violence, predatory mayhem, and terrorism with a publicly sponsored soapbox. One answer is to ensure that free speech is also open speech. It would be unlikely that anyone could anonymously mount a serious threat to the public interest from an open forum. Likewise, it would be difficult to conceive of an overriding public interest in the public sponsorship of private, encrypted exchange—which might be used to plot terrorist attacks, organized crime, violent revolution, or anything else contrary to the public interest.

Protection of Artistic and Literary Expression Artists and authors are sometimes unwilling or unable to publish under their own names. Although anonymity might also shelter those who act unethically in the furtherance of devious agendas, some provision should nonetheless be made for the protection of anonymous publication in cyberspace.

Often, creative and significant artistic contributions are made that grab society by the lapels and force it to face Dynamic Quality, however frightening the prospect of dramatic change. These works are often provocative and challenging—even scandalous; but as the Supreme Court held in the *McIntyre* case, "the interest in having anonymous works enter the marketplace of ideas unquestionably outweighs any public interest in requiring disclosure as a condition of entry."

Whistle-Blowing Many individuals, in the course of their employment or other involvement in the doings of government or an organization, discover facts that are unpleasant evidence of illegal or immoral activity by superiors or peers. Such an individual is invariably faced with a serious dilemma, which is often a no-win proposition: report the facts or stay silent. Many who are faced with such a dilemma choose to remain silent. Thus, the opportunity to provide anonymous feedback and thus trigger an appropriate investigation can be an important safety valve in government and business. For example, IBM has employed a "Speak Up" program successfully for years, which offers the option to remain anonymous. Organizations employing such feedback mechanisms not only mitigate the no-win aspect of reporting violations of policy and law, but also facilitate ethical conduct and adherence to the law by everyone in the organization.

Similar mechanisms should be protected in cyberspace, to enable reasonable suspicions to be voiced anonymously. Of course, it must be a two-way street. Such suspicions cannot be taken at face value, or the avenues for blowing a real whistle might soon be clogged with false reports voiced by those with hidden agendas. No accusation made anonymously should ever be taken more seriously than the corroborating evidence offered and verified warrants.

Elimination of Bias in the Consideration of Ideas In discussing ideas in cyberspace, on most forums, the acceptance of personal responsibility for those ideas and full disclosure are appropriate. There should also be avenues of expression, however, where all participants are anonymous. In such an environment, fewer ideas are dismissed because of prejudice and bias. The survival of ideas purely on merit is highly desirable, yet in many meetings or in public debate, some of the best ideas are stifled because the prevailing hierarchy of authority prevents the free expression or exchange of possibilities. Even in brainstorming sessions where management urges employees to speak their mind freely without fear of retaliation or judgment, almost everyone applies a mental filter on everything he or she says. In the public sphere, how often are valuable ideas dismissed when they become associated with an unpopular or discredited candidate or spokesperson? Only when all participants are on equal footing and anonymity is the rule is fully honest, unfiltered, open, unbiased discussion possible.

Cyberspace facilitates such discussions, whether the means is anonymous forums or group decision support systems. Although bias can never be completely eliminated from decision-making systems, in such an environment, bias in the expression and consideration of ideas is mitigated by the fact that all consider the idea on its merits alone, and thus biased ideas are less likely to survive an unbiased review.

Venting As I have stated before, one should resist the temptation to flame and vent online with or without exposing one's identity. However, because venting can be therapeutic, cyberspace should include arenas for anony-mous flaming and venting, just as traditional societies provide healthful channels of anonymous venting, such as counseling or religious confession, where a code of ethics protects the anonymity of the confessor.

A number of moderated conferences have discovered the benefits of establishing venting areas outside typical customer service channels. These arenas, such as monitored chat rooms or forums, increase a company's online image and effectiveness, because such complaints can be handled by seasoned professionals who carefully examine each complaint for merit and respond appropriately. Such ancillary forums should allow anonymous complaints against the a company or it's products—they should not be con-fused with the primary forum where serious discussion calls for the use of real names and affiliations.

Some claim that online anonymity offers escape from reality and can teach us about other cultures. They say that by posing, for example, as a member of the opposite sex, a teenager, a senior citizen, or a minority, we can better under-stand another culture or subculture. In such cases, anonymity might generate increased understanding and heightened sensitivity. Be aware, however, that no one really knows a great deal yet about the positive and negative conse-quences of such explorations.

It is up to the individual and, to a lesser extent, the regulators of the medium of escape to prevent healthful forms of escape from degenerating into negative forms of interaction. If participants are deceived or confused about whether the basis of participation is real or imagined, even though anonymous, serious problems could result. One must exercise caution in ac-cepting anyone in cyberspace at face value. Cyberspace is not a playground. Its participants must be aware of and adhere to the ground rules and the terms of engagement in forums where anonymity is acceptable to ensure valuable interaction.

Balancing the Dangers and Advantages of Anonymity and Pseudonymity

The fundamental problem with anonymity is that it is difficult to gain its advantages while minimizing its dangers. If anonymity is completely pro-tected, there is no way to track and punish serious wrongdoing, which opens the door to lawlessness in cyberspace. If anonymity is compromised by providing the means to track perpetrators, many of the advantages of anonymity are also compromised.

Various proposals have been offered as a means of dealing with this dilemma. There are numerous ways of requiring identification that also protect anonymity—which is how most online services currently operate.

In order to use the service, you must provide a valid credit card number, name, and billing address—but you are nonetheless free to choose any name you like (or even no name at all, in certain cases) for participation in the various forums and services. The online services will generally protect your identity unless there is evidence of wrongdoing on your part. This is, however, a weak form of anonymity that doesn't offer much comfort or safety to someone who, for example, might wish to inform on the mafia or a violent drug dealer.

A bit more security might be offered by some sort of escrowed registration process, in which an identity is carefully secured and protected in a safe and secure system with a third party, who would be legally obligated to protect the privacy of the registrations except as required by court order or warrant. This would, unfortunately, be a bit of an administrative and thus economic burden and would also require a just and fair court system and a competent government.

In his June 1995 column in *Boardwatch Magazine*, Lance Rose proposed a system where the societal costs of anonymity (as suffered by victims of fraud, tax evasion, terrorism and riots fomented online, libel, copyright infringement, etc.) would be borne in a system similar to statewide or nationwide insurance. Rose points out, however, that such a system would be open to a variety of abuses (such as anonymously injuring oneself to collect insured damages) and might simply reduce anonymity to an economically beneficial boon to those willing to exploit it for immoral purposes, thus perhaps making it prohibitively expensive—defeating the valued objectives.[26]

I believe at least part of the solution lies in restricting complete anonymity to certain limited forums specifically designated to achieve socially valued objectives. Everywhere else, responsibility and accountability can be encouraged by requiring that real names be used or by providing limited anonymity.

For example, encrypted e-mail IDs could be established in conjunction with certified anonymous remailers to receive e-mail from citizens willing to blow the whistle on such things as corruption in government or big business, criminal activity, or potential terrorists—with complete anonymity, even in interactive exchanges. Naturally, sufficient corroborative evidence would be required before an investigation into reported abuses would be deemed justifiable, in order to prevent such an avenue to be used for intimidation or revenge against the innocent.

Similarly, a series of anonymous forums could be established that provide for discussion and publication of political and other socially relevant topics.

With such a forum in place, an individual like the Unabomber would have less need to wreak havoc on the innocent in order to gain a widespread forum for radical ideas. Because the forum is interactive, such intelligent social misfits would have the opportunity to test their theories and get legitimate feedback—all in complete anonymity. Whether providing complete anonymity in such a forum would act as a safety valve or a pressure cooker remains to be seen, but the benefits should outweigh the costs.

In certain areas, however, such as chat rooms, fantasy worlds (MUDs and MOOs), or recreational forums, limited anonymity is probably most appropriate. Short of committing a crime, identities should be scrupulously protected. Each participant should be told upon registration or upon entering the forum exactly what the rules of engagement are concerning anonymity, so that only those willing to be fooled are likely to be confused or mislead.

On the other hand, certain forums and services simply don't lend themselves to anonymity. A forum for discussing investments and economic opportunities, for example, should require full disclosure and complete identification of participants. Anonymity or pseudonymity in such a forum should be considered completely out-of-line, since insider trading schemes, fraud, stock manipulation, and so forth could be easily perpetrated. Such a forum might be essentially worthless to serious investors if there were no accountability for the information provided. Forums for discussion of industry issues and standards would similarly be inappropriate for anonymous participation.

The bottom line is that anonymity is appropriate under certain conditions, but that we should begin now to build into the cyberspace systems we use the means to allow or prevent anonymous and pseudonymous participation as appropriate to the various purposes devised for cyberspace. If we provide too much opportunity for anonymity in contexts that are simply inappropriate by any standard, we will probably pay an unacceptably high societal price for the indulgence. If we provide too little opportunity for anonymity, we lose an opportunity to increase our freedoms and well-being. The answer lies in a wisely chosen balance, enabled by the distributed choices of the many thousands who will provide various avenues of anonymous or accountable participation in cyberspace.

LAW AND LAWLESSNESS

The real world is an intriguing mix of law and lawlessness. Security and order are not necessarily directly correlated with an increase in the number of laws on the books, and freedom and crime do not necessarily increase as the number of laws decrease. The only true security rests in the honor and decency of individuals. By that standard, the Internet offers about as much security as the world in which we live. It is a complex, noisy place full of every variety of human experience—both positive and inspiring and negative and horrifying. You can find WWW sites from which you can find a child to adopt from a foreign country, or you can find a site containing everything you need to know about bombs and explosives—including detailed discussions about how to be sure you kill and maim the intended victims (set the bomb to go off while a car is moving fast. If the bomb doesn't kill the driver, the crash will). Disney has a site. Penthouse has a site. Churches have sites. Devil worshippers have sites. You name it, you can probably find it if you go looking for it.

Cyberspace, particularly the Internet, was a lawless place for a long time. Although there have been a wide variety of rules that have been enforced by various online services, sysops, and others in a position to impose sanctions, the degree to which the denizens of cyberspace have been free to say and do whatever they please might as well have been a laboratory of anarchy in a world where you can't really reach out and touch anyone physically. In spite of the lack of law, it was a remarkably successful experiment in self-government.

In the 1980s, the discipline on the Internet and elsewhere in cyberspace was imposed by the other users and "superusers"—particularly the sysops—as well as by the intellectually segregating, technical barriers to access that seemed to grant the online community a distinctly idealistic culture of common concern. Since the Internet and other states in cyberspace were generally populated by researchers, college students, and professors, the Net was a nice place to exchange pleasantries and valuable information with strangers—many of whom didn't stay strangers for long. Law was virtually unnecessary and was in most cases deemed an intrusion on the freedoms so valued by those of us still marveling at the possibilities of being online, participating in the creation of virtual communities. One would hear about hackers and even encounter them occasionally on bulletin boards, but unless you were a sysop, they didn't seem to do much to cause concern except on the fringes.

Some time in the late 1980s, I noticed that bulletin boards began to impose restrictions and post disclaimers, referencing the Electronic Communications Privacy Act,[27] which had become law in 1988. These disclaimers were quickly viewed by the BBS community, at least, as legally necessary. No one can say precisely when the end of innocence for the anything-goes online culture arrived, but my vote would go to those days when sysops began to see the wisdom in embracing such laws—for their own protection.

In the relatively few years since then, there has been a snowballing increase in cyberspace issues coming before Congress, courts, and judges. There is not only more money at stake now than in the 1980s but also more people in cyberspace to get involved in disputes. In the mid-to-late 1980s, when Mitch Kapor and John Perry Barlow founded the Electronic Frontier Foundation (EFF), one was hard-pressed to find legal counsel familiar with cyberspace, much less cyberspace law. Little more than five years later, there's apparently enough interest to attract an entire convention of lawyers (please, no bus-going-off-the-cliff-jokes) at the Internet Law Symposium 95 held in Seattle during the fall of 1995. According to their promotional material,

> Evidence of the growing importance of Internet law abounds in scores of news reports of online gambling, online bingo parlors, FBI sting operations netting cyberspace kiddy-porn peddlers, legislative battles over free speech and civil liberties, and intriguing cases of intellectual property rights.

Robert Cumbow, an associate at Perkins Coie, a Seattle law firm, points out that "there are a lot of unanswered questions of what one can and cannot do on the Internet. And what kind of liability will apply."

Such a convention is necessary because the body of law that relates to cyberspace is still in a highly dynamic state. Many areas of law in cyberspace are still in dire need of additional legal definition, including jurisdiction, intellectual property, security, encryption, signatures and certification. According to EFF cofounder Barlow,

> In many ways, cyberspace is as extranational and anti-sovereign as the high seas. It appears that most existing laws, derived as they are for a very different social and commercial environment, may not serve us well as we try to assure order there. One of the many problems is that even if new laws need to be written, which they probably do, it is not clear whether any of the world's governments have clear legal authority to either write them or enforce them.[28]

In May of 1996, I attended the "9th Annual Computer Law Conference: Communicating and Conducting Business Online," sponsored by the University of Texas School of Law. Without describing the impressive proceedings, suffice it to say that the emerging field of cyberspace law is attracting well-deserved attention. Because cyberspace law is in such a state of flux, the following summary of important legal considerations in cyber-space are no more than my suggestions intended only to raise issues of importance to anyone who participates in cyberspace. I am not a lawyer (or, as you would see online: IANAL) and am ill-qualified to advise you on any specific legal matter. Nonetheless, I think it is important that I share with you the practical aspects of what I have learned as an online profes-sional. Another disclaimer is also in order: just like any matter involving law and legalities, anything you read about law in cyberspace is not only subject to change, but also may not apply to you or your situation. My personal involvement in cyberspace has indeed led me to consultations with attor-neys, on two separate occasions. The first occasion was the first time I had ever consulted a lawyer, so I understand a reluctance to consult attorneys. In each case, my consultations led me to conclude that my initial instincts were right on target, that the threats made against me were unjustified, that the danger to me personally was not serious, and that I would be better off not pursuing remedies, since an ongoing lawsuit could cause far more grief than a few misrepresentations made by some individuals.

As volatile a world as cyberspace is, it is not necessary to consult a lawyer before venturing into cyberspace. If it were, many of us would be either imprisoned or impoverished by now. I would nonetheless advise consulta-tion with an attorney if you have questions whether something you'd like to do online might be harmful to you or anyone else or if it might poten-tially entangle you in a difficult situation. If you have more time than money, then you might be interested in learning more about the law, begin-ning with Cornell's excellent web page at http://www.law.cornell.edu, which includes extensive legal resources, such as a searchable database of the United States Code—a starting point for studying federal law.

The following discussion reflects only my views on those elements of law and common sense most likely to pertain to typical activities in cyberspace. Entire books have been devoted to the subject of law in cyberspace—it would be foolish for me to even attempt to cover every angle and nuance of such a dynamic body of law. My purpose, instead, is to communicate those aspects of the law that have been most important to me during my fifteen years in cyberspace, trusting that my experience is somewhat representative of what most individuals will encounter in cyberspace. My bias is that we should abide by the higher laws of propriety and morality; law, by protecting our rights, is the foundation of our ability to pursue those higher laws.

Intellectual Property

Because cyberspace is a world focused in the minds of networked partici-pants, it is not surprising that intellectual property is one of its foremost legal issues. Issues surrounding copyright, trademarks, and trade secrets have been among the first issues related to cyberspace to be decided by the courts. Some issues have been determined, but on most, we might say that "the jury is still out."

Copyright

A copyright is a set of legal rights associated with the creation of certain intellectual work such as books, articles, essays, poems, songs, a newsgroup post or thread, pieces of music, pictures, and computer programs. Some of these rights are particularly important in cyberspace—including the right to copy, modify, distribute, perform, run (on a computer), or transmit a work. Note that these rights belong to the copyright owner, who can relinquish, sell, or share the rights with others. Thus, for example, the author of a piece of software may grant a license to individuals to use the program for 30 days on a trial basis. By joining a forum, the writer of a post might implicitly grant the sysop the right to delete or modify the post. By actually posting, the writer of a post grants others the implicit right to copy that post from the forum to their screen or even to their hard disk without compensation. A programmer might grant a company all rights to work produced by virtue of employment. An author or a publisher may own a copyright.

These rights might be granted to certain portions of the public or even the public at large. Many shareware licenses and even some commercial licenses grant a no-charge license for use by non-commercial users, while charging commercial users for a license. All copyrightable works are protected by international and United States copyright laws as soon as they are created. Although it is not necessary to place the familiar © notice on any such work, it is clearly worth doing to clarify the ownership of the work for anyone who might attempt to justify its duplication on the grounds that he or she thought it was public domain. The notice takes the familiar form of the copyright symbol (©), the year the work was created, and the name of the copyright holder.

Even though it is not necessary to register a work with the Copyright Office or label it as copyrighted to protect your rights under copyright law, it is nonetheless advisable. If infringement occurs, the damages can be greater if the work was labeled, and attorney's fees are recoverable if the work was registered before the infringement occurred. Before 1909, any work without a copyright notice could be assumed to be in the public domain. Numerous changes to the law have since then, however, mean that such an assumption is no longer possible. The only way a work can be known to be in the public domain is if the copyright owner clearly dedicates it to the public domain. One should treat files created since 1988, with or without a copyright notice, as copyrighted unless there is clear reason to think otherwise. With works created between 1909 and 1988, caution is the byword. Even though a work without a copyright notice might very well be public domain, one should err on the side of treating it as if it were copyrighted. Works before the turn of the century can be treated as public domain if there is no copyright notice displayed, and even if there is, chances are good that it can be treated as public domain because the copyright has probably expired. Fortunately, this includes most of the great works of civilization—many of which can already be found online. For example, I found Thomas Paine's *Common Sense* on the World Wide Web in less than a minute using Yahoo.[29] The Gutenberg Project has for years been making a number of the great works available online.[30]

It is the free availability of so much valuable public domain reference work that makes cyberspace already better than many libraries for quick and easy research. It is also perhaps why many law-abiding, decent people unknowingly violate copyright law. One of the reasons copyright law is sometimes abused is due to misunderstandings of "fair use" clauses. Fair use is a concept included in copyright law to relax what would otherwise be absolute rights that might work against the interests of all concerned. For example, without the fair use doctrine, excerpts from books would rarely be quoted, even in reviews; educational uses would be severely restricted; and photocopies of articles made for one-time personal use would be prohibited. The copyright owner would not receive valuable exposure and the public would be deprived of the free spread of ideas. There is, however, no clearly defined standard as to what constitutes "fair use." To illustrate an example of fair use, consider my use of the following quote explaining fair use from *NetLaw,* by Lance Rose:

> Your chances for fair use treatment of quoted or copied material are greatest when
>
> ■ you take very little of the copyrighted work.
> ■ you make the quoted portions a small part of your own work.
> ■ your own work does not interfere with the sales of the original copyrighted work.
> ■ you don't depend on the quoted material to sell your own work.
> ■ your use of the copyrighted work promotes a publicly valued objective, such as education or public commentary.[31]

This list, I trust, represents a perfectly acceptable example of fair use—I have used only a small portion of Rose's work; I've made it only a small portion of my own work; I hope my endorsement of Rose and his work increases rather than decreases the sales of his work; I'm not dependent on the inclusion of the above quotation for sales of this book; and my objective in quoting Rose is to promote a publicly valued objective—helping others understand fair use.

There are limits to the application of the fair use doctrine—there are numerous areas where fair use almost certainly does not apply to online use. One such limit, as the law exists today, would be the posting in a public forum of an entire article from a recent magazine or newspaper by anyone but the copyright owner or someone who has permission from the copyright owner. Another (as yet untested in court) would probably be the collection of a series of valuable threads of discussion from other forums in order to publish them in a collection or even make them available on your own forum for downloading. Clearly, scanning in pictures from magazines or books and making such pictures or collections of pictures available to others online, even for free, violates the copyrights to the pictures of those who own them. Similarly, making copies of a commercial software program available online or even transferring copies to a friend over the network are also copyright violations, unless specifically permitted by the software license.

There are other uses that fall into gray areas under law, where the companies and copyright holders would have us believe one thing, and the courts have held another. For example, the film industry would have us believe that it is clearly illegal to record any movie for any reason—yet the courts have determined that not only may a pay-per-view movie be recorded for the purpose of private, in-home time shifting, but even that certain unspecified nonauthorized copying is not an infringement of the movie maker's copyright under fair use provisions of copyright law.[32]

Absolute copyright is also mitigated by the concept of "implied license." For example, when you post to a forum or newsgroup, you are the copyright owner of your messages. However, if your copyright were to be enforced literally, no one could download or view your message—since that is digitally identical to making a copy of your message in your computer's localized memory space. Thus, you are, in effect, granting to anyone who wishes to access the forum or newsgroup, an implied license to make a copy of your message for the purposes of reading or even archiving your message. This implied license is derived from commonly accepted practice on bulletin boards and precedent. It is similar in concept to the idea of an access easement, whereby a property owner who makes his or her property available to the general public for long periods of time without restriction eventually loses the right to prevent the public from continuing to access that property as in the past.

Note, however, that implied license is not the same as "everyone does it, therefore it must be OK." In *Playboy Enterprises, Inc.* v. *Frena* (1993), *Playboy* won a summary judgment against a bulletin board named Tech's Warehouse that made images scanned directly from *Playboy* available for download, even though similarly infringing images were routinely scanned and uploaded to cyberspace.[33] The bulletin board operator's defense that "everyone does it" clearly didn't grant him right to violate the magazine's copyright without its knowledge or permission. If *Playboy* had been uploading those images to bulletin boards and had been actively promoting them as advertising, then it probably would have been a different story in court and the concept of implied license might have held. Be aware that if someone is violating your rights online, and you allow it to continue with your consent or knowledge, you may be giving up those rights, to some degree at least.

One area of controversy online, which has yet to be tested in court, surrounds cross-posting. For as long as there have been online communications, messages from one venue have been cross-posted and forwarded to other venues. For example, soon after the announcement that Microsoft intended to acquire Intuit, someone once posted a mock news release stating that Microsoft had announced that it was "acquiring" the Vatican. It didn't take long for this very funny work to spread worldwide throughout the Net, prompting Microsoft to actually issue a denial of any such intention—which was perhaps funnier than the original satire and which, in turn, was widely distributed. In most such cases, no one objects to the cross-posting and the original poster is honored that his or her post was considered worthy. In other cases, however, copyright owners such as newspapers and magazines have rightfully objected to the cross-posting of articles or stories. Even if there are no commercial interests involved, some participants object to wider distribution of their posts on the grounds that cross-posting of their works might expose them to ridicule or loss of status, or because the original context might easily be lost. Additionally, the owner of the forum in which the posting was originally made may feel that the post adds economic value to his or her forum and may object to its use elsewhere. It remains unclear whether cross-posting can be prevented legally. Some posters are making it clear, right in the post, whether they want the post cross-posted or redistributed via e-mail, either by explicitly stating the restrictions, or by affixing a copyright notice. In the absence any such explicit restriction, I personally believe that no publicly valued objective exists for not treating postings as public domain. Whatever the law relating to the matter, I believe it is usually appropriate to ask permission of the copyright owner before cross-posting any message as a matter of courtesy. If permission is refused, a decision must then be made regarding the propriety of any further distribution of the work under the concept of fair use. If, for example, you wish to criticize someone's idea or position, then you can probably quote the original text even without the consent of the original copyright owner, under the fair use provisions of copyright law. If your objective is to include the post in a newsletter you write and sell, then it would be clearly inappropriate to include it without the author's permission. Each case must be judged on its own merits.

Another ownership issue involves the creation of messages during the course of employment. State law or employer contracts signed by employees often give the employer rights to the intellectual creations of the employee. In that case, the employee probably shares the copyright with the employer and needs permission before sharing valuable information outside the company.

There is much yet to be decided about copyright law as it relates to cyberspace. I believe it would be careless to treat cyberspace as identical under law to any existing precedent—since there is so much that differentiates it from any physical model previously known. A great deal of information about copyright law and issues is available on the World Wide Web if you wish to do your own research.[34] Common sense is sometimes as valuable as a detailed understanding of the law—but when in doubt, consult an attorney.

Trademarks

The primary reason trademark law is important in cyberspace is because domain names on the Internet are the addresses by which individual sites are known. A domain name is also a key part of site addresses. Examples of domain names include: ibm.com, disney.com, mit.edu, whitehouse.gov, and lds.org. In the early days of the Internet, it was strictly first-come, first-served when it came to reserving domain names. One of the first disputes involving trademark law and a domain name involved MTV, the cable music network, and a former host named Adam Curry. Curry started a site under a domain name he had procured mtv.com apparently with the permission of MTV. After he left MTV, the cable network sued to recover rights to the domain name.[35]

Since that time, it has become increasingly understood that domain names should be included as an important part of the rights granted in association with a trademark. Thus, for example, nobody but International Business Machines, Inc., should be able to register and use ibm.com and nobody should be able to prevent IBM from registering and using `ibm.com`. InterNIC, the national body that assigns domain names, has tried to avoid playing a policing role, although it is becoming increasingly difficult for them to avoid such a role. If you register a domain name, you should check with a lawyer if there is any doubt as to whether you have a right to it under trademark law.

Contracts

A contract is essentially an agreement by which an exchange of value occurs between two parties. Online, there are numerous examples of contracts, whether explicit or implied. When you join an online service, you generally must signify that you have read and will obey the terms and conditions of participation before you can actually use any of the available services. When you log onto a bulletin board or sign up for the first time, you will probably be asked to read certain bulletins and agree to abide by the conditions established for the board by the sysop. When you purchase anything in cyberspace, whether via a toll-free telephone call or by filling in the blanks of an online purchase order, you enter into a contract subject to the terms of the agreement, or the Uniform Commercial Code, which designates contractual and legal obligations and agreements even in those circumstances where they have not been clearly stated between the contracting parties.

Contracts may be formed whenever there is a meeting of the minds. A signature on paper is not necessary to establish a contract. In most cases, before you enter into a contract, you will be asked to certify your consent by some legally enforceable and verifiable means, which is often as simple a matter of providing your credit card number or typing in "Yes" or "I agree" to an online question. On the flip side, if you wish to enter into agreements with online parties, you will probably wish to provide them with every bit of information necessary to ensure that they understand the precise nature of the agreement and that they have the opportunity to say "No" or opt out if they wish at each stage of the procedure. This information would include, as appropriate, such things as your expectations of the customer, what you are offering to the customer, unit prices for goods and services, follow-up phone numbers, delivery terms, shipping and handling and tax costs, and any other relevant terms and conditions. The greater the amount of information exchanged before an agreement is reached, the less likely the agreement will result in a later dispute.

Electronic Data Interchange (EDI) is commonly used for routine, structured commercial transactions between companies. EDI is a standard that defines the electronic format of transaction information exchange between parties to the transactions. Invoicing, payments, ordering, and other debits and credits between customers and vendors and intermediaries, such as financial institutions, are often handled using EDI. The contracts are built into the protocol of the exchanges. Although EDI is more likely to be used for common repeat transactions, it is possible, but more difficult, to use it for customized transactions as well. Companies considering doing business online should look into the benefits of using EDI—which include reduced transaction costs, increased accuracy, and faster turnaround times.

Other matters concerning contracts in cyberspace include the following:

■ Children cannot enter into legally enforceable agreements.
■ Both parties to a contract must sign or otherwise provide legally certifiable evidence of acceptance. This is particularly important in the case of services offered online, or any other offer made where some sort of clarification is required of the customer and of the provider.
■ Digital encryption will almost certainly be used more in the future to validate both ends of a contract. The public key system described earlier will almost certainly be the basis of the seamless signature and verification procedures, but no standard means of accomplishing this has yet been established.

Free Speech

Freedom of speech is a critical bedrock principle in cyberspace—it is therefore of critical importance that we examine the roots of free speech as a tradition in our society in order to understand how the principle should find application in cyberspace. The application of principle, carried to an extreme, can have harmful consequences. For example, the application of equality and fairness carried to an extreme would result in mind-numbing sameness and intolerance for difference and diversity. The principle of freedom of religion misapplied might sanction murder in the name of a deity. We should examine and understand the nature and importance of free speech to avoid carrying its application into the realm of harmful results.

There is a principle in law and society that any attempt to control thought or conscience is contrary to Good. This principle is deeply imbedded within our culture and traditions, and the sacred nature of our freedom of speech is derived from this principle. Thomas Jefferson described it in the preamble to The Virginia Statute for Religious Freedom, where he wrote:

That Almighty God hath created the mind free;—that all attempts to influence it by temporal punishment, or burthens, or by civil incapacitations, tend only to beget habits of hypocrisy and meanness . . . that the impious presumption of legislators and rulers, civil as well as ecclesiastical, who being themselves but fallible and uninspired men, have assumed dominion over the faith of others, setting up their own opinions and modes of thinking as the only true and infallible . . . that to suffer the civil magistrate to intrude his powers into the field of opinion and to restrain the profession or propagation of principles on supposition of their ill tendency is a dangerous fallacy, which at once destroys all religious liberty . . . and finally, that truth is great and will prevail if left to herself; that she is the sufficient antagonist to error, and has nothing to fear from the conflict unless by human interposition disarmed of her natural weapons, free argument and debate, errors ceasing to be dangerous when it is permitted freely to contradict them.[36]

In *A Man for All Seasons*, this principle was articulated by Sir Thomas More just after the perjury of Richard Rich, which left More condemned for treason for not declaring under oath a thing he did not believe: "What you have hunted me for is not my actions, but the thoughts of my heart. It is a long road you have opened. For first men will disclaim their hearts and presently they will have no hearts. God help the people whose Statesmen walk your road."[37]

Harry S. Truman, in his Inaugural Address of January 20, 1949, said:

The American people stand firm in the faith which has inspired this Nation from the beginning. We believe that all men have a right to equal justice under law and equal opportunity to share in the common good. We believe that all men have the right to freedom of thought and expression. We believe that all men are created equal because they are created in the image of God.

The First Amendment to the Constitution of the United States is the source of a U.S. citizen's rights to speak freely without interference by the federal government: "Congress shall make no law respecting an establishment of religion, or prohibiting the free exercise thereof; or abridging the freedom of speech, or of the press; or the right of the people peaceably to assemble, and to petition the Government for a redress of grievances." [38] Freedom of speech is important and protected because it is necessary to protect speech in order to protect beliefs and thoughts. Nonetheless, it should be noted that even though freedom of conscience may be an absolute right that outweighs all other rights, freedom of speech is not. As Federal Judge Buckwalter wrote in the District Court decision declaring the Communications Decency Act (CDA) unconstitutional, "it may come as a surprise to many people who have not followed the evolution of constitutional law that, by implication at least, the First Amendment provides that Congress shall make no law abridging the freedom of speech unless that law advances a compelling governmental interest. Our cherished freedom of speech does not cover as broad a spectrum as one may have gleaned from a simple reading of the Amendment."[39]

When speech crosses the line from expression of thought or belief and becomes a vicious or criminal act actually and demonstrably harmful to others, it should no longer be protected in principle or in practice. Even the provisions of the Articles of Confederation, which guaranteed freedom of speech and prevented the arrest of those debating the Constitution, specifically excluded "treason, felony, and breach of peace" from the protection of free speech. [40] Justice Oliver Wendall Holmes said, in a Supreme Court ruling, "The character of every act depends on the circumstances in which it is done. . . . The most stringent protection of free speech would not protect a man in falsely shouting fire in a theatre and causing a panic."[41]

Those haven't been the only limitations placed on free speech over the years. A teacher cannot offer a spoken prayer in front of a classroom each day. Obscenity is still illegal, however much it may have been redefined as community standards have changed. Exercising one's freedom of speech by joking about a gun at an airport security checkpoint is not likely to have a happy ending. Publishing damaging lies about someone is not protected by the First Amendment. Conspiracy to commit illegal acts can often be a prosecutable offense. False advertising and much commercial speech is unprotected speech. Threatening physical harm to another that causes them reasonable apprehension (assault) is also a criminal act.

Take the case of Jake Baker, for instance.[42] Although the case against Baker was dismissed, it is an appropriate starting point for a discussion concerning the limits of free speech. A student at the University of Michigan, Baker wrote imaginative but graphically violent, loathsome, pornographic prose depicting rape, torture, sodomy, and murder. He posted his first-person prose to the alt.sex.stories Internet newsgroup. Urged on by apparently sick and twisted readers, Baker grew increasingly bold in his writings, until he finally actually used the name of a student in one of his classes as the victim of one of his vile stories. The stories were written in a light-hearted style that made them all the more horrifying. A sixteen-year-old American girl in Moscow, Russia, was so shocked by the story naming the victim that she showed it to her father. He, in turn, showed it to an attorney friend who, as an alumnus of the University of Michigan, notified the president's office at the University to ask why such obscenity was coming from an account sponsored by the University. In the investigation that ensued, Baker cooperated fully, apparently confused by the "anything goes" nature of the Internet and not realizing that he had done anything seriously wrong.

In an introduction to one story, Baker wrote, "The following is just words. Words have no inherent meaning. Plato is dead." Plato may be dead, but words are still powerful and can bear serious meaning. After the university suspended Baker, it turned over various of Baker's writings and e-mail it had obtained from Baker during the investigation to the FBI. Among them were e-mail exchanges with a Canadian apparently using the pseudonym Arthur Gonda. These went well beyond fantasy, discussing detailed plans for abduction, bondage, rape, and murder—including plans to get together the next summer for that purpose. The exchanges exhibited a clear understanding of the distinction between imagination and reality and were thus impossible to read as imaginary fiction. On February 9, 1995, Baker was arrested by the FBI, which cited a federal statute against using interstate communications to transmit a threat. Baker was held without bond until mid-March, when he was released on bond following a psychiatric evaluation that concluded that Baker would not act out any of his savage fantasies. On March 22, a federal Judge dismissed all charges because the government had failed to demonstrate the presence of any action associated with the plans to carry out the crimes discussed or any imminent threat to anyone in particular. The word on the Net is that the government plans to appeal the case.

Cyberspace offers us an opportunity to re-establish common sense and fundamental values consistent with the static quality of the wisdom of the ages and the dynamic quality of a rising generation. The challenge is to reject the shrill sophistries of those who ignore the obvious in defending the indefensible. Too much focus on whether Jake Baker's First Amendment rights were violated neglects what should be obvious to anyone who has read his stories—that what he wrote was indefensibly wrong. Does his "right" to write any obscene thing he pleases outweigh the right of the "Jane Doe" named in his story to life, liberty, and the pursuit of happiness free from the horror imposed upon her by Baker? If Jake Baker escapes legal consequence in order to make a statement of how strongly we support the First Amendment and the principle that a person should not be prosecuted for his thoughts, that's one thing—but it's another thing entirely if we forget or neglect that what he did was revolting, immoral, and depraved. One Baker fan wrote, "You, sir, are sick. And I love it! Keep posting these great stories."[43] There seems to be a serious gulf between the assumptions of at least one subculture on the Internet and society in general. Perhaps if there's no law, there should be significant moral and cultural sanctions. If there are no such sanctions, then there ought to be a law. Have we gone too far in the protection of free speech, having forgotten the reasons we protect free speech is to protect freedom of conscience? What do we do when conscience is lost? Is this really a victimless act? Where is the Dynamic Quality worth protecting?

Online, seemingly absolute freedom of speech has been widely defended by those accustomed to the "anything goes" freedom of the Internet with much passion; yet believing that such "freedom" actually exists and acting irresponsibly as a result is foolhardy. Absolute freedom of speech in cyberspace has existed pretty much untrammeled until recently for several reasons, including the relative anonymity of cyberspace and the difficulty of identifying perpetrators, ignorance of the law, and the relative lack of moral and economic interest in the Internet. Those times are over. One disgruntled individual who posted an accusation of fraud against a company in a Prodigy forum for investors was sued, as a codefendant with Prodigy, for defamation in a case which was eventually settled with an apology from Prodigy and a much-criticized court ruling holding Prodigy liable. A magazine publisher I know tells me he has, with the help of his legal staff, asserted his rights against online bullies successfully on numerous occasions—although in talking to the bullies, they have a different perception of who's bullying whom, because not everyone has the benefit of legal counsel. But the lesson is clear: don't assume you can say anything you please in cyberspace unless you are willing to become a test case for new legal doctrine, as Jake Baker became. Specifically, let's examine some of the laws relating to free speech as they apply to cyberspace.

Defamation (Libel and Slander)

When you wrongly harm the reputation of another with written (libelous) or verbal (slanderous) public statements that are not true, you may be guilty of defamation. Therefore, it is not only important to be truthful and accurate in whatever you say online, it is generally wise to abide by a modification of Thumper's Rule: "If you can't say anything nice, don't say anything at all—unless it's true and needs to be said in order to help others." That will not only keep you out of legal trouble, but also a variety of other trouble as well.

Assault, Stalking, Harassment

As Jake Baker learned, there are laws against threatening others. Assault is a threat or attempt to inflict harm or offensive contact that creates fear or apprehension in the person threatened. Thus, some threatening flames might conceivably be judged as assault. Although you may think free speech gives you every right to tell people that if they don't stop doing whatever it is you don't like, then you'll find a rifle and shoot them in the knees because you know where they live, it doesn't. Don't threaten others in person or in cyberspace.

There are also laws against harassment and stalking. Like many laws, these laws have not yet been fully tested or defined in either the real world or in cyberspace. This is one area where the direct application of laws from the real world to cyberspace may not make sense. For example, if some stranger from afar is sending you annoying e-mail, it is more easily ignored than if someone is physically following you around. Nonetheless, I expect that we will see lawsuits and criminal charges filed that are based on the cyberspace equivalent of assault, stalking and/or harassment laws. To stay out of trouble, it is simply common sense not to deliberately persist in bothering others online after they have asked you to stop. Philosophically, peace will bring you more satisfaction than pride.

Conspiracy

When two or more people join in secret agreements to engage in illegal acts, a conspiracy may exist. Conspiracy is often illegal per se. Unfortunately, since cyberspace advances the state of the art for cooperative communications, it also facilitates conspiracy. One of the hot debates in cyberspace has been whether the government should be permitted to intercept and decrypt suspect communications. With the advent of unbreakable encryption coupled with online communications, the U.S. federal government is arguing that it will lose ground in the fight against organized crime, terrorists, drug dealers, and other conspiracies if criminals enjoy access to unbreakable encryption technology. On the other hand, most cyberspace citizens argue that conspirators already have access to such technology, but that the government's attempts to keep it from conspirators only results in keeping it from American citizens and businesses who might use it for their own protection.

Beginning in the early 1990s, the federal government has attempted to address what is suspected to be a loss in its ability to crack intercepted messages due to advances in civilian encryption technology. The means by which government security agencies hoped to reassert their advantage in decryption was a proposal known as the Clipper chip. Many leading cyberspace intellectuals and observers argued in a multitude of online discussions that forcing technologists to deliberately implement the means for government to override the security and privacy offered by the technologies significantly reduced their effectiveness. If the best security legally allowed to the people is, by default, insecure against the government, then the people will not only be exposed to some degree to the potential for abuse by their government, but will still be at the mercy of conspirators who can obtain their own fully secure encryption technologies and might be able to find ways to exploit the legislated insecurities. One of the first effective online petition drives was organized, and tens of thousands of electronic signatures in the form of e-mail notes were gathered. One brave government representative willing to argue that something needed to be done to secure the government's ability to track down and apprehend criminals, terrorists, drug rings, embezzlers, and so forth was "welcomed" with scorn and derision at a convention of hackers and cybernauts. Eventually, the government withdrew its proposal and has since been offering new compromise proposals.

Unfortunately, some in the cyberspace community seem unwilling to compromise, in spite of the acknowledged importance of trusted third parties even in civilian schemes. Brock Meeks, a leader in the nascent field of cyberspace investigative journalism, called the government's follow-on proposal to Clipper the "not-so-new 'Clipper II': a train wreck waiting to happen," and disparaged the new proposal with ad hominem idioms, vulgar language, crude clichés, and metaphor, without offering a glimmer of a substantive alternative to the government's proposals.[44] Meeks seems to assume that government is always corrupt; that it's better to be at the mercy of criminals and anarchy than to be subject to government and rule of law; and that eliminating the ability of the FBI and the CIA to intercept communications is not just a good idea but also necessary for the preservation of our freedoms and civil rights. In other words, the assumptions which underlie most of the arguments against any form of government intervention in cyberspace seem to be that government looms large as a threat to our civil liberties and rights and is ineffectual in protecting them. I believe that governments indeed can be a serious threat to individuals, but that the Constitution established a form of government that is more likely to protect our rights and well-being as citizens than it is to deprive us of them—and that the check on government abuse is an informed citizenry. I'm sure the debate is healthy in the long term—but if there is one crime that looks to be relatively undetectable and unpreventable in cyberspace for the foreseeable future, with state-of-the-art cryptography as readily available (even if not legally) as it is, it would be conspiracy.

Censorship

Is censorship illegal? In other words, do you have any recourse against someone who attempts to restrict what you can say online? Interestingly, for all the knee-jerk outrage directed against it, censorship is only illegal when practiced by the government to suppress protected speech. Actually, censorship, the act or process of deleting or suppressing matter which is found offensive or objectionable, is part of our everyday life. Parents censor their children's reading and viewing material, teachers are themselves prevented from saying certain things to students, editors pick and choose what to publish, directors and producers exercise "editorial control," and employers generally exercise near total control over what employees may say or publish publicly about the company. The cries of "censorship!" can sometimes seem overused to protest the exercise of authority over free expression, even when such exercise is legitimate and in harmony with the rights of those in authority.

Thus, when you are online, you are at the mercy of whomever is hosting the discussion group in which you are participating. Sysops of bulletin boards or forums may exercise total control over the forum, shutting you out as they please for whatever reasons they please. Fortunately, this does not happen often, but it is always amusing to see some unruly participant threaten a sysop with legal action if the sysop decides to censor the unwelcome guest. It may not be good business to censor customers, but it is certainly not illegal. The legal danger in a moderator modifying any message is from copyright and defamation laws and not from any anticensorship law. Even then, if the moderator has established his or her right to modify messages by force of contract via an agreement required of all participants, or if the moderator and participants are all employees of a company, which typically "owns" all employee copyrights, the moderator can "censor" messages according to their best judgment. But on private, moderated, or commercial forums, sysops and moderators should be able to delete any message they please in order to assert their right to create an appropriate environment for valued discussion. If the sysop or moderator represents the government, however, much more care must be exercised, lest the kind of censorship forbidden by the First Amendment is used to deny citizens their right to express themselves free of government interference.

Unfortunately, in *Oakmont v. Stratton*, the court found that Prodigy was also liable for libel based on its failure to censor libelous comments, since Prodigy had advertised that it was a "family forum." One unintended but ironic effect of the ruling has been that the commercial online services have become less willing to establish or enforce policies prohibiting offensive or illegal speech lest they be held liable for a failure to enforce the policy. The "Good Samaritan" clause of the Communications Decency Act was intended to exempt any such service which acted in good faith to censor abusive, offensive, or profane language—but even that statement of legislative intent backfired when the CDA was declared unconstitutional by a District Court. There will, no doubt, be further progress in this arena as cyberspace matures.

Gambling

Gambling has long been legal in various parts of the world, which have enjoyed enormous economic success as a result. International Gaming & Wagering Business puts the total legal wagering in the United States alone at one-half trillion dollars, and even though net winnings to the gambling industry is only about eight or nine percent of that amount, it is still bigger than the domestic motion-picture business and the recorded-music industries combined.[45] The future of gambling online is still unclear, in spite of its illegality in the United States, since the Interstate Wire Act and other laws prohibit online gambling. Specifically, the taking of bets over a network, such as the Internet, that crosses United States or state boundaries is prohibited by federal law. In spite of such laws, there are already offshore gambling sites appearing on the World Wide Web. Their defiance of the law relies on the fact that secure encryption offers safety for participants and that enforcing United States laws against foreign citizens or residents is so difficult. It will probably only be a matter of time before anonymous, electronic cash makes the enforcement of existing laws prohibiting gambling on the Internet impractical and very nearly impossible. Conceivably, legal action could be brought by the government to identify and shut down those domain names known to be hosting gambling, but it is doubtful whether such legal action would be long effective, given the ease with which a domain name can be procured and established when compared to the difficulty of bringing and/or enforcing such action.

One can debate the effectiveness of maintaining unenforceable laws on the books, but given our ambivalence towards gambling, it is quite likely that the laws will stay on the books, and gambling could nonetheless increase dramatically to the point that it could conceivably become a major societal problem. That is, unless individuals choose not to gamble.

Indecency and Obscenity (Pornography)

The laws surrounding indecency, obscenity, and pornography are extensive. Individuals trying to make money from pornography often complain that the laws are ambiguous, confusing and vague—perhaps due to the inherent conflict they face from attempting to market perversions on the fringe of legality while nonetheless staying out of jail. Pornography is essentially erotic and sexually stimulating material, which is sometimes indecent and sometimes obscene, with the line between those respective classifications of pornography often blurred and dependent on local community norms. Obscenity isn't the only thing illegal according to some of the laws in place—certain depictions of violence and other matters offensive to community standards of morality might also be considered indecent and/or obscene and thus illegal, depending on the context. Legal standards for broadcast television and radio, for example, are more strict than for books or magazines. In brief, pornography or erotica is not illegal per se—but a variety of state and federal laws exist that prohibit indecency in certain contexts and obscenity in general, in order to protect the public health, safety, and general welfare. Some of these laws

- prohibit the sale of obscene material.
- prohibit the possession or distribution of child pornography (where a child is anyone under the age of 18)
- restrict the interstate mailing of obscene materials.
- forbid indecency or obscenity on the public airwaves.
- permit indecent conversations by dial-a-porn companies only if the age of the user is verified.

The 1973 Supreme Court case of *Miller* v. *California* established a three-part test for obscenity. If all three of the following criteria are satisfied, then material can be considered obscene:

1. The material or work, taken as a whole, would be found by an average person to appeal primarily to the prurient interest according to "contemporary community standards."
2. The work depicts or describes sexual conduct specifically defined by the applicable law in a patently offensive way.
3. The work, taken as a whole, lacks serious literary, artistic, political, or scientific value.

In spite of seeming inconsistencies in the enforcement of pornography laws over the years, several BBS operators have been convicted of trafficking in obscenity in the last few years. In *United States* v. *Thomas*,[46] the operators of a California BBS named "Amateur Action" were given a jail sentence based on action brought and judged in Tennessee, where community standards apparently differ considerably from those in Milpitas, California. Their appeal has been denied.[47]

Tony Davis, the sysop of the Oklahoma Information Exchange BBS and a respected businessman in Oklahoma City, was given a ten-year sentence that almost seemed obscene itself for making available images from CD ROMs that were fairly openly advertised and sold nationwide. Worse, the police apparently had entered into an agreement with a local television show entitled "You're Busted!" to film the raid on Davis's operations.[48] Much has been written about these two cases, and much more probably remains to be written, but the fact remains that neither the consumption nor distribution of obscene materials should be considered to be a right.

It may seem unfair that laws are applied and enforced in a manner that might appear random—and it probably is; however, the realities of society are that there is no guarantee of fairness for anyone on the frontiers of legality and community moral standards—since laws are reflections of those societal standards of morality, which are typically in a state of flux. Perhaps additional clarification of the laws is in order, and perhaps clear lines should be drawn in order to leave no doubt in anyone's mind what constitutes legal and illegal activity; but the fact of life is that such lines simply cannot always be clearly drawn or evenly enforced.

The story is told of two truck drivers applying for a job. Each was asked how close he could drive a truck to the edge of a mountain road without going over the cliff. The first stated that he could drive indefinitely within one foot of the edge, even at 30 miles per hour, without an accident. The second simply said that he had no idea how close he could get because he always stayed as far away from danger as possible when driving. The second got the job.

In the absence of a clear lines regarding what is legal and illegal in the area of pornography, however, it only makes sense to steer clear of the line. No amount of money should be worth the risk of spending time in jail, and the morality of creating or trafficking in pornography, however great the demand may be for such pornography, is questionable at best. Note that we're not really talking about nudity—most pornography today is far more extreme. Those who defend pornography as free speech and pornographers as artists may be missing the big picture—what justification can there be for the exploitation and objectification of children and women? Free speech as the rationale for obscenity makes as much sense as arguing for the right to bear arms as justification for armed robbery. This will be discussed more as a societal pitfall of cyberspace, but for now, suffice it to say that the distribution of obscenity, as measured by prevailing community standards, is illegal. Until further clarification under law becomes available, the prevailing community standard should be considered the most strict community standard in the United States even if care is taken to ensure that only adults have access to the material. What's more, the Communications Decency Act (CDA) applies even more stringent standards. Even though it has been declared an unconstitutional infringement, its passage indicates that legislators and presumably their constituents have declared that enough is enough and are responding to the obvious failure of self-discipline in cyberspace to create an environment free from material that would be considered offensive by many concerned adults, much less one that is suitable for children.

As far as the consumption of pornography (as opposed to its production) is concerned, there are dangers there as well. One industry columnist I know told me the story of a man in Arizona who found himself under arrest after downloading a few images from an Internet site in Denmark. The man even claims that he didn't know the images were of child pornography—yet he faced legal problems and reportedly lost his job. Because even the possession of such images is illegal in the United States, such ignorance could be costly. Lest anyone be unduly concerned, the chances of downloading illegal images randomly from an unknown site is extremely remote unless you are in the habit of downloading files of unknown content from unknown sites, and the chances of getting arrested for doing so are even smaller. I've been quite active in cyberspace for over fifteen years, and have only encountered unwanted obscenity in cyberspace on very rare occasions. Indecency is more common, however, but can still be avoided by choosing the appropriate sites and forums to visit.

THE COMMUNICATIONS DECENCY ACT

Most recently, many of the most relevant legal issues have been brought to the forefront of public debate by the passage of The Communications Decency Act, an amendment of the recently passed Telecommunications Reform Act which was signed into law on February 8, 1996. This act has attracted significant controversy and was declared unconstitutional by a District Court in June 1996—yet in my opinion, at least some of the criticism is a smoke-screen to promote and protect ulterior motives, hidden agendas, and economic interests. The following represents a listing of what I think are the most important and relevant parts of the Act and the findings of the court. I have filtered out much of the less interesting legal wording, but I believe the essence is nonetheless intact. You should obtain and read each in its entirety to judge it for yourself, however.

FINDINGS — The Congress finds the following:

(1) The rapidly developing array of Internet and other interactive computer services available to individual Americans represent an extraordinary advance in the availability of educational and informational resources to our citizens.

(2) These services offer users a great degree of control over the information that they receive, as well as the potential for even greater control in the future as technology develops.

(3) The Internet and other interactive computer services offer a forum for a true diversity of political discourse, unique opportunities for cultural development, and myriad avenues for intellectual activity.

(4) The Internet and other interactive computer services have flourished, to the benefit of all Americans, with a minimum of government regulation.

(5) Increasingly Americans are relying on interactive media for a variety of political, educational, cultural, and entertainment services.

POLICY — It is the policy of the United States

(1) to promote the continued development of the Internet and other interactive computer services and other interactive media;

(2) to preserve the vibrant and competitive free market that presently exists for the Internet and other interactive computer services, unfettered by Federal or State regulation;

(3) to encourage the development of technologies which maximize user control over what information is received by individuals, families, and schools who use the Internet and other interactive computer services;

(4) to remove disincentives for the development and utilization of blocking and filtering technologies that empower parents to restrict their children's access to objectionable or inappropriate online material; and

(5) to ensure vigorous enforcement of Federal criminal laws to deter and punish trafficking in obscenity, stalking, and harassment by means of computer.[49]

I interpret other portions of the CDA to mean that it makes it illegal to use a telecommunications device" in "interstate or foreign communications" to

■ knowingly make, create or solicit (and then initiate) "the transmission of, any comment, request, suggestion, proposal, image, or other communication which is obscene, lewd, lascivious, filthy, or indecent, with intent to annoy, abuse, threaten, or harass another person."[50]

- knowingly make, create or solicit (and then initiate) "the transmission of, any comment, request, suggestion, proposal, image, or other communication which is obscene or indecent knowing that the recipient of the communication is under 18 years of age regard less of whether the maker of such communication placed the call or initiated the communication."[51]
- make "a telephone call" or utilize "a telecommunications device, whether or not conversation or communication ensues, without disclosing his identity and with intent to annoy, abuse, threaten, or harass any person at the called number or who receives the communication."[52]
- make or cause "the telephone of another repeatedly or continuously to ring, with intent to harass a person at the called number."[53]
- make "repeated telephone calls" or repeatedly initiate "communication with a telecommunications device, during which conversation or communication ensues, solely to harass any person at the called number or who receives the communication."[54]
- knowingly permit "a telecommunications facility under his control to be used for any activity prohibited"[55] above with the intent that it be used for such activity.
- use "an interactive computer service to send to a specific person or persons under 18 years of age, or uses any interactive computer service to display in a manner available to a person under 18 years of age, any comment, request suggestion, proposal, image, or other communication that, in context, depicts or describes, in terms patently offensive as measured by contemporary community standards, sexual or excretory activities or organs, regardless of whether the user of such service placed the call or initiated the communication."[56]

The CDA also makes it a crime to knowingly permit "a telecommunications facility under his control to be used for any activity" prohibited above "with the intent that it be used for such activity." [57]

The Act further provides defenses (exceptions) for those who

- are unwittingly involved in the transmission of such information but are not involved in the creation of the content and are not a "conspirator" with someone who knowingly creates or advertises the availability of, such content.
- employ someone who violates the Act
- have taken, in good faith, reasonable, effective, and appropriate actions under the circumstances to "restrict or prevent access by minors to a communication specified in the subsections, which may involve any

appropriate measures to restrict minors from such communications, including any method which is feasible under available technology."[58]

▪ have restricted access to such communication by requiring use of a verified credit card, debit account, adult access code, or adult personal identification number.

The CDA also provides protection for "Good Samaritans" who act in good faith to prevent minors from obtaining restricted material and also requires cable TV companies to scramble channels carrying indecent or offensive material.

Opponents of the law argue that it is an unjustified encroachment on free speech, that it will make criminals of anyone who discusses sensitive topics such as AIDS or abortion in public, that it will stifle valuable exchange, and that it is unenforceable. Some online activists have argued that Congress and President Clinton took the cowardly way out by passing a law they knew would be overturned by the courts. Opponents such as the Civil Liberties Union, the Electronic Freedom Foundation, and a coalition of other organizations and companies with a presence on the Internet banded together to bring action against the CDA. In July, in The United States District Court for the Eastern District of Pennsylvania, the CDA was ruled unconstitutional. In a remarkable decision that should be read by anyone wishing to understand the importance and nature of cyberspace, the court discussed 123 findings of fact before each of the three judges offered their conclusions.

Although there was no agreement among the judges concerning whether "indecency" was too vague, the judges were unanimous in finding that sections "223(a)(1)(b) and 223(a)(2) of the CDA are unconstitutional on their face to the extent that they reach indecency. Sections 223(d)(1) and 223(d)(2) of the CDA are unconstitutional on their face. Accordingly, plaintiffs have shown irreparable injury, no party has any interest in the enforcement of an unconstitutional law, and therefore the public interest will be served by granting the preliminary injunction."[59]

To understand why the CDA was declared unconstitutional, it's important to examine the actual text of the contested provisions. Section 223(a), the "indecency" provision, subjects to criminal penalties of imprisonment of no more than two years or a fine or both, anyone who

(1) in interstate or foreign communications . . .
    (B) by means of a telecommunications device knowingly—
        (i) makes, creates, or solicits, and
        (ii) initiates the transmission of, any comment, request, suggestion, proposal, image, or other communication which is obscene

or indecent, knowing that the recipient of the communication is under 18 years of age, regardless of whether the maker of such communication placed the call or initiated the communication; . . .
(2) knowingly permits any telecommunications facility under his control to be used for any activity prohibited by paragraph (1) with the intent that it be used for such activity.[60]

Section 223(d), the "patently offensive" provision of the CDA, subjects to criminal penalties anyone who

(1) in interstate or foreign communications knowingly-
  (A) Uses an interactive computer service to send to a specific person or persons under 18 years of age, or
  (B) uses any interactive computer service to display in a manner available to a person under 18 years of age, any comment, request, suggestion, proposal, image or other communication that, in context, depicts or describes, in terms patently offensive as measured by contemporary community standards, sexual or excretory activities or organs, regardless of whether the use of such service placed the call or initiated the communication; or
(2) knowingly permits any telecommunications facility under such person's control to be used for an activity prohibited by paragraph (1) with the intent that it be used for such activity.[61]

The court noted in its conclusions of law that "the CDA is patently a government-imposed content-based restriction on speech, and the speech at issue, whether denominated "indecent" or "patently offensive," is entitled to constitutional protection. As such, the regulation is subject to strict scrutiny, and will only be upheld if it is justified by a compelling government interest and if it is narrowly tailored to effectuate that interest."[62] The decision also explored the question of compelling government interest, noting that Internet communications are more like telephone communications than broadcast television communications and asserting that "even if a broad search will, on occasion, retrieve unwanted materials, the user virtually always receives some warning of its content, significantly reducing the element of surprise or "assault" involved in broadcasting. Therefore, it is highly unlikely that a very young child will be randomly "surfing" the Web and come across "indecent" or "patently offensive" material."[63]

Judge Buckwalter wrote, in conclusion:

Cutting through the acronyms and argot that littered the hearing testimony, the Internet may fairly be regarded as a never-ending worldwide conversation. The Government may not, through the CDA, interrupt that conversation. As the most participatory form of mass speech yet developed, the Internet deserves the highest protection from governmental intrusion.

True it is that many find some of the speech on the Internet to be offensive, and amid the din of cyberspace many hear discordant voices that they regard as indecent. The absence of governmental regulation of Internet content has unquestionably produced a kind of chaos, but as one of plaintiffs' experts put it with such resonance at the hearing:

What achieved success was the very chaos that the Internet is. The strength of the Internet is that chaos. [Testimony of March 22, 1996, at 167.]

Just as the strength of the Internet is chaos, so the strength of our liberty depends upon the chaos and cacophony of the unfettered speech the First Amendment protects.

For these reasons, I without hesitation hold that the CDA is unconstitutional on its face.[64]

The Department of Justice has stated their intention to appeal the findings of the U.S. District Court. Congress, perhaps expecting a struggle, provided "fast track" provisions for the CDA to be heard by the Supreme Court. Court decisions can be taken into account to draft new, Constitutional legislation. The battle over indecency in cyberspace is not over. Whatever happens, this Act and its purposes promise to provide the fodder for much welcome debate and discussion about the coexistence of morality and free speech in cyberspace. It is an important struggle, but until the details of the law and its enforcement become more clear, the safest road and perhaps most sensitive is to treat public cyberspace communications as if they were subject to the restrictions on broadcasting.

NETTING IT OUT

In most situations, we face choices about what we should do. Those choices are and should be influenced by our cultural norms, sense of propriety, ethical standards, and laws. It may be tempting to view cultural norms as constraining, or ethics as archaic hand-me-downs from ancestors who are clueless about the unique challenges of today, or law as something to be ignored when we can get away with it; yet there are sound reasons why most of the norms, standards, and laws of our day possess a high degree of value. Most of the rules and principles by which we live are derived from the lessons of history and the best thinking of the ages. They have been refined over millennia of thought and experience. In Pirsig's terms, they are often rich in static quality. Too often, we discover that some new version of morality is just the same old immorality. The dynamic quality of progress need not be made at the expense of the static quality of principle.

At the base of our shared cultural understanding of morality and values there should be a fundamental commitment to living in harmony with those around us. Culture, ethics, and laws should be constructed, understood, and enforced to increase that harmony.

One of the aspects of Jewish culture I have admired over the years is its devotion to understanding tradition and law as embodied by passion for scripture and discussing and even debating in an orderly turmoil the details of law and morality, as pictured in films such as *Fiddler on the Roof* and *The Chosen*. At the core of the debates there always seems to be a fundamental respect for one another and for the wisdom of those who have struggled with similar issues of right and wrong in the past. Surely, the extraordinary cohesiveness and durability of Jewish culture owes much to their core devotion to such a magnificent tradition. I get the sense that there are as many individuals as ever in our society who are highly concerned about these matters of right and wrong, but that they see the synagogues of our day, to draw a parallel, as the many courtrooms throughout the land that have been built to interpret a body of law as vast as entire libraries. Yet have we *really* relinquished responsibility for the mores of society to lawyers and judges? I trust not; I hope not. I also trust that many lawyers and judges yearn for an increase in morality in society as much or more than anyone else, but it may be that the most important arbiters of culture, ethics, and law in the next generation will be found in cyberspace, where the voices arguing matters of right and wrong can be seen far more easily than anywhere else.

Ultimately, culture, because it underpins so much of who we are and what we do, is the most important element in determining the future of our ethical and legal stance. Culture drives norms, ethics, and law because it is driven by our popular consumption of ideas, images, maxims, assumptions, beliefs, values, arguments, precepts, visions, and ideals. Cyberspace is already a world where such consumption is accelerated and enabled to an unprecedented degree. There, each of us, and not just those who pass by the barriers of editorial censorship, is better able than ever before to participate in the creation of culture. Thus, we must be more responsible than ever before for our moral stance. We should be open to others and sensitive to their concerns before we attempt to argue matters of common import from a purely selfish perspective.

Ultimately, the responsibility for our moral condition rests with each of us. We need not choose to sink to the lowest common denominator—there is no reason our personal standards should not be far higher than the minimum prescribed by law. There is no reason why laws should be passed to enforce morality at a higher level than is necessary to protect the basic rights of each individual—life, liberty, and the pursuit of happiness. Both those who decry national morality and demand new laws and those who decry the rising tide of law and demand more freedom could perhaps be more effective in eliminating the laws and increasing our freedoms by turning their attention and creativity toward solving the underlying problems that prompted the new laws in the first place. Law can never truly substitute for morality, but morality can indeed substitute for law.

I hope we can find opportunities to agree on the fundamentals of morality before we proceed to address the significant cultural, ethical, and legal issues of cyberspace. Solutions lie in mutual respect coupled with the technological means to build good fences and gates, i.e., in good neighbors. In cyberspace, not all dialogue needs to be argument, and not all morality needs to be legislated. Perhaps we can agree that the moorings of morality and the basis of culture, ethics, and law should be found in the degrees of excellence of static quality, and in Quality itself—building on the foundation of human rights that were the Dynamic Quality of the American Revolution. The emerging Dynamic Quality of the Cyberspace Revolution demands no less.

PART TWO

THE HUMAN DIMENSION

CHAPTER FOUR

*T*HE INDIVIDUAL AND EXCELLENCE

Freedom Through Discipline

We are moving into an era when the Information Superhighway will have the capacity to cut a wide path into our homes. With fiber-optic computer technology, it can link homes to an incredible assortment of messages and influences. This highway will be the conduit of information that will have the power to change our culture and, thus, our very lives. . . . The computer, television, satellite, microchip, and even the telephone, all can bless and enhance our lives—or can make them miserable.

—M. Russell Ballard

Quality of life is determined by individual beliefs, excellence in thought, word, and deed, and interactions among individuals—relationships. Our beliefs and interactions color our world. When our beliefs yield positive fruits and our relationships work, even something as otherwise insignificant as a brief exchange of words can be a joy. When a crucial relationship goes awry, however, suddenly nothing seems worthy of our time or attention. These interactions work when enduring principles of mutual respect and cooperation, justice and fairness, decency, compassion, and virtue are practiced. On the other hand, when even one party to those interactions adheres instead to thoughts, words, and acts that are more consistent with indifference, selfish disregard for others, brutal competitiveness, indecency, injustice, cruelty, or depravity, then all parties to the interactions suffer as do the relationships involved.

The contrast is often evident in cyberspace—where words have a quality of their own and individuals of every kind mingle more freely than they ever would elsewhere. The social stratifications we often take for granted blur to a significant degree, leaving us face to face with humanity, individual by individual. Our gravitation toward one or the other type of interaction reflects our beliefs and values. If we believe in peace and harmony, we eschew involvement with those who flame or with forums where fighting rules. If we value conflict and competition, we seek out others who are similarly inclined. In either case, we get what we bargain for.

Because the individual and the fundamental importance of each individual is at the heart of all that matters—including beliefs, relationships, family, principle, ethics, society, economics, politics, and so on—the importance of individual excellence in cyberspace cannot be overstated. That is what will make cyberspace a human dimension rather than an inhuman dimension. Freedom of conscience, freedom of speech, and freedom to assemble and associate are not important freedoms to possess in order to abuse one another in brutal competitions—they are important because they are the soul of that life and those liberties that are necessary in the pursuit of happiness.

In Part Two, I'll share with you a few of the things I've learned about the role of the individual, the community, business, and government viewed through the human dimension of cyberspace. I wanted to tell stories that might be fresh to me and more immediate to you. I wracked my memory and researched hundreds of articles and books looking for stories that supported the conclusions I had drawn from my own experience.

For the purposes of this chapter, my own stories are a good foundation for introducing the lessons I have learned. Although I prefer not to be the focus, I do have a story or two to tell about the revolutionary potential of cyberspace. At the basis of many of the arguments in the following chapters is my strong belief that cyberspace immediately affects each individual, presenting a challenge to our society, politics, and commerce. The stories have been told by others—and not always accurately—and many have urged me to tell them from my perspective; so I suppose they beg a telling.

ONE VOICE

From the time in the late 1970s that I first read about IBM as an employer that put people before profits and consequently (or perhaps nonetheless) generated profits that back then were the envy of every company on the planet, I was fascinated by the IBM mystique. While working for Price Waterhouse (also IBM's auditors) in San Jose in 1979, I was assigned to the Zilog audit. Zilog made the Z80 chip that stood at the heart of CP/M-based microcomputers. One day, I sought to satisfy my curiosity about personal computers and wandered through the front doors of a small Cupertino company named Apple to ask about their personal computers. I was amazed at what I saw and was quickly hooked on the idea that these small computers would change the world.

Returning to graduate school to get an MBA, I learned from David Hart, professor of ethics, that large organizations tend toward bureaucratic and unethical devaluation of the worth of individuals, unless there are deeply imbedded organizational cultures and structures in place to mitigate that tendency. Hart argue that IBM was indeed an exception and demonstrated that a large organization could value the individual, so as soon as IBM extended an offer in 1984, I accepted it to get to the heart of the PC revolution. I laughed off the famous Apple Super Bowl commercial that compared IBM to Orwell's Big Brother in *1984*—enamored instead by the image of IBM as portrayed in *In Search of Excellence* by Peters and Waterman.[1] I had read *1984* but hadn't even heard of William Gibson's *Neuromancer*, released that year—and thus had no appreciation whatsoever of the coincidence of the name of Orwell's novel, the coining of the term "cyberspace," and the timing of my joining IBM.

The Basic Beliefs

I welcomed the cultural indoctrination at IBM, excited at the prospect of working for the legendary company. At a week-long course for newly hired professionals, IBM's "Basic Beliefs"[2] were taught with a sincerity and honest concern bordering on religious passion that appealed to my spiritual side. The three Basic Beliefs, which were deeply imbedded in company literature, indoctrination, and policy, are detailed in the following list.

Respect for the Individual. This meant more than just not laying people off. It meant corporate practices, which protected employees from any form of unfair treatment, such as

- an "Open Door" policy that promised employees the right to speak with executives.
- anonymous "Speak Ups" that guaranteed a hearing for all grievances, however minor.
- regular anonymous opinion surveys to which management were held strictly and openly accountable.
- "resident managers" who were, if other procedures in place failed the employee, empowered by the chairman's office to resolve any employee grievance by taking any action deemed necessary, including the termination of anyone in management.

Employees were given as much time as required for sick leave, virtually without limit—although dishonestly abusing the privilege was a firing offense. IBM was a family company—a silver spoon was sent to an employee whenever a child was born into his or her family. IBM went to extraordinary lengths to demonstrate concern and offer time off or other assistance whenever a family medical crisis arose. When my wife, Serena, was told by a doctor that her pregnancy should be considered high risk, IBM flew me home from my assignment in Bethesda, Maryland, each weekend for several months. I thought I was devoted to IBM for life.

The Best Customer Service in the World. IBM celebrated employees who went to extraordinary lengths to serve customers. If a customer had a "critical situation" based on an IBM system that threatened the customer's business, IBM spared no expense to restore the system. "The blue suits falling from the sky" was an apt description of the customer engineers and systems engineers IBM would fly in to help with particularly thorny problems. Of course, when the product is a multimillion dollar mainframe on lease, such heroic measures are affordable and justified.

Pursuit of Excellence. Anything worth doing is worth doing in a superior manner. Hosting customers was inevitably a grand event, with every consideration planned in meticulous detail. IBM could afford the occasional extravagance of luxurious, all-expense paid trips to resorts for members of the Systems Engineering Symposium, Hundred Percent Club, or Golden Circle. The zeal for Quality was supported throughout the company. IBM's research facilities in Yorktown, Zurich, Almaden, La Gaude and elsewhere produced Nobel prize winners and were legendary worldwide.

These Basic Beliefs produced a distinctive IBM culture that was like that of a paternalistic family. There wasn't much question that working at IBM was an honor and a privilege—employees felt obligated and able to give their best to such a special company.

The man who had articulated the Basic Beliefs was a charismatic leader named Thomas Watson, Jr. The son of IBM's first great executive, Thomas Watson, Sr., the younger Tom Watson was an energetic risk taker who had made IBM *the* industry power in computers during the 1960s with a bold, bet-the-company project called the system 360—which created a standardized product line upon which businesses could build "legacy" software that could survive many generations of hardware changes and improvements without worrying about costly reprogramming. The zeal for computing architectures and standards was born.

IBM was known as the company that offered conservative, quality solutions. Information processing professionals knew that "Nobody ever got fired for recommending IBM." You may not have gotten the best price every time, but you knew you were getting a good value and reliable quality and service.

Watson had retired by the early 1970s but had left the company in good hands. By 1984, however, IBM had spent so much time and energy defending itself against the Justice Department suit and other litigation that it seemed the lawyers were defining company policy more and more often. Employees often talked about certain executives derisively as being an "empty suit" or as being especially well-qualified because he "talks nice and looks good in a suit." Akers came into power as Chief Executive Officer at the peak of IBM's prestige in 1985, not long after I joined the company. Little did either of us know that our paths would cross in person and in cyberspace half a decade later, with consequences neither of us would escape.

Collision and Explosion in Cyberspace

Soon after joining IBM, I discovered IBM's internal forums on the IBMPC Conferencing Disk. These forums had been created to enable employees worldwide to share information and solve problems relating to their use of the IBM PC, but employees discussed more than just PCs. The natural desire of employees to discuss the whole range of issues confronting someone at a company like IBM had not been stifled—largely because most of the half-dozen or so employees who administered the forums were as interested as anyone in exploring the possibilities presented by the new conferencing communications technologies. Although the forum administrators were constrained by corporate politics, policy, and funding issues, there were visionaries among them who understood the power of ideas freely shared, often joining in the discussions and inviting dialogue on the future and potential of conferencing communications in general and on IBMPC in particular. Even though the conferencing disk was fairly heavily moderated and required users to overcome technological and usability barriers, thousands of users developed an underground subculture in which I felt at home. IBM culture and company policy suppressed flaming, so these internal IBM discussions developed a distinctive tone and subculture. Consistent with the Basic Beliefs, participants were respectful of one another and differentiated between individuals and ideas. Lively discussion over ideas was valued and encouraged—but no one was allowed to attack or criticize other participants. The "appends" (posts) of anyone violating the rules were simply deleted, and any discussion of the moderators' decisions were also deleted. All such discussion (called "metadiscussion," or discussion about the discussions and the rules) was restricted to a few special forums devoted to that purpose. Employees were free to create forums on topics of their choosing if they agreed to "own" (review and moderate) the forum. Forums with names with only tenuous connections to personal computers were formed. Soon, forums such as "MARKETIN FORUM" (forum names on IBMPC are limited to eight characters), "WISDOM FORUM," "DEM-ING FORUM," "PIRSIG FORUM," and "QUALITY FORUM" were attracting fascinating discussion and facilitating creative brainstorming.

I was astounded by my new-found ability to reach thousands of employees companywide, and I was soon finding ways to improve my performance, widen the scope of awareness, and build a network of contacts within the company by using IBMPC regularly. I began by sharing tips and techniques for using PCs. I argued the merits of systems and software. When engineers in Boca Raton disregarded as "user unfamiliarity" problems I was having copying files from one prerelease Personal System/2 (PS/2) to another, I went to an IBMPC forum and, after asking if others were facing similar problems, used the affirming notes I received to force the development management to take another look. The result was an identified defect in a batch of thousands of diskette drives from a supplier. The systems weren't sold, thus saving a number of customers from a defect that might have given IBM's systems a black eye. I recognized that conventional communications would not have produced the same result.

I had joined IBM's marketing force in 1986 during a "redeployment" movement—a bold move by Akers meant to increase revenues by taking qualified employees from development, finance, and other supporting roles and moving them into marketing positions. It was the right thing to do to avoid layoffs in an environment where full employment was more than just a respected tradition. Unfortunately, little by little over time, judging from the discussions on IBMPC, the corporate passion for the Basic Beliefs was eroding as the company got so big and so powerful that arrogance set in and growth and prosperity were generally assumed rather than actively culti-vated. Inspired by one outspoken but inspiring old-timer named Dave McManigal, who often spoke out about IBM and the Basic Beliefs in these forums, I began to share my own ideas. I began to read and participate in discussions of company policy and practice—intrigued by the opportunity to experience the work environment and application of company policy in other sites through the eyes and experiences of others, as described on the forums in the process of seeking solutions to various problems facing employees. Most interesting to me, those problems seemed to be increasing. Hiring decisions were made more hastily as empires were built by ambitious executives. Resident managers were reassigned as a cost-cutting move because they were seen as unnecessary overhead. Some employees had self-ishly abused the concept of "Respect for the Individual" to demand some-thing for nothing—raises and promotions just for showing up at work and doing what they were told. Perks and cronyism began to flourish. Employee ranking systems were implemented to supplement the rating systems to "ensure equality" in the administration of merit pay systems. Profit growth slowed and was used to justify further tightening of the corporate belt. The gifts given to children at the employee Christmas parties were no longer quite as nice. Benefits were pared again and again in ways company officials hoped would be relatively painless to employees. Employee outings at theme parks were no longer an annual event. The famed IBM country club for employees was sold. An entire division (now Lexmark) was sold, and many employees in Lexington viewed the action with anger as a sell-out and a betrayal. Several anguished notes appeared on IBMPC. From within, the declining fortunes of IBM were a topic of many a lunchtime conversa-tion and were clearly visible from the IBMPC comments and discussion. As excellence was getting harder to find within IBM, those most passionate about the subject seemed to congregate with increasing frequency on IBMPC's forums to discuss what could be done to reverse the trends.

In 1989, I developed and began to enhance and maintain a series of tables to track the burgeoning compatibility issues stemming from the various combinations of systems, memory, software, and peripherals. I used the IBMPC Disk not only to discuss the tables and to gather suggestions, but also to advertise and distribute it as well. By 1990, over 100,000 copies of the tables had been distributed in softcopy and hardcopy formats, with less marketing and distribution effort than possible through conventional com-munications. In fact, without the word of mouth and convenience of con-ferencing communications, the tables wouldn't have been possible. IBM determined that the tables had saved it over $22 million in employee time and awarded Whittle a $150,000 Suggestion Award. To put those numbers in perspective, the $22 million represents one-fifth of the total savings real-ized by IBM through its suggestion program that year,[3] and the two inven-tors of the Scanning Tunneling Microscope *shared* an IBM award of the same amount I received.[4] Understandably, I was sold on the value of the forums and began a long, part-time process of convincing management that

IBM was overlooking an internal communications vehicle of enormous strategic value. Early successes were scattered—IBM management was interested in empowering employees, but these internal computer-mediated conferencing systems looked more like a Pandora's box than a genie waiting to be let out of the bottle. The selling of cyberspace within IBM was surprisingly difficult.

By 1991, I was well-known on IBMPC for my devotion to IBM's Basic Beliefs on a number of forums. I received dozens of responses to a long append I had made urging a revolution of sorts: a "New IBM" based on a change in culture but with a renewed and heightened emphasis on the Basic Beliefs. I applauded Akers's emphasis on customers, empowerment, and the need for change. An append I had made had come to the attention of Lee Reiswig, an executive responsible for the development of IBM's Operating System/2 (OS/2), and I had heard that it had made a significant difference in Reiswig's ability to "sell" my idea of opening the beta testing of OS/2 to tens of thousands of willing testers outside the company.

Soon after, in March of 1991, I witnessed what I believed to be an erosion of the Basic Beliefs at the gala launch of OS/2. Being a nondrinker, I was surprised to be in the position of refusing the wine that was served at the table. It was the first time I had been served wine at any IBM customer event—IBM was known as a teetotaling company during the Watson era. What was worse, in my mind, was that Akers took his wine glass to the podium and said that he suspected the audience was surprised to see IBM's chairman in front of everyone with a glass of wine in his hand, announcing, "This is a 'new IBM' "[5] and adding that he wanted to toast everyone for sitting on their "fannies" to listen to IBM tell them about OS/2. He went on to state that he had been persuaded that OS/2 would ship that year, but that he was holding the badges of the two executives responsible for that task (Lee Reiswig and Jim Cannavino), just in case. The wine, the reference to "fannies," and the threats, however jocular, made me, for the first time, ashamed to be associated with IBM. I returned from New York the next day and told coworkers who frequently debated company policy with me that I had changed my opinion of Akers, and I apologized to one longtime IBMer for having ever disagreed with him on Akers in the first place. A serious sense of betrayal, however, was still in its infancy.

In mid-May, I was in Dallas, Texas, for a week-long technical seminar. For the first time, I considered not spending my entire career at IBM. After registering and attending classes on the first day, I found a terminal connected to IBM's network of mainframes in the terminal room established to allow a few of the thousands of attendees at the seminar to keep up with their PROFS (e-mail) messages. On a forum devoted to discussing OS/2, I read a few short excerpts from a circulating PROFS note that quoted Akers's address to a meeting of high-ranking company executives at IBM's Advanced Management School. In the note, Akers was portrayed as expressing anger, using profanity, threatening marketing employees with their jobs if they lost market share or sales, complaining about the tension level in the business being too low and the comfort level being too high, asking management to downplay community involvement and social activities, ordering those in sales to sell and those in manufacturing to build, and so on. I was incredulous. After all of the online discussions on the vast potential of computer-mediated communications and the importance to IBM of a vision of networked communications, here was IBM's Chief Executive Officer urging employees to be even more focused on their own tasks—to actually *reduce* the amount of cross-pollinating communication and cooperation occurring within IBM. Where was the vision of worldwide networked communications so strategically important to the future of IBM? "Akers is not the man to be leading IBM," I thought. I wrote a response, showing it first to a friend at the next terminal. When the friend raised his eyebrows and chuckled, making a comment and a gesture indicating guts, I thought about it one more moment, examining my feelings and willingness to leave IBM if his management perhaps read the note. I hit the PF5 key and posted the note.

```
OS2ARENA FORUM
SUBJECT:   Mr Akers' Comments at AMS Roundtable
    REF:   Append at 01:35:33 on 91/05/18 GMT . . .
:TEST OF IBM CULTURE on.
```

I realize that criticizing an IBM executive is contrary to IBM culture, and that one's career can be limited by doing so; however, if IBM is truly devoted to Excellence, free speech must become more important than protecting executive egos. So here goes:

Mr. Akers appears to be revealing a lapse in character—he is not only willing to offend many who believe that such cursing is inappropriate for any leader, much less IBM's premiere leader—but more significantly, he has resorted to laying the blame for IBM's predicament on the shoulders of others. I believe he betrays his inability to see past a rapidly failing paradigm if he believes that IBM can market today as it did in the past, namely pushing "sales" without regard to product quality, timeliness, or marketability.

What's more, in today's environment, Reps aren't even aware of the existence of many revenue opportunities, much less being aware of when they lose. That's because they don't focus on "small opportunities," and the number of "small opportunities" is increasing dramatically at the same time Mr. Akers' cherished "large opportunities," a.k.a. "sales" are vanishing from our environment at break-neck speed. That's why I'm so breathtakingly encouraged to see Lee Reiswig take action toward that all-important shift toward IBM mass marketing.

One last thing I've noticed clearly that leaves me cold is that, in the face of adversity, many of us in marketing are being asked to abandon all "strategic and long-term" projects and focus instead on increasing short-term revenue, while we simultaneously cut expenses by as much as 50%. That is the kind of thinking that must have Toshiba and our other Japanese competitors grinning from ear to ear. In the name of short-term quarterly profits, IBM has been and continues to be willing to sacrifice almost everything. Why is it that so many first-line employees laugh at the mere mention of the Basic Beliefs these days?

I dearly hope that we can prove the "New IBM" paradigm successful by showing to the world that the dynamic efforts of EVERYONE on THIS SAME TEAM named IBM can be wildly successful by adopting a new paradigm of openness, cooperation, and careful listening and aggressive action to quickly address requirements. Lee is showing the way, so it's up to us to follow his example and do everything within each of our reach to make OS/2 successful, even if that means defying the assumptions of the old failing IBM paradigm.

I would love to see Mr. Akers himself (on this forum—chuckle chuckle) correct me in my assessment of his intent, but it seems difficult to me to accept that someone who makes millions of dollars while presiding over the crash of IBM shouldn't be anxious to accept personal responsibility and resign rather than continue to point to the failings of others as the reason.

:TEST OF IBM CULTURE off.

Dave WHITTLE at WSCVM

I had used a convention from IBM's General Markup Language (GML) to hedge my statements somewhat. In GML, formatting "tags" surround text to indicate its function. I intended this post to be read as a "TEST OF IBM CULTURE," hoping that it would soften the impact somewhat. Nonetheless, I believed that my audience was perhaps several hundred people, and my primary concern was whether any of those would forward the post to his manager—who would probably call me in for a little more of the dreaded "counseling" so familiar to IBMers who stray from the culturally correct path. Within IBM, there were strong cultural norms to "keep it positive," and to avoid "offering a public appraisal." I had violated both, either of which could be career limiting.

I moved to the referenced forum to read the entire note, posted by an employee who had apparently received the note without the IBM CONFIDENTIAL label that should have made it unsuitable for posting on the internal forums. The note had been written by a branch manager attending the "Advanced Management Seminar" in New York. Akers had addressed the attendees in a frank, straightforward manager. In addition to the quotes from the previous post, I read that Akers had complained that he wasn't able to communicate with employees and that his messages were being "filtered," had used profanity (seemingly in violation of a directive from Akers himself stating that profanity and vulgarity by management would not be tolerated), had seemingly berated employees for "standing around the water coolers" waiting for instructions, and told how he had reprimanded those executives reporting to him one by one. Here was Akers, according to this note, dressing down and chewing out each one of his direct reports. In public. Worse, the person writing the note, who had been there, applauded Akers for his comments. "It's reassuring to see that the man at the top understands the issues and has a sense of urgency to deal with the present situation. He earned my respect!"

How could Akers be so blind to the obvious? How could this sycophant taking notes respect him *more* after hearing all of that? I wanted to repudiate his earlier defense of Akers on these very forums; so I typed the following append into the old IBM 3279 "dumb" terminal:

```
MARKETING FORUM

SUBJECT:   Mr Akers' Comments at AMS Roundtable
    REF:   Append at 21:47:42 on 91/05/17 GMT . . .
I wasn't there, so I may be off-base; but what Mr. Akers has done
and is saying doesn't earn my respect. Of course, he doesn't need my
respect; however, if I represent a large number of IBMers, then he
does need our respect.
    Here's why I now believe Mr. Akers just may be a large part of
the problem:
```

1) He has abandoned many of those things that make IBM unique and have done a lot to earn industry respect over the years. . . . He appears to believe that when times are tough, offensive language and other visible signs of disrespect for individuals is justified.

2) He has continued to emphasize form over substance. . . . The IBM culture change needs to start at the top down, and Mr. Akers continues to put the needs of IBM stockholders ahead of the needs of IBM customers by focusing the attention of executives and employees on short-term profits and meeting schedules. . . . Of course his messages are being filtered--he literally demands them to be when he continues to shoot messengers of bad news!

3) Perhaps circumstances have made him look bad; however, in our culture tradition demands that he be judged by results. He has no results to show--worse, he has presided over the most serious erosion of everything that matters that IBM has ever experienced. He would be respected more if he were to resign.

4) He continues to cling to old paradigms when CLEARLY IBM is faced with the need to DRAMATICALLY change its culture, organization, priorities, and managerial assumptions. Instead, Mr. Akers clings to assumptions about Marketing being able to sell anything to anyone if they simply do their job well, about Development being able to meet schedules without drastic changes in process throughout the entire company. . . .

5) He's out of touch if he thinks that "the tension level within IBM is not high enough." From where I sit, it's so high that management is paralyzed and doing their best to paralyze any employee doing useful, productive work by forcing them to do things that will "save our jobs," such as creating 90-day panic plans.

. . . Perhaps it's not too unreasonable to hope that perhaps IBM will still succeed IN SPITE of management's furious attempts to bring it down faster by abandoning everything that made it great and by clinging to everything that is causing it to die. I'm seeing reasons for hope in some of the very things that cause Mr. Akers so much anger and consternation.

Dave WHITTLE at WSCVM

Without any idea of the magnitude of the furor that would be triggered, I logged off and went to meet friends for dinner. It wasn't until the next day that I learned I had played a catalytic role in a drama that was attracting the attention of thousands of IBMers worldwide, including executives and management. A friend told me at breakfast the next day that people couldn't believe my "courage." I made a beeline for the terminal room, only to find a line there—everyone else was busy with the buzz. One of those seated motioned for me to take over his terminal. Many watched, trying not to be obvious, while I checked the forums.

I quickly learned that my append had been a shot heard round the IBM world. My two original appends had been deleted and moved—but not until they had generated dozens of appends in response. The original appends had been replaced by a pointer to a new AMSROUND FORUM, which had been created the evening before for the express purpose of focusing the discussion of the Akers note and my response in one forum— but privately I was told that this was done to prevent the discussions from contaminating every forum on IBMPC. I checked PROFS mail—my typical morning load of ten messages had ballooned to well over one hundred. My append was being forwarded around the world, just as the Akers note had been, and friends and strangers alike were sending me long chains of such forwardings. The response was overwhelmingly positive. A few nasty notes berated me for my disloyalty, but I had expected controversy and criticism. Instead, I found that I had galvanized, through one cyberspace act, a movement of employee dissatisfaction that, under traditional circumstances, could not have taken shape.

Spurred by the opportunity to make a difference, I became the most active participant in the AMSROUND FORUM, which attracted a phenomenal 55,000 lines of text in only a few weeks in posts from over 1,000 different employees. The Akers note and my posts had opened the floodgates of self-examination for IBM, and after receiving a call from the chairman of the "Corporate Conferencing Review Board," I helped turn the forum from criticism of Akers and middle management into a clearinghouse of ideas, commentary, and suggestions. IBM's "keep-it-positive" imperative was evident throughout the outpouring of passionate interaction and devotion to the ideals upon which IBM was founded.

The media picked up on the incident and continued to report about it with fascination for over a year. In the middle of the week, the *Wall Street Journal* quoted from one of my posts in an article titled "IBM Wants Its Managers to Encourage Certain Workers to Leave the Company."[6] In another *Wall Street Journal* article, IBM vice president Mary Lee Turner insisted that the comments on the internal forums were idle "chit chat," "totally unrepresentative of what's going on at IBM."[7] *Business Week* wrote in an editorial on its back page that Akers "would be foolish . . . not to heed the outpouring of opinion from the company's rank and file. After all, Akers would be tapping a resource that no other computer company in the world can match: the thinking of some 373,000 workers."[8] *PC Week* noted that "IBM Chairman John Akers is breathing fire, but many employees there are blowing it back in his face."[9] *The Washington Post* began a lengthy article on IBM with a profile of me and my messages, followed by the sentence "This is the year the distress inside International Business Machines Corp. burst into the open."[10] An underground employee "newsletter of information and solidarity" ran an article entitled "Akers Opens His Mouth and the Electronic Rebellion Begins." The article used seven quotes that had also been featured in the news media—five of which were mine.[11] Many assumed that I was the source of the leaks, even though I had not violated IBM's confidentiality rules, which restricted the comments made on the forums to IBM's internal use (the rules have since been relaxed). *PC Week*, for example, got it wrong three times in one sentence when it reported in a 1992 article that I had "sparked controversy within IBM by releasing IBM Chairman John Akers' (sic) memo blasting lazy IBM employees on IBM's PROFS network."[12] I didn't release anything; it wasn't John Akers's memo; and it was an e-mail note and not a "memo."

Speculation was rampant that Akers would acknowledge the importance of this newly discovered, wide-open form of communication, where filtering is difficult if not impossible, by responding on the forum itself. It would have been a stunning, unifying move that would have riveted the attention of every IBMer—but Akers chose instead to reply with a letter in IBM's *THINK Magazine*, where he said, "In recent days, we have had a great deal of experience with communications, unfiltered and otherwise, especially concerning what I said to a small group at the Advanced Management School in Armonk." Akers quoted a statement made by Tom Watson, Sr., in 1945:

> It becomes increasingly apparent in my small sphere of observation, and I conclude the company as a whole, that the average IBMer has lost sight of the reasons for his company's existence. IBM exists to provide a return on invested capital to the stockholder. . . . Respect for the individual and employee satisfaction mean providing an atmosphere for personal growth and individual expression while carrying on a business, not assuring that IBMers are more prosperous than their neighbors or have more benefits than other companies can provide. It is the success of IBM as a business that enables the company to provide good salaries and ben-

efits. When everyone realizes that IBM is a business, run by businessmen and affected by the business environment and not a fraternity or club they've joined with lifetime benefits, then we can parade into the future to reap earned rewards.[13]

Akers urged IBMers to improve everything they do, saying, "A healthy level of concern and urgency, which I call tension, is essential for everyone in IBM."[14] Whatever the intent of Akers's communications, it was apparent that he had missed a notable opportunity to demonstrate leadership. Speculative discussions on the bulletin boards concluded that if Akers had actually availed himself of the opportunity to use the wholly unfiltered communications of cyberspace to engage in serious dialogue regarding the future of IBM, IBM employees would have been inspired to entirely new levels of respect for the individual, customer service, and excellence—and subsequent success and profitability.

Apparently, not all senior IBM executives agreed with Akers's approach to the incident, either. George Conrades, the much-respected heir apparent to Akers and a subject of particularly harsh criticism in the Akers note, published his e-mail address and promised to personally read and respond to every note anyone wished to send to him about what IBMers could do to improve IBM. Employees responded with enthusiasm. My note to Conrades suggesting more funding and development for computer-mediated conferencing and more widespread use within the company was met with a phone call from someone in Conrades's office, who included my recommendations in the strategic planning recommendations championed by Conrades. In spite of, or perhaps because of, Conrades's enormous popularity with the troops, Akers forced Conrades out of IBM. A reliable source suggested that Conrades had "brought the people too close to Armonk" (the location of IBM's headquarters and Akers's office).

In early 1992, Lee Reiswig recommended me to the Personal Systems Market Development corporate headquarters group for a position representing IBM on the internal and external bulletin boards. I took the position and the title "OS/2 Evangelist," believing that it would make a statement about the new attitude I believed was transforming IBM. As described in Chapter 5, I took advantage of my notoriety to start an online virtual team named Team OS/2. That fall, I was approached by an influential media friend I had met online who asked me to write a book with him. I agreed—and the book was completed even though the authors were separated by oceans and continents. I used cyberspace to solicit the help and support of dozens of IBMers—all necessary coordination and exchange of information was done via e-mail and over the phone.

In early 1993, John Akers was forced out of IBM and a very public search for a successor culminated in the spring 1993 selection of Lou Gerstner as Chairman and CEO of IBM, marking the end of an era at IBM and the last gasps of Watson's IBM. Thomas J. Watson, Jr., died that same year.

A few months later, Wayne Rash, a respected industry analyst, noted in an *OS/2 Professional* magazine profile, that

> Dave Whittle doesn't look like the kind of guy who would topple an empire. In fact, he looks a lot like what he is: A devoted husband and father, a leader in his church, a man of deep ethical principles and a man who cares about life. You can see the love that permeates his life as he and his children rise and fall above their backyard trampoline—a place that forms the center of closeness for this most caring of families.
>
> Yet, it is this same caring that led to a memo which some say led to the corporate landslide that ended the reign of John Akers as IBM's CEO.[15]

I transferred to Austin in 1993 as IBM's first (and perhaps only) Online Advocate. It was a difficult assignment on the "bleeding edge" of representing a company like IBM in cyberspace, facing a competitor like Microsoft—which seemed to take a greater interest in my online activity than IBM did. After over two years of struggle, caught between IBM and Microsoft's war over operating systems, and between IBM and increasingly unhappy customers, I left IBM in early 1996, telling friends that the IBM of today little resembles the IBM I joined in 1984. For better and worse, however, I attribute my IBM experience to the extraordinary leveraging power of cyberspace, which provided the corporatewide, worldwide dialogue and debate, without which I would probably still be a foot soldier in the IBM army, with online friends and less of an understanding of the real potential of cyberspace.

FREEDOM

Cyberspace brings new freedom to those who use it wisely. It brought me new opportunities, relationships, and financial reward. Cyberspace empowers individuals. It gave me the unexpected ability to touch and even influence the thinking of tens of thousands. Cyberspace breaks down barriers. It brought me face to face with corporate executives and media stars I never expected to meet, much less influence. Cyberspace extends the reach of an individual unlike any communications medium heretofore known. How else could my comments have gained such widespread attention so quickly and easily?

Within a decade, individuals will enjoy unprecedented freedom. As an online advocate for IBM, I could work from wherever I happened to be so long as I had a laptop and access—and could get just as much done in a mountain forest as I could in my office. Truth be told—I was more productive when I felt free. I'm convinced that the status-conscious, hierarchical assumptions of the last generation of companies will fall—to be replaced by a generation that knows its way around cyberspace and use it to great personal advantage. This generation will exchange information, humor, news, and ideas—in data of whatever form is convenient: voice, text, music, graphics, or video—almost without regard to place or even time. We might even be able to free ourselves of the burden of physical phone books, directories, and calendars, including the interminably mundane task of tracking changes. I expect we will more often be known by a single identifier—our cyberspace name. Such a name might even replace phone numbers, e-mail addresses, social security numbers, bank account numbers, and more. Protected by secure encryption, informa-tion about me associated with that name will be instantly transferred to others at my command. My cyberspace name, for example, is dave.whittle@usa.net. I expect to see such addresses evolve in function and usefulness—offering us more and more freedom. Phone calls and e-mail will follow us anywhere, using wireless technologies. As advanced as our ability to communicate and cooperate is now, it will be transformed and expanded—to a degree we almost can't imagine—over the next few decades.

This communication between free-thinking individuals is at the heart not only of cyberspace but of a free society. In the words of Charles Bradlaugh:

> Without free speech no search for truth is possible; without free speech no discovery of truth is useful; without free speech progress is checked and the nations no longer march forward toward the nobler life which the future holds for men. Better a thousandfold abuse of free speech than denial of free speech. The abuse dies in a day, but the denial slays the life of the people, and entombs the hope of the race.[16]

One might imagine that Bradlaugh had cyberspace in mind when he spoke of "a thousandfold abuse of free speech" that "dies in a day." Yet one might also imagine that he was speaking of the "search for truth," the "discovery of truth" and "the nobler life which the future holds for men." This is a pursuit worthy of our devotion and cyberspace is a means worthy of our serious attention.

Liberty and License

Anyone who spends much time in cyberspace is bound to discover discussions on freedom and liberty. It seems to be at the heart of why participants love cyberspace. It's a liberating experience. At times, however, it can seem almost obsessive. One might wonder whether the world's entire population of libertarians and anarchists haven't come together in cyberspace to celebrate liberty as the ultimate value and to bemoan every possible imposition on individual freedom. Consider these excerpts from over 10,000 posts and WWW pages found by searching for the phrase "individual freedom" in CompuServe forums, Internet newsgroups, and WWW pages:

■ "Libertarian presidential candidate Harry Browne . . . has already said he will pardon anyone convicted of tax evasion, a non-violent gun-control charge, or a non-violent drug offense. The Libertarian Party platform has long called for full application of the concepts of freedom of speech and of the press to new technologies, including computer networks, and opposes censorship in any form."[17]

■ "Some day, I hope that all people who work hard to make a better life for their families will become maroons (escaped slaves), and that they will be able to control their destiny and the destinies of their children, free from the self-serving machinations of those in tyrannical governments and monopolistic unions."[18]

■ "Government's role is to keep the peace, not have grand visions or lead the nation."[19]

■ "Once a right is gone, it's gone."[20]

These cries for freedom are often argued with great passion, and often with even more eloquence than any of the above examples. Inevitably, when I first hear of some of the possible encroachments on our civil liberties in forum discussions, I'm inclined to applaud and join in. After all, as the arguments are framed, if liberty is a good thing, then more should be better. Yet the longer I watch, the more often I see the arguments framed in extremist terms that leave me uncomfortable that those making the arguments don't understand that at the foundation of freedom is responsible action that displays concern others. Examples of views I consider extreme include the following:

■ "I believe that laws against prostitution and any drug that is not smoked are unconstitutional infringements upon freedom of religion. I believe corporations should be allowed to hire their own standing armies, provided they don't stockpile nuclear weapons."[21]

■ "It is immoral to continue having cannabis as an illegal drug because the current prohibition (a) creates smuggling cartels of a shady nature; (b) frivolously eliminates the freedom of those caught using it; (c) costs the taxpayers millions of dollars to chase down and lock up people who pose no threat to anyone."[22]

For every threat to freedom posed by unwarranted government intrusion, there seems to be another threat posed by careless or misguided thinking, unwarranted rebellion, and selfish disregard for law and society. It is rumored that right-wing militia have used and are using cyberspace to plot a new American revolution, including the bombing of the federal building in Oklahoma City. There are those who would love to create a crime-free society by eliminating all law. It is argued that pedophiles, pornographers, and perverts have used cyberspace to perilous personal advantage. We should not be surprised to discover that organized crime, money launderers, and international drug cartels are exploiting the electronic frontier. That leads us to a serious question: Whose freedom matters most?

There are those, such as many libertarians, who believe that the only laws required in our society are laws protecting life, limb, and property. Although appealing at first glance, such a position seems to me to ignore the larger realities of the social contract under which we live. If every individual behaved ethically and responsibly, then we could indeed dispense with law and even the protections afforded by rule of law. However, as we see more of the abuse of rights and the abdication of the associated responsibility, aren't we that much more likely to relinquish our so-called "right" to do something we'd never do anyway, for our own protection against those who would do it to our harm? Responsibility is a prerequisite of freedom, and yet many argue that freedom is defined by the absence of responsibility. In some of the arguments I see for civil liberties, the meaning of both words is largely hidden behind anarchic assumptions regarding "civil liberties." Should we perhaps consider civility a pre-requisite of civil liberties? One has cause to wonder when defamation, obscenity, and deception are often, directly and indirectly, among the "civil liberties" being defended on the networks in the name of free speech. Have we confused liberty with license?

Few of us truly understand freedom. As Goethe said, "None are more hopelessly enslaved than those who falsely believe they are free."[23] Many prefer to think of freedom as the absence of external constraints. Others see it as license to do as one pleases without consequence. Unfortunately, neither view is realistic. Constraints exist in nature and in dealing with others in any civilization. Ignorance of or refusal to accept the law of gravity doesn't give you the freedom to fly. We cannot escape the simple fact that our acts *do* have consequences, our ignorance of those consequences notwithstanding. So what, then, is freedom?

I prefer the definition of freedom as "the absence of necessity, coercion, or constraint in choice or action."[24] The key to freedom is, ironically, discipline and responsible cooperation with others, i.e., compliance with morality and law, natural or legislated. As Pope John Paul II said, "Every generation of Americans needs to know that freedom consists not in doing what we like, but in having the right to do what we ought."[25]

For example, we understand that we cannot escape our obligations to others to be civil and responsible and treat them as we would like to be treated. If we were to suddenly decide that kindness and civility presented an unwarranted imposition on our freedom, we could rebel, urge others in cyberspace to be rude to one another, and spend a great deal of time online discussing how nice it would be if our rude and insensitive natures were allowed complete and unrestricted license. We would soon suffer the consequences, however, of lost friendships and an impaired ability to gain cooperation and sway others to our point of view. It must be said that there are certain immutable natural principles that exist independent of our recognition of their existence, our knowledge of their application, or our unwillingness to heed others who have experienced the consequences of ignoring those same principles. Liberty should not be confused with license.

Truth and Consequence

To the degree one gains knowledge and applies it wisely, one can gain freedom, including freedom to explore new possibilities and freedom from the harmful consequences of our ignorance. An understanding of the array of choices one faces increases as knowledge increases. An understanding of and sensitivity for people, history, language, reason, and culture can help us avoid the unpleasant results of acting in ways that bring us into conflict with others.

Truth, like freedom, is often misunderstood. Some may try to make it into a grand statement of omniscience, while others might ridicule the concept that truth has meaning as being worthless because the word is abused. Truth can be defined metaphysically as being synonymous with the knowledge of God, or more practically and usefully as personal knowledge that has lasting or significant value. Truth can be as epochal as a revelation or as simple a thing as the knowledge of a great restaurant. You find new "truths" every day of your life—in the form of information. It is the search for this truth that often motivates us. We seek truth through knowledge.

Knowledge is gained as we gather information and test it by our experience. Hugh Grant was quoted by *Newsweek* as saying, "I don't believe in truth. I believe in style." What he says is, ironically, "true"—in a narrow sense as an apparently honest statement of belief for Hugh Grant based on his experience, and an apparent narrowing of the meaning of truth—which would ordinarily be a superset of style. As Nicolas Boileau-Despreaux said, "Nothing but truth is lovely, nothing fair." Style won't endure—it is of the moment; but truth endures. Cyberspace offers a radical new perspective— its style will surely change over the years, but what will endure, I believe, is truth. Cyberspace has unprecedented potential as a source of information, but are we prepared experientially to determine truth from error, substance from style, and right from wrong?

Today, cyberspace offers information to a degree unimagined even a decade ago. We arguably have more information available to us now as individuals than did all but the most powerful men and women of a generation ago. The possibilities for us to increase our freedom and fulfillment through an ardent search for truth are so seemingly endless that the present concern is information overload, not lack of information. We have so much information at our disposal that it is difficult to sort through cyberspace garbage in search of truth. The sorting process, however, is a valuable learning tool.

We love to learn. We learn instinctively. Babies learn. Adults learn. It is simply part of our nature to learn. We are, however, limited in what we can learn in life. We must choose our own truth. We believe only what we choose to believe, so we must choose carefully. Nobody can or should make those choices of belief for us—for on such choices hinge our happiness. Our behaviors might be dictated by law, but our beliefs can never be determined by others unless we surrender our conscience to others through laziness, fear, superstition, or apathy.

One of the first things we should learn, is that not all truth is created equal. Some truths are more relevant than others to our lives. The knowledge of the circumference of Pluto, no matter how accurate and scientific, is usually of less value to you than the knowledge of the circumference of your waist. What's more, the truth surrounding the immeasurable—such as love and beauty—is often even more valuable than the truth surrounding things that are more concrete and measurable, such as wealth or waist size. Learning isn't easy. Life is difficult, however blessed.

Cyberspace is arguably the most significant individualized learning tool in the history of civilization. It represents an opportunity for personal learning that Aristotle, Newton, Galileo, and Einstein probably never dreamed of. In theory, the knowledge of the world can and will be made available to us wherever we happen to be. We can test our ideas against the ideas of others. We can come face to face with others who are more or less able to challenge not only our beliefs, but also our knowledge and ignorance. As we face more and more information, experience becomes more important than ever to us in our search for truth.

Anyone who has "surfed the Net" knows how quickly time passes as we explore new areas of knowledge to our heart's content and engage in exchange with others. No library or teacher ever satisfied the unfocused search for "interesting things" with a concentrated presentation of knowledge as quickly or easily as does the World Wide Web. We can learn and gain knowledge with unprecedented ease. Or we might we find the arteries of our ignorance hardening as we face the extraordinary challenge of facing the flaws in the infrastructure of our knowledge and experience. As the maxim on the wall of the Granada Hills High School boys locker room proclaimed: "Life is a grindstone—whether it polishes you or wears you out depends on the stuff you're made of." I don't know of any place on earth that consists of higher concentrations of giving, taking, teaching, learning, cooperation, competition, genius, foolishness, nastiness and love than cyberspace. It is as if the laboratory of life has been condensed and focused for our hastened learning—and the opportunities to choose the right and eschew the wrong are, thankfully, prolific.

For example, following the death of a London police officer in the line of duty, Detective Constable Jim McNulty of Scotland posted a note on CompuServe. Some individuals responding to the post asked why the officer hadn't worn a bulletproof vest. When McNulty explained that British police officers aren't provided with bulletproof vests, it wasn't long before policemen from the United States and Canada were offering to send their extra vests. Eventually, over 1,500 bulletproof vests were sent to Great Britain, with some airlines even providing free transportation.

Online friends of Dale Llewellyn, a well-known and much respected *PC Magazine* editor, learned of his untimely death when the news was posted on a ZiffNet forum. Some quickly established a memorial fund for Dale's children and spread the contribution details to other forums. Others gathered the notes posted in various ZiffNet forums as eulogies and presented them to his family.

Texas columnist and writer Joe Barr, a rather vocal Microsoft critic, learned about a Microsoft initiative and set aside differences long enough to work with a Microsoft manager, Rick Segal, to obtain donated software for a local school.

Such things happen regularly online. Most cybernauts can relate story after story of learning leading to personal help received from and provided to strangers online. The truth—when we find it, at least—truly sets us free and brings us peace of mind and satisfaction.

Yet in the same mountain of material in cyberspace that contains the genius of the ages and the goodwill of our age can be found unspeakable trash, mind-numbing trivia, and a lifetime's worth of time-wasting pursuits. On the same nets where volunteers give of their time and talents freely can be found greed, deception, and corruption. Because all events and facts differ in relative value to each of us, we assign different degrees of importance to the various facts and information we encounter. The outcomes of our choices are significant and laden with consequences: our choices can lead us to either happiness and freedom or misery and restriction—and even though many of those consequences are predictable and consistent for each of us, others are as unique as our lives and beliefs.

How often do we consciously examine our lives—asking the real value and cost of our favorite habits and vices? Or do we instead try to muddle along, uncertain about the dictates of our conscience, seeking freedom by attempting to avoid consequences? I've found that the situations and individuals I've faced in cyberspace have forced me to make tough choices I didn't want to make, but in the end, I was glad I made them. Sure, cyberspace is no different from life itself in this regard, but for me, the lessons of cyberspace came in ways life never would have presented. I learned costly but valuable lessons, and it somehow feels right to be not only older, but also a little wiser—at least if we define wisdom as knowing not only the truth of a matter, but also the consequences.

DISCIPLINE

One of the criticisms that has been leveled against cyberspace (at least by some managers I've known) is that individuals in cyberspace are less likely to be thoughtful and disciplined than their typical real-world counterparts. No one can prove such things, of course, but many who have been online for years speak of such impressions—admitting that there indeed has been a higher-than-average ratio of individuals online who might be categorized as social misfits. It only makes sense—cyberspace has been the ultimate egalitarian soapbox as well as the ultimate intellectual playground. Further, the nature of the medium might be expected to attract, or at least display, those who are perhaps noisier and more aggressive and who might be more socially adept at writing than in speaking.

It is all too easy to be distracted in cyberspace. In a hypertext medium such as the World Wide Web, where scattered and distracting words and images beg to be clicked, the medium may contribute to a loss of discipline. In cyberspace, one can abandon discipline and balance and leave the simple pleasures of life behind in an orgy of discovery. Some are tempted to adopt and defend extreme positions, only "because you can." For example, in one exchange on CompuServe's CANOPUS forum, a business owner said he wanted his employees to follow his every order and when challenged about the ethics of such a position candidly replied that he probably would have made "a good Nazi." Others could begin flirting with danger because such dangers seem less real in cyberspace. For example, "harmless little affairs" in cyberspace can lead to marital strife and divorce. Lawsuits are brought against those who are either not aware that certain actions are as illegal online as they are off. Other lawsuits are threatened as a means of manipulation and intimidation. Lack of discipline might be considered a significant source of pollution of cyberspace.

When new horizons beckon, traditional restraints are often forsaken in the rush to break new ground. Just as individuals and businesses and governments are tempted to rush in to control the new territory with rules and technology and laws never considered in more familiar territory, so do criminals rush in to exploit the new territory before civilization arrives. Such lack of discipline harms us all in cyberspace just as much as it harms us in the real world. It seems to me, then, that discipline and balance are the toughest but most important lessons any cybernaut can learn.

Constraint and Restraint

Those who live by discipline and personal restraint don't need to live by external constraint—which is necessary to protect our rights against those who would exercise against us their liberty and lack of discipline. In an interdependent society, there is a tension between the rights of its respective elements. As James Madison said,

> It is of great importance in a republic not only to guard the society against the oppression of its rulers, but to guard one part of the society against the injustice of the other part. If men were angels, no government would be necessary.[26]

Thus, a keen conscience can be more valuable than a thousand laws. Somewhere between the two extremes of untrammeled government power and unlimited criminal activity exists a happy medium. However difficult it is to find that happy medium (truth), it is a search we neglect to our own loss. Restraint is imposed from within—often for our benefit; constraint is imposed from without—often to our harm.

Modern culture tends to trust more in the science and technology than social sciences or liberal arts. Thus, some believe only those facts that arise from scientific evidence and neglect the valuable truths of philosophy, religion, ethics, morality, language, and the social or family sciences because they're governed by the complex interactions of individual choice rather than by the deterministic inevitability of technology.

Restraint, however, comes from within. Its benefits to those who exercise it can't be measured in a laboratory. Rather, the benefits of restraint are unquantifiable in such things as a clear conscious, one that is free of guilt, doubt, and shame.

While the individual benefits of restraint are immeasurable, the societal benefits are quite measurable. Societies whose members practice restraint, in theory at least, should suffer fewer constraints in the form of legal and governmental interference in individual activities. Thus, sociologists might find a correlation between the number of police officers and the number of individuals failing to exercise restraint or, as social scientists might say, delayed gratification.

For example, the failure to follow one's conscience might be considered an act of self-betrayal, or a failure of restraint. I have found in my life that failures to follow my conscience consistently lead to frustration, anger, shrill attempts to justify my choice, contention with others, and unhappiness—at least until I recognize and correct the error. From personal self-betrayal often springs harm to others.

We cannot escape our responsibilities to ourselves and to one another if we wish to enjoy the fruits of society and association with others, because rights cannot long exist in a vacuum independent of our responsibilities to one another. Restraint is especially needed in cyberspace—where we are tasked with the responsibility and opportunity of forging a new culture. If we wish to avoid the imposition of external constraints on cyberspace, then we must exercise appropriate restraint in our dealings with others.

Rights and Responsibility

In forging a frontier as vast and awesome in potential as cyberspace, it is critical that we maintain a balance between our rights and our responsibilities. Those who wish others to respect their rights must be committed to the rights of others. If we wish freedom of conscience for ourselves, we must defend it for others. If we want to teach our children our own values, we must respect the rights of others to teach their children their values.

184 ■ CYBERSPACE: THE HUMAN DIMENSION

Our culture and civilization has been built upon the balance between individual rights and our societal responsibilities. We must be careful, as we examine the liberties we should preserve and extend into cyberspace, not to abandon that balance. If we demand absolute free speech without limitation, then we must be prepared for the consequences. If we demand absolute privacy, then we must forego a measure of public life. There are no easy answers in the unidimensional online platitudes so often used to argue for positions that are essentially an escape from responsibility. You can't sow wrongs and reap rights. You can't plant harmful acts and harvest worthwhile rewards.

As I see it, we are caught in a struggle for the future of cyberspace. The battle lines this time are not drawn between conservative and liberal, black and white, East and West, freedom and slavery, or even between the government and the individual. Rather, from my perspective, the battle is between two philosophical approaches to cyberspace. On the one side, the benefits of cyberspace are viewed as a natural right with only those purely technical issues necessary to access cyberspace viewed as associated responsibilities. On the other side, the benefits of cyberspace are viewed as ancillary rights derived from and granted by government, with the associated responsibilities (such as creating and enforcing the law) traditionally associated with government extended to apply to individuals in cyberspace. The cyberspace controversies surrounding franchise, civility, decency, intellectual property, security, and the appropriate role of government can be more clearly understood when seen from the perspective of this struggle. The implications of this struggle are momentous.

The prospect that either of those two sides will win is grim. If those who view rights expansively and responsibilities narrowly prevail, then cyberspace could contribute to the realization of some of our worst nightmares: brutal power struggles in cyberspace might regularly spill into real-world violence, online thugs might enforce their desires with technical prowess with viruses and the bombardment of their enemy's e-mailboxes with thousands of randomly generated e-mail messages (mail bombings), the destruction of our privacy could easily occur when the private details of our lives are published and freely available online, defamation and ad hominem personal attacks might carry more weight in debates and dialogue than reason and principle, and a new ethos of lawless confusion might prevail. If those who view responsibilities expansively and rights more narrowly prevail, then cyberspace could lose its distinctive potential: discussion of topics on the fringes of dynamic quality might be suppressed, the ideas of individuals might never develop, government might dictate operational details and content in cyberspace, our privacy is surrendered to big business and government, dialogue is lost to fear, and a new ethos of over-regulation and stagnation prevails.

Whichever way the struggle goes, I'm confident that most of us will spend more time in cyberspace in the future. Cyberspace, like most technology, is morally neutral. It enables anyone who uses it without regard to values or morality. I'm therefore confident that neither of the two extreme positions I've outlined will prevail. I believe we can indeed redefine the terms of the essential cyberspace debate. We will find solutions and balance through dialogue, debate and the natural workings of academia, society, law and economics. We will find a basis by which we can make significant and lasting judgments of truth if we are to avoid the many pitfalls in cyberspace and fulfill instead the many possibilities.

Respect for Individual Excellence

Do you know these people? Lucio Aleman, Jr. (33), Teresa Alexander (33), Ted Allen (48), Richard Allen (46), Baylee Almon (1), Diane E. Hollingsworth Althouse (44), Rebecca Anderson (37), Pamela Argo (36), Saundra Avery (34), Peter Avillanoza (age unknown), Calvin Battle (65), Peola Battle (51), Danielle Bell (1½), Oleta Biddy (54), Cassandra Booker (25), Carol Bowers (53), Peachlyn Bradley (3), Woodrow Brady (41), Cynthia Campbell Brown (26), Paul G. Broxterman (43), Bruce Gabreon (4 months), Kimberly Ruth Burgess (29), David N. Burkett (47), Donald E. Burns (62), Karen Gist Carr (32), Michael J. Carrillo (44), Rona Chafey (35), Zackary Chavez (3), Robert Chipman (51), Kimberly K. Clark (39), Margaret L. Clark (42), Anthony C. Cooper II (2), Antonio A. Cooper, Jr. (6 months), Dana L. Brown Cooper (24), Harley Cottingham, Jr. (46), Kim R. Cousins (33), Elijah Coverdale (2), Aaron Coverdale (5), Jaci Coyne (14 months), Katherine Cregan (60), Richard Cummins (56), Steven Curry (44), Brenda Daniels (42), Sgt. Benjamin L. Davis (29), Diana Lynn Day (38), Peter DeMaster (44), Castine Deveroux (48), Sheila Driver (28), Tylor Eaves (8 months), Ashley Eckles (4), Susan Ferrell (37), Carrol "Chip" Fields (49), Katherine Ann Finley (44), Judy J. Fisher (45), Linda Florence (43), Donald Fritzler (64), Mary Anne Fritzler (57), Tevin Garrett (1), Laura Jane Garrison (62), Jamie Genzer (32), Margaret Goodson (55), Kevin Lee Gottshall (6 months), Ethel Louise Griffin (55), Colleen Guiles (58), Marine Capt. Randolph Guzman (28), Cheryl Hammons (44), Ronald Harding (55), Thomas Hawthorne (52), Doris Adele Higginbottom (44), Anita C. Hightower (27), Thompson E. "Gene" Hodges (54), Peggy Louise Holland (37), Linda Coleen Housley (53), George M. Howard (46), Wanda

Howell (34), Robbin A. Huff (37), Charles Hurlburt (73), Anna Jean Hurlburt (67), Paul D. Ice (42), Christi Y. Jenkins (32), Alvin P Justes (age unknown), Valerie Koelsch (33), Carolyn A. Kreymborg (57), Teresa L. Lauderdale (41), Catherine Leinen (47), Carrie Lenz (26), Donald R. Leonard (50), Airman 1st Class Lakesha R. Levy (age unknown), Rheta Long (60), Michael Loudenslager (48), Aurelia "Donna" Luster (43), Robert Luster (45), Mickey Maroney (50), James K. Martin (34), Gilberto Martinez (35), Tresia Worton-Mathe (28), James Anthony McCarthy (53), Kenneth McCullough (36), Betsy J. McGonnell (47), Linda G. McKinney (48), Airman 1st Class Cartney J. McRaven (19), Claude Medearis (41), Claudette Meek (44), Frankie Ann Merrell (23), Derwin Miller (27), Eula Leigh Mitchell (64), John C. Moss III. (51), Patricia Nix (47), Jerry Lee Parker (45), Jill Randolph (27), Michelle Ann Reeder (33), Terry Smith Rees (41), Mary Leasure Rentie (39), Antonio Reyes (55), Kathryn Ridley (24), Trudy Rigney (31), Claudine Ritter (48), Christi Rosas (22), Sonja Sanders (27), Lanny L. Scroggins (46), Kathy L. Seidl (39), Leora L. Sells (57), Karan D. Shepherd (27), Chase Smith (3), Colton Smith (2), Army Sgt 1st Class Victoria Sohn (36), John T. Stewart (51), Dolores M. Stratton (51), Emilio Tapia (49), Victoria Texter (37), Charlotte A. Thomas (43), Michael Thompson (47), Virginia Thompson (56), Kayla M. Titsworth (3), Ricky L. Tomlin (46), LaRue Treanor (56), Luther Treanor (61), Larry L. Turner (43), Jules A. Valdez (51), John K. VanEss (67), Johnny A. Wade (42), David J. Walker (54), Robert N. Walker (52), Wanda L. Watkins (49), Michael Weaver (45), Julie Welch (23), Robert Westberry (57), Sharon L. Wood-Chesnut (47), Ronota A. Woodbridge (31), and an unidentified black female.[27]

Do you know these people? Timothy McVeigh (27) and Terry Nichols (41).

McVeigh and Nichols are charged with federal murder and conspiracy counts and could face the death penalty if convicted of the April 19, 1995, bombing that destroyed the Murrah Federal Office Building in Oklahoma, City, Oklahoma, and killed the 168 individuals whose names you just read and injured more than 500 others.

Chances are that you are much more familiar with McVeigh and Nichols than you are with any of the victims. The mass media, alleging constraints imposed by time and space and audience desires, focus less on the details from the lives of the victims of tragedy than it does on the details of the lives of suspected perpetrators. The individual identities are often buried in the mass grave of a statistic. As Joseph Stalin said, with insight that was tragically consequential, "A single death is a tragedy; a million deaths is a statistic."[28]

Recently, in a televised cyberspace experience, I joined the survivors of the tragedy in Oklahoma City. As the 168 seconds of silence passed, one long second at a time, the senselessness of the tragedy was clearly evident. This single terrorist bomber had torn the threads of those lives from the fabric of humanity, and no amount of mending can compensate. The mind staggers as we contemplate the loss of our own life—yet the senseless loss of so many lives is so far beyond our capacity to understand that it almost seems to demand that we minimize the individual identities of victims in order to cope. Now, however, cyberspace offers us something that the traditional media does not—an opportunity to focus on individual excellence (Quality) as the fundamental unifying principle of cyberspace.

In the rotunda of the Jefferson Memorial, I first read Jefferson's famous oath: "I have sworn upon the altar of God, eternal hostility against every form of tyranny over the mind of man." The statue of Jefferson looms in heroic proportions, befitting his status as one of the intellectual creators of America. Yet, in spite of the acknowledged greatness of Jefferson and the inspiring grandeur of his memorial, it is not the most visited monument in Washington, D.C. Neither is the Washington Monument nor the Lincoln Memorial. The most visited monument in the capital of the United States is about a mile away, celebrating the individual excellence of more mortal Americans. Not far from the Lincoln Memorial, slabs of black granite line a discreet, angular slash in a gentle slope. The granite of the Vietnam War Memorial begins on one side of the angle as a sliver and gradually increases in height as it descends into the slope toward the crest of the angle. It then decreases symmetrically on the other side until it is just a sliver again. On the granite are the chiseled names of those who died in the Vietnam War, beginning with the first casualties on one side and ending with the last on the other. Approaching the monument, it is difficult to anticipate the emotional experience ahead. Walking beside the granite as the number of names per slab gradually but dramatically increases, one gradually but dramatically realizes the enormity of the nation's loss—one name at a time. The flowers, stuffed animals, medals, and other memorials left at the monument daily add to the pathos as one realizes that these 50,000 names represent an incomprehensible, immeasurable tragedy and not just a statistic. The Vietnam War Memorial affirms our innate respect for the excellence of every individual.

In his landmark philosophic work, *Personal Destinies*, David L. Norton articulates a philosophy, called eudaimonism, based on the importance of a passionate and personal devotion to one's own individual excellence, or genius. On the surface, this may seem like a selfish philosophy, but surface appearances are deceiving.

> What the world acclaims is often unworthy and deserving of scorn. The common belief that one man's gain means others' loss is amply supported by appearances. Nevertheless, as a philosophical undertaking, eudaimonism cannot capitulate to appearances, but must plumb for the buried truth. And the truth that eudaimonism finds is rich with implications, promising a better way. In formal expression, this truth is the principle of the complementarity of excellences. It affirms that every genuine excellence benefits by every other genuine excellence. It means that the best within every person calls upon and requires the best within every other person.[29]

In cyberspace, personal excellence and passion can be nourished and will thrive, if we establish a culture that nourishes a complementarity of excellences. Those who care must join together to apply individual talents to creatively construct cyberspace with the technological tools of encryption, user interface, connectivity, exclusion, security, and so on to build a cyberspace infrastructure that respects individual excellence. We need protection from the dangers of anonymity and psedonymity, as well as the protection of appropriate avenues for anonymous expression. We need public spaces and private spaces—for our children and for the protection of the rights of adults. We need the benefits of self-government in cyberspace without territorial imperatives and tyrannies. We need policies that broaden choices with a minimum of coercion. We need freedom of information and truth in labeling to enable those choices. We need effective means to communicate with authority as necessary. We need structures that facilitate cooperation without eliminating competition.

Every human being is unique and extraordinary. Cyberspace offers unique opportunities because it does not yet suffer the same time and space constraints as traditional media. Individuals will be able to be their own reporters and publishers. Victims can tell their own stories. One Web page I've seen honors grief—as dozens of real people share the story of the loss of a child or other loved one, with a singular eloquence that no reporter or editorial team could hope to capture.[30] It was in cyberspace where I first learned the names of the victims of the bombings. It is in cyberspace that I can read the first-person accounts of victims that the mass media neglect. It is in cyberspace that I can observe individuals as they are and as how they present themselves, unfiltered, to the world. In cyberspace, the excellence of an individual need not be buried in a statistic. Individuals may go there, instead, to recognize and show respect for individual excellence, which is found in the juncture of freedom, truth, discipline, cooperation, passion, and achievement.

PITFALLS FOR THE WIRED INDIVIDUAL

On the flip side of individual excellence, however, is self-betrayal (the denial of conscience and excellence) and social betrayal (the denial of others' excellence). Half the key to fulfillment online is a passionate devotion to genius and excellence in self and others—but the other half of the key is finding your way around the gaping pitfalls and potholes that plague the Information Superhighway. These pitfalls are real and demand our attention and focus. Problems solved now will pay dividends in the future; problems ignored now will return to haunt us time and time again. There aren't enough pages in a book to document in detail all of the pitfalls or possible solutions, but please consider the most common pitfalls I've encountered in cyberspace, as they relate to individuals.

Self-Betrayal

I remember watching in amazement once as a person came online and quickly made enemies of almost everyone with inane comments, disruptive behavior, flames, and ridiculous assertions. When asked about his state of mind and happiness, this humorless individual responded that he was "happy as hell!" He was obviously anything but happy, and his sarcastic answer was ironically appropriate. He was betraying his best self, and thus his individual excellence. Unhappy with the results, he resorted to blaming and lashing out at others.

Many of the pitfalls in cyberspace can be described under the category of self-betrayal.[31] Ill-adjusted individuals can often find, in cyberspace, the illusion of validation and attention that might elude them in the real world. Online, the absence of visual and other aids that generally guide us in our communications can encourage damaging, insensitive behaviors. Individuals may not have to face such feedback as the raised eyebrow of a friend that might rein him or her in to focus on the presence of real individuals rather than words on a screen that are easily misjudged. Even the most outrageously antisocial seem to get enough reinforcement in cyberspace that a variety of unhealthy individual conditions rooted in the denial of one's best self can be unleashed and rewarded.

Addiction

In the opening pages of *Neuromancer*, Case, the protagonist, is struggling with withdrawal symptoms after having been cut off from cyberspace— "he'd cry for it, cry in his sleep, and wake alone in the dark, curled in his capsule in some coffin hotel, his hands clawed into the bedslab, temperfoam bunched between his fingers, trying to reach the console that wasn't there."[32] Gibson was remarkably prescient.

Perhaps the most common serious challenge faced by many who go online is that cyberspace can be as addicting as gambling or any other psychological addiction. Many of us who have furiously typed through the night in dynamic interchange with others have wondered whether such behavior is evidence of addiction. Others may freely admit to an addiction, but in reality, aren't addicted. Too much time spent online has led to lost jobs, neglected families, divorce, and others negative consequences—often for little gain other than intellectual stimulation and interaction. A sense of balance can be easily lost when one has an audience of hundreds.

In my experience, online addiction manifests itself when an individual's online interactions interfere with more important external activities. The addicted individual may be unable to go to bed or to sleep until the Net has been surfed to the point of exhaustion, may be unable to stop to eat until every conference has been read and digested, and may not be able to go to work in the morning until every last e-mail has been answered.

Individuals are most likely to manifest the symptoms of addiction when discussions are centered around the addicted individual—almost inevitably, "ego-surfing," chat-room exchanges focused on self, and other such self-centered activities are potent predecessors of much online addiction. Just like a rat pushing a lever to get a reward, there is a temptation to discuss individuals and personalities, critically and uncritically, simply to watch participants comment. I speak from personal experience. Although I don't have an addictive personality, I have at times exhibited obsessive behaviors—and have learned much about myself and others in the process. I've observed that many of those whose financial stability is seen to be connected somehow to cyberspace are probably more prone to this excessive regard for image. I've seen that the need to be understood is often a far more powerful motivation than the need to understand. I've noticed that it is very easy in cyberspace to lose track of time and important real-life activities.

It can take enormous willpower to differentiate between the truly important and the merely controversial and then exercise the discipline to spend no more time on either than is available without sacrificing those other things in life that matter most. If you find yourself exhibiting the signs of addiction online, you may wish to consider a 12-step program or, ironically, an online support group such as `alt.recovery`. The key to solving online addiction is in recognizing the addictive temptations and those aspects and behaviors in cyberspace that are harmful. Once that giant leap is accomplished, then make a plan to eliminate the need to fulfill those aspects of your life online. Determine to find fulfillment in ways that are more productive and satisfying and consistent with your best self, and then just do it. In other words, the cure for online addiction is to "get a life."

Anxiety

In its existing state, cyberspace can arouse feelings of fear, concern, and uneasiness—even in those who are experienced with the medium. I consider myself an emotionally healthy, stable, self-confident individual; and yet I have faced several periods of rather extreme anxiety online (including the Akers incident) when the online threats promised to translate into real-world consequences. I believe this anxiety over the unknown potential of cyberspace is not only justified, but is one of the primary forces preventing more individuals from venturing into cyberspace. Although anxiety is a reasonable response to many of the threats one faces in the electronic frontier; it can also be a real pitfall if we allow our anxiety to dominate and deprive us of the many very real possibilities presented by cyberspace.

I've concluded that the risk/return ratio applies to online activities as much as it does the stock market or in starting a new business. The greater the potential for gain, the more significant the risks required—and the more likely one is to encounter anxiety. If the promise of cyberspace includes reaching many more individuals who can offer help, support, friendship, and information, it is unreasonable not to expect it to also leave one more vulnerable to the reach of those who would use the medium to exploit, threaten, deceive, and intimidate. The more one tries to accomplish online, the greater the likely anxiety a reasonable person will face.

Some occasional anxiety is justified—but it should be mediated by a careful analysis of what you are trying to accomplish. If your goal is to change the world or alter the balance of power between industrial giants, then you probably have much more to be concerned with than someone who wishes only to find a recipe for roast duck. One of my goals in this book has been to help those who may be facing the cyberspace experience with some degree of anxiety. Preparation, knowledge, and experience (personal or vicarious) are the best means of minimizing anxiety and risks and maximizing results and return.

Identity Crisis

The split personality affects of cyberspace have been much observed, but little understood. The long-term effects of pretending to be someone you're not online have not been well studied, but Sherry Turkle's *Life on the Screen: Identity in the Age of the Internet* is a giant step in that direction. Turkle examines the meaning of "identity in the Age of the Internet," suggesting that the ability to create and model new selves "on the screen" may "help us achieve a vision of a multiple but integrated identity whose flexibility, resilience, and capacity for joy comes from having access to our many selves." She points out, however, that "if we have lost reality in the process, we shall have struck a poor bargain."[33] The loss of reality she describes is when the cyberspace experiences and selves of individuals become more compelling and attractive than real life, when people fall in love with and are seduced by their dreams, become addicted to etheroality, and forsake the more immediate concerns of real life relationships and living. Turkle notes that before the 1970s, multiple personality disorder was rare, but that now, "cases of multiple personality are much more frequent."[34] In cyberspace, the threat of an identity crisis is more real than ever.

In one case, a male police officer pretended online to be a woman. Eventually, he became confused about his real-life sexual identity and suffered a nervous breakdown. He left the police force, divorced his wife, and filed for bankruptcy.[35]

At times, it almost seems as if the only thing considered abnormal in cyberspace is to assert that anything about anyone should ever be considered abnormal. For example, Graham Lea, a respected British analyst and columnist, suggested that the person behind the Bartko name (see Chapter 3, under the heading "Irresponsibility") might have chosen that name in a conscious attempt to link the genius and idiosyncracies of Bill Gates and the autism and Asperger's syndrome of Hungarian composer Bela Bartok.[36] Lea was heavily criticized by those who asserted that the mental health or identity crisis of the person pretending to be Bartok or Gates was nobody's business but theirs. This led to discussion of whether the mental health of such a powerful man as Bill Gates wasn't actually a matter of great public interest after all, considering the much-documented win-at-any-cost tendencies of Microsoft.

So does cyberspace in some way contribute to mental disturbances, or is cyberspace merely a mirror of such disturbances? After many years, including personal observation, I believe that living in cyberspace can concentrate some of life's experiences to such an extent that some otherwise rational individuals can indeed be driven over the edge—without being aware that they have crossed the line. Certain aspects of cyberspace make it easy to lose touch with reality. You often have far fewer visual or auditory clues. What you experience there is usually a filtered and posed representation of reality. There is little or no accountability for words except that imposed by the virtual community. Even though that virtual community can be quite accurate over the long run, clarifying every detail of an issue with relentless precision, it can often be surprisingly difficult to know who is trustworthy and wise and who not in the short term or after only a few postings.

It is easy to perceive cyberspace as a "sandbox," or a "playground," or as somehow independent from the real world. That is why I call for a distinction between public and private places in cyberspace. There needs to be a place for role playing and the use of pseudonyms and anonymity, but those places need to be clearly defined. Cyberspace can be a pleasant and enlightening experience if everyone plays by the same rules. When people behave by an entirely different set of rules and norms, one can easily lose track of the purpose of the discussions and his or her own pursuit of individual excellence and enter a private world governed by fear, paranoia, superstition, lack of trust, and even dementia. Avoid this pitfall in cyberspace just as you would in the real world: focus on positive personal goals, achieving your objectives, and helping others.

Seclusion

Ironically, just as cyberspace can bring a world of strangers to one's computer screen, so can it lead one to withdraw from physical society. Some, I'd guess, even spend significant amounts of time online without ever making their presence known, truly lost and alone in cyberspace. The real danger here is that one inadvertently and unconsciously substitutes quantity for quality in his or her online interactions. Many of those participating online seem to spend so much time reading or writing or both that one wonders how they can do anything else. When I represented IBM online in a full-time position, I was a prolific reader and poster—often responding to dozens of posts a day and reading thousands. Yet I found others who contributed as much or more to online forums than I did, who supposedly had full-time jobs in addition to their contributions. It leads me to wonder if a large share of many lives isn't being lived online.

During a time when one of the forums I frequented was discussing the online pathology of using pseudonyms and faking identity, one member came under scrutiny because he had consistently refused to tell us anything about himself. Although he frequently criticized others using whatever they might share about themselves, he steadfastly refused to respond to personal questions. Someone learned that this self-described "resident curmudgeon" lived alone in a Chicago high-rise apartment, which led to a series of phone calls to the individual whom he described as harassing—apparently in an effort to discover whether he was a real person. Perhaps this man was a modern hermit—deliberately secluding himself from the outside world, content to fulfill what few social needs he might have in cyberspace.

It's easy to do. In cyberspace, if someone challenges our weaknesses, we can react in arrogant disdain, flame, or pull the plug on future interactions with that person. In real life, we must often deal with our problems: escape is not so simple an option.

Cynicism

David Shaw reports, in an article in the Los Angeles Times, that a growing cynicism in the news media is being cited by the unprecedented number of senators and representatives who are electing not to run for office again. He quotes Senator Paul Simon as saying, "The great weakness of journalism is cynicism."[37]

Based on my experiences in cyberspace, journalists aren't the only ones facing the great weakness of cynicism. Many online participants, for example, seem philosophically more like tired and bitter old men than youths full of enthusiasm. At least a portion of the online culture seems to be built around the twisted cliché of "do unto others before they do unto you." Some hackers and cybernauts download credit card numbers, purloin phone card numbers, manipulate markets, run all kinds of scams, and attempt to steal government and industrial secrets—justifying their behavior with suggestions that everyone does it and that they are only testing and pushing the limits of the security measures in place. To believe and act as if everyone is selfish seems to lead to more selfishness—although there is clearly a chicken-and-egg issue here. Perhaps those who are cynical merely reflect an arrogant self-righteousness, or their own selfishness. In either case, cynicism is not a healthy attitude likely to increase personal happiness.

After being exposed to the wide range of human behavior, one may have a natural tendency to remember the negative more than the many daily miracles of kindness, helpfulness, and altruism one is likely to encounter in cyberspace. This suspicion that everyone is purely selfish in turn can easily lead to an unjustified and harmful cynicism that can, all by itself, sap the joy from life. The challenge is real: make every effort to keep a balanced perspective, fully expecting that anything that can happen in cyberspace will happen, trusting that the miracles of interdependent, free cooperation by strangers far outweigh the everyday nastiness of those few bitter individuals who make up in quantity what their contributions might lack in quality.

Despair

In a well-known incident on The WELL, a regular participant of that virtual community named Blair Newman first committed an act of cyberspace despair by deleting all of the postings he had made over the years and then, within a short time of this online act of despair, Newman committed real-world suicide.[38]

Did something about the online experience drive Newman to his drastic decision? Is there something dangerous there we must guard against? Of course—it is too human a place for us to expect a Utopia there.

Online or off, when despair finds you, attack it head on. Go online and find something nice to do for someone or to say about someone. Identify your interests and pursue them. Take a walk. Start a hobby—anything to get your mind off your sorrows and focused instead on a productive use of your time.

Mutual Betrayal

In online forums and newsgroups, one phenomenon that has fascinated me is the "school of fish" shifts in dialogue. Factions almost always develop in discussing any given idea, but many participants seem to be merely following the lead of others in any argument. Individuals may loudly proclaim their independence while uniformly parroting one cliché after another. The facts and examples may change, but the clichés do not. Individuals can sometimes seem to lose their unique identity as they begin to echo a party line, seemingly indistinguishably from other participants vested in the same position and also vying for attention. A sociologist could have a field day studying groupthink online.

One wonders: Are those who fancy themselves rebels, loners, and revolutionaries actually insecure in the position they take? Do most people simply seek intellectual safety in numbers, oft-repeated clichés and bland sophistries? Or is it simply that some people prefer to be wrong in a crowd rather than to be right but alone? Whatever the reason, it seems as if this "school-of-fish" groupthink is part of a larger and older phenomenon: misery loves company. In other words, self-betrayal often leads to mutual betrayal—or a collusion of self-betrayers. Each of us tend to normalize or generalize our own behaviors, even when they are harmful, resulting in damaged relationships and tears in the social fabric.

Propaganda

Make no mistake about it—cyberspace is and will be used for all manner of propaganda. We are already awash in this explosion of this type of information. According to *The Age of Propaganda,* each year, the average American watches 1,550 hours of TV, listens to 1,160 hours of radio, spends 180 hours reading newspapers and another 110 hours reading magazines. More than 30,000 new books are published annually, and you are likely to see or hear about 100 television commercials per day and another 100 to 300 print ads daily. In the 1980s, you probably received, in an average year, several hundred pieces of direct (junk) mail advertising and over fifty phone calls from telemarketers. Over five million sales agents were paid approximately $150 billion per year to sell to you.[39]

Persuasion and propaganda are everywhere and such a pervasive share of American life that I suspect cyberspace will be more of a refuge, since no one in cyberspace can really be considered a captive audience. Remember that junk mail is expensive and usually results in much less than a five percent return rate for mailers—many will probably move in droves to targeted e-mail or any other cyberspace medium that proves to be either less expensive or more effective. It's possible that as targeting mechanisms become more sophisticated and enable consumers to exercise more choice and control over the filters, we will face less unwanted junk mail. We should have greater control over the kinds of advertising and propaganda that capture our awareness and consciousness, at least when technologists cooperate.

Contention

Nothing seems to attract attention and a crowd like a nasty fight—online or off. The relative anonymity of online participants seems to promote incivility, since the consequence of online contention can seem to be roughly on a par with that of teasing the class nerd: you *might* get caught, but the supposed "fun" can seem to make it all worthwhile.

Flame wars are all too common but actually seem to be diminishing in intensity as more participants begin to flood cyberspace and tame the frontier. Hopefully, as we learn to separate our ego from our ideas, we can also learn to treat one another with respect and dignity—even when undeserved and unrequited. It takes two or more to have a contentious flame war, and refusing to respond to an invitation to tangle and failing to bite the bait is generally one of the most significant evidences of online maturity to be found.

Abuse

In cyberspace, verbal abuse, psychological abuse, manipulation, and other varieties of abuse are still rather common. A common motivation for such behaviors is to attempt to build one's social standing or economic interests by tearing down another group or a even a weaker member of the same group. I've sometimes succumbed to the momentary temptation online to twist the knife myself in a vainglorious attempt to demonstrate the moral bankruptcy of an opposing position. While satire and humor can be used to argue ideas quite effectively, when used against individuals, even seemingly positive devices can be devastating and destructive. Cyberspace abuse can be recognized when the selfish purposes of an individual or group trigger attempts to manipulate, exploit, trivialize, condemn, belittle, or vilify others, causing them harm, fear, distress, or offense.

A Korean girl "committed suicide as a result of hatred and abuse directed at her in IRC (Internet Relay Chat),"[40] according to Colin Gabriel Hatcher, CyberAngels Director. Following a group discussion on the religious conversion of a forum member, the sysop sent the member an e-mail message, asking that friend to consider the possibility that his recent conversion and religious experiences shared on the sysop's forum weren't just some "spiritually onanistic phantasies," heaping criticism and abuse on another forum member who had been instrumental in the conversion. That abuse not only ended the members participation on the forum but led to a groupthink discussion on the forum that resulted in the destruction of much of the goodwill that had been built surrounding the discussion of the conversion.

On one forum, I espoused an unpopular opinion and soon found myself subject to personal attacks, ad hominem discussion of my motives, and a variety of abuse coming from so many directions that another forum participant eventually wrote, "I personally find (and don't understand why more of the others do not) his voice to be sincere and principled and will not see him shouted down by others . . . who from where I sit, are behaving like a pack of dogs yapping after a wounded stag. . . . I was taught by one of the Great Moral Teachers (my mother!) to extend a helping hand and sympathy to worthy people who are oppressed by the capricious tempers of the herd, and by my lights that is exactly what is going on."[41] I have also seen this same abusive lynch mob mentality on numerous other occasions.

Abuse of power can be a problem as well. One middle manager of a dominant software company handled several particularly effective critics on the Internet by contacting their employer, the U.S. Government, and complaining that taxpayer funds were being used to interfere with his business.

A liberal application of the Golden Rule is probably the best way to avoid the pitfall of the myriad forms of abuse that are not only possible, but probable, over time, in cyberspace. I've seen that it just doesn't pay to try to fight flame with flame, or abuse with abuse—so the only answer I've found for handling abuse is to "hold a mirror to the ugliness." In other words, free speech coupled with a respect for principled decency makes for better virtual communities.

One of the best overall approaches I've seen to the problems associated with online abuse and social betrayal is that advocated by CyberAngels, an all-volunteer Internet safety organization started in June of 1995. Over a thousand members unite in an organization dedicated to "fighting crime on the Internet, protecting children from online criminal abuse, supporting and advising online victims, and promoting preserving, and protecting netiquette, helping preserve Internet freedom of speech, and teaching cyber-streetsmarts to new users." They rely on individual effort and individual responsibility, rather than a posse or vigilante approach. They teach volunteers the appropriate principles and let them act independently to support law-enforcement efforts without usurping them. They urge members to "strive to be role models for self-regulation and responsibility."[42]

The Seven Deadly Sins

Talking about sin may be out of style, but discussing the Seven Deadly Sins (pride, avarice, sloth, gluttony, wrath, envy, and lust) seems to be enjoying a renewal of interest. The movie *Seven* dealt with a serial killer obsessed with these particular sins, and a search for Web pages containing the words "seven deadly sins" produced hundreds of pages. Although "deadly" may be an overstatement, these "sins" are among the choices we must proactively guard against if we are to maximize our experience in cyberspace. They are often at the root of the self-betrayal and mutual betrayal that leads us away from individual excellence. In any case, it is worth taking a brief look at the associated pitfalls.

Pride

Many of us have an ambiguous view of pride, believing it to be both a positive and negative factor in our lives. We speak of pride of ownership, pride in our heritage, pride in our work, and so on; yet we condemn haughty, arrogant pride and praise humility. The sin of pride is often described as an exaggerated sense of self-importance, or excessive regard for self. Yet any form of pride can be a real threat to our own happiness if we let it interfere with relationships because at its heart, as noted by Ezra Taft Benson, Secretary of Agriculture under President Eisenhower, pride is a form of enmity—that which separates people from love and keeps us from positive relationships.[43]

The nature of online dialogue seems to encourage or at least highlight pride, as evidenced by many seemingly endless rounds of self-justification. One rather sad tendency is for wounded individuals to vent their grudge online, as if such a futile attempt might heal the wound. One is likely to encounter newsgroups with names like "`alt.john.doe.is.a.big.fat.jerk`," or see threads with subjects lines that seem to go on forever such as "`John Doe is a !%^#$+! idiot!`" One disgruntled divorcee created a web page of the story of her divorce, complete with a picture of her naked husband. Revenge is not so sweet, when you get right down to it.

I confess my own ambivalence here—nursing an online grudge is something I might be accused of having done a few times myself. In hindsight, I must confess that I was sometimes driven by pride rather than a genuine concern for others. One of the most difficult lessons I learned is that whether we are interacting with others in cyberspace or in real life, achieving unity with others goes farther to contributing to our personal happiness than does being right or gaining the upper hand. If you are humbly generous and confident, you will be far more effective in gaining friends and respect and persuading others than if you are an arrogant know-it-all willing to be at odds with others at the drop of a hat.

Avarice

Is greed good? Does it make our capitalistic economy work? Many seem to believe that the less regulation in cyberspace the better, because allowing each individual to pursue their ambitions without interference or guidance ultimately results in the greatest good. So the question is pertinent: is greed, or avarice, the "invisible hand" spoken of by Adam Smith in *The Wealth of Nations* that drives the economic engines that bring prosperity to all?

Not according to Adam Smith. *The Wealth of Nations* was published in 1776, but Smith's first work, *The Theory of Moral Sentiments*, was published seventeen years earlier, and has been widely recognized as a classic that lays the moral groundwork for the free enterprise system described in *The Wealth of Nations*. Smith taught that self-love, not greed or avarice, was the guiding light of successful economic activity. This love of self must not even be confused with selfishness—because one who truly loves one's self must necessarily have empathy for others, desiring their goodwill, knowing that positive relationships are a critical ingredient in a happy, successful life. The root of free trade is an understanding of the needs and desires of others and a willingness to apply one's own specialized knowledge and skill to fulfilling those needs and desires in exchange for the currency by which we can motivate others to apply their specialized knowledge and skill to the fulfilling of our own needs. Greed disturbs the balance of such a system, whether it be cyberspace or our national economy, to the degree that enabling capital and information is hoarded selfishly and removed from the system or used to subvert or pervert free exchange in the raw exercise of power. Although self-love naturally promotes ones own welfare by promoting the welfare of others as well, greed brings unhappiness and suffering through a disregard for anyone but oneself. As Smith said, "The great source of both the misery and disorders of human life seems to arise from overrating the difference between one permanent situation and another. Avarice overrates the difference between poverty and riches: ambition, that between a private and public station: vainglory, that between obscurity and extensive reputation. The person under the influence of any of those extravagant passions is not only miserable in his actual situation, but is often disposed to disturb the peace of society in order to arrive at that which he so foolishly admires."[44]

Too often, I see an immature selfishness and greed at the heart of many of the arguments made in cyberspace and even in *Wired* and *Boardwatch* and the other influential publications to which many look for guidance as cyberspace develops. However appealing a philosophy may be which exalts self-interest alone as the most noble pursuit possible—we would be wise to reject such thinking for the simple reason that our well-being is ultimately integrally linked to the well-being of others, and working together we are capable of far more achievement and prosperity than we could ever achieve working alone. Hoarding those resources, whether intellectual property or information or monetary capital, that others might gainfully employ represents a very real threat to the maximization of the potential of cyberspace.

Sloth

Sloth, indolence, laziness, and sluggishness is often manifested in the intellectual realms of cyberspace as a follow-the-pack lack of intellectual discipline. I've observed that some individuals carefully craft their messages, including what they say and how they say it, and inevitably I find that I respect and follow the contributions of such individuals carefully. Those who take the easy road and say whatever comes to mind about any subject, without much effort to research or support what they say, seem to cheapen the online discourse.

The quality and value of online discussion is increased significantly when those of who might tend to be slothful can avoid the temptation to speak up even with nothing to say, and learn from those wiser and follow their lead.

Gluttony

It's tough to see how gluttony represents much of a menace in cyberspace—although it's always interested me that there seem to be more overeaters per capita among the cyberspace crowd than one might typically encounter. Perhaps that's because most of the many opportunities I've had to meet these cyberspace "names" have centered around arranged dinners; but somehow I doubt it. My operative hypothesis is that one of the last bastions of allowable societal prejudice and discrimination is against obesity—and cyberspace offers a refuge and an opportunity for those who are overweight to be judged by the quality of their ideas and minds rather than according to their physical appearance.

Envy

Envy is an enemy to peace of mind and encourages hostility toward others as we compare our fortune with theirs. At its worst, such envy can be a complex piece of the motivations leading to hatred, racial prejudice, and bigotry. The most common temptation we may face in cyberspace, however, is envy stemming from the good fortune of others. When others share their good fortune and sources of joy with you online, learn to rejoice with them, even if you are not so fortunate. The positive feelings generated just may turn things around for you as well.

Lust

Lust, as one of the seven deadly sins at least, is an insatiable appetite or craving for impure pleasures, usually in reference to unbridled sexual appetites. Nobody should deny the importance of healthy attitudes toward sex and procreation; yet the topic attracts inordinate attention in our society. If lust is an unbridled obsession with sex, then we may have to admit that we are culturally guilty. Unwanted pregnancy and venereal disease are serious social problems. Lust leads to irresponsible sexual activity. By that standard, cybersex or Tinysex (the simulation of sexual activity with strangers online using words and pictures) is a more responsible approach than promiscuous sex. Pregnancy is impossible, and contracting a disease is likewise out of the question. So is cybersex safe and without pitfalls?

I would argue that although it is less dangerous, it is nonetheless not without serious hazards and challenges. If one is married or in a committed relationship, an online affair is arguably a form of disloyalty and can lead to marital conflict. Going online for sexual experimentation can lead to inappropriate patterns of behavior, gender confusion, addiction, and other dysfunctions. Sherry Turkle is breaking ground in serious sociological study of the complex issues involved in virtual sex. In *Life on the Screen*, she explores numerous aspects of virtual sex, including violation of trust, psychological confusion, "gender trouble," children and netsex, and deception.[45]

One could argue that the online experiences of cybersex aren't the only cause of such unhappy consequences, but I believe that the fantasies indulged in online certainly don't help and can easily contribute to the problems. Such examples are becoming increasingly common—just because the capacity to indulge in these new forms of behavior exists doesn't mean that our lives can or will be improved by indulging ourselves and exploiting that capacity.

On another level, children who venture into cyberspace risk coming face to face with pedophiles, perverts, and even ordinary people who may assume they are dealing with consenting adults. This failure to keep separate the public and private is discussed in depth in the next chapter—suffice it to say here that the National Center for Missing and Exploited Children publishes a brochure entitled "Child Safety on the Information Superhighway," which recommends parental involvement, supervision, and teaching. The brochure is available by calling the NCMEC at (800) 843-5678.

POSSIBILITIES FOR THE WIRED INDIVIDUAL

For all the hand-wringing (including mine) about the fall and decline of society and of the evils and pitfalls of cyberspace, it should be noted that good old-fashioned virtue is still by far more popular than vice, crime, and evil. Try an experiment: find a good web search engine, such as Alta Vista or Lycos, which counts the number of finds for a given word, and enter a few words representing good and a few words representing bad—you define which is which. Chances are, you will find, as I did, that hits for the "good" words far outnumber the hits for the "bad" words. In other words, it would appear that there is more discussion and presentation of good than bad—

which fits my belief that individual excellence can thrive in cyberspace even more easily than it does in the real world. I truly believe that cyberspace holds more possibilities than pitfalls.

Principled Personal Choices

I've been told that three books have topped the charts and dominated sales this past decade: *The Bible*, *The Road Less Traveled*, and *Seven Habits of Highly Effective People*. The dominant themes of each of these books are the principles of spirituality, and morality. I find it enormously encouraging that those principles still matter after suffering decades of apparent assault in our culture. The promise of cyberspace to bless our lives is rooted in our pursuit of excellence as determined by the principles we put into practice there.

As Stephen R. Covey notes in *Seven Habits of Highly Effective People*, shortly after World War I, the basic view of success in our country shifted from what he calls the "Character Ethic" to the "Personality Ethic." In his review of success literature in American history, he noted that the writings of the past 50 years have been largely "superficial," "filled with social band-aids and aspirin that addressed acute problems and sometimes even appeared to solve them temporarily, but left the underlying chronic problems untouched to fester and resurface time and again." Covey points out that this "Personality Ethic" viewed success as a "function of personality, of public image, of attitudes and behaviors, skills and techniques, that lubricate the process of human interaction." In contrast, the "Character Ethic" as more evident in the earlier literature, such as Ben Franklin's autobiography, was more focused on "things like integrity, humility, simplicity, modesty, and the Golden Rule."

Cyberspace will not be a "good" place wholly consistent with your personal values—in fact, I can guarantee you that it will not be any more than the world is so. The issue is how your values help you to achieve your life's goals in cyberspace. If you want to make money from cyberspace, does it make sense to spend your time in chat groups? If you wish to develop relationships and share your expertise, should you allow yourself to be drawn into a heated exchange with someone obnoxious? If you value your privacy, will you post your phone number and address on the Internet? Obviously not.

So why is it so easy to get off track? Because it is. We're human. A carelessly worded or reasoned post takes only a moment to make, and yet can consume hours of our time and others time. Constant discipline is required to keep discussions on track, meaningful and productive. The challenge is to make deliberate choices consistent with our deeply held convictions.

To illustrate the importance of principle in cyberspace, consider love. I was surprised to discover, in a search of DejaNews (an incredible, searchable arhive of virutally all newsgroup postings) that the word "love" is mentioned over a half million times—almost four times more often than "sex" or "evil" and even more often than "peace," "freedom," "beauty," "virtue," and "family" combined.

It has always been helpful for me to think of love as an active regard for the well-being of another; a proactive choice rather than a reactive emotion. In cyberspace, this regard for others is manifest in a myriad of ways. Individuals answer the questions of others. They share knowledge and experience. They willingly become involved in the problems of others. They offer words of support and encouragement. They affirm the value of the individuality of others.

Love is at the heart of what makes cyberspace a uniquely human experience. Love is magnified there, because the kindness we show one individual is often a kindness shown to many others. The inspiration and support provided to one inspires and supports any who read it. There are online support groups for every imaginable personal tragedy ranging from cancer, AIDS, leukemia, cystic fibrosis, alcoholism, and multiple sclerosis to victims of rape, suicide, crime, incest, or abuse. There are pages that honor grief, full of stories of those who have lost loved ones. There are participants in forums who share freely, often with little expectation of return. There are personal web pages galore that honor the uniqueness of individual excellence. Volunteerism is alive and well in these groups, as individuals with common experience and concern share of themselves and their love. Love is not just an altruistic moral principle—it makes sense from a personal perspective because it makes the time we spend in cyberspace more enjoyable and fulfilling.

How we choose and apply values and principles such as trust, respect, peace, understanding, and fairness can make a significant difference in determining the quality of our life and experience in cyberspace.

THE DIMENSIONS OF PERSONAL EXPERIENCE

I believe the quality of life for any individual is a function of the choices he or she makes in five dimensions: physical, emotional, social, intellectual, and spiritual. Each of us is born into unique circumstances and with a unique set of genetic gifts and challenges. In spite of this inherent and obvious inequity, we are each blessed with one universal endowment: freedom to believe as we choose. Our happiness and quality of life is more dependent on how we exercise that freedom than it is on our genetic or environmental circumstances. Although the dimensions of our personal experience are influenced by many things, our beliefs and responses to those things ultimately make all the difference. Thus, someone who faces a life of untold challenge, such as a Helen Keller, might actually be happier and live a richer and fuller life than someone who has it all but squanders it away in vain and selfish pursuits.

Physical

The physical impact of cyberspace—as nonphysical and abstract a place as most of us will ever encounter—can be significant. Many of the physical separations between families, friends, coworkers, and even strangers become less limiting, as communications occur more regularly and more easily than ever before. Simultaneously, we are able to impose physical separations between us and others for our safety and convenience. You can't be physically assaulted in cyberspace, as brutal as the personal attacks may seem at times. As technology progresses, more of our business and personal interaction will occur in cyberspace rather than in the external world—and we will spend more and more time in our homes as it becomes less necessary to venture outside cyberspace to accomplish the fulfillment of many of life's needs, including intellectual stimulation and social interaction, procurement of goods and services, work, and even recreation.

Yet concurrent with the need to leave home even less, I see an increased desire to leave home to interact in person with cyberspace friends—as discussed in the coming section on the social impacts of cyberspace.

Just as baby-boomers have countered the couch-potato effect with an increased emphasis on personal fitness, I presume the increased involvement in cyberspace will merely open the doors for an increased awareness of the importance of diet, exercise, nutrition, and health—all of which can be improved by the kinds of knowledge and discussion available online. Already, there are exercise groups on television, the means to plug in a treadmill or ski machine to a video simulation of walking or skiing through the woods, and virtual reality exercise machines. Perhaps before long, keeping in shape will become a thoroughly enjoyable social experience we accomplish with friends connected in real time over a network as we engage in physically strenuous races and contests without leaving home.

Safety and security of person and property is one of the foremost concerns of our age. Steady increases in the crime rate are probably at least partly responsible with the increased trend to stay at home, rent videos, watch cable TV, and play video games. There are significant increases in home-based activity such as shopping, home food delivery, pay-per-view movies, TV watching, and, of course, net surfing.

Physically going out to do what can also be done in cyberspace entails risks to person and property and inconveniences that can be simply avoided by staying at home and using cyberspace. For example, compare going to the library with researching the same subject in cyberspace. Going to the library means making yourself presentable and spending time in transit, facing the potential inconveniences of not finding what you want, standing in line, not finding a parking place, getting a traffic ticket, getting lost, running out of gas, or the minor risks of accident or crime.

Those who value safety and convenience will find that the equivalent risks to physical safety are minimized in cyberspace, and the only potential inconveniences to be faced are hardware or software problems, rude and discourteous people, and overcrowded or slow connections.

It is also likely that cyberspace will begin to play a more important role in individual and family health. Several of the online services and television networks have already sponsored the availability of licensed physicians to answer questions from those who call in or post questions. I foresee doctors who will take a few moments daily to answer questions online for their patients who have questions that aren't emergencies but don't wish to make an office visit to get them answered, as a means of cutting costs and increasing patient well-being and satisfaction with their health care provider. Already, many of those online are increasingly able and willing to self-diagnose and self-medicate such common maladies as colds, flu, insect bites, and other common health problems. Self-help books and CD ROMS, such as *The American Medical Association Family Medical Guide* (New York: Random House, 1982), and *Family Doctor* (Creative MultiMedia, 1995) are increasingly popular, and cyberspace will certainly allow us access to a body of information about health and physical well-being that has heretofore been available primarily only through library research or health-care professionals during an office visit.

Even our homes—our physical surroundings—are likely to change in order to conform to cyberspace. We will probably find that televisions and computers will eventually be replaced with high-resolution, portable flat panel displays that incorporate processing hardware and software into a single unit that needs only be plugged into a wall jack to be actively connected to cyberspace, following a brief personal login. When not in use, the panels might display artwork or kinetic patterns in stunningly realist resolutions. In *The Road Ahead*, Bill Gates describes his multimillion dollar home in Seattle as a harbinger of homes to come—complete with individual "electronic keys" that assist the house in tracking your movements, turning lights up or down as you go into or out of a room. This home also features computerized consoles that adjust to and learn your own requests, preferences in music and lighting, and phone handling. If you get a phone call, only the phone near you will ring.[46]

The division between the real physical world and the abstract world of cyberspace will continue to blur. There will be more evidence of cyberspace in the real world, and more aspects of the real world will be available through cyberspace. For example, our television guides will probably no longer be physical books with listings of time slots—but rather online catalogs with indexed and searchable listings of content available for instantaneous delivery via cyberspace.

Our physical world will be changing even more in the future than it has in the past half-century. Bear in mind that as recently as 1946, there were no color televisions, no microwave ovens, few fast food restaurants, no personal computers, no boom boxes, no cassette recorders or players, no video cassette recorders (VCRs), no computer games, no intelligent appliances, no push-button phones, no fax machines, and no compact disc players. In the next 50 years, we'll begin to buy and use all kinds of personal communications devices, cyberspace access devices, virtual reality helmets and games, 3-D flat panel displays, speech recognition and control, real-time video exchange, digital video capture and editing, music devices with programmable storage for customized downloaded music (imagine a juke-box the size of a Sony WalkMan), and much more. Cyberspace promises to rearrange our physical space and lives even more dramatically over the next 50 years—in ways we can't even begin to fathom.

Emotional

The online experience can be an emotional one. Every range of human emotion can and does find its way into messages and exchanges that can enrage, sadden, cheer, or inspire readers. Cyberspace is a great place to find affirmation, consolation, and understanding. One rape victim in Scotland was too ashamed to report or discuss her experience with anyone in person but was willing to share it anonymously with others via e-mail. Ironically, the physical distancing that is inherent in the cyberspace experience can facilitate an emotional intimacy that can be healing. The rape victim took the first steps on the road to emotional recovery in cyberspace. The attention and kindness of strangers can be a significant aid following a traumatizing experience inflicted by strangers.

I believe this unfiltered, raw emotional edge that is often found in cyberspace can be one of its most appealing attractions. Participants not only seem to wear their thoughts on their sleeves, but also their hearts. I've often seen things said online in a public display likely to be seen by hundreds, that would probably never be said in meetings with friends. These comments can range from confessions to boasts. In one series of exchanges, one online participant boasted of having pulled an elaborately deceptive ruse on a competitor while another confessed that he had ordered a load of manure to be dumped on his boss's lawn using his boss's credit card number.

One intensely emotional issue that lends itself to the reach and even the distancing of cyberspace is adoption. In spite of scattered concerns related to privacy, there are numerous adoption sites where potential parents can review biographies and pictures of children who need parents. The Texas Department of Protective and Regulatory Services, working with the Texas Adoption Resource Exchange, put together the first state-sponsored page at http://www.dhs.state.tx.us/tdprs/homepage.html following the lead of Annette Thompson, who established the "Precious in His Sight" web page (www.adopt.org) in 1994, working out of her home in Waco, Texas. There are also numerous forums to assist those who are adopted or those who have given up children for adoption to find one another. My wife was adopted at birth but was fortunate enough to find her biological mother not long after we were married. A meeting was arranged at the home of my wife's parents, and we now count this delightful woman and her family as dear friends. Cyberspace is an ideal place to facilitate such happy reunions.

Social

If anything, the social significance of online communications is staggering, as I hope you'll conclude after reading the next chapter. One's circle of acquaintances is increased to an enormous degree, while the quality of the friendships might be diminished by the relatively limited range of interaction possible over the Net when compared to physical interaction. Yet there is no doubt that cyberspace communications can strengthen family ties— especially between parents and siblings who have left the nest. Similarly, there is no doubt that the virtual communities that form in cyberspace are often motivated by a desire among participants to gather in physical space. Time and again, I and online friends and associates have gone to great lengths to get together for dinner or some other occasion to extend the cyberspace relationship to physical space. In most cases, it strengthens the ties that bind, but in some cases, it has had the opposite effect. That person who was so genuine and interesting online might be a boor and a bore in person. In any event, it can be a fascinating lesson in personal awareness.

For example, I once met someone I had respected and admired online and discovered to my great surprise that he was severely obese—perhaps 400 pounds—and found myself somewhat shocked at the discovery. Given the fact that I am no longer the stick figure I once was, my reaction gave me cause for self-examination. On the other hand, I once met someone for dinner who was often rude, direct, and grating online; only to find him charming, sensitive, and warm offline. I have since concluded that there are certain social prejudices that many of us harbor unknowingly. Attractive people thrive in business and other social settings, while the obese, ugly, physically challenged, or verbally obnoxious are often simply the victims of widespread discrimination. I believe that cyberspace attracts a disproportionate share of those who have been disenfranchised for such reasons, especially to the degree that they can communicate effectively using the written word. In other words cyberspace can be an empowering social haven.

Online dating is already turning into a social trend. Rush Limbaugh met his wife online. So did my brother-in-law. Individuals can find, with far greater ease than ever before, like minds and hearts online, because the social risks are so small. Somehow, it must seem easier to be rejected by words on a screen than by a face at a dance. The "meat market" aspects of the dating scene are absent online, where judgments are made based on ones command of the language and ideas. We could even see a cultural revolution as the majority who are plain and ordinary in appearance recapture the upper hand in an ad-rich culture that stresses perfection in appearance over perfection of character to a dismaying degree.

Over the next decade, I believe that cyberspace will force us to confront our vestigial prejudices and will thus further the social cause of every individual. Hopefully, the hard lessons of acceptance will be dictated by the social covenants that emerge in cyberspace. In cyberspace, the next Forrest Gump may not be a fictional character.

Mental

The most obvious benefit in this dimension is that our means of gaining an education stands to be fundamentally altered. When I went to college, a healthy share of one's learning was obtained in study groups or in social discourse. One's learning was, quite naturally, somewhat limited by the number of those involved in the sharing and in the quality of their knowledge and experience. Not now. Most students nowadays are assigned an Internet account and ID when they enter college. That ID becomes an extension of their ability to communicate and stay in touch with others, much as calculators and computers extend anyone's ability to process information and solve problems. For example, students could literally watch the furor surrounding cold fusion unfold in cyberspace as posts came directly from those who were closely involved. No longer was it an academic exercise in understanding the workings of scientists through boring and sterile journals: it was a real life drama involving people whose words showed up on computer screens worldwide within moments of when those words were released.

Musicians and artists are also flocking to cyberspace. The distance between artist and audience has been reduced. Never before has the reach of either been so extensive. More importantly, cyberspace is becoming more than a mere channel or medium—it is often part of the work, art itself. In numerous "art galleries" in cyberspace, the presentation becomes almost as important as the art itself, as the thin line between marketing and art is blurred indistinguishably.

Some of the best writers in Texas joined forces in serial collaboration in cyberspace to produce short stories. Some of the other "writers" in cyberspace (which encompasses just about everyone out there) joined forces to create a story with as many authors as it has paragraphs. However art in cyberspace evolves, I'm confident that individuals will find ways to portray the best that is within them, and we will all be the better for the sharing.

Spiritual

The spiritual effects of cyberspace could be significant. In my experience, there is a great deal of inspiration to be found online—even if spirituality is atypical for such a public medium. By the nature of that medium, where agreement is silent and usually invisible, intellectual conflict is more evident than spiritual unity. It can be very difficult to have a spiritually uplifting exchange with cynics ready to pounce on every word. Yet in certain contexts, such as private e-mail exchanges, support groups, and tight-knit online communities; spirituality can indeed be enhanced by the more focused communications often possible using the written word, even among strangers.

Searchers and seekers have long used cyberspace to learn more about various religions and spiritual ideals in religion forums, and will certainly continue to do so. Cybersects and online churches are already arising in cyberspace—including both serious and satirical forms. Virtually every denomination I can think of has a web page, although it can sometimes be difficult to distinguish between an officially sponsored site and one run by a believer. There are, not surprisingly, numerous pages devoted to criticism of other religions or churches. There are, or will be, a wide variety of apologetics, 12-

step programs for cyberspace and other addicts, spiritual leaders and gurus attracting online followings, proselyting and fund-raising in cyberspace, and, of course, all manner of sincere spiritual exchange between individuals.

PURPOSE

Individuals go online for a number of reasons, primarily for communications, convenience, commerce, education, and entertainment. Although the purposes often overlap, it can be helpful to look at the possibilities for each of these primary purposes.

Communications

We've already explored the foundations of cyberspace communications, but even if we devoted this entire book to the possibilities, we'd probably be scratching the surface. Consider the many possible uses of e-mail alone:

- compose a letter with a child to send to Santa Claus
- send a love note to your spouse
- submit a resume to a potential employer
- suggest an idea for a strip to a cartoonist
- apply to join an association
- complain to a company
- correspond with a pen-pal
- tell an artist you liked his or her work
- send a tip to a reporter
- brainstorm possibilities with a business partner
- compare notes on homework with a classmate
- send away for freebies
- make a date
- keep in touch with family
- offer a suggestion to a web-page designer

I'm sure you can think of a hundred more if you spent the time. Sure, all of these things are possible without e-mail—but I've found that since e-mail makes it easier, we are more likely to actually do it. It's easier and less time-consuming for both the sender and the reader. The volume we can handle seems to be greater as well. Some well-known cyberspace personalities get as many as several hundred e-mail messages a day—and handle them without assistance.

Many-to-many communications add another entire range of possibilities. Because your communication is addressed to a forum with a topic rather than to an individual, you don't know who is likely to read your message or be motivated to respond. What's more, you can see the questions and answers and messages and responses of everyone else interested in the same topic, and are quite likely to often glean important little tidbits you didn't know anything about, such as ways to solve or prevent problems before they occur. Since the conversations and queries are real-life, the knowledge you gain there is more likely to be practical. But if you need the theory explained, you might just find someone who will do that for you too.

If you're an expert on a particular subject, what better way than to get a reputation as such than to help others online? Many a consulting or job opportunity has come when someone has recognized those who knew what they were talking about online and simply made them an offer. Of course, this is a two-edged sword: you may learn that you're not as smart as you think you are when you expose your knowledge to the world. In either case, though, you win.

One great way to introduce yourself to others is to be able to give them an address for a personal Web page. I'm often surprised and delighted at what some of these contain. One web page had pictures and very frank descriptions of a brother and parents under the heading: "I Didn't Choose 'Em, but I Love 'Em!" Another contained an apparently forgotten link to a girlfriend's web page, where the girlfriend issued a pithy disclaimer about the former boyfriend. In any event, having your own Web page or reading the personal Web pages of others is a great way to communicate who you are to others—and not that difficult or expensive, if you don't get too fancy.

Convenience

Many of those chores that now require trips outside, standing in line, long phone calls (often on hold), or waiting by the television for the right segment to come on, are rapidly migrating to cyberspace. Imaging doing any of the following with a few clicks of a mouse and a keyboard from the comfort of your own home or office with speaking to anyone or requiring their time:

■ making appointments with doctors and dentists and other professionals
■ banking
■ checking the current traffic and weather
■ ordering tickets to the theater
■ finding your way around using online directions, maps, and addresses
■ investing

- ordering postage for delivery to your home or mailbox
- paying bills
- placing a classified ad
- library research
- tracking an overnight-delivery package
- shopping
- applying for a passport
- renewing vehicle registations
- choosing and scheduling reservations at a restaurant
- voter registration
- voting

Most of the above conveniences are available today, in one form or another. Some of these conveniences deserve special note. There are, for example, traffic sites available in Seattle and other cities that display a color-coded map of the various arterial roadways in the city—various shades of green, yellow, and red mean; well, you can guess. These web pages could be tied directly to sensors in the roadways themselves to provide real-time, accurate information about traffic patterns. Combined with historical and predictive data, you could even conceivably order a map of expected traffic densities fifteen minutes or one hour from the time you check.

Classified ads, when placed online, have a few benefits over newspaper classifieds: they don't cost as much and are more easily found (using search tools) by those you wish to reach. Some cities, including Austin, Texas, where I live, already have newsgroups for unclassified ads—I even received a query from as far away as Atlanta about a printer I had advertised.

Many excellent restaurants provide information online such as their menu, user comments, reviews, location maps, and so on—in short many of those things that you simply can't find now without taking your chances and going into the restaurant. What's more, various travel, hotel, and restaurant guides are available online.

Obviously, cyberspace isn't going to walk your dog, do your gardening, exercise for you, or do your laundry. But you might find discussion groups ready and willing to share tips to improve your ability to do just about anything you do. The sooner you go online, the sooner you begin to discover the conveniences.

Commerce

I've devoted an entire chapter to this aspect of cyberspace, but let me just briefly highlight a few of the most relevant possibilities as they relate to individuals here. For starters, imagine a national clearinghouse of jobs and available employees—or assuming we can move beyond the employer/employee paradigm, of the ability to match opportunity and resource. Today, the system seems bogged down by endless copies of resumes nobody reads, boring job postings for jobs nobody seems to want, and an entire industry of matchmakers (headhunters and career consultants). A clearinghouse in cyberspace should serve everyone's purposes more readily—except for those matchmakers who love their work as it is today. Already, a number of graduate schools are providing web sites of resumes—including my alma mater, Brigham Young University. So when I'm looking to hire someone like myself except 20 years younger, I'll just visit http://www.byu.edu/acd1/msm/carser/resumes and have my pick of the litter—although I suspect it won't be long before we see links to the personal home pages of the more desirable candidates, complete with descriptions of the bidding wars for his or her services.

In a survey by Robert Half International conducted in early 1996, over 76 percent of the corporate executives surveyed indicated that they believed that a strong understanding of the Internet will be important in their career advancement in the future. Another 14 percent were neutral on the issue, with only 10 percent expressing no concern with a lack of such skills. That's an extraordinary result indicating the growing economic importance of experience in cyberspace to individuals and employees.

The most obvious potential for cyberspace commerce is home shopping. More of us than ever are willing to buy sight unseen via mail order—especially if we can get top quality and money-back guarantees for less money. Cybershopping promises to offer all of the above: prices should be lower on some products (but not all) with the dramatic reduction of sales commissions, marketing costs, and other overhead. In theory, at least, you should have better information about quality as well—not only from manufacturers, but from others in cyberspace sharing their opinions of products, similar to what *Consumer Reports* delivers to subscribers.

Most important, the opportunities to make a living directly from the web will be one of the most liberating aspects of the ascendance of cyberspace. The enormous, pent-up demand for fulfilling at-home work coincides nicely with the explosion of opportunity for web page designers, writers, content creators, artists, marketing mavens, small businesses selling product, and a wide variety of entrepreneurs. Networked marketing, hobbies, and a wide variety of possibilities for new niche markets arise on the Web. Those who see this phenomenon as somehow temporary remind me of the IBMer who, in 1985, made a concerned attempt to convince me that I was killing my otherwise promising career when I insisted that it stay tied to personal computers. Sure, the web has its share of challenges and problems at the moment, but they'll be solved somehow; and things will fall together such that the big companies may not even need to lay people off in order to downsize—we may find employees leaving big companies in droves to secure the benefits of working at home in some Web-enabled enterprise or another.

Education

Ultimately, I think education is what cyberspace is all about. Learning is the cornerstone of individual excellence. Using cyberspace, we can both teach our children and learn how to better teach them. We can share experience and avoid the pitfalls experienced by others. We can build self-esteem, create memories, discover the secrets of life, find kindred spirits, develop new hobbies, increase our enjoyment in our present pursuits, break habits, build habits, and even find and develop new talents and skills that can lead to new careers.

Research has already been dramatically altered by cyberspace, as results and knowledge can be shared in days and weeks instead of months and years. Scholarly print journals are facing a rising challenge from electronic publishing that threatens to change some of the traditional processes by which information is vetted and shared.[47] Universities are already wired; now kindergarten through twelfth grades (K-12) are coming online. During California's Net-Day initiative, thousands of volunteers wired hundreds of schools. Voters in the Austin Independent School District recently approved, by a wide margin, a bond issue to install networking and Internet access in its schools. Utah is pursuing an ambitious high-tech initiative to bring commerce and education together to use distance learning and other cyberspace technologies to foster lifelong learning, prepare its citizens for a knowledge-based global marketplace, "cultivate social responsibility and commitment to ethical values, improve the quality and understanding of life, and promote cultural awareness and appreciation of diversity."[48] With the help of a grant from 3M, the Web66 project is helping to integrate the Internet into K-12 school curricula.[49] As part of the Web66 initiative, the University of Minnesota, and Hillside Elementary School in Cottage Grove, Minnesota, have collaborated to publish student work, access information, conduct research, commmunicate, and share ideas. As a result, students in every grade at Hillside have created some delightful Web pages which share their work and information about themselves.[50]

As cable, phone, and television companies work together in a mad rush to wire homes in order to maintain and increase share of the home entertainment dollar, and government and volunteers and even businesses work to ensure that schools are wired, a likely benefit will be classrooms and family rooms that are easily connected. Parental involvement in the education of children could be increased dramatically. By prior arrangement or invitation, parents could join classrooms via a two-way video link, watch special lectures, or join in participatory exercises. A teacher might maintain a Web page for each class to keep parents informed about course requirements and focus throughout the year—hopefully reducing the overall workload by reducing the number of parental inquiries demanding the teachers time and attention. Parents could be more involved without feeling that they are intruding on the teacher's valuable time.

Perhaps cyberspace will help us face our reluctance to invest as much as we should in education. William Gibson himself makes an interesting proposal: all public school teachers should receive free long distance calls and free software licenses. Gibson argues for the proposal by asking,

> What would this really cost us, as a society? Nothing. It would only mean a so-called loss of potential revenue for some of the planet's fattest and best-fed corporations. In bringing computer and network literacy to the teachers of our children, it would pay for itself in wonderful and wonderfully unimaginable ways. Where is the R&D support for teaching? Where is the tech support for our children's teachers? Why shouldn't we give out teachers a license to obtain software, all software, any software, for nothing.[51]

Applause. One wonders why we hear about laptop credits from Newt Gingrich but nobody but Gibson proposing free software for teachers. In cyberspace, perhaps we can make a difference. We can work into our business plans special promotions for teachers and students, much like NetScape has done with its free licensing policies for education and nonprofit use of its software. Although most high-tech companies, including Microsoft, IBM, Apple, HP, Corel (WordPerfect), and many others offer discounts to educators and students, much more should be done.

Education will be increasingly viewed as a lifelong pursuit complementing other goals and activities rather than as an exercise that consumes the first 20 to 25 years of our lives in preparation for the rest of our lives. Individuals will continue to learn the essentials of reading, communications, math, history, and other disciplines in K-12—but will also focus on a foundation for gathering our own information and knowledge as problem solving in cyberspace begins to occupy its share of the curriculum.

Colleges will not, of course, disappear—but over time they will be dramatically altered in nature as students and professors adopt cyberspace as their primary window into the laboratory of life. The distinctions between academic and applied research will become blurred as academic and commercial researchers begin to tap into the same sources of information and exchange in cyberspace.

Of course, not all of the world's knowledge is available online yet—but at the rate I'm seeing things added to the WWW, nothing would surprise me when it comes to timetables. Dr. Jerry Pournelle, author of *The Mote in God's Eye* and influential *BYTE* columnist, predicted in 1977 that "by the year 2000 anyone in Western Civilization will be able to get the answer to any question that has an answer." In an e-mail message dated September 25, 1996, he told me that "we're pretty well on schedule."[52]

Entertainment

Our entertainment options are exploding. Television and VCR didn't eliminate the demand for the experience of viewing a film at a movie theater. Instead, it simply drove the movie-going experience into new directions, including more choices, lower prices, and better acoustics. Similarly, I expect cyberspace will provide us with far greater choices in entertainment and could even trigger a dramatic leap in the quality of those choices. George Gilder, fellow at the John F. Kennedy School of Government at Harvard and senior fellow of the Discovery Institute in Seattle, writes that "television is the tool of tyrants. Its overthrow will be a major force for freedom and individuality, culture, and morality. That overthrow is at hand."[53] I don't believe that television will disappear quite as quickly as Gilder believes, but I do agree with him—much of the nature of television programming will be transformed for those of us who want it to be, as video on demand becomes technologically feasible and we are liberated from the tyranny of television scheduling.

Standard television fare barely scratches the surface of the potential for entertainment in cyberspace. Already, live concerts are sent in real time across continents. Cartoons have been created expressly for cyberspace, such as Kevin and Kell—about a couple who met online. The husband, a rabbit, is a sysop for the HERBIVORE FORUM and the wife is a wolf with a day job in marketing. Humor well worth downloading from CompuServe's FUNNIES FORUM.

When I finish this book and have a spare moment, I may learn to play bridge just to find those games that James Gleick and Bill Gates have admitted playing in cyberspace. Half the fun may be guessing who I'm really playing out there. Then there are the thousands of computer games I haven't yet tried, and the many more popping up on Web sites using Java— the interactive adventure games, checkers, chess, and every imaginable board game, probably licensed by Parker Brothers or Milton Bradley at a few cents a play.

Not even computer games as we know them today can touch the potential of virtual reality to attract, entice, and addict the current and next generation. Imagine putting on a helmet and a pair of gloves and finding yourself in a dogfight with the Red Baron so real that you sweat. Imagine exploring the corridors of a pyramid as you walk on a treadmill, changing direction as you turn your head. Love pinball? Pretend you're the ball as you zoom up and down the face of the playing field, trying to remember to push the right button as you get near the flippers. Spend a minute thinking about every possible simulation that can be imagined. If you can't do it, someone out there can and will.

NETTING IT OUT

We should make the principle of individual excellence and the complementarity of excellence the defining foundation of cyberspace. When freedom, conscience, and discipline meet, great things happen. Cyberspace can and should be a great thing in our individual lives.

Cyberspace should be liberating. The ability to communicate with so many others, in many-to-many computer-mediated dialogue, is a breakthrough communications technology that transforms lives. Its potential for good won't be automatic, though. Without the discipline of proactive choices consistent with our strongest personal values, our lives can easily be consumed with unrewarding distractions and time-wasting pursuits of little consequence. I've been there and have wasted many hours trying to prove things that ultimately didn't matter, with results that served nobody well.

Cyberspace should be safe. The threats inherent in cyberspace to our well-being, mental health, happiness, and values are real. So is our chance to use cyberspace to make a big difference. Just as we make our children "street smart," we have to make them and ourselves "online smart." On an individual level, we face the challenges and opportunities of any unsettled frontier. Let's tame it. Happily, the physical threats are minimal. Instead, the dangers and threats are psychological, social, intellectual, and spiritual. If we take the low and easy road and conduct ourselves differently in cyberspace than in real life, the pitfalls can be deep and distressing. If we choose our options wisely, however, the possibilities are endless.

That is the real choice we face—not whether we will enter this new dimension. We can perhaps delay the timing of our involvement with cyberspace, but that merely delays the inevitable. Cyberspace most needs many of those who think they least need cyberspace. Thoughtful and civil individuals often seem less likely to get involved in the culture-setting discussions of cyberspace than do the individuals who shout empty clichés and wear out anyone who dares to dispute them. And there are no score-cards—whoever gets the last word seems the victor. Those who aren't competing are at a distinct disadvantage. This debate on cyberspace is too important not to have all of our voices heard.

So what do we do? In the next chapter I'll discuss what we can do working together—but this is the chapter to discuss what we can do as individuals. Follow your best instincts—your individual excellence. The First Amendment was founded to ensure that fundamental freedoms are part of the nation's social and political fabric. Freedom of conscience is a responsibility. The Founding Fathers assumed that we would follow that conscience if given the chance—cyberspace gives us another opportunity to prove them right.

Identify those unifying values and purposes that give your life meaning and offer fulfillment. Read *Seven Habits of Highly Effective People* and *The Road Less Traveled* if you haven't already. Many values are universal, such as harmony, fairness, open-mindedness, love of learning, accountability, and personal fulfillment. Others, such as respect for nature, financial independence, loyalty to family, freedom of worship, and effective use of leisure time, may be more individual.

Focus on your objectives. Goals can also be shared—but be sure that yours are consistent with those of the online groups you join. Your most important goal, however, is likely to be unique. Define that goal. Find your singular purpose, your cause, your destiny—whatever makes you special and unique. When you do, use those values to set your short and long-term goals and priorities for your activities online. Then reconcile those goals and priorities with your real life objectives. Consider how your cyberspace communications and communities help or hinder the achievement of your goals. Consider whether your current activities in cyberspace contribute or detract from your enjoyment of those things most important to you. Simplify. Unburden yourself of any online activity inconsistent with your priorities. Fill voids with things consistent with those priorities.

Ask yourself whether you are true online to your best self. If you don't like fighting online, then stop. If everything else in your life seems dull in comparison to your time online, ask yourself why and fix it. Demand fewer rights and privileges of others and take more personal responsibility. Consider the ways in which cyberspace can assist you in many of the preceding processes. Find friends there and share personal insights and experience. Learn from others, and impose the discipline necessary to sort through the dross to find those things of lasting value.

Decrease your dependence on the news media by finding unfiltered and filtered sources in cyberspace. You will not only decrease your level of frustration but will also increase the effectiveness of the time spent analyzing current events. Continue to use your preferred news sources, if you enjoy them, for the variety, but identify and use a customized "online clipping service" to scan a wide variety of periodicals and topics according to your primary interests, providing you with focused reading. Don't give up if the initial results seem discouraging—keep working at fine-tuning your search word profile until you easily find the clippings you're looking for.

Communicate freely but moderately. Learn the power of words and reason, and exercise it with due care. Consider the value of your two-cents worth from the perspective of others. Be protective of those things you suspect others may not respect as much as you do. Whether your online communications become a distracting burden or an enabling convenience depends on your approach to them. Participate in carefully selected newsgroups, but don't spread your participation over dozens of newsgroups or forums, attempting to boil the ocean. You will too quickly find yourself in the thick of thin things as you waste many hours accomplishing little of value.

Choose the newsgroups and forums you will follow carefully, according to your real interests, values, and proactive choices. Look for forums on the topics of your choice—those with less contentious fighting and more mature dialogue. There are plenty to choose from' and each has its own culture. Become a member of one virtual community. Again, choose it carefully; it will influence you probably even more than you will influence it. Bring something of value to that community without looking for the reward. It will come.

Be chary about your reading choices online. Don't subscribe to mail lists unless you are fairly confident that you really do want to see everything said about the topic. You could easily find your mailbox filled with clutter. Don't continue an e-mail exchange when you both have run out of productive things to say. Rather than read every post made to newsgroups of only moderate interest, use DejaNews on the WWW (http://www.dejanews.com) to research particular topics as required. You don't need to be an expert on everything. It's often more important to know where to find the information than to have it memorized.

If you read this chapter and said "Of course, this all makes sense. This is how I conduct my life," that's great. Now make sure you do the same thing online. Be your best self online. Since it is so easy to put your best foot forward, do it. Don't give in to cynicism, fear, or selfishness: it's a dead end that leads nowhere. Embrace instead the enduring principles of individual excellence that constitute a fulfilling and happy life: discipline, respect, love, passion, sharing, and simplicity. The world of cyberspace is one that can be yours—on your own terms. Make sure those terms consider what's best for others too. If you're struggling with how to prepare your children for life in cyberspace, I can't stress enough the importance of laying this solid foundation for a quality life.

CHAPTER FIVE

SOCIETY AND COMMUNITY

The Value of Values

Virtue is not left to stand alone. He who practices it will have neighbors.

—Confucius

I magine that you are suddenly the last person on earth. Everyone else has vanished. It is as if you are "home alone." The world and its treasures are yours, and yours alone. You are unconstrained. You have no more responsibility to anyone but yourself. You can do whatever you please, when you please, and how you please. You have all of the power and wealth in the world.

Tough questions then arise: What would you then miss most? What would you learn about your current values? How many of us would choose to return to the status quo rather than lose all of our relationships and sense of community in exchange for all the world? I believe the majority of us would draw the same conclusions about the long-term undesirability of such a lonesome situation.

In the words of Benedict Spinoza, a seventeenth-century Dutch philosopher, "Man is a social animal." Indeed, humankind lives in societies in which we learn the values necessary to function effectively in relationships with others, whether in a family, tribe, school, corporation, state, or nation. But what happens when a wrench is thrown into the works of society—a wrench so large that it threatens the society's values and viability?

In *The Gods Must Be Crazy*, a 1984 film, an airplane pilot flying over Botswana, Africa, throws an empty Coke bottle from his plane. It spirals to earth, landing in the Kalahari Desert, where a bushman named Xi witnesses the descent of the bottle, examines it, and takes it back to his clan. His people marvel at the "thing" the gods have sent them. They don't know why the gods have sent it, but in their experience, the gods always have sent them only good things; and this is a good thing—at first. Every day, they find new use for the thing. It is a toy, a musical instrument, a rolling pin, a pestle, and a snakeskin curing device. Its uses seem endless. But the gods have been careless; they've sent only one. It isn't long before people argue over possession of the thing, which introduces unfamiliar emotions into the society—anger, selfishness, hate, violence. One woman hits another over the head with the thing as they struggle over it. Xi throws the thing into the air, screaming to the gods, "Take back your thing!" The gods won't have it—it falls back to earth, hitting a child. Xi buries the thing. A hyena, smelling the blood on it, digs up the bottle but then drops it, where it is rediscovered by one of the children of the clan. Another struggle for possession ensues. The people are very unhappy that night as they sit around the campfire discussing the dilemma presented by what they now call the "evil thing." It is decided that the evil thing doesn't belong on earth. Xi says he will take the evil thing to the end of the earth and throw it off.

Clearly, when the value of sharing is undermined by ego—individual cries of need—the integrity of the society can be so threatened that the object of the instability has to be done away with. What lessons can modern societies glean from this movie? I think there are several. We must recognize that a "Coke bottle," in the form of cyberspace in its broadest sense, has "fallen" into our midst. We must recognize that the "thing" is amoral—that it has the potential for both good and evil vis-à-vis our societal values. We must discuss and define the dilemma and weigh the ramifications of its amorality. As modern society, we have opted to integrate the thing into our society, rather then "throw it back to the gods," and therefore we must identify which values the technology has threatened and resolve to find and take measures to reinforce them in a way that will both accommodate the technology and preserve the integrity of the society.

Granted, the bush society of the Kalahan bears little resemblance to modern society, but both societies value many of the same principles such as harmony and sharing. Modern western societies, however, also value individuality, an incongruity that historically has lent a dynamic tension to our societal pursuits. Further, the population of the bush society of the movie was sparse and homogeneous, and it occupied, at any one time, only a small geographical area; its society was not further challenged by the dense, diverse, and widespread populations of modern western societies. It was a simple matter for the bush people to gather around the campfire to discuss the thing in order to resolve the problems its presence engendered.

But modern societies have also had "campfires" around which to gather and discuss things—legislatures, town meetings, congresses, conventions, and conferences. Ironically, cyberspace—the thing itself—now presents us with a new campfire around which everyone can gather and discuss things. Cyberspace represents a revolutionary advance in our means of interactive socialization. Never before has it been possible for groups to assemble, cooperate, explore, organize, discuss, transform, synergize, and progress around such a large campfire, with so little interference from the barriers of time and space. Millions are pursuing these new possibilities to get together (online first, face-to-face, or FTF, second) with astonishing energy.

I first became convinced of cyberspace's incredible capacity for socialization, and the limits of that capacity, as a result of my participation in a cyberspace society named Team OS/2. A variety of fascinating forces converged to trigger this amazing and unexpected cyberspace phenomenon, and an understanding of those forces lends insight into the possibilities and pitfalls that arise when the "gods" drop some new thing from the sky.

VIRTUAL VOICES

Operating System/2 (OS/2) was announced in 1987 by IBM and Microsoft as the personal computer operating system that would replace the aging but ubiquitous Disk Operating System (DOS). Since then, industry debates have constantly raged over the relationship of IBM and Microsoft, the tactics Microsoft used to establish Microsoft Windows as the operating system standard instead of OS/2, and the relative merits of Windows and OS/2. As recently as 1991, Microsoft was flatly denying rumors that they intended to abandon their support for OS/2; yet by the time John Akers stood before customers at the Crowne Plaza Hotel in Manhattan that March to profess the "New IBM"'s unwavering commitment to OS/2, Microsoft had decided to turn from their cooperation with IBM to an all-out war. During an IBM executive presentation there, Windows crashed, prompting the executive to tout the benefits of the "crash-resistant" OS/2. Bill Gates interpreted such actions as IBM bullying. According to the biography *Gates*, "Chairman Bill decided it was time to sever the cord with Big Blue for good. 'They did these demos where they personally crashed Windows and they said nasty things about Windows,' he recalled."[1]

By the time I made my comments about Akers and IBM and the slow slide of IBM's desertion of the Basic Beliefs in May of 1991, it was clear that IBM's relationship with Microsoft was in serious trouble. The trade press called it a divorce. To me, it was counterproductive, regrettable foolishness which would lead to the loss of a single IBM-compatible desktop operating system standard as well as a serious dilution of the industry's efforts to develop quality software. Some software developers would develop for OS/2, others for Windows, and some for both—but it seemed that it would be more difficult than ever to see dramatic increases in creative new software, since the base operating system market would be divided, thus working against smaller vendors trying to establish themselves against market leaders. I believed Microsoft wanted it that way. But even then, I didn't want to accept the idea that a war was inevitable and that Microsoft had every intention of destroying OS/2 and IBM in the marketplace in an attempt to establish Windows as a monopolistic, proprietary standard.

By that fall, I realized that Microsoft would outmuscle IBM in the software sales channels unless IBM began to do some very creative marketing. My experience with the power of the Akers (AMSROUND) incident had left me convinced that the creative application of online communications were the answer. In IBM's traditional marketing, you identify the decision-maker in an organization, convince him or her, and then work your way down the organization if necessary. This didn't work in personal computers, because the decision-making often worked in reverse, with the individual users and the media influencing purchases and standards to an extraordinary degree. In fact, the personal computer revolution was just that— escape from a bit of the "tyranny of the glass house," where information systems departments were rarely as responsive as users wanted. What I believed would work effectively to market OS/2 was a word-of-mouth approach based on the principles of geometric acceleration: sell two people, who each sell two people, who each sell two people, and so on. Cyberspace communications facilitated the rapid spread of word-of-mouth communications, and also enabled new possibilities for principle-centered socialization and dynamic teamwork. In this particular case, I felt that there were other reinforcing factors as well—OS/2 was a great product and a lot of people had a lot invested in OS/2.

In January of 1992, I joined the IBM group marketing OS/2. On February 12, I created an online forum I called TEAMOS2 FORUM on IBMPC, "for the discussion of those things that empowered IBMers, working as a team can do to promote the success of OS/2," focused on "synergy and combining talents to achieve results greater than the sum of individual efforts through teamwork." I announced the forum on several other forums, and before long, the movement began to grow. *PC Week* provided it with significant impetus in an article they ran not long after: "IBM Creates Post to Push OS/2 2.0 Into Mass Market." According to the story, "Whittle . . . has been appointed to a new post to help sell and support the yet-to-be-released OS/2 2.0 in the consumer community via popular bulletin board services such as Prodigy, CompuServe, and MCI." Later, the article stated that a "key part of Whittle's charter will be to foster grass-roots support for OS/2 2.0—an effort he kicked off by soliciting bulletin board users for suggestions on his new title. . . . Whittle claims top IBM executives have given him the charter 'not to spout the party line,' and to give users a forum to share OS/2 problems, ideas and support issues . . . 'If OS/2 2.0 is going to fly, it has to win over end users,' said an IBM insider. 'Whittle's been given carte blanche because before, when IBM went through the field and came back with feedback, by the time it went through management, it came back sanitized.' "[2]

The real-space article gave the cyberspace movement the kick-start it needed. I believed the article and assumed that I had indeed been given carte blanche—in every way except, of course, funding. Once other IBMers began to notice that something different was happening, some long-standing cultural prohibitions at IBM seemed to dissolve, and soon TEAMOS2 FORUM became another IBM phenomenon similar to AMSROUND FORUM. Team OS/2 members voluntarily joined this virtual association that was without rules, by-laws, dues, or obligations. The only requirement I had specified was that members needed to make a personal sacrifice to share the benefits of OS/2 with a stranger or friend not already using it.

Team OS/2 members, brainstorming on the forum, came up with a wide variety of ideas for promoting OS/2 with minimal help from IBM. Some members made software developed by IBMers available for OS/2 on the networks under the terms of a no-charge license, some worked with Prodigy to create an OS/2 section on Prodigy, some compiled and shared electronic text concerning OS/2, some created and shared demonstration techniques, and others responded to the "To Do" items I was posting and coordinating based on e-mail input from others worldwide. One enterprising Team OS/2 group in Chicago obtained and placed a large OS/2 banner outside the window of the IBM offices on a prominent skyscraper during the Comdex conference at which OS/2 was announced. An individual or team achievement was cause for an energizing report posted on the forum, which was often followed by a round of kudos. The Director of Market Development for OS/2, Lucy Baney, sent "LuvOS/2" T-shirts to many of those who reported successes online. The excitement and energy were palpable.

Throughout the nation, small groups of supporters presented OS/2 at trade shows, user groups, computer and software stores, and anywhere else the could find an audience. One enterprising IBMer organized ongoing demonstrations of OS/2 in a booth at the nation's largest air show, with attendance of over a million flight enthusiasts. A group in Washington, D.C., represented OS/2 with a fully staffed booth at the Maryland State Fair. A gathering of over 100 marketing representatives and systems engineers at a seminar in Dallas, Texas, turned into a full-fledged party, raffle, and fund-raiser for charity.

The first formal Team OS/2 event sponsored by IBM was held in April 1992 at Comdex. One enthusiastic Texas "Teamer" paid for his own ticket to Chicago to deliver a hundred special-ordered T-shirts, with an OS/2 logo stamped with the superimposed word TEAM on one side and "ibm/2" (the new IBM) on the other. We gave away prizes donated by OS/2 software vendors and gave the winners an opportunity to nominate someone they knew to the "Team OS/2 Hall of Fame" for creative ideas. So much excitement and goodwill were generated that IBM executive John Soyring noted to the crowd, "This is the first time I've been to an IBM event which gave me goosebumps." The leather-clad leader of the Chicago blues band that had been playing said he'd never been to a party quite like it and asked for one of those "hot T-shirts" for each member of the band.

Many of these Team OS/2 events resembled parties much more than they did formal marketing events—and as such, you didn't need to look like a starched collar, white-shirted IBMer to participate, with IBM's blessing. Suddenly, you didn't need to have IBM marketing training to represent IBM. The culture change was exhilarating for those involved. Many IBMers who knew little about OS/2 joined because they liked what they saw. *PC Week* wrote us up: "Team OS/2 is Preaching IBM Gospel," writing about groups of IBM "employees who spend their off-hours promoting IBM's new operating system, which is scheduled to be released this week." The interviewer, however, asked me a few questions I didn't like about failure. In his words, "What happens, if, in spite of all the evangelism and the promotions, IBM loses? Whittle disputes the premise behind the question. 'I think the win-lose mentality is Bill Gates's gift to the computer industry,' he said. 'We're not an army out to destroy Microsoft. We're out to have fun, help customers and enjoy these computers.'"[3]

I believe that another significant factor in the movement was that cyberspace enabled individuals to contribute their talents to a cause in a way that was visible and growing. Someone came up with the idea of identifying Team OS/2 members in cyberspace using a number of devices, including tag-lines, adding the keyword TEAMOS2 in online directory entries, and maintaining lists of members and e-mail addresses. Soon, a search on almost any major city in North America would yield several dozen Team OS/2 members—many of whom began to demand local forums to discuss possibilities. I established a series of more local forums on IBMPC named TEAMNY, TEAMDC, TEAMFL, TEAMTX, and TEAMCA. These forums quickly attracted enthusiastic followers who coordinated plans for real-world activities, volunteered to help, shared good humor and success stories, and creatively applied what they were learning from one another. It was obvious that people love to associate with others who share a common cause. The movement was outgrowing its roots and taking a life of its own.

By August of 1992, I stepped aside as the de facto leader of the group when IBM created, according to my recommendation, a "Grass Roots Marketing Department" within a new organization built around OS/2 to compete with Microsoft—Personal Software Products (PSP). Team OS/2, with the able help of Janet Gobeille and Vicci Conway, began to grow dramatically outside of IBM. As it grew, so did the enjoyment and the subsequent attention the phenomenon attracted. Thousands were signing up worldwide—not through any carefully cultivated grass roots organization, but solely through the reach of cyberspace. Team OS/2 forums were established on FidoNet, the Internet, on America Online, Prodigy, and CompuServe. It became impossible for one person to keep track of Team OS/2—I know; try as I might, I couldn't keep up.

In the fall of 1992, PSP shipped the one millionth copy of OS/2—and for the next year, it seemed as if OS/2 was going to be the smash hit that we all knew it could be. John C. Dvorak, widely thought to be anti-IBM after his column several years earlier titled "My Dinner with IBM" had castigated IBM for arrogance, started using and recommending OS/2 after noting with approval the Team OS/2 phenomenon. Will Zachmann, an industry analyst who had coined the term "downsizing" and had first predicted an unprofitable IBM, wrote persuasively that OS/2 would succeed because it was superior to Windows and backed by IBM. Dave Barnes, an IBM evangelist with a dramatic flair that mesmerized audiences, went head-to-head with Microsoft in "Operating System Shootouts" and won convincingly with good humor and razzle-dazzle demonstrations of OS/2's prowess. I remember Philippe Kahn, then Chairman and CEO of Borland, standing with Barnes and me onstage at a Team OS/2 party, saying rather poignantly, "This is the way the industry used to be."

Over 10,000 volunteers joined Team OS/2. I exchanged messages online with literally hundreds of those thousands, and most saw cyberspace as a powerful vehicle for uniting individuals with a common cause. In a feature story in *PC Week* in early 1994, one Team OS/2 member, Richard Frank, was asked why he spent 30 hours a week promoting OS/2. "Personal satisfaction. When I see other people who are using it, they're happy, they're excited."

What none of us anticipated was that the wild frontiers of cyberspace would facilitate not only a positive movement but the onset of its decay as well. OS/2 was all that seemed to matter to many of the new Team OS/2 members, and friction with Microsoft and fans of Windows became increasingly intense. Dvorak began to call the shrill chorus of Microsoft boosters "Microsoft Munchkins," and the Munchkins responded by calling Team OS/2 members "Teamsters." At times, it got downright ugly. Some who signed their notes using the familiar "Team OS/2" tag lines became increasingly abusive, and some even sent threatening notes and death threats to journalists who weren't so positive about OS/2. Because Team OS/2 was so egalitarian, anyone could join (including Microsoft employees and supporters) and there was simply no way to know exactly who was giving Team OS/2 a black eye—or worse, how to prevent them from doing so. Rumors were rampant that it was another Microsoft plan to neutralize effective competition—and my talks with industry contacts did little to assure me that such a possibility was out of the question. I watched with discouragement as the group seemed to change and decline, until in the fall of 1995, one week before Comdex, IBM "surplused" (IBMese for "laid off unless you can find another job within IBM") everyone working on Team OS/2 except for one contractor.

John Dvorak, the best-read columnist in the PC industry, with an audience estimated by one survey to be almost seven million readers, wrote "[Team OS/2] traces its roots to early efforts by Dave Whittle, a very religious man dedicated to starting a smiley-faced, feel-good, grass-roots group. To prevent it from becoming a cult or empire, he set up Team OS/2 as a nebulous organization with no leadership. Whittle, perceived as a threat, was endlessly harassed by Microsoft advocates in various on-line forums and was bounced around IBM. His feel-good vision of Team OS/2 began to fade as its membership reached nearly 10,000 members and fragmented. OS/2 failed to meet market expectations and Microsoft did its best to submarine interest in the product by deriding it. . . . Team OS/2 suddenly emerged as a revolutionary force . . . Microsoft always sensed that something was up with Team OS/2, and reckoned that by spending a ton of money and making a lot of noise, it would drown out Team OS/2 and other Microsoft bashers. Microsoft began to characterize them as 'thugs' and then copied the Whittle model to form its Team OS/2 clone. Club Win is their equivalent, which sounds more like a casino. None of this helps anyone . . . I blame Microsoft's win-at-any-cost mentality for this sickening turn of events."[4]

My biased opinion is that Team OS/2 is one of the most interesting social experiments in shared values and beliefs that cyberspace has seen to date. It is certainly one harbinger of the possibilities (and pitfalls) for society in cyberspace. The "gods must be crazy" to have dropped such a useful and threatening thing into our midst, and yet it is by understanding our reactions to such a thing that societal progress is possible.

Meetings, conventions, negotiations, and other interactive social transactions once required propinquity; so large expenditures on travel by businesses and other organizations have long been considered necessary. Now, Team OS/2 is but one example of the many individuals (mostly strangers) who are gathering in online groups of anywhere from two to many thousands devoted to the pursuit of common interests. More and more commercial, political, media, and social interaction occurs in cyberspace every day, supplementing and enhancing face-to-face meetings. A new class of acquaintance has emerged: virtual friends and associates—those we feel we know well but have never met.

Yet the power of cooperation in cyberspace that is being unleashed is still in its nascent stages. Scholars have had at least a decade's head start on the rest of the world and are therefore understandably at the forefront of using the network to collaborate on research, share their findings, and brainstorm about future possibilities. Now, others are catching up. Many businesses are using the networks aggressively; but there are really rather few well-organized, openly cooperative initiatives online as yet. But they will, I'm sure, become more common as soon as they make a bit more sense technologically and sociologically. Virtual corporations, virtual communities, virtual societies, virtual governments, virtual clubs, virtual gangs, virtual neighborhoods, virtual malls, virtual universities, virtual enterprises, virtual associations, and even virtual families are coming to a screen near you.

How will such rampant socialization affect our lives? It is too soon to say, but not too soon to hope and work for the best—which is why there seems, on the surface at least, to be a cottage industry of cyberspace utopians. It is entirely possible that cyberspace can fundamentally alter the social system under which we live, but the cultural assumptions that will determine the shape of the changes are not yet in place.

The challenge of our generation and every generation is to choose the enduring values of cooperation and goodwill over the types of selfishness that lead to corruption, contention, enmity, and war. In the ups and downs of Team OS/2, the ups came from cooperation, or at least good-natured competitiveness, and the downs came from the aggressive competition of win/lose thinking. This tension between cooperation and competition seems to me to be at the roots of every culture and at the heart of every society—for no society can long exist where the choice is made again and again to compete in win/lose struggles rather than cooperate towards win/win ends when offered the choice.

John Perry Barlow told *NetGuide Magazine* that "we're in the middle of the most serious cultural change since the capture of fire."[5] At first glance, that may seem like hyperbole—but if we step back and take a closer look at what is happening around us, it is not difficult to be persuaded that we are in the midst of an enormous social and cultural upheaval. Whether we emerge from the upheaval with a paradigm of cooperation and unity for cyberspace or one of competition and divisiveness, or whether we will ever emerge from it at all, is still very much undecided.

DANGERS OF CULTURAL UPHEAVAL

Many nations and cultures are experiencing dramatic challenges to their defining assumptions and values—perhaps nowhere more dramatically than in the United States of America. The notion that the United States is "one nation, under God, indivisible, with liberty and justice for all" no longer seems to reflect the realities of the divisions created by such things as its cultural diversity, the secularization of its government, and the marginalization of some groups of its population.

Indeed, even the concept of a nation as the cradle of cultures is vanishing. The new fountains of modern culture are those entities that produce easily identified assumptions with which we can pick and choose according to our fancy—the sound-byte media, Hollywood, tribes, political parties, musicians, special interest groups, and even commercial brands (such as Nike, Calvin Klein, Ralph Lauren, and even Team OS/2). The aggressively competitive assumptions of big business competing for mind and market share, the mass media competing for ratings, and our two-party system competing for votes seem to permeate every aspect of our culture, yet rarely does anyone question the underlying cultural assumption: competition is good and healthy, and the more of it, the better. Even if competition *is* good and healthy, we must strive to accept values that pay more than lip service to "we the people."

Unless we can somehow reverse this cultural trend towards combativeness and divisiveness, cyberspace will only hasten the fragmentation of our national culture coupled with the corresponding strengthening of subcultures and tribes. Whether those subcultures are Team OS/2, Greenpeace sympathizers, Shriners, Dogberts New Ruling Class, or the Church of

Scientology, it will be easier than it ever has been to identify others who share one's assumptions and to band with them in "defense of the faith"—for better or worse.

The better might be much, much better. Cooperation between men and women of goodwill brought together online could revitalize neighborhoods, find solutions to societal problems, improve and rejuvenate schools, energize civic organizations, teach disadvantaged youth, increase social capital, reclaim nature, renew civic virtue, and restore political purpose to the grass roots. Unfortunately, the "worse" in banding together online might be much, much worse. Drug dealers, gambling barons, pornographers, pimps, gangs, hate groups, and weapons dealers could create black markets that cover the globe, recruit new members, incite riots, and plot destruction.

So where is the cause for optimism? Simply this: the world has always been a place of great contrast and varying degrees of such things as good and evil and cowardice and heroism, but the choices are more easily made when they are seen in the light of experience and we are free to seek association with whomever we choose. Is it unreasonable to expect that this light of experience won't outshine the influence of the media when experiences are more easily shared, unfiltered, directly with others in cyberspace?

Culture Clash

In *Thriving on Chaos*, Tom Peters documents "a world turned upside down," pointing out that things aren't nearly as predictable as they once were, that companies are struggling to keep up with the pace of technological change, and that "big" isn't better anymore and that the interaction of the many dynamic new forces are simply creating an environment of chaos and turmoil where those who are quick on their feet, responsive, and adaptable will thrive. Tom has always been a few years ahead of the rest of us (cyberspace networks were novelties when Tom published *Thriving on Chaos* in 1987), but those same dynamic, interactive forces that are driving us economically are also driving us culturally and socially—towards cyberspace.

The competition of ideas in a free society can easily become, as we have seen in American culture, a free-for-all of special interests and a cacophony of competing influences, each demanding attention. To the degree this becomes a process of perpetually divisive competition rather than a unifying search for accord, it is likely to be at least as destructive as productive.

These ideas, beliefs, and values over which we struggle are derived from a broad diversity of personal and cultural experience, information, and interpretation. Fundamental core beliefs are often so closely associated with identity and thus self-esteem and values that it is often difficult to see disagreement as anything but a personal threat and attack. Hence, the cultural battleground upon which we are engaged embraces race, gender, class, age, appearance, politics, profession, and religion. Our culture is undergoing dramatic changes in the bedrock of cultural assumptions themselves, seemingly triggered by our struggles to deal with those factors at the heart of our individual differences. It seems evident that, as a society, our attitudes towards feminism, environmentalism, technology, and civil rights—at the very least—have changed significantly in the past several decades. When such foundational ideas concerning the very nature of our interactions with others and nature are in a state of enormous flux, cultural change and conflict is inevitable, since culture rests on shared assumptions and ideas. These changes result in social and cultural upheaval—culture clash.

In an environment where cultures clash, the tragedy of the Luddites comes into focus. In nineteenth century England, the rise of manufacturing threatened the economic foundation of an entire way of life—the agrarian society surrounding Sherwood Forest and Nottingham. Free men working the land with their own tools at home at the mercy of nature were being replaced by wage slaves working artificial machines in factories at the mercy of other men. Ned Ludd and his followers fought against the effects of industrialization, destroying both factories and machinery in raids and battles, but the insurrection was squashed and the Luddites failed in their attempts to resist the industrial revolution. Since then, "Luddite" has come to describe those who resist technological change. On the other hand, the word "technocrat," from the 1930s technocracy movement (whose supporters advocated the reorganization of society based on technological principles), is often used to denote those who pursue and embrace technology as if it were salvation itself. Where the two extremes meet, we have culture clash.

What can we do to minimize such clashes and their effects? How can cyberspace facilitate that minimalization? The answers lie in trusting in turmoil, enlarging the focus on the mutual benefits of individual and social similarities and complementary excellences while minimizing the arena of conflict (the public differences) by narrowing the focus on divisive differences to those immediately affected.

In the turmoil of technological change, we cannot afford to neglect those things which are purely human, personally or socially. A cyberspace access device makes a strange bedfellow and a cruel taskmaster. Technology is amoral. Just because we have the capacity to do new things doesn't guarantee anything other than that those new things will be used to further whatever purposes are held by those who learn to exercise that capacity. And that brings us back to square one: do we make positive proactive choices driven by shared values or do we default and accept the baser instincts of competitive animals as our natural lot in life? The former leads to constructive cooperation and increased well-being for all, while the latter leads to wearying and destructive fights.

We can and must trust in turmoil to provide new opportunities to be seized. If we are to embrace change without losing our lives or lifestyles, those who uphold the static quality of traditional values must embrace and exploit the dynamic quality of technological change more wisely than those who pervert technology to selfish ends destructive of community. The story of security whiz Tsutomu Shimomura and his takedown of the taunting hacker Kevin Mitnick, through patient waiting and tracking of break-ins and cellular phone signals, resonates because it seems so easy to recognize the "good guy" from the "bad guy." It indicates that the guy standing for respect and decency and security can indeed outwit the guy standing for theft and taunts and undisciplined immaturity. Not all virtue is so patiently modest as Shimomura's, and not all iniquity so evident and arrogant as Mitnick's— but the fundamental principle shines through: if the "good guys" are "better" and "smarter" than the "bad guys," then technology will serve us well.

Still, most situations are more ambiguous than that. The choice is often between multiple goods or compromises. Trusting in turmoil requires a certain humility as we examine the various choices. If we recognize that we may not have all the answers, we may be able to find the answers more easily. If we begin every debate with a search for agreement, we enlarge the focus on the mutual benefits we seek. We are more able to extract value from diversity and find the complementarities of excellence which enable us to minimize the conflicts which otherwise make culture clash a destructive social force.

Many places in cyberspace can be found where the mix of a wide range of newsmakers, reporters, company executives and representatives, twits, analysts, kibitzers, and even everyday people creates opportunities for discussions and perspectives on the news and culture seldom, if ever, seen outside cyberspace. Cyberspace is fundamentally different from any other media source I know: the only differences that are visible in cyberspace are those we voluntarily reveal and admit to during a discussion. The "battleground" can be transformed. We can, if we learn how, make cyberspace a place of pure ideas and thus, conceivably, escape the crippling effects of prejudice, hatred, discrimination, envy, and class warfare. If the culture clash can be reduced to the essence of ideas, we may be able to come face to face with more of those revealing understandings that precede peace.

As we have greater ability to participate in and read such interactive, real-time exchanges, the breadth of our exposure to ideas and influencers will increase; the depth of the analysis we have available will be extended; and the diversity of our interaction will expand. As more of us seek to obtain our news and information from cyberspace, and more of the news-makers tell their stories and plead their cases directly to the public there, we should see a much greater availability of influential information, at lower cost, to more people, with a higher level of quality—if, that is, we can build into cyberspace cultural or structural resistance to the pitfalls I describe in this book, many of which are the same forces that have made today's mass media less effective than it could and should be.

In the public square, the diversity that is surely with us to stay can be energizing and healthy IF only we can reach a cultural consensus on a few key points such as respect for individual excellence, the difference between a person and his or her ideas, and a healthy respect for the boundaries sep-arating societal authority and personal rights—i.e., a keen recognition of the difference between the public and the private.

Blurred Boundaries

As a people, we demand privacy on the one hand and yet, on the other hand, tune in while others give up the most intimate details of their lives to the public in the televised spectacles hosted by such as Geraldo Rivera, Jerry Springer, and Jenny Jones. Is there even a line to be drawn between the public and private anymore? If there isn't, there should be. It may be the only hope we have to resolve many of the issues that face us.

It seems to me that many of the most divisive issues we face today as a society are derived from attempts to bring what is essentially private into the public arena. Many argue that the right of free speech is the basis for their supposed right to go public with private matters. Yet freedom of speech is based on the freedom to follow the dictates of one's conscience, consistent with allowing others to follow the dictates of their conscience—which demands mutual respect. That respect is diminished when we attempt to eliminate the boundary by which we judge that which is private and force the acceptance of our private decisions and morality on others publicly. Whether the issue is abortion and the right to choose, prayer in schools, gay rights, the media coverage of Presidential candidates and Presi-dents, welfare, or obscenity and pornography, euthanasia and the right to die, the core issue is related to the blurring of boundaries between what is public and what is private. The consequences are especially severe when the confusion over public and private results in a broadening of the arena of public conflict and the accompanying perception that we are losing our cultural base of shared values and assumptions. That shared base of values and assumptions is the essence of what should be "public," and to the degree that we enlarge that sphere, thus narrowing the sphere of that which is "private," we expand the opportunity for culture clash, conflict, and turmoil.

In cyberspace, the distinction between the public and the private can be and should be built into to the structure of cyberspace, technologically and culturally. The genius of public and private key encryption is perfectly suited for this, as are other technological solutions such as filters and gateways. Many programming languages have already made a somewhat similar distinction—when private variables are clearly delineated from public variables, the possibility of conflicts between software modules written by different programmers are eliminated. Although the words public and private have a different meaning in that context, the underlying lesson should not be lost on a society seeking to minimize our public differences and thus increase the public peace and welfare. By delineating the public and private, we can minimize conflict as we increase the sphere of the private concerns and decrease the sphere of public concern.

It won't be as technically difficult to accomplish this distinction in cyberspace as some might contend, either. The challenge is primarily political and social. For example, the Communications Decency Act represents an attempt to solve a political problem with a legislative solution. A technical solution, such as the Platform for Internet Content Selection (PICS), can easily allow the distinction between public and private to be made by individuals. PICS is a voluntary rating system whereby the content provider rates his or her own content in relation to a variety of distinct categories, including nudity, sexual acts, violence, racism, profanity, satanism, alcohol, or tobacco use, militancy, firearms use, or illegal activities such as gambling or illicit drug use. Popular browser software could be programmed to access only those sites specifically rated in the ranges defined as acceptable in each category, with conservative defaults. Changes to the defaults should require proof of age or some sort of adult key or PIN code, in order to prevent children designating themselves as "parents" when downloading and using new copies of browsers. Unrated sites would be inaccessible, thus encouraging all sites interested in broad exposure to be rated. Consumers could be protected from mislabeling by minor modifications to existing consumer protection laws that forbid false or misleading advertising or labeling.

In order for PICS to work, it must reach a critical mass of public acceptance—which is a social and political problem. Users who enable PICS filtering in their browser will face a serious handicap unless PICS support is almost universally enabled, since any site that doesn't support PICS standards will not be available to anyone using the PICS standard on the view-ing end. Thus, a solution might be elegant technically and yet still fail for political or social reasons. For a standard such as PICS to become viable, it must be supported commercially by those creating the enabling tools for cyberspace as well as by the providers of content. Because it is not in the best interests of most Web site designers or content providers to label their content and thus potentially reduce their audience, the only way a standard like PICS will reach a critical mass of acceptance is because demand for it on the viewer side reaches critical mass, or through legislative fiat. No one can predict the outcome at this point—but my best guess is that PICS will be adopted only if legislative pressures (similar to the passage of the Communications Decency Act) provide the impetus.

Whatever the means used, cyber spaces should be created and designated either public or private. Private forums and sites should be considered bas-tions of free thought, free speech, and privacy—and can and should be remarkably free of regulation or interference from government. Public forums and sites should be considered places which are not only consistent with but also reflective of shared societal values. Private space in cyberspace can and should be clearly labeled as such and should be protected by pass-words, encryption, or a universal rating system to ensure privacy and pro-tection. The owner of the private space should be responsible for the control of passwords and thus for the welfare of any children allowed into a private space. There should be means to create temporary private spaces for specific purposes—children can then be taught to simply avoid such places while in cyberspace. "Don't take candy from strangers" can become simply "don't enter private spaces with strangers." However elegant we make filtering software to protect children in real-time exchanges, it can never be the ultimate solution, because it shifts the responsibility for even clearly offensive and inappropriate material from the originator to the recipient. If we believe that "you own our own words," then accountability must be built into the system.

Certain private spaces might even have larger audiences than most of the public spaces, since adult or sensitive topics could only be discussed in private spaces. General and nonsensitive topics of public interest could be discussed in public spaces. Filtering software could add an additional safe-guard for those public discussions that necessarily discuss matters of adult concern. Government censorship should not be necessary in the public space, because self-enforcement there could be exercised similar to what already happens on the Internet in relation to the cultural prohibitions against spamming. Diversity would thrive in both the public and private spaces—and even to a degree that is seemingly impossible at the moment while we spend so much time fighting over who "owns" the public space, since that is essentially the only space we recognize as available to us. The barriers to private property (or spaces) in cyberspace are high—and those who own such spaces in cyberspace get little cultural or legal support for imposing the constraints that would truly distinguish such a space as private. Thus, most spaces pretty much resemble public spaces.

Technology can also be harnessed to make information about ourselves either public or private. Although such technologies are still in their infancy, individuals should have the option to make valuable private demographic information (age, gender, income, etc.) available to interested parties anonymously. The information denoted as public would be available to anyone, while private information would be protected and available only to those we choose. This would benefit all, since those offering products, services, or information could target their offerings more effectively and the individual would face fewer uninteresting solicitations or invasions of privacy. Such technologies are perhaps just as likely to develop commercially as the content filtering mechanisms, but might also need prodding from the government to develop in publicly beneficial ways.

When boundaries become blurred, backlash often results when average citizens and politicians begin to feel threatened by the changes. One example, arguably, is the Communications Decency Act. Soon after the Act was declared unconstitutional in June of 1996, Web pages with a variety of pornographic images began to proliferate, promising to trigger further action by those who oppose such readily accessible public pornography. Many advocates of restrictions such as those embodied in the CDA believe that the use of cyberspace for many broad public purposes will be severely hampered if pornography and indecency continue to be little more than a mouse click or two away in the public places of cyberspace. Many business leaders are troubled by their inability to prevent employees from accessing sites that serve no business purpose and impair productivity, which has been partly responsible for significant interest in Intranets. I believe some sort of legislative mandate is inevitable unless commercial interests band together to ensure an industry-wide social solution, similar to what the movie and cable TV industries have created.

If we can make the public spaces acceptable to the public and if we are free to choose our own private virtual communities consistent with our values and interests, then through mutual respect for one another's individual excellence, we might begin to rebuild our sense of community and the quality of our communities as we enter the cyberspace age.

THE QUALITY OF COMMUNITY

Will Zachmann's CANOPUS FORUM, the virtual community I've known best outside IBM, is not, for me, an online Nirvana, but it has an interesting quality that has often given me cause for thought. Here, the rules against personal attacks and such things as ad hominem arguments are rarely enforced—almost anything goes (and often does). At times, there seems to be balanced amounts of genius and witlessness, virtue and immorality and amorality, and humor and gloom. I joined CANOPUS shortly after its creation in 1992. During the first several years of its existence, I was one of the forum's most active and, often most controversial, participants. Although I have largely abandoned it because it has steadily deteriorated in value to me, I came to personally appreciate this community for various reasons, most especially because it provided me with valuable community experience in cyberspace—experience that has forced me to bridle my enthusiasm for the virtual communities of cyberspace.

Culturally, CANOPUS is much like New York—there's plenty of attitude and arrogance, but enough stimulation and raw goodness to be quite endearing. For me, the appeal was to not only stay current with chatter about the computer industry but to get reactions to ideas in a hostile environment. Cyberspace provides us with the opportunity to play devil's advocate in a forum of diversity. It is in this type of environment that we can truly test our ideas, which is probably what has kept me returning to CANOPUS long after I tired of the anarchic incivility there. It is a peculiar characteristic of learning that we often, perhaps without being aware of it, seek out and cultivate relationships with those who are surprisingly *dissimilar* to ourselves—opposites attract. IBM's Thomas Watson, Jr., spoke of the importance of cultivating a "mighty opposite"—someone who would force you to think twice about almost anything. Nonetheless, it is also important to be able to readily disengage from the mighty opposite if things get too heated. Freedom to leave the community when you find that its values ultimately conflict with yours is important. When we have less freedom to choose those relationships freely and find ourselves instead surrounded by those with dissimilar values or even prejudices towards us—and have no choice in the matter—we can often feel cheated and violated by that very community if we have little hope of escape. Frustration can erupt. I wonder if that isn't one of the challenges of living in the inner city, or as a minority in America—the inability to choose or find a community that can help us achieve even our most limited objectives may lead to frustrations and rage. What is missing in at least some of today's communities may well be this sense of control. A community that hasn't been chosen is a community of lesser quality.

At times, the only thing that made CANOPUS bearable for me was the notion that I was free to leave at any time. The only reason I stayed was because I was genuinely fond of many of the people there. Eventually, the increases in what I considered the "low-quality" aspects of the community prompted me to exercise my freedom to come and go to withdraw from the community—a decision made after considerable deliberation as I wrote this book this past year, and not without personal distress. The quality of any community in which we invest ourselves is a compelling and powerful personal force.

In cyberspace, we are rarely forced into a community we don't deliberately choose for ourselves. Cyberspace can fulfill our yearnings for the quality of community in a number of ways. It offers us unprecedented freedom to choose our associations. It enables us to participate on our own terms—as much or as little as we please, when and even where we please. We can log on at any time, night and day, to retrieve waiting messages and posts—and it's as if the community is there whenever we will it to be. Individuals can control the pace of their own participation and the amount of time spent in participation. The other members of the community make few, if any demands. Giving is voluntary, not pressured. Everyone may, in turn, speak his or her piece. People are not silenced involuntarily unless they consistently violate community norms in a serious way and, after much warning, are shut out—an excommunication of sorts. Even though a hierarchy of relative status develops over time, the class structure is usually noticeably absent. The risk of participation in these communities is low—individuals on the fringe of such communities come and go. Interestingly, those who have been active in such a community often feel obligated to let others know whenever they'll be absent for more than a few days. If they don't, other regulars begin to notice and ask questions. Newcomers are often welcomed as such.

Ray Oldenburg wrote, in his 1989 book *The Great Good Place,* about these "great good places" such as coffee shops, bars (such as that in *Cheers*), general stores, community centers, beauty parlors, barber shops, cafeterias, service stations, and truck stops where individuals could gather, converse, socialize, shoot the breeze, and pass the time without being alone.[6] Virtual communities represent a new variety of great, good places—where we can learn from friends and mighty opposites alike, where we can fulfill many of our social, spiritual, and intellectual inclinations, and where we are free to come and go as we please. Ultimately, though, as I learned from the Team OS/2 experience, the full power of cyberspace may be realized when we are not only be able to choose our communities, but also to create and build communities as well.

EXPANSION OF COMMUNITY

Just as the automobile and airplane changed the dynamics of distance between communities and thus expanded our sense of community to include state and nation, so have computers and modems and networks expanded our sense of community to include those with shared interests without regard to distance. One of the critical elements in establishing quality communities in cyberspace will be enabling individuals not only to choose their own communities freely but also to be able to create their own communities if they are so inclined. Right now, unfortunately, only a select few have the resources and connections to be able to form such a community and generate the critical mass of interest. Just as the automobile helped families overcome the constraints of distance and liberated a generation to choose their community, so will a modem and the right software enable individuals and families to choose and create their own communities in cyberspace.

The "right software" remains elusive. Currently, a healthy share of online activity is "chatting," or real-time, contemporaneous, on-screen written exchanges. This is horrible software for building a community. It is temporary, fleeting, and shallow, usually limited to one-sentence outbursts. It lends itself to cybersex, insults, and quick warm fuzzies and platitudes, but for the exchange of carefully considered ideas and the development of community, it is virtually worthless. On the other hand, the forum and conferencing paradigm of lasting postings made in threaded conversations is ideally suited to community building, but there is really no common standard. USENET newsgroups are quirky at best, even when managed by software such as Agent or Netscape's newsgroup reader, since they include so much irrelevant routing information. Most of the major online services have proprietary forum-handling software, on both the user (client) and service (server) side, that lends each a distinctive look and feel. For example, the only units of division in a newsgroup are messages within threads, whereas on CompuServe, each forum has a dozen or so sections containing messages within threads. Also, most of the existing virtual community software is still text-only. Theoretically, any variety of information that can be digitized can be communicated and shared in these communities. That includes not only text, but voice, music, pictures, video, and interactive computer programs.

Creating the structure to enable individuals to join and create interactive groups and support true communities is strictly a matter of programming and inspired design. That responsibility (or opportunity) rests with Netscape, Microsoft, Sun, IBM, and perhaps other free-market players who have not yet entered the fray. The race is on. Netscape seems to be the most visionary of the companies competing in this arena to date. They acquired Collabra—thus acquiring the collaborative software base necessary to move in that direction, and have based their strategies on open standards and cross-platform interoperability. IBM acquired Lotus for much the same reason—to buy Lotus Notes, the commercial leader in "groupware," which can and should evolve into community building networking software. I'm not sure I'm ready to trust Microsoft—with their proprietary standards, Windows-centric view of computing, and admitted hyper-competitiveness—with the task of teaching a hungry nation the concept of cooperation and virtual community building, but they've proven me wrong before. Sun looks to be a winner with the WWW-based programming language Java, which will probably be used to enable community-building software due to its support of interactivity. Ideally, users will begin now to speak up and be heard—because the platforms upon which our future will be built are being built now, and market forces favor vocal customers as much as political forces favor vocal voters. When communities can form as freely as Web pages on the WWW, enabled by excellent software, I expect to see an explosion of virtual communities of every kind there. In the meantime, however, virtual communities are expanding at a measured pace governed by the respective business cases of the online services and the technological savvy of newsgroup creators.

This expansion of our sense of community can work for the benefit of society as a whole, or against it. The ability to find like minds more easily online than in real life can either enhance the quality of our associations and generate civic renewal or breed ideologues and alienation. Groups that might otherwise have never found like minds can now form, for better or worse, over networks. The same communications technologies that can enable support groups for victims of rare diseases and marshal resources on their behalf can also put terrorists in touch with one another. Like minds can unite where once they were isolated. If hatred is the common cause of those so united, however, the results might be terrifyingly destructive. On the other hand, it is certainly possible that the ability of social deviants to find like minds, or even a good argument, in cyberspace will also act as a safety valve. As Thomas Erskine (1750-1823) said:

> When men can freely communicate their thoughts and their sufferings, real or imaginary, their passions spend themselves in air, like gunpowder scattered upon the surface—but pent up by terrors, they work unseen, burst forth in a moment, and destroy everything in their course. Let reason be opposed to reason, and argument to argument, and every good government will be safe.[7]

Even primitive bulletin board communication technologies proved their value to the Yeltsin faction during the Soviet putsch attempt of August 1991. The Soviet faction knew that its control of communications and transportation channels played a significant role in overthrowing the tsarist regime in 1917, so again in 1991, it secured those traditional channels. However, it failed to consider the impact of distributed forms of mass communications. I still remember reading with excitement the e-mail coming right from the Russian parliament building, describing Yeltsin's position, holding out hope, and rallying resistance. Interested parties in cyberspace quickly forwarded the messages around to friends, and it spread like wildfire. Yeltsin and friends were using fax machines, modems, and copiers to distribute information to the people and were receiving messages from such supporters as British Prime Minister John Major. Two years later when I visited a Moscow computer show in 1993, several of our guides and government officials spoke with pride of the role that cyberspace communications technology had played in bringing a more democratic form of government, via a form of free press, to the Russian people.

Will totalitarian governments be able to survive in an environment where the citizenry is informed by anyone with access to cyberspace? If the Russian example is any indication, it's highly unlikely, unless a technologically savvy dictator uses the ability to monitor and manipulate the bulletin boards world wide for surveillance and propaganda. Who knows? It is indeed a leap of faith to trust that power can be subdued by the goodwill and knowledge of an informed electorate—but a leap that has been made in the past to consistently positive results. The power will indeed accrue to the people if individuals seek ways to increase positive socialization, economic well-being, and civic virtue; after all, that process is the desired end of a functioning community.

Isolation vs. Cooperation

Robert Putnam struck a resonant chord with the publication of an article entitled "Bowling Alone: America's Declining Social Capital" in the January 1995 issue of *Journal of Democracy*. In the article, Putnam points to significant declines over the past few decades in voter turnout, participation in public meetings, trust in government, weekly churchgoing, union affiliation, Parent-Teacher Association (PTA) participation, League of Women Voters membership, Boy Scout and Red Cross volunteerism, and the activity of fraternal organizations. Those groups that have enjoyed significant increases in membership, such as the American Association of Retired Persons (AARP) or the Sierra Club, are less likely to demand actual socializing or networking. Putnam titled his article after the fact that even though the number of bowlers has increased since 1980, the number of those bowling in leagues decreased by 40 percent. Putnam pointed to a decline of the "vibrancy of American civil society," referring to a body of work by James S. Coleman and others in which "social capital" refers to features of social coordination such as "networks, norms, and social trust that facilitate coordination and cooperation for mutual benefit."[8]

Might cyberspace be a factor in the reverse of this decline in social capital? Although the simplicity of the WWW should be ideal to trigger such a reversal, the WWW seems currently to be based on a "surfing [the Net] alone" paradigm. Most of the collaborative communications during the 1990s have been occurring in newsgroups and commercial online services. Although there is nothing which would prevent collaboration on the WWW, it has been slow to arrive. It would be a tragedy if the dynamic socialization that occurred on a limited scale online during the 1980s gave way to a subsequent generation where the prevailing online experience is a solitary one because the prevailing cyberspace standards support isolation. Such a tragedy can be averted if we cooperate in the social and political process of encouraging the development of the appropriate technologies and standards supporting interactive socialization. When new technological tools are developed, by whatever company, that will make the creation and participation in virtual communities as easy as the creation and interaction with Web pages, a dramatic increase in social capital will almost certainly result.

Unfortunately, the same trends that Putnam observed may be working against such participation. What's more, competing special interests are making a new and modern music as each attempts to strike one key on the piano more loudly than others strike their key—with the resulting cacophony accepted uncritically as the price of diversity. Imagine instead what Chopin might have composed if there were a piano where each key had its own player. Trending towards individual and familial isolation and failure to cooperate might very well be a recipe for an increase in "poverty and backwardness," according to a work by Edward Banfield published in 1958. As he demonstrated, the underdevelopment of a community in Southern Italy could be traced to a culture of "amoral familism"—"Maximize the material, short-run advantage of the nuclear family; assume that all others will do likewise."[9]

Assume, for a moment, however, that enough concerned individuals can work together towards a single focused objective: encouraging the development of social capital in cyberspace. Could cyberspace itself then be used to enable an orderly revolution based on cooperative achievement? I believe such an outcome is not only possible, but likely.

The Virtue in Virtual

Since cyberspace affects not only our perspectives on physical reality but also our ability to communicate and share ideas, it is a powerful, if abstract, means of transforming cultures. Whether in the form of television, telephone, online communications, or any of the other transforming, enabling, perception-altering digital technologies, the leveraging power of cyberspace technologies can be liberating or destructive. The virtue in virtual rests not in the technologies or the structures themselves but in the positive cultural elements generated by those technologies and structures. Two of the most important of these elements are the absence of prejudice and the consequent facilitation of cooperation.

In a famous *New Yorker* cartoon, a dog with a paw on a computer keyboard turns to another and observes, "On the Internet, nobody knows you're a dog."[10] This is one of the greatest virtues of cyberspace: the traditional physical trappings of self are not manifest online and we can thus rise above the traditional constraints of physical appearance that often burden our judgments. We can loosen the bonds of prejudice. This unburdening is already occurring. There is a disproportionate share of journalists, writers, executives, and other opinion-makers online. It's no surprise—the benefits of cyberspace to those in the idea sciences are compelling. It's like tapping a mother lode of freely expressed sentiment, opinion, and information. Interestingly, now that so many have access, and that access is so relatively egalitarian, there seems to me to be more cooperation between journalists and other idea professionals.

In cyberspace, most participants either know or seem to have learned the importance of cooperation at a fundamental level. It's built into the structure of the Internet, bulletin boards, and most online services. An everyday event like sending an e-mail requires enormous (but automatic) cooperation. My system works with the telephone line which uses the phone company switches to tie to CompuServe while my software connects to CompuServe's software to hand off the e-mail, which e-mail is then routed through CompuServe's network onto the Internet, where other people's networks are used, without charge to me or CompuServe, to hand the e-mail from one router to another, until it eventually gets to its destination. Without the architectural cooperation built into the Internet, it simply wouldn't work. Even though the flame wars draw most of the attention in cyberspace, the sense of community and the willingness to share is far more common and seemingly second nature for most cybernauts. Just this morning, I received a thoughtful e-mail containing the details of how to cite online sources—from someone who had recently engaged me in a lively debate online over copyright issues. Judy wasn't trying to prove a point that related to the argument at hand—she was trying to be helpful in response to a request I had made. Therein lies the nature of the appeal of cyberspace, I believe, for most regulars. The sense of possibility derived from this new culture of cooperation and helpfulness is one of the most exciting human developments we expect to face in our lifetime. Never before have so many been brought together so easily. To me, this is the primary virtue to be found in the virtual.

Assumptions Worth Sharing

The reduction of prejudice and a renewal of cooperation may be the primary values required in order for an increase in social capital to become reality, but other widely held assumptions and values we must share include cooperation, harmony, peace, law and order, honesty, helping others, sharing, self-discipline, self-reliance, hard work, financial security, fairness and equality, a love for learning, open-mindedness, personal freedom and liberty, achievement, and freedom of conscience and expression.

So I see no reason that cyberspace shouldn't be given the chance to thrive by imbedding these core values right into its very structure—the servers, browsers, networks, agents, and protocols which act as spaces, gates, and fences. We should create mechanisms that enable more sharing and less competition. We should create simple mechanisms such as automated micromoney exchanges with extremely low overhead and uniform file and information exchange standards for all forms of data and value that would go a long way to making an economy based on ideas and their expression (as well as goods and services) much more feasible. We should encourage more choice and less coercion by building into cyberspace software such features as voting, anonymity controls and enabling (as appropriate), demographic targeting, copyright notification and tracking, security, and so on. We should imbed self-enforcing security into the whole of cyberspace, providing free-market mechanisms that reward or pay those who give and tax or charge those who take. We should strengthen the role of parents by encouraging them structurally to accompany their children into cyberspace.

There are simply no good reasons that we must agree to disagree on everything in order to avoid conflict. We simply need to unleash the creativity that already exists in cyberspace to solve the problems. Coordinated, moderated electronic discussion forums among some of the leading lights and experts of our day, sponsored by the Electronic Freedom Foundation or some other such group, might go a long way towards identifying the problems, the solutions, and the opportunities for dramatic progress through cooperation and considerate debate.

PITFALLS FACING A WIRED SOCIETY

I may be overly optimistic in my hope that others will agree with me that cooperation is better than competition. Even though I believe that the possibilities that cyberspace offers individuals outweigh the pitfalls facing individuals, I believe the pitfalls that threaten our societal cohesion and the foundations of shared values and assumptions might easily outweigh the possibilities facing society. As our societies become larger and more diverse, with competing values rather than the shared values of strong cultures, we may never recapture the unity more characteristic of smaller groups. Worse, we are more likely to choose unproductive and counter-productive values as individuals and small groups lose sight of the benefits of civic virtue or their ability to grasp those benefits.

Domination

Selfish zeal to control cyberspace, whether by any individual, group, or government, poses one of the primary threats to its culture of cooperation and its ability to contribute to social cohesion and civic virtue. Government seems to be rushing in, threatening to tighten online regulation in ways that would never be considered outside the misunderstood realms of cyberspace. Yet even before the government got involved, control and "ownership" have been hot issues in cyberspace. The meaning of "property" in such an abstract medium is still a matter of considerable discussion. On The WELL, for example, one value is that participants "own" their "own words." But how do we interpret ownership? Many in cyberspace seem to view *all* of their words and intellectual creations as valuable property that, even if they are shared freely and publicly, needs to be protected against copying, reuse, misappropriation, quoting out of context, republication, and so on.

For example, in one exchange on CANOPUS FORUM where I indicated my intention to quote from the exchange in this book, a debate over the interpretation of ownership ensued. The exchange triggered an outpouring that left me surprised. The outpouring wasn't focused on the issue of prejudice or incivility that I was seeking to highlight with the quote, but rather on the issue of control and ownership. Perhaps half a dozen individuals who jumped into the discussion truly believed that copyright gave them absolute control over every word of their online public statements, and that it grants them the right to prevent anyone from quoting them in a magazine article or book. Some seemingly ignored arguments that the fair use exemptions of copyright law in the United States protect selective quoting of individuals in order to protect free speech and the spread of ideas, which was arguably the original purpose of copyright law in the United States. Ironically, most ignored the fact that in most exchanges I've seen in cyberspace, selected quotes from the messages of others are freely and continuously used in new posts. Some claimed that there was an ethical prohibition against quoting because messages in such a forum are private, even arguing with the careful analysis of a law student who advised them that an online service was indeed a public place rather than a private one.[11] Some argued that even if it is legal to quote from posts, it is unethical to do so without permission, especially if the intent is to present another in a bad light.

The principles involved here are important. Because the competing objectives served are complex, copyright laws are complex. While the author of an e-mail message may "own" its content, there is a gray area concerning message threads in forums, which also could be owned in their totality by the respective sysops who participated in their creation and management or by the online services which provided the software by which the threads were created. The ownership of these threads and messages could also be covered by contract law, because they are specifically addressed in user agreements when a user signs up or agrees to be a sysop. Copyright protection is not a guarantee against someone else's saving in long-lasting computer file archives statements you wish you had never made.

Ironically, copyright law, privacy, and defamation are often used as the primary rationale for what I view as the attempt to control and suppress free speech by some of the very individuals who argue that free speech is inviolate. Is copyright law then a threat to the principles of free speech? I would argue that, if it isn't already, it could very well become a tool of the competitive corporate and media cultures to do exactly that. The United States Constitution originally granted the federal government the authority "to promote the Progress of Science and useful Arts, by securing for limited Times to Authors and Inventors the exclusive Right to their respective Writings and discoveries."[12] The intention seems clear—to promote intellectual and cultural progress through the protection of creative works for a limited period of time. The Supreme Court has said that "the copyright law, like the patent statutes, makes reward to the owner a secondary consideration. . . . the primary object in conferring the monopoly lie in the general benefits derived by the public."[13] In the Copyright Act of 1909, Congress also had this to say:

> The enactment of copyright legislation by Congress under the terms of the Constitution is not based upon any natural right that the author has in his writings, . . . but upon the ground that the welfare of the public will be served and progress of science and useful arts will be promoted by securing to authors for limited periods the exclusive rights to their writings.[14]

It is therefore difficult to reconcile the public welfare with proposals to expand the application of copyright protection to further restrict the spread of useful information and ideas, especially when that information has little or no economic value. Copyright law should not be so complex and restrictive that an average individual can't understand how it serves useful public and societal purposes.

Efforts to control words and ideas, from whatever source, outside the publicly beneficial purposes of copyright law and a desire to be quoted correctly and in context, represent a serious threat to the free exchange of ideas in cyberspace. Individuals should not be constantly concerned that they are infringing on the copyrights of others when their intentions are simply to facilitate the spread of ideas. It might even be argued that in cyberspace, neither ideas nor words nor their distribution should be controlled or afforded any more protection than technology can provide. Consider the views of George Washington:

> For if Men are to be precluded from offering their sentiments on a matter, which may involve the most serious and alarming consequences, that can invite the consideration of Mankind, reason is of no use to us; the freedom of speech may be taken away, and, dumb and silent we may be led, like sheep, to the slaughter.[15]

or Adlai Stevenson:

> I yield to no man in my belief in the principle of free debate, inside or outside the halls of Congress. The sound of tireless voices is the price we pay for the right to hear the music of our own opinions. But there is also, it seems to me, a moment at which democracy must prove its capacity to act. Every man has a right to be heard; but no man has the right to strangle democracy with a single set of vocal cords.[16]

One particularly dramatic example of how copyright law can be used to control publicly valuable information and data and thus thwart the purposes of free speech involves the privatization of law citations. Even though legal decisions are public domain—owned by citizens—a single publisher, West Publishing of Eagan, Minnesota, has been able to establish its page-number citation system for all circuit and district court decisions as the standard used by almost all courts and lawyers. Court decisions are cited based on the copyrighted page numbering scheme maintained by West Publishing, and the courts held that anyone publishing the decisions using an identical page number scheme was infringing on West Publishing's copyrights.[17] In other words, there is no widely adopted, open public standard for referencing the law. It's almost as if the chapter and verse numbers of the Bible (as opposed to the text or translation of the Bible) could be copyrighted and controlled by the Vatican, and no one could publish a version of the Bible using the standard chapter and verse numbers without infringing on the copyright of the Roman Catholic Church. Thankfully, no such copyright on the system of referencing the Bible actually exists—and there is no confusion or ambiguity when anyone of any faith or persuasion references a standard Bible book, chapter, and verse. In referencing certain key portions of United States law, however, the fact that the standard referencing scheme could be copyrighted thwarted, not furthered, the purposes of free distribution of valuable information. Providing the public domain court decisions to the public in a form that could be referenced using the standard referencing format was prevented by interpretation of copyright law, and therefore the text of the law itself was essentially unavailable outside libraries and the offices of lawyers. The increase in popularity of cyberspace as a research medium, however, has brought attention to this particular issue. In early 1995, a task force of the American Association of Law libraries issued a report examining the issue and offering recommendations for a new system of citation based on "case name, year of decision, court, opinion number, and, where a pinpoint citation is needed, paragraph number."[18] Dissenters to the conclusions pointed to the potential for disruption to the legal profession that would result from the "balkanization" of reference formats and the failure of such a citation system to actually help readers find the referenced source. The potential for confusion is highlighted by the fact that the American Bar Association also appointed a "Committee on Citation Issues" to study the problem.[19]

The lack of a standard citation system and the control exercised by a private company means that individuals wishing to access and use the law, which is public domain, have no acceptable way to reference their findings to a judge or lawyer or anyone else until alternate citation proposals are widely accepted. West can't be blamed for attempting to assert and retain such control—but the government and the courts should be held accountable for failing to establish publicly owned standards and allowing West to control the information and thus serve narrow financial interests rather than the more valuable public interest.

Pamela Samuelson, John Perry Barlow, Esther Dyson, and other cyberspace visionaries argue that we must fundamentally reexamine the nature of intellectual property as it applies to cyberspace. They have each written, for *Wired Magazine*, of the stimulating challenges cyberspace presents to copyright law and its foundations. Barlow argues that Thomas Jefferson and those who provided the framework for copyright law in the United States did so as a practical necessity in order to maximize the availability of ideas, not private rights to control ideas or profit from them.[20] Barlow quotes Jefferson:

> That ideas should freely spread from one to another over the globe, for the moral and mutual instruction of man, and improvement of his condition, seems to have been peculiarly and benevolently designed by nature, when she made them, like fire, expansible over all space, without lessening their density at any point, and like the air in which we breathe, move, and have our physical being, incapable of confinement or exclusive appropriation. Inventions then cannot, in nature, be subject of property.[21]

In Jefferson's day, the spread of ideas was aided significantly if the ideas were captured physically on the primary medium of that time—the printed page. In order to ensure the widest possible distribution of ideas, the creator was granted the right to publish, control, and profit from the creation of copies and to ensure the integrity of the original work. Today, however, when copies that are perfect replicas of the original (song, writings, video, audio, pictures, etc.) can be accomplished so easily and cheaply, the nature of copyright in relation to its original purpose has changed. Besides encouraging the spread of new and valuable ideas for the benefit of all, copyright law is now also limiting their spread to those who can afford the price of consumption, for the benefit of the wealthy who control the means of distribution and the mass media. I believe the result has been a weakening of respect for copyright law and intellectual property. Bootleggers are ignoring copyright laws. Ordinary citizens and the courts are beginning to interpret "fair use" more broadly. Copyright law is becoming more difficult to enforce. Government attempts to tighten control over the expression of ideas by passing more restrictive copyright laws only serve to invite further noncompliance. As Barlow says, "the increasing difficulty in enforcing copyright and patent laws is already placing in peril the ultimate source of intellectual property—the free exchange of ideas."[22]

Radical new ideas and perspectives surrounding the very nature and value of information and creative endeavor are required in order to avoid drifting away from the original importance placed on ideas and their spread by the Founding Fathers.

Esther Dyson, also one of the intellectual giants of the digital age, argues that "intellectual property in a Net-based economy can lose its value," and that although this "horrifies most owners and creators, . . . they'd better get over it." Like Barlow, Dyson recognizes that controlling the distribution of copies is no longer practical or even desirable. Dyson, however, takes a more practical, economic approach to the coming clash between those who would tighten the controls of intellectual property law and those who believe, as I do, that we must modify the law to conform to the realities of cyberspace without abandoning the original intent of copyright law in the United States. Dyson says that "in the new communities of the Net, the intrinsic value of content generally will remain high, but most individual items will have a short commercial half-life. . . . The problem for providers of intellectual property in the future is this: although under law they will be able to control the pricing of their own products, they will operate in an increasingly competitive marketplace where much of the intellectual property is distributed free and suppliers explode in number."[23] The implications are significant: relationships with customers and the reputation of creators of content will increase in economic value. Traditional means of "winning through intimidation," domination, and control will be less effective in such an environment.

The possibility of free information, the free sharing of ideas and content, and the economic impact of these developments will be explored further in the next chapter, but for now suffice it to say that a reexamination of the laws dealing with intellectual property is inevitable.

I should point out that creators of content should retain some level of control of their respective works. Most of the best books, films, and music simply don't appear on the Net, and won't until the creators put them there. There is little incentive for anyone but counterfeiters to digitize those works from another medium. Even with existing copyright law and economic models, it is economically feasible to physically distribute content through controlled and rationed channels while the value is highest, and gradually reduce the cost of distribution and broaden the channels as the value of the content decreases. Most books are first sold in hardback for a price of about twenty dollars, then in paperback at about ten dollars, then at larger discounts, and finally end up as either worthless and out-of-print or a classic, available at Wal-Mart in paperback, two for a dollar. Movies start out in theaters for $5-$8 per ticket, move to discount theaters at $1-$3 per ticket, pay-per-view for $3-$4 per showing, video for $1-2 per rental, and eventually end up gathering dust at Blockbusters. There is little reason that the Net couldn't be used to extract the last bit of marginal profit from aging works as a natural progression down the value curve.

Unfortunately, this natural economic progression could be thwarted by excessive legislatively control. Rather than working to relax copyright law consistent with the natural trends, lawmakers are moving in the direction of increasing restrictions and control. According to Vinton G. Cerf, MCI Senior Vice President and cofounder of the Internet, "Legislation pending in Congress could change the Copyright Act and bring the new and ever expanding Information Superhighway to a crawl. If this legislation is passed in its current version, companies like MCI that provide access to the Internet may be forced simply to stop providing information services or dramatically raise prices to cover their liability that would put Internet access out of the reach of many Americans."[24]

Copyright law isn't the only area of law where ignorance of cyberspace trends, philosophy, culture, and technology is causing havoc through unwarranted attempts to dominate and control. Less than a decade ago in the 1980s, cyberspace was virgin territory. Few precedents existed. Steve Jackson became a cause célèbre in 1990 when federal agents, acting more like jackbooted thugs than law enforcement officers, confiscated the computers of Steve Jackson Games in Austin, Texas, with no more cause than the fact that Jackson was running a BBS supporting his role-playing games business that was suspected of harboring illicit information. Whether Jackson was aware of the information on his board (which later proved to be fictional accounts of hacking activities related to Jackson's games) seemed irrelevant to the investigators, who seemed to assume that anyone hosting a bulletin board must be a coconspirator with anyone using such a board for illegal purposes. Jackson prevailed in court and those who had raided his business were given a very firm legal slap on the wrists.

Today, the courts are still struggling with numerous thorny problems relating to control. One is whether online services are publishers or service providers and thus whether they can be held liable for the defamation and copyright infringements of members and customers. Another is that the laws and standards of one jurisdiction are used to convict those in other jurisdictions. Federal law is brought into play because cyberspace communications are oblivious to state boundaries—yet it should be apparent that, by the same reasoning, international law should be applied. The fact is, arguments from lawyers and libertarians notwithstanding, we need new laws altogether in many areas. Even determining where any given cyberspace case should be pursued is still moot.

The struggle for control of cyberspace isn't going away anytime soon. Everyone has an interest, from international agencies to national governments to local governments, from large corporations to local proprietorships, from creators of information to consumers of information. Especially in the area of intellectual property, we cannot afford to permit the domination of cyberspace by those who would squelch the free exchange of ideas with onerous and controlling laws that serve special interests at the expense of the general public.

Escape from Social Accountability

Cyberspace as it exists today offers escape from social accountability. The relative anonymity and illusion of isolation offered when we deal with human beings as if they were words on a screen leads to a variety of socially irresponsible behaviors. Defamation and carelessness with the reputation of others seems almost commonplace online. Violations of privacy and decency are far more common in virtual worlds than in the real world. Many associate cyberspace with the "hacker" culture of existential amorality—breaking into computers just for the fun and the challenge of it. The media sometimes paint a dark and disturbing picture of social misfits engaged in the dark pursuit of violation. Cyberspace is considered a dangerous place for children. Anonymity encourages irresponsibility. These aspects of cyberspace born of the relative lack of social accountability threatens the social benefits that might otherwise come from cyberspace. On the whole, cyberspace could benefit significantly from more secure structural constraints that enforce personal accountability in cyberspace.

The dilemma is that much of the success of cyberspace to date has been based on the lack of such constraints. Secure networks have traditionally been more expensive and limited in acceptance than more open networks.

While IBM and other companies have spent decades building highly secure global networks based on IBM's Systems Network Architecture (SNA), the market for such networks proved to be those commercial and government enterprises that depend on secure transmission of "mission critical" information—the lifeblood of business. IBM's failure to recognize the power and appeal of the "personal" in personal computing led IBM to also miss its opportunity to lead the world into a more secure cyberspace—although it isn't likely that the Internet as we know it could have ever developed under the assumptions that prompted secure networks in the first place.

The Internet, on the other hand, began as an experimental project funded by the military to develop a robust means of information exchange under any set of conditions, and became a revolutionary insurgency intent on exploring the frontiers of human interaction and the quest for pure knowledge. This community has attracted millions of users in the last decade. One of the primary attractions of the Internet has been it's considerable flexibility, which empowers users in ways no centrally controlled, secure network has before. Internet users can learn to participate in newsgroups and mailing lists, log onto other systems, browse files on other systems, obtain Internet addresses (including domain names such as ibm.com or usa.net), extend the network by providing access to new users, establish World Wide Web home pages, and much more. The only limitations are technical know-how and the finances necessary to purchase the hardware, software, and services—and even those financial costs are lower than they could be, because the Internet has been traditionally subsidized by the U.S. government and other providers of the network nodes and connections.

Although personal physical safety is enhanced when greater social interaction occurs in cyberspace, social accountability is weakened by insecure networks. Cooperation is enhanced when we trust those we work with, but it is more difficult to know and trust those we work with in cyberspace without reliable means to accomplish such simple tasks as verifying identity to tie a person to the real world for the purposes of legal accountability, entering into contracts, engaging in cash transactions, and exchanging personal and confidential information with the assurance of privacy. Without unobtrusive security built into the systems we use, we cannot expect cyberspace communities and civic virtue to be as strong, vibrant, or rewarding as real-world communities. Security cannot, therefore, be ignored or refused:

it must be applied wisely to facilitate trust. When applied too strictly, however, it demeans and undermines the pillars of community, trust, and cooperation—when applied not at all; it makes community impossible. Unless we find the balance, cyberspace could indeed be more destructive of our sense of community and social systems than constructive.

New Views of Vice

As I've come face to face with a variety of ideas in cyberspace that oppose many of my own, I've realized that I'm witnessing society's reconsideration of what constitutes vice. *Webster's Dictionary* defines vice as a moral depravity of corruption, an evil habit, a degrading practice, a moral fault or failing, or sexual immorality. In cyberspace, I've found many who argue that pornography, no matter how obscene, is as harmless and healthy as art or sex—a victimless crime. With state-sponsored lotteries and more and more regions legalizing gambling, gambling seems to be more generally accepted as well. We seem to have made celebrities of a strange sort of the Mayflower Madam, Heidi Fleiss, Martin Sheen, Hugh Grant, Divine Brown, Sherry Rowlands, and many others who have provided or purchased the services of prostitutes—shame seems to be anachronistic. I was first exposed, in cyberspace, to these surprising revisionist notions of vice in the fall of 1992. Robin Raskin, then an editor at *PC Magazine*, had asked for readers' opinions in an online forum about its then-regular ads for adult CD-ROMs. I responded to her query with my opinion that her magazine, found in many homes including mine, would be best served by a policy that excluded tasteless ads for sexually explicit material. I knew that such an opinion would incite a discussion and was prepared for some controversy, but I was little prepared for the brouhaha that ensued. There were venomous outpourings of personal criticism and a sustained willingness of some to argue in favor of pornography as well as for a liberal advertising policy—even to the point of asserting that porn has no negative social consequences, i.e. that there is no evidence that pornography contributes to or is even slightly associated with, for example, the degradation of women or pedophilia. Arguments that pornography demeans women were rebutted not only by males, but also by a few women. My protestations that children could be harmed by freely available pornography were met with admonitions to step up to the task of being a good parent and to quit attempting to shift that responsibility to others. Many argued that snuff porn (images of actual death and dismemberment) didn't exist, that the problem with child porn is deliberately overstated by blue-nosed conservatives, that pornography is no one's business since it affects no one but consenting adults, and that feminists and the religious right are way out of line to say that pornography is wrong or immoral and thus attempt to legislate morality.

One of those who argued unemotionally and with great intelligence on the issue had been a regular and much respected contributor to many of the forums I frequented. Even though I sometimes disagreed with this man, I considered him a voice of reason who often made astute observations on both sides of an issue. I had even met and had dinner with him at a "Pizza Madness" dinner party in New York in June of 1992, and had found him to be thoughtful and intelligent. I had often enjoyed and profited from my exchanges with this man, both public and private; so when I logged on for the first time in the new year, 1993, I was stunned to see a posting with the news that he had been murdered—shot by a robber trying to make an escape through a Times Square porn shop. I was stunned by the coincidence and irony.

Since then, I've realized that pornography is a seriously divisive emotional issue. Nothing seems to fire the printing presses like stories of erotica and pornography in cyberspace and the related legal and legislative struggles.

In a June 1994 editorial, *Boardwatch Magazine's* editor, Jack Rickard, commented on the 1994 conviction and sentencing of BBS operator Tony Davis to 35 years and $25,000 for violation of 5 counts related to the distribution and possession of obscene materials by an Oklahoma City jury. Comparing that conviction to the trials of the Menendez brothers and Jeffrey Dahmer, Rickard wrote: "We are not on a slippery slope of freedom lost. We now live in and at the largesse and behest of precisely the kind of totalitarian, authoritarian, monolithic 'state' evil empire so many Americans fought and died to prevent. It is corrupt, venal, and evil. You will be more severely punished for what you say, or what pictures you view, than you will for serial murder."[25]

The release of a study entitled "Marketing Pornography on the Information Superhighway: A Survey of 917,410 Images, Descriptions, Short Stories, and Animations Downloaded 8.5 Million Times by Consumers in Over 2,000 Cities in Forty Countries, Provinces, and Territories" (whew!) was one of those triggers. The study, which has since been discredited, was released by a research team, led by Martin Rimm, at Carnegie Mellon in June 1995 (not long after the Senate approved the Exon amendment, which banned indecent material from cyberspace), and was followed by a flurry of related stories. Journalists and broadcasters jumped on the conclusions of the study and soon it might have seemed to the inexperienced that there was little BUT pornography to be found in cyberspace.

Newsweek ran an article entitled "No Place For Kids? A Parents Guide to Sex on the Net." Steven Levy, a respected writer in cyberspace, said of the Carnegie Mellon study,

> [Rimm] provides solid evidence that there's loads of hard-core stuff in cyberspace. Rimm wrote a computer program to analyze descriptions of 917,410 dirty pictures (he examined about 10,0000 actual descriptions). His conclusion: "I think there's almost no question that we're seeing an unprecedented availability and demand of material like sadomasochism, bestiality, vaginal and rectal fisting, eroticized urination . . . and pedophilia."[26]

That same week, the cover of *Time Magazine* featured a photo of an eerily pale wide-eyed pre-pubescent boy, fingers on a keyboard, face awash in the monitor's glow, looking as if he had accidentally stumbled upon something unexpected and shocking. Inside, the cover article by Philip Elmer-Dewitt is accompanied by a naked man shown sitting on a keyboard embracing, with both arms and legs, a glowing computer.[27] In a sidebar describing "The Marquis de Cyberspace," *Time* deftly complimented Robert Thomas, in jail, for his "flair for marketing." Thomas had earned over $800,000 for gathering, labeling, and marketing thousands of pictures of bestiality, sado-masochism, nude children, and other such material for his BBS, which he had portrayed as "the nastiest place on earth."

This article caused a furor in cyberspace. Elmer-DeWitt was ferociously attacked by individuals who charged that his article contributed to the cause of Internet censorship and created the impression that the Internet was nothing but a pornographic cesspool. These online critics blasted *Time* for its uncritical publication of the article, thereby strengthening public opinion against the continuance of cyberspace as an unregulated frontier. Mike Godwin, legal counsel for the Electronic Frontier Foundation, was particularly vocal in voicing his disapproval—claiming that he had been "betrayed" by Elmer-Dewitt, who in turn claimed that Godwin was a "professional lobbyist" on an "orchestrated campaign" to discredit Elmer-Dewitt and the Rimm study. Elmer-Dewitt said, "This may be self-serving, but it feels like poor Marty Rimm is being lynched here. He's not getting a fair trial; his study's not getting a fair trial. Mike Godwin has organized an attack, and there are precious few voices that are not already prejudiced to one side."[28]

Brock Meeks revealed that Marty Rimm had obtained an ISBN for a self-published, 64-page book named *The Pornographers Handbook: How to Exploit Women, Dupe Men & Make Lots of Money*. The Carnegie Mellon study was ambiguous enough to serve the various purposes of pornographers, feminists, legislators, journalists, and libertarians.[29] Although many of the critical attacks on the study were indeed justified, many of the attacks on the study, Rimm, and the conclusion that pornography in cyberspace represents a serious problem were unfortunately characterized by speculation, ad hominem arguments, and character assassination. Consider the concluding paragraph in the chapter in *Sex, Laws, and Cyberspace* titled "The Barnum of Cyberspace."

> Mike Godwin had the last word on Rimm by saying 'The more you research Rimm, the more a portrait emerges of someone wily, subtle, glib, manipulative. Even when he tells you he's being totally honest, totally frank, you have this lurking feeling that below the surface he's calculating the precise effect his choice of words—both his admissions and omissions—will have on you.

Whether that statement accurately portrays Rimm, it is clearly representative of the battle over pornography in cyberspace, where personal judgment and opinion are often given greater weight (the last word?) than the facts and truths we should be using as a base for policy.

The issue of pornography is tough to discuss online. I've often seen that those who side with the laws outlawing obscenity or with law enforcement officials seeking to track and snare offenders are often attacked using appeals to emotion, labeling, and sophistry. When it appeared likely that Senator Exon would succeed in imposing constraints on cyberspace speech, many online denizens began to urge the substitution of various politician's names for profanities in posts, yielding arguments like, for example, "That Exoning Exon Amendment is the most outrageous, stinking piece of Leahy legislation that this Exoning country has ever produced." When Brock Meeks titled a column in *Wired* "The Obscenity of Decency," he reflected similar disdain for those holding opposing views.[30] Most online participants know better than to waste too much time arguing about pornography in cyberspace—civil argument even with those who otherwise routinely engage in civil arguments is often all but impossible on this subject.

Yet it is difficult to tell whether those who argue so fervently in favor of pornography represent a loud political minority or a groundswell change in our societal attitudes towards vice. The Communications Decency Act, even though unconstitutional, passed with overwhelming bipartisan support. A "blue ribbon campaign" designed to show the extent of support for "free speech" (opposition to the CDA) by "blacking out" the background on Web sites—a fairly trivial technical matter—apparently garnered support from less than 15 percent of the Web sites, according to personal observation and at least one reasonably supported estimate.[31]

Many net denizens believe that the public is being brainwashed about the amount of pornography in cyberspace and is thus unwilling to support legislation for tighter controls on indecency and pornography. They point to statements from the National Center for Missing and Exploited Children that fewer than twenty children are known to have been affected by cyberspace-related incidents. They argue that pornography is difficult to stumble across and even tougher to download and view, and that you aren't likely to confront pornographic material unless you go looking for it. That was essentially true until just after the CDA was declared unconstitutional—in my many years in cyberspace, I had encountered pornography only twice. Recently, however, it seems to be proliferating on the WWW. A recent search I did on PICS yielded hundreds of sites with descriptions that bordered on the pornographic. Given the point-and-click nature of the WWW, anyone with unrestricted access to the Internet has immediate access to a wide variety of free pornography.

Pornography is neither ubiquitous in cyberspace nor an artificially created issue. It is simply a serious societal problem demanding attention. The stakes are high for parents and the producers and consumers of pornography alike. Lance Rose, cyberspace legal authority and author of NETLAW, reported in *Boardwatch Magazine* in November 1992 that many bulletin board sysops attending the ONE BBS CON sysops convention that August in Denver "wanted a magic formula, a rule of thumb, to help them feel a little more secure against the possibility of being busted by the vice squad" and that they were puzzled and concerned over antiobscenity laws. He noted that "adult materials are practically a sure ticket to financial success" for commercial bulletin boards and that many sysops thus had a difficult time accepting the fact that those boards which dealt in hard core pornography were "at some risk of being raided and shut down at any time." According to Rose, these sysops argued that since they hadn't heard from the police, they must be OK. "What had me stumped," wrote Rose, "was how these people could see the screen displays of their BBS computer systems with their heads in the sand."[32]

That same issue included dozens of pictures from ONE BBS CON, including one picture, of a couple of ordinary guys standing in the midst of a dozen or so who were seated, with the rather chilling caption: "Pete White and Tony Davis (center) with Friends—Ain't this fun. . . ." Chilling because, two short years later, the smiling Tony Davis found himself convicted of 5 counts related to the distribution and possession of obscene materials by an Oklahoma City jury and sentenced to 35 years in prison. Although I believe that sentence is an injustice, what is clear is that confusion regarding the law and pornography can have a high price.

There is a need for standards that are clearer and more useful. Few outside the pornography business would disagree, I hope, that the predatory forms of pornography are obscene and rightly illegal. The right of free speech has often been, but must not be, confused with absolute license of expression. The commission of a crime, even in the process of expression and the creation of art, is criminal per se. It is easy to equate suppression and censorship in any form with totalitarianism and fascism; but we must not abandon the protection and promotion of innocence and decency. The importance of moderation and balance in understanding true and important principles such as free speech cannot be neglected except to our harm. Yet this issue has broader societal implications than might be evident if the only yardstick we use to measure its import is how much of it we must accept in order to protect free speech.

Traditionally, pornography has been seen as wrong and judged illegal based on whether or not it offended public sensibilities and community standards. It can be argued that pornography is a biased, often unrealistic, public expression of the ultimately private, personal and even, to many, sacred. The flaw in the arguments of pornography defenders is that they aren't defending healthy, joyous, affirming sexuality—they are, more often than not, demeaning it by endorsing distorted substitutes. However, under this view, the laws against obscenity have progressively lost their strength as the standards of communities change.

Attracting increasing attention are the views on pornography articulated by persuasive feminists such as Catharine A. MacKinnon and Andrea Dworkin of the University of Michigan.

> Pornography sexualizes inequality and the hatred of women so that men get sexual pleasure from hurting women and putting women down. It creates bigotry and aggression. It desensitizes men to rape and other forms of sexual violence against women so that they do not recognize the violence as violence, or they believe the women provoked and enjoyed it. Pornography is used as a blueprint for sadism, rape, and torture.[33]

This view of pornography as sexism and exploitation could trigger a redefinition of the standards and references by which we judge its legality. We could conceivably move from a standard rooted in community values toward a standard rooted in the harm pornography does to women and their civil rights. Claims that pornography is harmful to society are supported by research. As noted by Steven Hill and Nina Silver,

> Opponents of the Ordinance [which would redefine pornography as obscene based on whether it subordinates, degrades, or dehumanizes

women] inevitably claim that there is no scientific evidence of the connection between "unreal" pornography and violence against women in the "real" world, but this claim is untrue. There have been hundreds of such studies, and the results of some of the most comprehensive of these studies have been published in books like *Pornography and Sexual Aggression* edited by Dr. Neil Malamuth and Dr. Edward Donnerstein (New York: Academic Press, 1984) and *Connections Between Sex and Aggression* by Dolf Zillman (Hillsdale, New Jersey: Lawrence Erlbaum Associates, 1984) and in the work of sociologist Dr. Diana Russell (see "Pornography and Rape: A Causal Model" by Russell in *Political Psychology*, Vol. 9, No. 1, 1988).[34]

These documented effects of pornography include decreased sensitivity towards violence to women, increased acceptance of the idea that women "enjoy" rape, increases in the stated willingness of males to commit rape if assured that there would be no negative consequences such as prosecution, a distortion in the development of healthy attitudes towards sexuality by younger men, and decreases in feelings of guilt or accountability for replicating the behaviors seen in pornographic books or images.[35]

Cyberspace may yet play an unexpected role in actually reducing the availability of pornography. Awareness of the harmful effects of pornography might be increased as a result of Web pages such as the ones I found detailing the research. Discussions of pornography might be changed if the focus is shifted from a civil libertarian approach that emphasizes free speech to one that emphasizes its harmful effects. The controversies triggered by the availability of hardcore porn in the public spaces of cyberspace as the conflicts over the Communications Decency Act and similar legislation escalate could lead to a national referendum on pornography under the terms of a redefined debate.

In addition to the issue of Constitutionality, those who argue against such laws as the CDA make a point that cannot be ignored: government censorship and a ban of all adult material on the net is as unenforceable, unrealistic, and intrusive as laws that attempt to govern private sexual behaviors. Even the technology that lends the Internet its "power-to-the-people" flexibility makes enforcement of such total bans at least as difficult to enforce as bans on illicit drugs. John Gilmore's statement that "the Net interprets censorship as damage and routes around it" is true enough that policy makers would be wise to consider alternatives (such as the development of "public" and "private" spaces in cyberspace, each labeled as to content and purpose), which will be more effective and less offensive than outright bans and censorship.

Erotica and pornography take several forms on the Net—each of which should be considered separately. Unfortunately, they are often lumped together into one category: cyberporn. Some of these forms include

- private chats, where two individuals online engage in concurrent erotic exchange, exchanging "written sex" in real time.
- e-mail exchanges, where two individuals engage in erotic exchanges over longer periods of time, but not concurrently.
- libraries of pornographic images and writings available to be downloaded.
- forums, where sexual matters are discussed by forum participants and are available for perusal by anyone who chooses to access the forum or newsgroup.
- multimedia Web pages with pornographic images, audio, text, and video, including real-time visual exchange.

Note that private chats and e-mail exchanges are similar in almost every way to private conversations and mail. It would be just as offensive to free speech and privacy to attempt to regulate and enforce the on-line forms of private exchanges between individuals as it would be to legislate against the usual forms. Yet the libraries, forums or newsgroups, and Web pages are essentially more publicly accessible and unrestricted than any real-world library. Children and teenagers who have unrestricted access to the Internet now have free access to sexually explicit material that would almost certainly be declared illegal by most community standards. If the Internet is to achieve its potential, such material should not be so readily accessible, consistent with current public practices in other media and public places.

Technologies such as PICS should be employed to register spaces in cyberspace (such as locations on Usenet and the WWW) for content of various types (language, violence, adult sexuality, etc.). Then, one of two approaches could be adopted. Under the first approach, the list would be used to allow access only to those who actively pursue the access. For example, a "password key" could be required for access to any of these restricted locations. This "key" could be obtained through a process that confirms the age of the requester somehow. This method is opposed by many who argue that it eliminates one of the key "benefits" of online porn—the ability to obtain it anonymously. Philosophically, though, I would side with those who assert that if you would be ashamed if someone knew what you're doing, then you shouldn't be doing it.

Under the second approach, a list of such spaces could be maintained and used to allow parents to restrict access to them. This is roughly the approach proposed by those in favor of filtering as a means of controlling access to pornography. I think this approach is backwards—because it assumes that parents must place blinders on their children before allowing them to explore. The first approach is more consistent with current societal standards: children should be safe in a public place, and if adults wish to pursue adult interests, they are free to do so by leaving the public space and entering private places that restrict access to adults.

I've highlighted the issue of pornography in this section on vice because it has attracted the most attention and seems to be one of the most divisive issues. Similarly, though, I expect that society will need to come to grips with other vices, such as gambling, drugs, and prostitution. Our societal ambivalence towards gambling coupled with the unenforceability of territorial boundaries in cyberspace could lead to a vast gambling underground. Secure, encrypted communications between users, dealers, and international suppliers in cyberspace could facilitate the availability and use of drugs in ways that could make the public defiance of the prohibition of alcoholic beverages from 1920 to 1933 look mild in comparison. Similarly, if we prosecute prostitutes one week and make them celebrities the next, we need to be prepared to see cyberspace used to advertise and negotiate both the availability and the celebrity of prostitution.

Once again, I emphasize the importance of personal discipline and excellence. Children must be taught—hopefully by parents—the shared values by which we determine the protective laws necessary, at a minimum, to preserve peace and harmony in society. Cyberspace communication technologies already make available to children large numbers of voices competing unconsciously with the voices of parents, swaying impressionable youth as never before. Although no voice outside the home can effectively compete with the voices of loving parents, not all homes have loving parents. For some children, others will probably replace parents as the primary conveyers of values. It is incumbent upon the voice of society, therefore, to promulgate positive family values, even in a pluralistic society. Those shared societal values need to be transplanted in cyberspace.

Teetering on the Brink

For many years, with the Internet serving as the bastion of the academic research community, the online arena of cyberspace seemed rather insignificant and was mostly ignored by the mainstream press, politicians, law enforcement, and business. Now, however, we are beginning to face the difficult task of playing catch-up; but the terms of the debate have often been dominated by those who speak up most loudly. Sometime in the next few years, when the cable and telephone companies iron out the kinks, and the television becomes a cyberspace access device, and the point-and-click simplicity of the World Wide Web is available through a television set or a $500 box-and-screen-with-keyboard-and-pointing-device (whatever we call it), and unlimited access to cyberspace costs about $10 per month or less— then the rush to cyberspace will begin in earnest. If we're not ready by then, it will be too late. The cow trails of culture and community we're creating now will be worn from so much use that the only sensible thing to do will be to pave them—and if those cow trails lead in circles or to cultural or moral gridlock, our once-great society could face more fundamental challenges and chaos than ever before. We are teetering on that brink. The balance of powers that was designed to prevent the growth of the power of a centralized, federal government at times seems to have become a gridlock preventing the reduction of that power.

At times it seems that only one bond—the Constitution of the United States of America—holds us together as a society. Even when the melting pot seems to be boiling over with a stew of competing interests, no one argues that we start over and draft a more modern version of the Constitution. It has stood as an inspired document that informs all that we do as a society. And now we face new challenges and threats to our Constitutional republic: cyberspace will, I'm sure, unleash societal forces that will shake our institutions and government to their very foundations.

Our strength is that protecting the Constitution seems to be our common objective. Our weakness is that many take it for granted and forget what is required of us to defend the good that it represents and why it is important. In online debates, I often see the Constitution used as a club by the poorly informed, rather than as the fundamental source of societal authority. "So you would deprive me of my Constitutional rights to do whatever I please? Well, off with your head and go to hell!" Such wholly selfish arguments undermine the primary goal of the Constitution to provide for the common good—the orderly functioning of society and government.

The more of us who neglect, misunderstand, or abuse the Constitution, the nearer we are to that brink. On a trip to Russia in June of 1993, I saw firsthand how fragile the welfare of a society can be. The critical importance of information and shared purpose was never more evident. The decisions of the government were made behind the walls of the Kremlin, and their impact on the lives of the people was out of the people's hands— even though they had made the transition to democracy. Ordinary people had little but rumor, hearsay, and a free press still in diapers to help them sort out the choices facing them. Pensioners had seen their savings and retirement allowances vanish in the rampant inflation. We Americans could literally purchase a month's worth of work from Russian artisans for $50 without dickering or $10 if you pushed. The streets were filled with people hoping to sell cherished possessions and heirlooms to put food on the table.

One realized that enormous economic opportunity existed in Russia, but that necessary, reliable information was indeed one of the most valued and scarce of commodities. The black market flourished. There were significant differences between the exchange rates quoted on the street and in the banks, enabling savvy and aggressive young men to make a living doing nothing but buying and selling currency. Prices even of commodities fluctuated wildly. At a Moscow flea market, I was able to purchase a silver-dollar sized coin from the time of the tsars for five American dollars—probably less than the value of the silver it contained. Information on such basics as commodity prices seemed to be simply unavailable. There was a conspicuous absence of information sources that many of us might take for granted, such as catalogs or magazines. They were no longer teetering on the brink—they had fallen. It was obvious that they were struggling to deal with the dissolution of a strong government as much as the aftereffects of decades of suppression of free speech and a free press. They had grown up believing that the profit motive was evil, and many had come to accept the status quo of seeking only that information which was approved. There was little evident cooperation except among the well-educated. The culture of cooperation was latent. Children fought one another for your attention. Owners of cars kept their windshield wipers locked in their cars, putting them on only when it began to rain, to avoid theft.

The magnitude of the positive effects of our cultural bias for civic cooperation, virtue, and our Constitutional emphasis on free speech and freedom of the press cannot be overstated. Yet that same emphasis (as opposed to the effects) can be and often is overstated. In the name of promoting free speech, we often protect and promote those evils which undermine civic virtue to our own harm. Although we must tolerate enormous differences in political opinion, and even much that is angry, asinine, abusive, and wrong, we need not tolerate everything evil and treacherous in the name of free speech. There is a line, even in the law—a line drawn at the point where there exists a clear and present danger or threat to the purposes of the Constitution. As articulated by Oliver Wendell Holmes, a noted Supreme Court Justice, in 1919:

> But the character of every act depends upon the circumstances in which it is done. The most stringent protection of free speech would not protect a man in falsely shouting fire in a theatre and causing a panic. It does

not even protect a man from an injunction against uttering words that may have all the effect of force. . . . The question in every case is whether the words used are used in such circumstances and are of such a nature as to create a clear and present danger that they will bring about the substantive evils that Congress has a right to prevent. It is a question of proximity and degree.[36]

Whatever society should and will tolerate, of necessity, to protect the rights of individuals; the self-imposed limits on our own individual speech should be more stringent than the limits imposed by law. As noted by John Underwood, a former senior editor for *Sports Illustrated* and feature writer for the *Miami Herald*, in Stephen R. Covey's *Executive Excellence* magazine,

> "Censorship" is not the issue. The aggrieved party is not "civil liberties" Nowhere in the history of man have civil liberties been granted in such abundance and defended so doggedly as they have been in this country. We remain pretty near, to borrow the words of The 2 Live Crew, "as nasty as we wanna be."
>
> No, the real issue is decency—what all civilized societies demand. The real threat is not what might happen to the "artistic rights" of a few lightweights, but what is happening to a society out of touch with its own standards and values. We are being desensitized to almost every form of degenerate behavior.[37]

We need creative brainstorming and cooperation between government, business, media, and the people. Unfortunately, the law and government alone can't make it happen. Competitive political assumptions and cynicism are killing the will for public service. Committed politicians everywhere seem to be bailing out in surprising numbers. Business could, but won't, make it happen. Our corporate structure leaves executive management supposedly accountable to nameless, faceless stockholders and quarterly profits. The media—which should be the conscience of America—are too busy reflecting the growing cynicism and frustration of the masses to do the good they could. As the conscience of America, the media are so busy tearing down every possible person in government and business that the few who survive the assault can rarely be classified as leaders.

And the voice of the people? It is precisely the voice of the people that gives me hope. If they band together in communities, both real and virtual, intent on taking action and making things happen, things could change. The voice of the people might well use cyberspace as a megaphone. Voters might continue to force accountability and even revolutions at the ballot box. Virtual communities might generate the saving grace of great ideas, backed by genuine grass-roots support—an offer that politicians and businesses simply can't refuse. And one can always dream that we somehow find ways to resurrect a more cooperative spirit from the wreckage of several decades of the social destruction that is the legacy of the raw competitiveness of the media, big business, and our two-party system.

POSSIBILITIES FOR A WIRED GENERATION

It may be happening even now. The media are writing with great hope about cyberspace. We're seeing significant bipartisan agreement on technological issues. Who can fault President Clinton or Vice-President Gore for helping wire a school for cyberspace, or Newt Gingrich for talking about laptops for the disadvantaged? The media, perhaps triggered by *Breaking the News* and other well-argued criticisms, may be doing some soul-searching. Bill Gates is building a family, not just an empire. Businesses are beginning to question the wisdom of constant downsizing because it undermines employee loyalty and morale. We should reexamine our hypercompetitive assumptions about everything around us and start asking ourselves what more we can do to cooperate for the benefit of society: it's the least we can do for the next generation. Cyberspace can be a platform for that cooperation.

Loosening Constraints

Throughout history, humankind has been overcoming barriers only to find unexpected consequences and new constraints. Time, space, distance, class distinctions, tribal and racial consciousness, intelligence, culture, and technology have all, in one form or another, combined to limit, hinder, and even frustrate—as well as to empower and enable. In the past, when our interdependence on neighbors was often important to our very survival, shared assumptions about life were critical prerequisites to trust and association. Entire races, tribes, religious adherents, and families were forced to band together for physical survival, emotional support, and the achievement of mutual goals—and the close associations often meant that fundamental differences in perspective and values had significant consequences, such as whether a family would survive on the frontier. Let's focus on the potential inherent in overcoming these barriers using cyberspace.

Time

Time places limits on our freedom in many subtle ways. Who cannot relate to the frustration of telephone tag? We must adjust to travel schedules, work schedules, TV schedules, school schedules, meeting schedules, exercise schedules— ad infinitum. It's enough to make us feel, almost literally, scheduled to the point of exhaustion.

No wonder products that offer relief have been so successful. These products—such as video rentals, daily planners, fax machines, pagers, answering machines, cellular phones, and microwave ovens—are all designed to assist us in shifting time and overcoming the constraints of time in our lives, even if we are unaware that that's what we are doing. Because we live by the stress-inducing competitive assumptions of our culture, we live a harried and fast-paced life of our own making.

One of the significant appeals of cyberspace is that, once again, we are free to treat time in as carefree, unhurried, and unpressured a manner on the Electronic Frontier as we once did on the Western Frontier, where a "neighbor" was often anyone who lived within a few hours of you, and leisurely visits were a welcome event. We can now send an e-mail and forget about it until the reply comes—and even when it comes, it's not intrusive. It'll be there when we feel like checking e-mail. We can make a post or ask a question and at our leisure check back for replies. We can check in to our chosen "great good place" whenever we please, limited only by our proximity to the access device. We can time shift our communications with e-mail and voice-mail such that they no longer become time-wasting interruptions. Even better, cyberspace can help us bring time under our control in most aspects of our life—not just the time we spend online. We can postpone part of our workday to those hours after we put the children to bed, or get a head start before breakfast. Through the wonders of e-mail, we can keep a journal and keep parents or friends constantly informed of what is happening in our life at the same time. We can maintain social relationships with a much broader range of friends and associates than ever before, in less time and inconvenience.

Space

One of the most striking facts when you are in cyberspace is that distance, as well as time, is suddenly warped. Your Russian friend in Moscow will probably receive your e-mail only seconds later than will your friend next door.

Given the economic realities of the current global network, it will cost you no more to send a note to Russia than it will to send it next door for the simple reason that the net is subsidized, in effect, by the owners of existing networks and their donation of the idle line time of their networked lines and connections. In fact, the bits in a note to your friend next door may travel even farther—as they are routed around the world to avoid traffic—than would the bits in a similar note to your Russian friend. Cyberspace, then, doesn't need to be a respecter of time or distance.

What difference will this make socially and culturally? Imagine having a network of friends that spans the globe. Imagine the impact on foreign policy when you (and millions of others) can view, as it happens, the eyewitness testimony of the victims of the horrors of war. Imagine asking some obscure but challenging question on a forum devoted to a topic of interest to you and getting an answer from the world's foremost expert on that topic. Imagine being able to sell information to anyone in the world with access to the network. Now imagine that you don't have to imagine such things any more—they are real today, at least for some segment of today's population.

Class

"Class" has a dual meaning worth noting. It can mean the social stratum to which one belongs or refer to something or someone of elegance and quality. In cyberspace culture, being a member of the cultural or social elite doesn't seem to count for as much as being a "class act." I have seen multimillionaires engage in online exchanges with thousandaires, and it is often quickly obvious that the differences are not so great as one might expect. I have also known of instances where the famous have gone online pseudonymously. In cyberspace, the rich and famous can be like anyone else. The traditional barriers simply aren't there in cyberspace.

Class in cyberspace is often used to describe behavior that demonstrates concern and sensitivity for others, even if it isn't necessarily altruistic. For example, a company often described as "a class act" named Indelible Blue in North Carolina got its start responding to online OS/2 aficionados who were complaining that the local retailers weren't carrying OS/2 applications. The founders would often simply respond to online notes complaining about the situation or stating a problem with answers to the problems. They offered a toll-free telephone number, an e-mail address, and the simple statement that Indelible Blue had been founded to provide the OS/2 applications that customers were looking for, via online mail order. Without advertising or other traditional marketing overhead, Indelible Blue was soon doing millions of dollars' worth of business from helping consumers and word-of-mouth. They were truly and sincerely helping people (in a win–win manner), and it worked.

Contrast the Indelible Blue class with the lack of class demonstrated when two lawyers, seeking clients, sent out thousands of messages that were posted on numerous newsgroups without regard to the applicability of the message to the respective newsgroups. The Internet community was out-raged at this violation of net norms, but the lawyers were defiant, pointing out that there was no law against what they had done, and that it was not much different from direct mail.

In cyberspace to date, there has been a welcome tendency to judge a person by the classiness of his or her behavior and not by his or her social and economic station in life. To paraphrase Forrest Gump, "classy is as classy does."

Age

Online, all ages are finding enormous benefits from their experiences there. Many of the elderly have found in cyberspace many answers to some of the most pressing problems of aging. Many widows and widowers are lonely no more. Minds that are more active than bodies can roam free in cyberspace. The fear of rejection is lessened by the ability to observe unnoticed before participating. Friends are easy to find with no more effort than reading and writing. Retirement homes in every state are listed at length. A recent visit to the SeniorNet Web site revealed that six couples had met and married through SeniorNet. A detailed report on the visit of Tipper Gore, wife of Vice-President Al Gore, to a SeniorNet convention made surprisingly interesting reading.

On the other side of the age spectrum, children and teenagers can pretend to be much older than they are—and often find reinforcement that their self-perceived maturity is helping them gain respectability and credence that they probably don't or wouldn't get outside cyberspace. Perhaps for that reason, youths are attracted to chat rooms, where they can learn social skills through participation and observation in a low-risk environment. In many cases, age *is* usually an indistinguishable aspect of online persona. Some of the most creative programmers and Web page designers are teenagers who earn $25 per hour or more for their talents. In cyberspace, young and old alike can relate and participate as equals.

Gender

Personal observation leads me to believe that fewer than 30 percent of the current participants online are women. Worse, sexism is alive and unseemingly "well" on the Net. It is widely known that venturing into a chat room or MUD using a female name will result in a greater amount of masculine attention.

On the bright side, the number of women in cyberspace seems to be increasing. CompuServe has long had a number of forums with a majority of female participants, including several forums with sections on women's issues. MCI and Disney have each announced plans to draw women into cyberspace with targeted services and information, including fashion, consumer news and tips, shopping incentives, parenting, and women's issues.

Because names usually convey the sex of the bearer, sexual prejudices may not be so easily dispelled in cyberspace as racial prejudices or class distinctions. I found myself somewhat confused, as were many other participants, when someone named Nolly Unvala joined a series of discussions on one forum. Eventually, the question of Nolly's gender was broached, and Nolly had fun with the rest of us as he (she?) played on the ambiguity to full effect. When he showed up at a "Canopus Madness" party in New York, and we had the chance to see for ourselves that Nolly was very much a male with a healthy sense of self, as well as a delightfully keen-edged sense of humor. Many of us learned something from the confusion we had faced.

If men and women really *do* think and communicate differently, it might be argued that communications will be more effective if we are aware of the sex of those with whom we interact in cyberspace. If, on the other hand, there are no inherent differences, then cyberspace can enable the communications by which gender-based prejudices can perhaps be eliminated, thus enhancing communication between the sexes.

The Content of Our Character

> I have a dream that one day this nation will rise up and live out the true meaning of its creed: "We hold these truths to be self-evident that all men are created equal."... I have a dream that my four little children will one day live in a nation where they will not be judged by the color of their skin but by the content of their character. I have a dream today.

This dream of Dr. Martin Luther King is within reach in cyberspace. There is no question that no one in cyberspace can be judged by the color of their skin, which no one can see—the greater question is to what degree we are judged by the content of our character rather than by the sophistication of our rhetoric.

Many elements of character are surprisingly easy to spot online. For example: a sincere apology, the ability to deflect or ignore personal attacks without returning fire, a hearty laugh at oneself or even at jokes made at one's own expense, a soft but intelligent answer to a probing personal question, consistently researching and providing the answers to the questions of others, and offers to help others are quickly noticeable in online exchanges.

By judging others by the content of their character and keeping race as invisible a factor online as it deserves to be, we show respect not only for the principles behind Dr. King and his dream, but also for other online participants who are our new neighbors in cyberspace.

Improving the Social Dimensions

The varieties of social experience seem to depend on the opportunities for interaction between individuals. Metcalfe's law states that "the value of a network grows as the square of the number of users." In other words, "A network becomes progressively more valuable as it reaches more users."[38] That value is derived, I presume, by individuals from the increased opportunities for interaction. That value, in turn, is dependent on our shared values, such as cooperation, sharing, respect, and knowledge. Values have value in our pursuit of our individual and social good. When values clash, such as the case in which a selfish individual poisons the well of our mutual discourse with the pollutions of fallacy, hostility, reckless rhetoric, vulgarity and profanity, or bigotry, the value can also decrease for all— hence the importance of some degree, at least, of normative or cultural constraint.

It is likely that cyberspace will facilitate the achievement of social objectives by offering communications and information that take advantage of the primary benefits of cyberspace communications technologies: a savings of time and money, increased effectiveness, increased efficiency, increased convenience, enhanced currency, and a reduced possibility for errors. Let's examine those social subsets of the human experience that will benefit most: the environment, our legal system, our intellectual and academic experience, our religious perspectives, and our cultural awareness.

Environmental Opportunities

I'd like to address the environmental opportunities derived from cyberspace from two angles—the natural environment and the abstract cyberspace environment. Cyberspace offers a chance to improve our natural environment, but we must also address the influences and structure of and surrounding cyberspace itself.

I would hope that the impact of cyberspace on the natural world is a positive one. Cyberspace, an unnatural, artificial space, will, ironically, probably contribute to a renewal of our natural spaces as well. It could contribute to conservation of natural resources through a reduction of driving and commuting. It should also contribute to enhanced environmental awareness. Environmental activists are already cooperating in cyberspace to distribute information to thousands of interested individuals.

Imagine the day when you don a virtual reality helmet and can sample, as if in a helicopter, the natural beauty of the national park of your choice preparatory to scheduling a real visit by filling out a form on the Web site for that national park. The natural beauty of our skylines might, in some measure at least, be restored when or if we can ever replace in-the-sky telephone wires with some form of wireless communication technology. Collaborative research via the net could easily unleash creative solutions to energy problems. When it comes to applying our creativity to preserving and renewing our abundant natural resources, the sky's the limit.

Focusing on the cyberspace environmental infrastructure, certain factors will require some degree of regulatory attention and cannot be left entirely to the commercial marketplace to develop and refine. These include

- workable escrowed key encryption mechanisms.
- worldwide e-money and exchange standards.
- universal standards for the labeling and filtering of obscenity exploitation, violence, vulgarity, and other potentially harmful or offensive material.
- the carving up and distribution of the incredibly valuable resources of the air-waves.
- a bill of rights for cyberspace.
- minimalist cyberspace bodies and authorities, subject to proven checks and balances, which operate independent of all governments to ensure universal consistency of a very small body of cyberspace laws and their enforcement in cyberspace.

Cyberspace is too important to ignore or to leave its definition and development to anarchy and private power alone. It is too important to allow any existing government full control, either. We must have the courage to face up to the towering task of balancing the lessons of the past against the possibilities of the future in determining an appropriate environment in which cyberspace can promote the good, quality, and shared values.

Changes to the Legal System

Numerous online legal resources are already available—including copies of cases and court rulings. Lawyers are already using Lexis and other online databases to great advantage. States and counties are making and will make more and more public records, such as probate records, titles and deeds, marriage licenses, birth records, dockets, etc., available online. Law school education methodologies might change significantly, since computer-mediated conferencing debates and moot courts can be used hand-in-hand with classroom debate, discussion, and pleadings to leverage the time spent on each case and allow a much greater depth of individualized exploration and understanding. The rest of us will have increased opportunities to watch lawyers debate the law—which can be a significant and eye-opening experience. On CANOPUS, I've been blessed by the goodwill and expertise of several retired lawyers and one budding law student—and I expect we will see more such opportunities to understand the foundations of legal thought.

Organizationally, we currently have a variety of legal structures which facilitate the development of the social environment, including various types of partnerships and corporations, trusts, councils, utilities, legislatures, churches, educational institutions, and so on. I expect we will see new legal entities created which recognize the new demands and opportunities of cyberspace. For example, the unique situation of service providers almost demands that legislatures create a new status to protect those who provide access to cyberspace. Otherwise, we will continue to see legal action brought against deep-pocket service providers who are in a no-win situation. If they attempt to control the content of their forums and libraries, they are accused of censorship and lose business; if they don't, they find themselves the target of a lawsuit for facilitating the passage of illegal material from one user to another. Prodigy, CompuServe, Netcom, and several Internet services providers (ISPs) have all faced such lawsuits, accused of being accessory to defamation, copyright infringement, and violation of obscenity laws. The courts have struggled, not often successfully, to determine whether these service providers are publishers, common carriers, or something else covered by existing legal doctrine. Laws that define new legal entities such as "cyberspace service provider," or something similar, that would hold a business or individual who provides access to the Internet or to cyberspace harmless for the acts of its customers, unless gross negligence can be clearly demonstrated, are overdue. In return for holding such providers harmless, the law could require that the ISPs work with the relevant Internet committees to develop a workable infrastructure that embraces safe encryption, provides for the distinction between public and private spaces, and harmonizes with law, technology, and culture.

Cyberspace also offers myriad opportunities to increase the efficiencies of our system of justice. Online mediation and arbitration might become increasingly popular options, especially when everyday people have access to the law and inexpensive legal resources online. Arbitration procedures and rules of evidence could be modified based on the unique characteristics of cyberspace and conferencing communications, and more could be done online in discovery, preparation, and discussion of the facts and issues of the case before the face-to-face hearings. Even in courtrooms, lawyers are using technology for presenting the facts of the case, and juries might even someday use cyberspace decision support systems to aid deliberations.

Finally, special legal status and protection for virtual teams, virtual corporations, and virtual communities may promote valuable social purposes. Virtual corporations, for example, should be afforded the limited liability and distinct legal status of a real corporation, but could benefit from increased flexibility in relation to ownership and securities trading issues. Virtual communities might be permitted to establish laws within the online boundaries of that community, enforceable by force of real-world law and subject to overarching cyberspace law. Since no one would be required to join or belong to any particular cyberspace community, granting such sovereignty to virtual communities would actually serve to enhance individual freedom as well as social cohesion.

Cultural Awareness

Without a doubt, cyberspace will expand our opportunities for exposure to the humanities. The world's great literature, art, music, film, and media yet to be developed will be, quite literally, at our fingertips. Study groups are already forming, drawn by common interests in art and music—to whatever degree of detail is possible.

The Gutenberg Project, a longtime labor of love, will make available, in text form, many of the great works of literature throughout history. Over 250 museums and galleries are already online with everything you might need to know and see to make an actual trip that much more valuable. Notably, you can already find outstanding sites for a wide variety of museums, including the Louvre, the Istanbul Museum of Paintings and Sculpture, the Los Angeles County Museum of Art, the Metropolitan Museum of Art, the Smithsonian, the Whitney Museum of American Art. Even better, we will have available searchable indexes to the world's great art. Want the names of every work of Van Gogh? Search the index. Want to view every such work? Well, there are still intellectual property laws and ownership issues to deal with, but I believe that eventually, such images should be made available to everyone. I doubt artists created the works so that many years after their death, someone else could "own" the work and prevent everyone else in the world from looking at it.

Unlike mass media such as television, cyberspace encourages individuals to develop specialized tastes by offering an incredible variety of cultural choice and opportunity. Cyberspace should thus encourage an explosion of the arts and letters, to the improvement of our individual and societal cultural experience.

Intellectual Expansion

Cyberspace technologies will stimulate intellectual exchange. Instead of the emergence of a Newton or a Jefferson or an Einstein or a daVinci once in several generations, we are likely to see more cooperative genius emerge and won't truly be able to identify the individual geniuses as easily because they'll be engaged in so much interdependent collaboration. Imagine the stimulation of watching the public debate between renowned scientists and intellectuals unfold each day as it occurs—which is exactly what I enjoyed many years ago as IBM scientists monitored and participated in the cold fusion debates, making available much of the discussion in a forum devoted to the subject. Even though there is a strong tendency for scientists and academics to seek individual recognition and guard their research until it is complete, cyberspace increases the opportunity for collaboration, and those who collaborate may find the results significant enough to warrant more collaboration and less hoarding. And, of course, there is simply some research that can be accomplished only by using cyberspace. For example, the migratory patterns of Monarch butterflies have been tracked using the Internet: school children in North America were invited to report their first sightings of the butterflies along with the date and city where sighted.[39] From those data, which would perhaps be prohibitively expensive to gather using alternative, noncooperative means, trends and patterns could be plotted. I expect to see many other such projects emerge in cyberspace.

The socially unifying effect of finding intellectual soul-mates or "mighty opposites" should be greatly facilitated. Many of the great artists and writers of history have been associates from the same social circles in New York, Paris, Athens, London, and so on. I believe that genius is more of a social phenomenon than we imagine—and now that such soul-mates and "mighty opposites" can find one another across oceans and continents, we may well see an explosion of genius.

Religious Experience

Although religious experience is a compelling element of the social dimension, it is also deeply personal, even when shared. Thus, for my purposes here, I'll note simply that cyberspace will certainly enhance our ability to share our religious beliefs, learn about the religious beliefs of others, and interact with others on religious matters.

Many religions have doctrinal roots in ideas that might be construed to be related to cyberspace, such as collective consciousness, infinite knowledge, an oversoul, the all-seeing eye, and shared visions. These ideas may begin to influence religious perspectives in many ways as we interpret scripture and prophecies, share insights, and study sacred religious traditions with the help of cyberspace resources. Even the irreligious may seek ammunition to refute the fallacies of religious tradition in cyberspace.

No matter what one believes about religion, cyberspace will surely influence the religious dimension of social experience. Learning to respect one another's faith and beliefs is a critical first step. That is, I believe, easier in cyberspace where individuals gather to learn, where the "enemy" is abstract, and where indignation cannot be vented in ways quite as harmful as in a Crusade, Jihad, or Inquisition. It is certainly not outside the realm of possibility that the enormous challenge of learning to live together in cyberspace might inspire a new renaissance of faith, hope, learning and love worldwide.

Revitalizing Social Bonds

The reasons for joining together and forging social bonds in cyberspace are probably as varied as the number of individuals who have done so—but such reasons can usually be described in the familiar five terms introduced and briefly described in Chapter 1.

Communication

The ease by which we can stay in touch with families, old friends and neighbors, and anyone else with whom we have developed social ties will simply make it easier to stay in touch with a wider circle of friends and family. Even the tracking down of those old friends has been simplified. Already, there are national directories with phone numbers, addresses, cyberspace names, and other such information. At the Infospace Web page (http://www.infospace.com), you can enter a name and retrieve that individual's phone number, e-mail address, and home address and by clicking on the address, view a detailed street map of the area surrounding that address. Maintaining relationships and staying in touch will be easier than ever; but finding excuses for not staying in touch may get more difficult.

Another aspect of social communications is language. It is with increasing frequency that one encounters many in cyberspace to whom English is a second language. I believe that, ultimately, cyberspace will prove to be the most significant factor in making English the de facto international language. Although some companies, including IBM, are making every effort to provide multilingual support on their WWW home pages, most do not. English is clearly the primary language of the Internet, and there do not appear to be any forces that will likely turn the tide away from English as a "cyberstandard" language of choice. Most nations and peoples will eventually develop their own systems similar to France's Minitel, which will tie into the Internet and will no doubt use native languages, but English will probably remain the most universal of the languages of cyberspace.

Convenience

Social convenience largely falls around setting up opportunities for communication and exchange—which cyberspace improves significantly by enabling time shifting. Without cyberspace, arranging a meeting can often be just as difficult as actually meeting; but now with voicemail and e-mail and group scheduling software, such arrangements can be made quickly and easily. The nature of iterative decision-making can also change using e-mail. Often, decisions are made at meetings simply because a decision must be made, and everyone must be consulted before it is made. Going back and forth over a question at a meeting, with little time for thought between iterations, can often result in a hasty, suboptimal decision; whereas making the same decisions using e-mail or group conferencing software such as Lotus Notes, if there is adequate time before the decision needs to be made, can result in a much better decision, because each party will have had time to think and research each of the various rounds of subordinate questions and considerations.

The primary socializing convenience offered by cyberspace, however, is simply opportunity to "meet" and communicate with people without regard to time or distance. That alone is a radical development that enables most of the other possibilities in cyberspace.

Commerce

The social impact of cyberspace on business and commerce is already being felt. On the one hand, intracompany cohesiveness and insular corporate cultures will probably continue to diminish, as within IBM, as it becomes increasingly difficult to shelter employees from customers and competitors and vice versa. Intercompany and extracompany socialization will no doubt increase significantly, as contact with customers becomes more personalized, more important, and more easily accomplished using cyberspace communications. Large, hierarchically structured companies will continue to downsize in the face of dramatic shifts from traditional corporate jobs to newly created opportunities in the burgeoning world of small business, entrepreneurial activity, networked marketing, telecommuting, and online commerce. On the other hand, it will become increasingly difficult, I hope, for companies to maintain control over employees—who will often have better access to information than will their superiors and will also have a better understanding of how to cooperate with others to apply the information in productive ways. Because cyberspace increases employee awareness of opportunities and corporate awareness of who's doing good things, I would expect to see more job hopping than ever as loyalty to company rapidly becomes as much an anachronism as corporate loyalty to employees. All the while, online commerce will explode, changing the social nature of shopping, customer fulfillment and brand loyalty.

Education

Cyberspace will almost certainly make a big difference in the social aspects of education, more so than personal computers, because cyberspace technologies are more pervasive, offering more function and power to individuals with less investment in time and training. This is not to say, however, that education and cyberspace are perfectly paired, without controversy.

Chris Whittle (no relation) has already spurred controversy with Channel One, an innovative marketing arrangement whereby schools get free satellite dishes and televisions and a targeted daily news and current events broadcast in exchange for providing an audience for a few minutes of commercials. If that's a harbinger of debates to come, then we could see increased pressure for a voucher system as parents demand that government and the public school systems step up to the tough task of using available technology to do a better job of educating our children for today's challenges, not necessarily yesterday's ideas of what constituted a worthwhile education.

The trends in higher education have been unmistakable: higher tuition and yet pressures to cut costs and a demand for and serious competition for higher quality education. These trends increase pressures for the best schools to add "distributed education" (education using interactive videoconferencing and networks to replace physical presence at universities) to the range of available options for higher education. When interactive videoconferencing technologies mature, students will be able to attend "class" in cyberspace from their own homes or apartments, viewing the professor and the chalkboard or overhead but not the other students. Students will "raise their hands" by clicking and typing in a question, and the professor, with the aid of an assistant, will have increased control over which questions to answer publicly and which to answer privately. Homework assignments will be "collected" via e-mail or file exchange, and open book or honor system testing will be administered over the Net. "Testing centers" might spring up to handle all manner of competency assurance, based on all manner of continuing, university, and self-education. Of course, in such an environment, one of the key peripheral benefits of a university, social cohesion, would occur on the same level as most cyberspace socialization—in the mind. Students participating in such distributed education will gain their social education locally, probably using cyberspace to discover what's available to them wherever they are. The intimate ties between social groups and universities will probably expand so that fraternities, sororities, and other such social groups will be tied to locality as well as to university.

In relation to these possibilities for distributed education, the sheer number of social issues relating to education in cyberspace that will be affected is almost staggering. Teaching methodologies, home schooling, accreditation, standards for interactive studies, distributed campuses, testing, publishing standards, student guidance, grants and expectations, financial aid, entrance and graduation requirements, and vocational education are all issues that must soon be addressed. Forward-thinking educators are already hard at work addressing the possibilities. We could see a dramatic rethinking of education over the next decade as the existing social forces for reform meet the forces unleashed and enabled by cyberspace technologies.

Entertainment

In addition to the significant increase in entertainment options for individuals, there will be an increase in entertainment options available for groups. Played in cyberspace, group games become a new experience. Bill Gates and James Gleick have mentioned that they play bridge over the net. Numerous writers are working on interactive fiction—and after reading some of the results, I'm inclined to put this under "entertainment" rather than "culture." There are already contests of all kinds springing up on the Web, including sites that provide a wide variety of information about nationwide contests of all kinds. Virtual reality will become increasingly sophisticated, and it is likely that some forms of interactive illusions will eventually enable socialization in real time and three dimensions in cyberspace.

Theme parks have long been an escape. Information about theme parks is not only readily available in cyberspace (including first-person reviews of various roller coasters and attractions), but theme parks themselves will increasingly take on many of the characteristics of cyberspace but with a decidedly physical tone. Who knows? Disneyland may add a "Cyberland" full of rides into consensual illusions and interactive nerve impulses.

Theater schedules and ticketing will be available via cyberspace—whether for Broadway plays or high school musicals. Even better, reviews of such plays and of movies, books, and art will also be available. You might even be able to assign a rating yourself and then in return get a ratings summary from those who are similar to you in ways you define.

Devices connected to the Web will also provide some noteworthy amusements. One of the first such devices was a camera pointed at a coffee pot at Oxford—presumably to let those who use it know whether it's empty without leaving their desks. One Japanese robotics Web site allows people worldwide to "adopt" a patch of garden in Japan in which to grow a flower—dependent, of course, on the willingness of those who adopt a patch to visit the site regularly to instruct the robot to water and fertilize the plant. Who knows what other entertainments will emerge in the future.

Reinforcing Family Values

For all the talk of family values in the media, the only thing that is clear is that the word means different things to different people. A cyberspace search on the subject revealed that we haven't even reached agreement on what family values are. Some believe family values are the values associated with any two or more people who live together, and others believe family values are those designed to assist a father and a mother raise healthy, happy children. For our purposes, perhaps we can agree that family values are those universal values which strengthen relationships, including respect for one's self and others, helping others, honesty and integrity, accountability, a passion for education and knowledge, and being open to new ideas, cooperation, and self-discipline.[40]

I think we can also agree that the education of our children is of unmistakable importance and that as parents and as a society, we should teach children those values that strengthen families and society. Unfortunately, as it stands today, most of the spaces in cyberspace are probably not quite as supportive of those values as are the local schools. In my experience, a concerned parent usually needs to accompany a child into cyberspace. Still, the possibilities for enhancing the fundamental bonds of society through the careful application of cyberspace technologies are bright.

Uniting Families

The confines of time and space affect us all and our families in ways we may not even realize. Only a generation ago, it was not uncommon to find several generations living in close proximity to one another, with family ties one of the primary sources of foundational values. Our American culture was defined by the shared assumptions born of the demands faced by families working hard to provide a better life for themselves and their children. That in turn necessitated strong communities in order to provide for those needs that families alone could not meet. The limitations of time and distance prevented most individuals in local communities from more direct contact with the many variations to be found in the world except through exotic means such as prized subscriptions to *National Geographic*, preserved as valued windows into a world of incredible diversity.

These assumptions and values were largely defined by the Bible, the Constitution, and the works of the great minds of western civilization, as transmitted by the schools, churches, local newspapers, friends, and families. There was little room for alternative views, including differing cultural views. Repression of racial and religious minorities, who were viewed as a threat to the established order, was built into the fabric of those same strong communities that often reacted violently to threats to their insularity. My own fourth great grandfather, Thomas White McBride, whose father had fought as a soldier in the Revolutionary War, was murdered in the Haun's Mill Massacre, where seventeen were killed and a dozen wounded, including women and children. The perpetrators, an armed mob intent on driving all Mormons from Missouri, had been emboldened by an executive order from Lilburn W. Boggs, governor of Missouri: "The Mormons must be treated as enemies, and must be exterminated or driven from the state if necessary, for the public peace."[41] While historians argue over the cause of such repeated violence in frontier America, few would argue that the tolerance of those times did not leave much to be desired.

The norms established by the times were largely a function of spatial proximity and the relentless pressures of time and season. On the harsh frontier, lives were often placed at stake over such issues as slavery, ownership of land and horses, weather, relations with Native Americans, one's faith and religious beliefs, the movement of the stage and mail, and illness. Families and neighbors were not only a source of friendship and community, but also critical resources for survival.

The diminishment of the role of the nuclear family in modern life has occurred in generations whose children were finally able to pull up roots and live wherever their careers or interests might take them—freed geographically if not economically. Because it helps overcome the limitations of time and space, cyberspace can reunite families that are separated by time and distance. Even now, families are rediscovering the lost art of letter writing, as the simplicity and currency of e-mail strengthens and supports the ties that bind.

For example, I received the following note from an IBM friend in response to my request for insights into how cyberspace had affected his family:

MSG FROM: Calvin Arnason, White Plains, N.Y.
      TO: Dave Whittle, Ausin, Texas
 SUBJECT: (A) More Cyberspace

. . . currently about 15 members of my extended family have
Internet ids. The total number of letters I used to receive via the
mail from that group was about 35 per year. I estimate that I
currently receive an order of magnitude more now—350 per year. And
the letters are more up to date and pertinent, often responding
directly and immediately to what I wrote. Cyberspace truly brings
our geographically dispersed family closer together. It also lets
me participate in discussions and events that I would not normally
know of within the family. My sister's daughter might write to her
mother before, but would not copy me; now if it involves me in any
way I will get copied on it. The same applies to friendships
outside of family. . . .
Locations involved (Portland, Ore - Salt Lake City, Utah - Austin,
Texas - Davis, California - Granite Springs, New York - Dallas,
Texas - Philadelphia, PA - New Brunswick, NJ - Provo, UT).
A colleague became an Anglican missionary to Africa, Tanzania. The
only way I can reach him is via Internet. Mail never makes it.

Let's compare two real–life families. The first is a historically close family. All of the children are married and all but two live within an hour of the parents. They have annual reunions, and the mother stays in close contact with the others. Periodically, she even gathered and compiled family information for a newsletter, which she sent to each of her children and their families. Unfortunately, it was not only a lot of work but also dated by the time it was completed. Therefore, the newsletter idea was abandoned, and the annual reunions and infrequent phone calls became the only way this family stayed in touch—with the result being that the two families separated by distance from the others were less aware of family happenings and were not as often able to enjoy, even vicariously, the more frequent gatherings of those family members who lived in closer proximity.

The second family has been much less close over the years. One child lives near the parents, but the others are scattered across the country. This family has never had a family reunion, and the father often expressed concern about the breakdown of family that occurred as a result. Then the family discovered that every child had an e-mail address, whether on

CompuServe, the Internet, America Online, or Prodigy. One son helped each sibling iron out the technical difficulties of mailing lists and common Internet format e-mail addresses, and soon the family was exchanging notes regularly. The many-to-many communications meant that everyone suddenly was much more aware of what was happening. Although it took a while before they started sharing what was happening regularly, the exchanges drew everyone together in such a way that the more geographically dispersed family was soon closer than the historically close family living in geographic proximity. They discovered the value of being able to correspond quickly, easily, and informally; with the added bonus that arguments were much less frequent because one has the opportunity to collect ones thoughts and thus be more sensitive in cyberspace than in an "interactive, real-time mode" family discussion (argument).

Although I have not yet seen it, we should consider the possibility that the enticements of community in cyberspace might draw family members away from the family. I would expect teenagers and young adults to be especially attracted to an accepting and validating community online—even when such a community holds values distinctly different from the person's family. This possibility alone might have a serious negative impact on families—especially those whose bonds have weakened through such things as geographical separation.

Fortunately, though, even as the family unit faces serious challenges in society, the role of the family in the transmission of values in society can easily be strengthened by the wise use of cyberspace. Few doubt that the family is the primary means whereby society can be strengthened and improved, and hopefully few will argue with the assertion that cyberspace could and should be a family-friendly place. In its present state, however, it would seem that cyberspace is decidedly not family friendly. The cultural assumption instead seems to be this: cyberspace was created by adults for adults, and if children wish to join our space, then they should be supervised by responsible adults.

Transmitting Values

So what is the next generation learning about values? What will they learn about values in a wired world? *Wired Magazine*, in its February 1994 issue, contrasted "Gene Autrey's Ten Cowboy Commandments," used as guidelines for making his movies in the 1930s, with those of making a video game in 1993, based on the "Nintendo Video Game Content Guidelines" (from "Nintendo Parents' Informational Brochure"). The comparison is amusing and thought-provoking:

One needn't wonder where our cultural heroes have gone—it would seem obvious that the Gene Autrey "good-guys-in-white-hats" defending

Cowboy Hero	Nintendo Games
He must not take unfair advantage of the enemy.	No random, gratuitous, and/or excessive violence.
He must be a patriot.	No subliminal or overt political messages.
He must be gentle with children, elders, and animals.	No domestic violence and/or abuse.
He must not possess racially or religiously intolerant ideas.	No ethnic, racial, religious, nationalistic, or sexual stereotypes and language.
He must neither drink nor smoke.	No use of illegal drugs, smoking material, alcohol.
He must help people in distress.	No graphic illustration of death.
He must respect women, parents, and his nation's laws.	No sexually suggestive or explicit conduct.
He must be a good worker.	No excessive force in sport games.
He must always tell the truth.	No profanity or obscenity.
He must never go back on his word.	No sexist language or depictions.

truth and justice have been replaced by the "don't-do-anything-offensive-or-too-stupid" Mario Brothers trying to get out of one pickle after another in a relentlessly claustrophobic representation of what might be described as a blandly inoffensive, politically correct heaven.

It would seem that the values of a previous generation were positive assertions of proactive values. Have they been replaced by a generation whose best hopes and values rest in the avoidance of negative values? Could a failure to promote proactive values in schools be tied to declines in the quality of education? IBM's Chairman, Lou Gerstner, pointed out in remarks at the National Governors' Association Annual Meeting that corporate America spends $30 billion per year on remedial education for workers and called for a "fundamental, bone-jarring, full-fledged, 100% revolution that discards the old and replaces it with a totally new performance-driven system. . . ."[42]

One of our many challenges is to pass along positive values. I, for one, want my children to have a childhood firmly founded on a value system that will contribute to their future happiness and fulfillment. I'm not sure they need to see the world as it is in every detail, or endure attacks on faith and other closely-held but tender beliefs at such a young age. I'm not convinced that a young teenager is old enough to make every choice for himself or herself. I'm not persuaded that I should turn any child loose in cyberspace. Venturing into the bowels of cyberspace is an eye-opening experience for *anyone,* much less the impressionable and vulnerable.

Fortunately, most parents are not so naive as to turn their children loose to fend for themselves. The transmission of values to children is and should remain the primary responsibility of parents. Fortunately, cyberspace can be an amazing resource to parents in the fulfillment of that enormously important responsibility.

As we teach children the importance of our principles and values, cyberspace can be a wonderful laboratory of human interaction. We can demonstrate, in real time, whatever principles of happiness and unhappiness that we may wish to teach them. We can use the conversations we find in cyberspace to teach our children to recognize, trust, and heed their own quiet voices within—their best selves. That may be the most significant challenge life has to offer—but the social laboratory of cyberspace may just make it a little bit easier.

NETTING IT OUT

Whether the common cause is making a success of a computer operating system or solving the problem of world hunger, communities form around common interests and purposes. Whether those common interests are constructive or destructive, the social bonds of cooperation at the heart of those communities are what make them most effective and thus most valuable to those who belong. Those values have weakened, however, in the United States over the course of several decades, for various reasons.

The history and future of cyberspace is intimately tied to these reasons. The social decline seems, to my untrained eye at least, to coincide with the advent of cyberspace, in its broadest meaning, including telephone, television, and radio. Cyberspace is a force to be reckoned with: it is arguably either a cause and perpetuating factor of the social disjuncture or the agent by which society can rebuild itself and renew civic virtues. Which purpose cyberspace serves will depend on us. We can argue and compete or seek understanding and cooperate. The nascent structures of cyberspace do reflect and will reflect our choices, determining the nature of the cyberspace experience for generations to come just as the pruning and shaping of a young tree determines its shape and the shadow it casts forever. If we continue to neglect the differentiation of the public from the private; if we tighten the screws on copyright until we have tortured free speech; if we neglect the creation of community in the software we use; if we control without cause; if we fail to impart values to our children—then cyberspace may facilitate the erosion of community and not its revitalization. We face a moment of cultural choice—individually and as a society: will we find self-interest in defeating our enemies or in boosting our neighbors?

John Perry Barlow perhaps says it best:

> I believe that the essential properties of humanity—the central characters in my mother's tales are semi-independent creatures that inhabit the human spirit. They are virtues like faith, hope, and charity. They are also the Seven Deadly Sins. And they are all the oft-repeated loops of human glory and folly that are negotiations between those two communities of behavior.
>
> But if you look for the native home of these abstractions, virtuous or sinful, you and they don't live solely inside individuals' heads. They live in the spaces between people's heads. They dance in the field of interaction. As with technology, they live inside us and we live inside them. The human virtues are about connection—achieving it, sustaining it, believing in it—while the sins, as Nietzsche held, are about separation. Human sins are creatures whose behavior amplifies the separateness of the flesh until they create a separateness of the soul.
>
> I find it hard to believe that the current explosion of digital technology, which seems to be about connecting everything to everything else, will do anything but pump energy into the space where the virtues live. Given new tissue of glass and electricity to bridge the danger zone between bodies, the old deserts of physical separateness may fall with a psychic rain forest of global interaction.[43]

Neither community of which Barlow speaks will go away. Which community we as individuals and families choose for our cyberspace experiences will have lasting consequences for the physical communities in which we live.

CHAPTER SIX

Business and Economics

Information, Innovation, and Prosperity

Many reasons may be assigned for the amazing economic development
of the United States. . . . In my judgment the greatest factor has
been . . . that there was created here in America the largest area in the
world in which there were no barriers to the exchange of goods and ideas.

—Wendell Willkie

Wendell Willkie had no way of knowing that he exaggerated in stating that "there were no barriers to the exchange of goods and ideas" in early American economic development. He may have meant that there no government-imposed barriers or that cultural and social factors presented no barriers to such exchange. In fact, however, significant natural barriers—most notably, time and distance—have always challenged commerce, even in the United States.

Yankee ingenuity has steadily reduced these natural barriers to commercial exchange and the exchange of information. The Erie Canal brought goods, people, services, and information to points along the canal in less time than previously possible. The steamboat did the same for cities along the Mississippi River. Alexander Graham Bell created the foundation for an entire industry dedicated to reducing one simple barrier by enabling people to communicate with one another instantaneously even when separated by short and long distances. Thomas Alva Edison not only extended the number of useful hours in a day with his electric lights but also laid the foundation for the industry serving our leisure time with his invention of audio and video recording and playback. The advent of airline travel has fueled the growth of modern multinational business and the global economy.

289

In fact, in looking back at the most significant contributions to our economic well-being, we find that most if not all of them reduce or eliminate certain barriers to commerce and knowledge involving time, distance, or both. What's more, government has been taking an increasingly active role in regulating and deregulating business—sometimes to positive effect and sometimes to deleterious effect. As competitive pressures have increased internationally, time and distance have become increasingly important factors in serving customers. Modern transportation and distribution systems have combined with cyberspace information and communication technologies to shrink the barriers of distance or translate those barriers into a matter of time and/or money. In turn, according to George Stalk, Jr., and Alan M. Webber, in the mid-1980s, "all across the business landscape, time became a new and powerful dimension of performance, expressed in a variety of ways: cycle time, time to market, new product development time, time elapsed between order and cash, real-time customer responsiveness. Time defined a new way to practice strategy."[1]

In such an environment, cyberspace is perhaps the most significant breakthrough of our era in terms of further reducing the barriers of time, distance, and even regulatory constraint to the exchange of goods and ideas. We will probably see, in our lifetimes, unparalleled economic growth and opportunity as cyberspace further reduces many of the remaining barriers regarding time, distance, and excessive regulatory interference to the free exchange of goods, services, and ideas.

CYBERSPACE MARKETS

Bill Gates predicts the rise of "friction-free capitalism" on "the road ahead."[2] He points to some of the existing currency and commodities exchanges as one example of a nearly perfect market, where buyers and sellers have almost identical access to instantaneously available information and can engage in real-time transactions electronically. He predicts that a wide variety of goods, services, and information will also be bought, sold, and traded in cyberspace through similar markets. The information superhighway and technology will be the "ultimate go-between, the universal middleman," and that technology (computers and software agents) will be able to find the best prices and even haggle with sellers.

According to Gates,

Information about vendors and their products and services will be available to any computer connected to the highway. Servers distributed worldwide will accept bids, resolve offers into completed transactions, control authentication and security, and handle all other aspects of the marketplace, including the transfer of funds. This will carry us into a new world of low-friction, low-overhead capitalism, in which market information will be plentiful and transaction costs low.[3]

In spite of the enormously significant barriers that will fall, we cannot be blind to the other barriers, natural and human, that exist. These barriers include language, culture, law and regulation (necessary and unnecessary), the state of technology and our knowledge of the natural world, ruthless and harmful competition, and inadequate rules, agreement, and standards. Understanding and overcoming these barriers will be key to maximizing the economic benefits available from cyberspace. In this chapter, I hope to shed light on the economic and commercial importance of cyberspace and some of the possibilities it engenders and barriers it faces—barriers that might be seen as incredible opportunities for those creative enough to overcome them.

Cyberspace will rapidly become an important global marketplace where goods, services, and ideas are advertised, provided, exchanged, and obtained. The form that this marketplace will take, however, is not yet entirely clear. Most of the investment and effort has been focused on the World Wide Web, the online services, and more secure, private commercial networks, such as IBM's Global Network. Although analysts such as Bob Metcalfe, one of the inventors of Ethernet and a columnist with *InfoWorld*, have predicted seriously tough times ahead (a crash, actually) for the Internet and the Web, the trust in technology is so strong that the stock market has been running up the initial public offerings of numerous Internet-related companies coming to the market, even though many such companies still haven't demonstrated a profit. Microsoft redefined its entire company strategy around Internet and Web standards in December 1995, essentially betting its future on the success of those cyberspace technologies.[4]

I believe that creative technologists, cooperative efforts, and demanding customers will find ways to address and solve the many problems plaguing the Internet and the Web, such as slow response times, the inability of Internet Service Providers to guarantee response times or service levels, lack of security, unclear legal jurisdictions, and inadequate standards. There is talk of a high-performance "Internet II" designed for noncommerical use just as was the original Internet. Whatever form the solutions take, there is simply too much invested in the Web already to believe that the many common interests won't bring together interested parties for the purpose of solving these problems. Indeed, the number of interested parties is ever increasing.

The Internet is expanding at phenomenal rates. In May 1996, there were an estimated 40 to 50 million users, and that number was expected to increase by 10 to 20 percent per month![5] Cyberspace is being settled at a rate exceeding that of any previous technological phenomenon, including the personal computer. The explosive growth of both the Internet and the WWW coincides with changes in the National Science Foundation's "acceptable Use Policy" that permitted increased commercial access and use of the Internet. When I first moved to Austin, Texas, in the fall of 1993, I had lunch with a friend who told me that commercial Internet access had just become available in Austin at reasonable rates. Today, less than three years later, there are literally dozens of providers, although only a handful of them have yet demonstrated any significant degree of marketing maturity. Many of these providers simply wanted the fast, high-bandwidth connection to the Internet provided by a high-capacity telephone link (usually called a T1 or T3 line) and found themselves selling the excess bandwidth to dial-up customers willing to endure the relatively slow modem access. Demand is literally forcing supply into existence as the free market works its magic. Although the actual sale of goods over the Internet was a relatively paltry quarter of a billion dollars in 1995 (which represents about one half of one thousandth of a percent of total retail sales in the United States), it is already apparent that we are witnessing a phenomenon that will revolutionize the global marketplace. It might even contribute to a new understanding of economics, which is a study of those principles related to the material welfare of humankind.

INNOVATION AND PROSPERITY

Capital is any form of wealth capable of being employed to produce more wealth. Labor is productive human activity. Capital includes natural and created resources, while labor includes work and the intellectual product of the human mind, including the application of knowledge and creativity. Together, they make up the engine of economic growth. Labor and capital are quantifiable factors that are valued according to a variety of sophisticated mechanisms, but the intellectual and creative factors of innovation that have been considered part of labor by economists are not easily measured and calculated, even though the impact of such factors is undeniably significant. We need only recall the genius of such men as Alexander Graham Bell, Thomas Edison, and Henry Ford to illustrate the impact of innovation on our economy. When breakthrough ideas come from within a typical corporation, the value of even one such idea may impact the bottom line for decades to come; yet accountants have few ways to quantify that impact in advance. Accountants and economists measure today's profits and historical growth rates, from which they extrapolate future earnings and cash flows—thus ignoring the impact that recognizably great ideas, not yet implemented, will have on the prospects of that company in the future. The impact of great ideas cannot usually be predicted with quantitative measures, so the best reflection of the value of those ideas to a company is often found in the subjective elements of the valuation of a company on open markets such as the stock market. Could our existing economic theories and accounting measurements, based as they are in the assumptions of the past, which downplay innovation, be dampening our collective economic growth?

Valuing Abundance

The difficulty faced by economists and accountants to measure and quantify such subjective, even irrational, factors as innovation has a price—as Tom Peters has long taught, the purely rational model has severe limitations. As he and Robert Waterman demonstrated in *In Search of Excellence,* "the exclusively analytic approach run wild leads to an abstract, heartless philosophy," "to be narrowly rational is often to be negative," and "the rational model causes us to denigrate the importance of values."[6] Economics is steeped in the assumptions of scarce resources that must be allocated against unlimited human wants, thus often creating self-fulfilling predictions that there will never be enough to go around. Stephen Covey calls the belief that resources are scarce and limited a "scarcity mentality," which spawns win/lose thinking, adversarial competition, and the socioeconomic scripts of the zero-sum game, where every success is perceived to come at someone else's expense.[7] Innovation and leadership, which look to the creation of new resources, are often less important in many companies than controlling and management, which look to the care and preservation of existing resources. In many large companies, the all-too-common failure to properly measure and fully reward innovation is almost certainly a barrier to economic growth and prosperity. The knowledge and creativity of workers involved in inflexible processes is often wasted when those individuals involved in any given process are not given the opportunity to exercise their expertise to full economic effect. When the natural innovative capacity of people is suppressed or directed at self-centered, political, or competitive activity, the result is often scarcity, real or perceived.

Consider again the contrast between the "civilized" world of steel and concrete and the Kalahari Desert world of the bush people in *The Gods Must Be Crazy*. In the civilized world, a woman gets in her car, with her hair in curlers, to drive one block to mail a letter. People are driven by clocks and schedules and competitive necessity. Time and space are indeed viewed as scarce resources. People own land, cars, and other abundant forms of wealth, and yet seem to enjoy them less than the bush people enjoy their relatively limited resources, where even water is difficult to come by. The "civilized" people, apparently driven by a scarcity mentality, seem to find less joy in their abundant possessions than the bush people, an innovative people who enjoy the positive fruits of an abundance mentality. Before the discovery of the Coke bottle, nothing they needed or wanted was so scarce that they needed to struggle over possession, and when that struggle was introduced into their society, the solution they chose was to eliminate the scarcity—the "evil thing"—even though they had found valuable uses for it.

Because many resources are indeed scarce, many of the beliefs underlying the scarcity mentality are true and valid. Yet there is great danger in accepting at face value the associated scripts that play out in our lives, leaving us unsatisfied with life and constantly feeling deprived. We may feel that natural or created resources are so scarce that none can be spared for consumption or enjoyment, even if renewable. We may destroy and consume natural resources in competitive haste lest someone else consume them first. We may view others as competitors rather than potential friends and partners in the adventure of life. We may feel that we don't deserve to enjoy something we believe we have taken from someone else. A scarcity mentality and the associated scripts can play a major role in our lives and thinking.

There are, on the other hand, many wonderful possibilities that accompany new scripts that focus on the abundance that is possible, even in the face of a genuine scarcity of natural resources. When the innovative creativity of individuals and teams can be unleashed, the result is prosperity and abundance. Covey calls a belief in this concept the "abundance mentality—a bone-deep belief that 'there are enough natural and human resources to realize my dream' and that 'my success does not necessarily mean failure for others, just as their success does not preclude my own.'"[8]

Only recently have economists and researchers such as Paul Romer been able to demonstrate the critical economic importance of knowledge and the creative ideas that spring from knowledge. Romer's work provides reason to believe that the spread of ideas and the encouragement of innovation made possible by cyberspace might benefit us all. Romer agrees that resources are scarce, but that resources can be reconfigured by human ideas—technology—to produce almost unlimited abundance. For example, sand (silicon), perhaps the most abundant mineral on earth, can be reconfigured through the collective and cooperative efforts of creative individuals and the application of their ideas, to be a microprocessor. The amount of sand consumed in the process is negligible—the environmental impact of the creation of even billions of microprocessors is virtually nil. Yet the microprocessor together with the software (which is, in turn, almost pure innovation and intellectual capital) that runs on it can contribute enormously to filling human needs and desires.

If we are indeed undergoing a shift in the primary sources of wealth, then the implications are significant. In times past, abundant natural resource created much wealth and material welfare—whether that resource was land for farming or mining to create food or obtain metal, forests for lumber to create homes, or sources of water to sustain life. Now, the cumulative innovations of centuries (often triggered by legal mandates and constraints) combine to facilitate the creation of more food by fewer farmers on less land, more homes using less lumber from fewer (but faster growing, carefully managed) forests, and more and cleaner water without as much sacrifice. Innovation, born when knowledge, creativity, and cooperation meet, enables us to enjoy abundance even in the face of scarcity.

This view could have a profound effect on traditional economic theories rooted in the scarcity paradigm of rational human beings spending intellectual effort competing for existing goods rather than in creatively reconfiguring available resources to create new resources. As Romer says, "On the ideas side you have a combinatorial explosion. There's essentially no scarcity to deal with."[9]

Business Week says that Romer's work demonstrates that technological change and innovation have been shown to be as important as labor and capital in determining which economies thrive and which stagnate.[10] Intuitively, one can see that labor and capital applied without an infusion of creative new ideas can be more wasteful of resource than productive. This in turn can lead to the decline of entire industries, such as the American automobile industry in the 1970s. The new ideas generated (and borrowed) in the face of the threat from innovative Japanese production technologies arguably saved the industry from further decline and stagnancy.

Thus, we can be assured that the information industry, where new ideas and innovation are the primary product class, will continue to flourish. If cyberspace fosters innovation by bringing together its prerequisite elements (knowledge and information, creativity, and awareness of opportunity), then cyberspace will almost certainly contribute to significant economic growth and greater abundance.

Valuing Information and Innovation

Businesses have long understood the inherent value of the right knowledge, effectively applied, even though it requires a leap of faith to invest in employee education. Companies invest billions of dollars a year to educate employees above and beyond the minimum requirements of performing their jobs and to foster pure research and development efforts that are independent from product applications. What's the payoff on such investments? More often than not, a significant return on the education investment as measured at the bottom line—but only in the long term. Before the investment is made, there is rarely proof that such investments will pay off. IBM has long been a leader in valuing employee education and research and development, yet even with its strong foundation of trust in employees and the value of their knowledge, IBM almost completely missed the boat when it came to recognizing and exploiting the value of cyberspace. The internal cyberspace network I have referred to in earlier chapters was funded on a shoestring budget and stayed largely unrecognized by executives as a major corporate resource. IBM had the ideas and technology to develop similar conferencing mechanisms for customers, but completely missed the market. It wasn't until IBM purchased Lotus and Lotus Notes that it became evident that top IBM executives understood the fundamental importance to business of collaborative communications—even though thousands of IBM employees had demonstrated the value again and again to IBM management. The links between cyberspace communications and innovation perhaps require as large a leap of faith to accept as the value of education and pure research.

Unfortunately, IBM is by no means unique in respecting knowledge and innovation yet overlooking the potential of networked, collaborative communications in fostering innovation. Few companies understand how to exploit cyberspace communications to enhance the teamwork and knowledge of its employees, even though employee creativity can be improved and nurtured by providing employees with opportunities to learn and share. The hierarchical structures of most bureaucracies (therefore most companies) are so highly specialized in terms of job responsibilities that it is often difficult in a hierarchy to create jobs that tap into any more than a small portion of the knowledge of any one person. Managers who know less about the details of any decision are often appointed to arbitrate between competing ideas and make decisions. Although cyberspace enables experts to collaborate directly in a team, many companies still insist on hierarchical organization structures originally designed according to a military paradigm to ensure that the most informed and expert individual was responsible for the decisions. The pyramid structure of most companies rewards individual knowledge and encourages competition but stifles group creativity and discourages cooperation. Recalling the diagrams of communications structure in Chapter 2, collaborative networked communications are better suited to emerging organizational structures, such matrix or spherical structures. A variety of firms, including Nike and Motorola, are experimenting with innovative approaches to new communications and organizational structures that have paid off with increased trust, institutional cooperation, and innovation.[11]

Those companies that value and reward intellectual capital seem to do very well indeed. Microsoft's success cannot be separated from the fact that it so highly values knowledge and intelligence. Microsoft's success is wholly dependent on the creativity of its employees—what does Microsoft have to sell if not the intellectual product of its employees? Microsoft's interviews are well known to be more similar to a grueling quiz than to a conversation; it is therefore not surprising to learn that the entire company culture revolves around e-mail and collaborative communications rather than meetings and bureaucratic political considerations.

Creativity itself might be described as the synergy that arises when disparate knowledge is combined to unique effect. The World Wide Web itself was the brainchild of one person—Tim Berners-Lee, who was trying to overcome a problem of distance and complexity and enable easy collaboration between high-energy physicists in different parts of the world. The economic value of his brainchild is certainly immeasurable—and yet he will probably profit much less from it than Marc Andreessen, who built upon Berners-Lee's work by programming the Mosaic browser and is now one of the founders of Netscape, whose initial public offering made Andreessen an instant multimillionaire. Both contributed knowledge of immeasurable worth to cyberspace, but the valuation of their respective knowledge by the marketplace, or at least their respective fortunes in being able to cash in on that valuation, has varied measurably and significantly. The disparity can be attributed to the difficulties in the valuation of knowledge and contribution, and the inefficiencies of the market when it comes to recognizing and assigning value to knowledge and creativity.

The challenge, then, in the economy of cyberspace at least, is to find new ways to value and reward the useful dissemination of knowledge and information more directly and fairly than in the past. Because information is prerequisite to the creative application of knowledge that is the essence of innovation, improving the means of valuing and rewarding the providers of information stands as critically important to our economic future. Fortunately, this need is likely to be met because history reflects nothing if not an ongoing pattern of innovation and creation to fill human needs. There are encouraging signs in cyberspace that progress is being made. In spite of the difficulties, there are numerous ways which currently exist to price knowledge and information as well as a few additional means we might anticipate in the not-too-distant future when enabled by technology.

Bookstore Model

In this one-time purchase model, each book or magazine or newspaper sold in a bookstore represents a store of information on multiple topics. Each item is priced according to its production and delivery costs rather than by its perceived value.

Subscription Model

This recurring purchase pricing model is used for newsletters and magazines. Most online services are moving from variations on the bookstore model to the subscription model. It has the advantage of simplicity and predictability for both the provider and the consumer. One subscribes because the information is perceived to have sufficient recurring value to warrant a prepayment to have it available on a regular basis. The disadvantage is that consumers generally pay for more information than they consume or find valuable. Providers are likely to overprovide to ensure that all subscribers are pleased with at least one bit of information gained through perusal of the product; while consumers are burdened with information overload and duplicate information.

Portions of cyberspace seem to be shifting to a combination of the subscription and the bookstore models. For a set monthly fee, you can choose to explore any forum or home page you wish that is included in your basic subscription. Some specific information sources, such as news clipping services, investor services, and small business support resources, however, assess an additional charge for usage.

Menu Model

Another obvious means of pricing information is via a direct, one-time charge for specific required information. I call this the menu model because the required information is often selected from a menu of single, specific choices, each with a different price. This is a less common means of charging for information and is usually associated with highly valued information, such as a consultant's report, product research, or strategic or competitive information.

One problem with this model that prevents its more frequent use is that it is often difficult for a business or consumer to place a value on specific, expensive information that isn't yet known to the purchaser. Thus, when spending money for something that is, by definition, an unknown until purchased, the credibility of the provider is a key concern. Most potential customers will spend time and money on research or sampling to help address concerns with credibility. We are generally willing to pay for single pieces of knowledge beforehand only when we are clearly able to understand the value of the information to us, are satisfied with the credibility of the potential provider of the information, and the value of the information exceeds the cost of gaining an assurance that the information will alleviate the pain of our ignorance.

Donations Model

Helping users choose to support pages they value with voluntary donations is another good way to assign a price to information. Many public broadcasting stations have been subsidized by the donations of individuals, corporations, and government, as are many museums that solicit donations. On television, requests for donations pre-empt the product, but in cyberspace, such solicitations could be fairly unobtrusive. The same page that provides information could ask for donations without being annoying or pre-empting the content. If a Web page provided information worth hundreds of dollars, many would be willing to "donate" $10 to the provider of that knowledge. This method of assigning monetary value to knowledge has the advantage of providing information freely, while nonetheless subsidizing the efforts of the creators and providers through the goodwill and self-interest of patrons and contributors.

Advertising Model

The price of information is also affected by whether the information is sponsored or subsidized by advertising. Although in some cases sponsors and advertisers might be indistinguishable, in others cases they are easily differentiated. In the committed sponsorship model, for example, an athletic shoe company may pay all of the costs of maintaining a Web page highlighting its superstar representative for fans. It might then display its logo on the ad with a link to a sales and advertising page. In the advertising model, a company pays a set fee to the owner of a Web page for the opportunity to provide an ad or a link on that page. In some cases, both might apply.

Yahoo! provides us with another example of the effects of advertising and sponsorship. Early in the life of the World Wide Web, two Stanford students created a set of menu pages to reference the many pages being created and named it "Yahoo!"—Yet Another Hierarchical Officious Oracle. Simply by being comprehensive, well-organized, and fast, Yahoo! soon became one of the most popular sites on the Web—a starting point for those wanting to surf the Net. Eventually, the two young men dropped out of Stanford, found dedicated sponsors, such as Netscape, and began making money from doing what had started as a hobby. The sponsors of Yahoo! eventually became advertisers. Users get a valuable service at the price of the minor annoyance of a small ad, which nevertheless often contains its own valuable information. Everyone wins. Yahoo! recently went public, to the delight of Wall Street and investors.

One problem with the advertising model to date has been confusion over the meaning of the term "hits"—the most common measurement currently used. The number of hits is not the same as the number of visitors or even visits to a given page. It is a measure of the number of files loaded for any given page or site and is thus less than desirable as a measure of impressions or actions. In cyberspace, the desired results (impressions and actions) will ultimately be easier to measure than they are now—and "hits" might happily be retired as a relatively meaningless measure.

Shareware Model

One trend well worth noting in pricing information is that of voluntary reimbursement for value received as exemplified by the "shareware" concept. The shareware concept was developed in the early 1980s, when many individuals had written marketable software but were unable to afford or arrange the formalities of packaging and retail distribution. A former IBMer named Jim Button came up with the idea of uploading the software to bulletin boards and online services, in a package of "archived" or "zipped" program and documentation files, one of which included a request for payment if the user found the software useful. A software license was granted for a 60 or 90 day trial period, after which the user was expected to pay a prescribed fee if he or she continued to use the software. Although many users wrongfully ignored such requests for payment and used the software anyway without remuneration, many others sent in their checks or provided a credit card number online. A creative new marketing approach provided voluntary payment for useful information in the form of software. The response was positive, and soon a shareware cottage industry arose around these noncommercial programs distributed in cyberspace—supported entirely by the goodwill and voluntary choices of software consumers wanting to support individual programmers writing valuable software. Eventually, as firms graduated from shareware success to commercial success, the shareware concept made multimillionaires of many individuals and companies who might otherwise have never had a chance to make it into the big time, including PKWare, Inc. (compression software), Apogee (games), DataStorm (ProComm Plus), and Id (Doom).

Even larger, more powerful companies are now beginning to use variations of this "try-before-you-buy" model. The shareware model is essentially the model originally adopted by Mosaic, which popularized the first Web browser written by Marc Andreessen, who was also responsible for the development of Netscape's Navigator. Now, Netscape also uses this method for the distribution of their Navigator Web browser. Users can download the browser and use it for 90 days, after which time they are expected to register and pay for the software, online or by phone. Nonprofit and educational users are granted a no-charge license for indefinite use. In the fall of 1996, Microsoft allowed users to download and use hundreds of dollars worth of software under a royalty-free license good for 1996 only, after which, presumably, users will purchase a license in order to continue using the software.

The shareware concept deserves support. It not only makes it easy for "the little guy" to get started and compete effectively, but it demonstrates an essential trust and respect for customers. It is a true win-win—users can try before they buy, and the variable costs associated with letting someone try is essentially zero to the vendor.

Unfortunately, the shareware concept has not been as broadly successful as it could be. One of the things that appears to have kept more people from registering and paying for their shareware has been the inconvenience of printing the remittance slip, filling it out, writing a check, and sending it all off. This inconvenience will be eliminated on the Web with the advent of electronic cash and microtransactions (financial transactions in very small amounts). Currently, overhead and transaction costs are too high to permit transactions of a few dollars or less, since it costs a credit card company a few dollars to process each transaction. When an extremely low overhead system of online currency exchange can be developed for cyberspace, however, I expect to see a significant increase in valuable content on the Web made available under the "sharesite" or "sharepage" concept—where information is made freely available on a trial basis, or even indefinitely supported by voluntary donations.

What if, for example, you could contribute voluntarily any amount you chose to those World Wide Web sites that offered you the information you found valuable? The Web site might have a ten-cents button you could press, according to your sense of fairness and value, as often as you chose to electronically transfer a dime from your checking account to its online "cybercash" account. Many Web pages are receiving 100,000 visitors each day. If only one in ten of those visitors pressed a ten-cents button on any given day, the daily revenue to the Web page would be $1,000. Looking at it from another angle, imagine the value of a single site provided by an excellent writer, musician, photographer, humorist, or artist willing to work for $100,000 per year. That artist would need to produce, in one year, only one work that could attract 25,000 people a year willing to pay a mere $4 each for the right to enjoy that artist's work indefinitely.

I believe this model has tremendous potential and should be broadly supported. It is fair, progressive, simple, democratic, and rewards goodwill.

Electronic Money

The key to making information a commodity is an easy to use, standard means of monetary exchange. Electronic money of some sort, i.e., e-cash, cybercash, virtual currency, etc., seems a virtual certainty within the next five years. Many are already paying bills electronically using CheckFree, Prodigy's BillPayer, or Intuit's Home Banking through an online banking account. Also, simply providing your credit card number online has been a widely used method to make payments online. Because any use of a credit card number limits the buyers liability to $50 by law, using the Internet to make a purchase is no less secure than placing a similar order over the phone. Consumers and businesses needn't be concerned with using credit cards in cyberspace until widely accepted electronic money alternatives are available. Nonetheless, over $10 billion is lost annually to credit card fraud[12]— which is passed along to consumers in the form of higher prices and bank charges—so highly secure and efficient electronic money promises to reduce overhead, losses, and transaction costs associated with checks and credit cards and even cash. Those savings will benefit business and consumers both.

The form these monetary exchanges will take remains the primary open issue. A variety of debates are currently raging concerning these new forms of potentially untraceable and undocumented transactions. How will the availability of such a currency affect the banking industry? How will the choice of exchange method affect the money supply and other critical measurements important to economists and governments who establish monetary policy? Won't criminals, especially sophisticated international criminals, have an easier time of money laundering than ever before? What is the jurisdiction of taxation authority in cyberspace, which essentially operates outside the traditional geographical boundaries and where the bits comprising any transaction may cross many such boundaries between the two points of contact? Do we attempt to preserve our privacy by enabling completely untraceable, anonymous exchange, even though such exchange would ensure that anyone who wished to launder money or evade taxes could do so with absolute impunity? How should digital signatures be implemented? How can we prevent redirection of otherwise secure transactions? How can we ensure that the interests of both parties in the transaction from the beginning until the end have been appropriately fulfilled, i.e., that one party doesn't take the goods and run, canceling the payment transaction, or that the other party doesn't take the cash and withhold the goods? How can such transactions be made so that neither party can repudiate the transaction fraudulently, while either party can repudiate it if necessary in the event of fraud? Tough questions, which we will no doubt be grappling with for years to come, even after consumers begin the mad rush to cyberspace commerce by accepting one or more of the several currently offered forms of electronic money.[13] Electronic money (e-money) will probably take one or more of several possible forms, including digital credit, digital checks (digital debit), or digital cash.

Digital Credit

Digital credit, the most commonly available form of electronic money available now, is similar to the use of a credit card to make a purchase—a financial institution extends credit to the purchaser through a previously established account. The financial institution pays the merchant immediately, accepting responsibility to collect the debt from the customer. The online services have been providing relatively secure environments for credit card customer shopping for years, but serious effort is currently being expended to enable credit transactions on the Web. MasterCard and VISA were pressured by merchants, software companies, and consumers into combining forces to hammer out a standard to enable secure use of their credit cards online, and that standard will certainly have a major influence on online commerce. Another firm offering a form of digital credit is First Virtual, a company started by former celebrity manager Lee Stein. First Virtual uses a credit card registration concept, whereby you must open an account with First Virtual and provide your credit card number in exchange for a purchasing number you then use. First Virtual acts as a bank to clear transactions.

Current implementations of this method have the disadvantage of relatively high overhead costs and an approval delay at the point of sale. Because digital credit has the significant advantage of allowing consumers to pay for something even if they don't have money in the bank, it will remain available in one form or another, although it is likely that credit limits and account numbers and other relevant information will be encrypted and tokenized to eliminate the approval delays and minimize the overhead.

Digital Debit

In this method, which is similar to the existing debit card model of payment, a third-party clearing house or a bank is used to verify the availability of a specific amount in the buyers account, transferring the funds in that amount immediately to the sellers account. Passwords, digital signatures, and encryption of the transaction details would provide security. This method is already seeing some limited use, but is not an adequate long-term solution because it delays transactions and has relatively high overhead costs.

Digital Cash

Most experts agree that some form of electronic cash will be in common use within the next few years. However, the conceptual challenges are significant and few, if any, vendors have fully addressed such issues as ease of use, the potential for abuse such as counterfeiting and laundering, and the balance between anonymity and traceability. Cash, today's anonymous form of money, is inconveniently bulky and difficult to use for large transactions. It can also be marked and traced using the serial numbers on the cash if necessary to hinder or document criminal activity. Truly anonymous electronic cash would almost certainly encourage seriously profitable criminal activity due to the easy ability to store and spend even large sums of money electronically. On the other hand, if such cash transactions are fully traceable, then the digital "audit trail" might be used in ways that violate consumer privacy even more severely than those violations and inconveniences we face today. For example, following the use of electronic cash to pay a speeding ticket, the payer might receive notification of a resultant rate-hike from his or her auto insurance company. Most systems are struggling to deal with these tradeoffs between cost, security, privacy, and convenience. Consider the implications of the following two implementations of electronic money.

Digital Tokens In this method, digital tokens called "coins" containing a pre-established amount of money are issued by a bank. Each token is secured by a randomly selected serial number large enough to be probabilistically unique, which is tied to the buyer's account and encrypted using the bank's private key. The recipient can then "spend" the tokens online, in which case they are transferred to the seller. Since any form of digital cash can be copied, this method requires the seller to turn the tokens into the issuing bank immediately to receive either credit in his or her account or fresh tokens tied to the seller, which he or she can then use elsewhere. The seller cannot simply use the digital coin in a new exchange, although turning in the coins for new ones is a quick and easy process. The traceability of the serial number built into the token and the requirement for instant verification of the fact that the token has not been previously spent provide the protection against counterfeiting, copying, or double payment. This method will probably not see widespread use because it enables the bank to gather information about the buyer's spending habits, and because it provides no assurance to the seller that a token has not already been spent.

Blinded Tokens This method shows a great deal of promise, and some form of this system will probably become a standard for electronic cash. In this method, the buyer request tokens, i.e., coins, from the bank in a certain amount. The buyer's computer automatically and transparently generates a random, probabilistically unique serial number, "signs" it using the buyer's private key, and then sends it to the bank along with the information about the buyer and the amount. The bank withdraws the amount from the buyer's account and validates the buyer's serial number by "signing" it again using the bank's public key and returns the validated "coin" to the buyer. The buyer's computer then strips the coin of the original "signature," leaving the bank's validating "signature" intact. The coin can now be spent with relative anonymity—with one exception. If the buyer tries to spend the coin twice, a mathematical trick in the signature processing reveals the identity of the person who spent the coin twice. This is essentially the model invented by electronic money pioneer David Chaum of DigiCash.

DigiCash is piloting these sophisticated ideas in a form it calls "e-cash" with thousands of beta testers and merchants. It appears to offer a viable solution to many of the problems associated with electronic cash. Its Web site at `http://www.digicash.com/publish/ecash_intro/ecash_intro.html` contains perhaps the most lucid explanation of any of the sites dealing with the topic, including a detailed description of how it actually works on existing systems. The original criticisms of e-cash have been addressed— although e-cash is anonymous for the buyer, it is not anonymous for the recipient, who would need to turn in the cash upon receipt, thus eliminating the complete two-way anonymity that would facilitate tax evasion and money laundering.

Mondex and VeriFone have joined forces to take a bit of a different approach, using proprietary (vendor-specific and vendor-controlled, i.e., nonstandard) chips and encryption methods embedded in hardware to provide "smart cards" that store electronic cash. Mondex provides the payment system and the "electronic cash," while VeriFone provides the card readers for the physical world merchants who will accept those cards at checkout stands. The Mondex system is being piloted by thousands of retailers and 40,000 consumers in Swindon, England.[14] It is not likely that multiple electronic cash systems will thrive in parallel. Consumers will probably, or at least should, demand a single standard of exchange. I anticipate that the VISA/MasterCard standard will be used for digital credit, and that Chaum's system will become increasingly popular for online purchases, thus forcing Mondex and VeriFone to provide transparent compatibility in their systems with e-cash or face the risk that their system will suffer the same fate as Sony's BetaMax. Monetary value will be stored on the hard disk of a computer or in the magnetic strip of a card in a wallet. Whatever method prevails, electronic money offers security, flexibility, convenience, and economy as a means of exchange, even in fractional cents.

Fortunately, one result of improved efficiencies in providing the structural support for the valuation of knowledge should almost certainly be a dramatic decrease in the *price* of knowledge, or information. The lower the costs, the more people can share the knowledge, and the greater our resulting prosperity.

THE INFORMATION REVOLUTION

Traditionally, commerce has been the interchange of goods and services. Goods are material objects of commerce and services are the performance of helpful work or professional activity for another. For the past few decades, however, we have been witnessing the emergence of an important new addition to the stew of commercial interchange: information.

The information sector of our economy is enormous—including the mass media (newspapers, magazines, books, online services, movies, radio, and television), information systems, educational institutions, and more. No industry or enterprise is untouched by the pervasive influence of the information revolution. Understanding this revolution requires an examination of the determinants and sources of the value of information and the impact of that value on the organizational infrastructure of business and commerce.

Information's Value

The right information can have enormous value and command a high price. Management consultants can charge clients millions of dollars a year for products that are essentially information—gathering it, digesting it, and communicating it. Even a nonconfidential, nonexclusive Gartner Group study—which amounts to a single report on a single topic in the information industry—can cost a company thousands of dollars.

Information can also be free. The census department provides extremely high quality, valuable information to the public without charge, as do many other government agencies. The Small Business Administration provides for free the same information that you might find at a bookstore for twenty or thirty dollars. The reason such information is "free" is because its costs have been borne equally by all taxpayers.

Information is anything but a commodity—its value varies person to person and its price often has little to do with its value. The supply of most information exceeds the demand, and since the cost of sharing it is less than the perceived value in sharing, the price quickly approaches zero. On the other hand, when there is a monopoly on the information that can be sustained by the possessor of the information, then the possessor is likely to be able to derive significant economic advantage from the information for as long as the supply of the information can be restricted and for as long as the knowledge imparts perceived value to the new possessor. In the case of patents, copyrights, trademarks, and other intellectual property recognized as valuable, the monopoly is granted by the government and by international law. This is so because it is widely recognized that to overcome the market forces that would encourage the hoarding of valuable information, it is in the public interest to grant legal protection to the authors and creators of information and intellectual property in order to encourage the sharing of the information without fear that its value will be lost in the sharing. Without such protections, there would be less incentive to create valuable works requiring significant investments of time and creative thought.

Note, however, that ideas are not protected: only their expression, or the physical manifestation of the idea. This curious distinction is deemed important and necessary in order to maintain the information monopoly necessary to reward innovation monetarily without discouraging the free exchange of ideas which stimulates creativity and innovation. Thus, the recipient of a patent agrees that the underlying ideas contained in a patent application may become a matter of public record in exchange for the legal protection offered by the patent.

Intellectual property laws have arguably nurtured the entire information industry, particularly the mass media. One of the reasons that the news is ferociously competitive is that "news" is most valuable as information while it is still "new." Aside from its historical value, few want to waste time reading old news. Therefore, reporters are always looking for and zealously guarding "scoops," nurturing sources they perceive as unique.

Thus, cyberspace has been a favorite haunt of journalists, writers, opinion makers, and others dependent on information for their livelihood. The same qualities that make cyberspace valuable to them, however, also make cyberspace a bit of a threat to their livelihood. When anyone can learn about things direct from the source in cyberspace, the role of a reporter as middleman is diminished in importance. If observers to newsworthy events are offering their observations directly to millions in cyberspace freely, the economic value of that information is lost to the journalist, or at least diverted to those who provide the connections between readers and observers. There are already many, including journalists, who get their news directly from cyberspace. From personal experience, I can vouch for the fact that many get much of their news sooner and more accurately in cyberspace than from those who process, filter, amplify and transmit the news through more traditional channels.

Even though the cyberspace ethos of "information was meant to be free" may solve one set of thorny philosophical and legal questions, it clearly raises another set of economic questions. If information is freely shared, then what will be the incentive for anyone to spend significant amounts of time to gather it or provide it? Will free information in cyberspace wreak havoc on those industries that create and market information? What impact would free information in cyberspace have upon the print and broadcast media?

Again, there are no answers—only trends and directions. By those standards, I believe cyberspace will be both evolutionary and revolutionary. Esther Dyson wrote:

> In a new environment, such as the gravity field of the moon, laws of physics play out differently. On the Net, there is an equivalent change in "gravity" brought about by the ease of information transfer. We are entering a new economic environment—as different as the moon is from the earth—where a new set of physical rules will govern what intellectual property means, how opportunities are created from it, who prospers, and who loses.
>
> Chief among the new rules is that "content is free." While not all content is free, the new economic dynamic will operate as if it were. In the world of the Net, content (including advertising) will serve as advertising for services such as support, aggregation, filtering, assembly and integration of content modules, or training of customers in their use.[15]

Dyson's vision is of a future where information loses much of its economic value in cyberspace, just as crops lose much of their dollar value to farmers when yields increase. Yet that doesn't mean that profits or wealth will necessarily decrease. Wealth will increase if we respond appropriately— not by trying to hang onto the past, but by facing the future with optimism and hope. There is no turning our back on the progress unleashed by the barrage of choice that is being unleashed by cyberspace.

Information available in cyberspace will be characterized by its immediacy and sheer breadth and scope. There are databases of all kinds—including high-priced legal databases serving every aspect of legal research, financial and stock market information and quotes, encyclopedias, dictionaries, style guides, thesauruses, jokes, pictures, papers, software, and more. Reference and exploration are ideal applications—and have driven the bulk of the early use and development of the World Wide Web—where providers are motivated to provide information about their products and services freely. Just yesterday, my wife asked me to help the daughter of a friend who had been frustrated by her search in libraries for information about the effects of radiation on the human body. Within twenty minutes on the Web, we had printed out five papers on the subject, along with a guide on how to cite papers taken from the Web. Total cost: about $0.40 for the online time and another $0.10 for the printouts. If she had known how to use the Web and had access through her school, that method of research would have saved her time over any alternative.

Easy distribution is another key advantage of cyberspace that will virtually ensure the increased use of cyberspace as a delivery channel for digital information. If you are selling something that can be delivered in digital form (music, text, video, news, stock quotes, reference materials, poetry, communications, software, formulae, instructions, documentation, stories, etc.), then you need do nothing to fulfill an order except take the money to the bank—no, scratch that—you might need only to spend the money. On the other hand, you may not be comforted to know that anyone else can make perfect digital copies of what you're selling and share it with others. Even in the software industry, where the need for good documentation discourages bootlegging, software piracy (even neighborly sharing) is a problem. However, if the cost of acquiring the new content is low, then the motive for such pirating is seriously diminished. Human nature finds ways to rationalize the theft of a $100 piece of software that it probably wouldn't find for a $0.25-cent package.

The primary disadvantages of cyberspace as a commercial vehicle are, for the moment, difficulty of access, bandwidth constraints, a wide disparity in the quality and applicability of information, and lack of security. The access to cyberspace is complicated by immature technologies and the lack of a pervasive infrastructure. The user interface isn't quite polished and is overly complicated, and the lack of infrastructure is the primary source of the bandwidth constraints, or the inability to access cyberspace quickly and at high speeds. There isn't a digital "cyberspace wire" running into every home. The telephone wire is being used in its place, and coaxial cable TV wire will probably be used in most homes for the next decade or so until forward-looking governments and companies decide to cooperate and lay fiber optic cable to every home in the country, at a cost variously estimated at between $1,000 and $5,000 per home. The disparity in the quality of the information is already being addressed as we develop better methods of filtering and searching. The lack of security is being addressed head on by most of the vendors pursuing solutions in cyberspace and by the inclusion of public and private key encryption in key cyberspace products.

In determining the future of the information economy and the extent to which information in cyberspace will have commercial appeal, it would be helpful if we consider some of the more distinctive characteristics of information that make it valuable. Some of these factors favor cyberspace as a delivery mechanism, and others favor traditional channels for the mass media. Some of the key factors that affect the value of information include convenience, quality, granularity, accessibility, suitability, and scarcity.

Convenience

Convenience is closely related to purpose: it is more convenient to surf the Net if you wish to gain new knowledge quickly, but printed media is better suited for portability, content, and permanence. Cybernauts jokingly point to the bathroom or the beach as ultimate justification for books and magazines.

What's more, there is a certain amount of convenience in knowing where information is on the shelf and knowing that what was there yesterday is still going to be there today—unchanging as an historical record. Cyberspace, on the other hand, is in a constant state of flux. This embodies a convenience all its own, inasmuch as information we rely on is often kept current without effort on our part. Unfortunately, that currency comes at the expense of history and uncertainty. It is likely that by the time you read this, some of the cyberspace sources in the footnotes will no longer exist. Much information on the Web is similarly transient—when you wish to refer to previously useful information later, it's simply gone. The cost of archiving some information may outweigh the value of doing so for providers. Saving and accessing back issues of *The Wall Street Journal* and magazines containing your favorite columns is easier and more economical, for most people, with hard copy than it is with computers, although that could certainly change given the right computerized tools. Conceivably, archiving, storage, and subsequent access should be a significant advantage of cyberspace—since digits are more easily stored and remembered by computer than visual or audio information can be remembered by the human mind—but the practical realities will probably mean a loss of permanence for most information.

In short, the convenience of cyberspace relates to the fact that you have access to far more information than anyone would ever keep in his or her home. The convenience of traditional media is that it is portable and more accessible.

Quality

There is something else about the printed word that you don't always get in cyberspace—the value added by an editor. There is a lot to be said for the process whereby an editor encourages the best in an author to make a work more useful, stimulating, and well reasoned. There is a lot to be said for *any* writing that has been critically reviewed before it reaches the public. You don't yet often find that level of quality in cyberspace. What you do find, however, is the raw material of ideas, in rich abundance.

Yet it appears that those of us in cyberspace may be able to have our cake and eat it too—magazines are putting many of the same articles on the World Wide Web that are available in their magazines. *Upside*, *PC Magazine*, *Wired*, *Boardwatch*, *Money Magazine*, and many others make their content available on the World Wide Web. With over one-half million Web pages currently in existence, and with the expectation that many times that many will be available within ten years, the novelty of looking at new Web pages will surely give way to demand for quality content.

Granularity

If you're like me, at least some of the money you spend on subscriptions is wasted. Not that you don't think the subscriptions are a good value; it's just that you may only read one article in a particular magazine—but that one article now and again may be worth the entire subscription price to you. That leaves much of the rest of the magazine as wasted content to you. This wasted excess stems from the problem of granularity.

Granularity is a concept involving the size of the pieces of information. Think of granularity in this context as the degree to which the information can be broken up and still be worth more to the consumer than the price at which it can be profitably delivered. For example, you simply can't easily subscribe at the moment to Ann Landers or Dilbert without subscribing to a newspaper. The granularity of information offered to you is coarse—not very fine. If the granularity of information were more fine, then you would be able to order only those portions of the newspaper you wished to receive.

Most media can be targeted only moderately well. The ability of advertisers to target those consumers most likely to value, rather than resent, the advertising has been limited by the technologies of distribution. The only way to effectively deliver small bundles of information at a low cost has been via direct (junk) mail. With traditional, physically limited information, in general, the finer the granularity, the more expensive that information is to deliver and the more narrow the market. Even the recent success of narrowly targeted "zines" (a class of narrowly targeted, inexpensively produced magazines) demonstrates the importance of this problem with granularity and yet falls short of solving it completely. Even if you are reading a zine, you are probably exposed to a great deal of unwanted or unneeded information.

Now, with cyberspace, targeting and delivery technologies can take a dramatic step forward. For example, Scott Adams, the creator of Dilbert, has a "Dogbert's New World Order" mailing list that enables him to deliver perfectly targeted advertising information about books and related products in the same regular e-mail in which he delivers, to requesting fans only, humorous information about himself, Dilbert, Dogbert, and his comic strip. In the same e-mail, he even provides information about how to best send him ideas for his strip. I would expect to see similarly dramatic increases in the granularity of the information available through cyberspace, resulting in an increased ability of advertisers and vendors to reach the right customers—willing customers—with a resulting decrease in prices and unwanted information for the consumer.

I'm confident that the information delivery models will evolve as we advance the technologies of money exchange and information identification such that we will be able to order only the information we want including advertising. This increase in granularity should enable a significant new market for information that has heretofore been free, conglomerated, or filtered. For example, new cartoon strips might be popularized and supported without ever entering a single newspaper or finding advertising sponsors. The subscription price of one cent per cartoon (per workday) would provide a budding cartoonist with an audience of only 100,000 enough to make an outstanding living of over $250,000 a year, with no agent to be paid and minimal overhead. The examples of such opportunities are everywhere—pick up a newspaper or magazine and you'll see plenty of economic potential for more granular information. Puzzles, stories, tips, columns, humor, and more will all be more available from more people for less money. Writers wishing to sell their information would include article profiles which sophisticated software matching algorithms could compare against your profile. When this increased granularity is coupled with the ability to purchase such information in microcash increments, subsidized by focused, invited advertising, these cyberspace developments could easily change the dynamics and economics of the mass media. Information flow (including advertising) will be much more efficient, and therefore the price of information will decrease and the amount of time and money we spend to gather and digest information will either decrease or become more productive. The impacts will be far reaching, if not immediate.

Accessibility

Accessibility is the ease with which information can be obtained and understood. One currently significant barrier to going online today is the difficulty in getting the right hardware, software, and connections in place. Most of us are accustomed to the requirements for a phone and a connection with the phone company before we can access that piece of cyberspace, but we are much less familiar with those things necessary to establish a connection with the Internet or an online service.

No matter how much information is available in cyberspace, it is worthless to any given individual who does not have access to it, which can cost upwards of $1,000. A national telephone survey of households with annual incomes of at least $35,000 by Response Analysis Corporation showed that 60% of such homes have computers and 38% had computers with modems—but only 18% access online services and 10% access the Internet. Many of those with computers and modems weren't even aware that their computer had come with a modem.[16] Businesses recognize the value of Internet access for the universal e-mail capability it provides, if for nothing else, and usually pay for the expertise necessary to connect everyone in the company to the Internet and train them to use it. As dramatic as the growth of the Internet may be and no matter how great its potential, it will not become an everyday part of most lives until it becomes at least as accessible as a Nintendo game or cable TV.

Even if one overcomes the current barriers to actually going online, cyberspace can often be an inhospitable place. Online services have made great strides in making their services easier to use, but judging from the amount of time I've spent helping my family use and troubleshoot America Online, Prodigy, and WOW!, they still have a ways to go. Learning to access the Internet can be a dauntingly formidable challenge, even though the advent of the Web and one-button configuration options has made it much easier than it once was. Setting up a server is still a process not recommended for anyone lacking extensive technical expertise or access to such expertise. Bulletin board systems and online systems have only recently gotten friendlier for novices; for many years they were anachronistic reminders of the DOS days of character-based computing. The popularity of the World Wide Web is that it is a point and click medium with lots of links—usable to almost anyone who can get access to it in the first place. Web page publishing tools are rapidly becoming common. Corel, Microsoft, and Adobe, for example, have made available add-on software for WordPerfect, Word, and PageMaker, respectively, that translate and save their respective documents in the Web's HyperText Markup Language (HTML) format, thus making it easy for anyone to use common word processors to create easy-to-understand and visually appealing Web pages.

The most important factor in accessibility is how universal access to cyberspace will be. I believe that within the next few years, government, private, and business initiatives must move to rectify the imbalances between the information haves and have-nots. We must consider the critical importance of universal access and the potential social and legal ramifications of severe imbalances in access to cyberspace.

Nicholas Negroponte has called for ideas about how to fund and provide inexpensive access devices to underdeveloped countries, and proposes a volunteer army of 500,000 from developed countries to serve a year in "school corps," like the Peace Corps, to teach individuals in those countries how to access the Net. He claims that "running such an effort would cost about as much as a few F-15s." I assume he would somehow include the training of the underprivileged in the developed countries in his proposal as well, although his initial brainstorming was restricted to the "48 countries considered by UNESCO as the 'least developed.' "[17]

This matter of cyberspace access depending on economic status deserves serious attention. As a nation, the United States devoted billions of dollars and a healthy share of the best intelligence of the 1960s to access a wholly inhospitable sphere in space and extend our frontiers by putting a few men on the moon. Now, we are faced with a virtual frontier far more alive, far more human, and with a potential far greater than anything we could have imagined in the 1960s. Will we miss a more important opportunity to shape the future of humanity?

Unfortunately, until visionaries and activists unite to reduce the gap, access to cyberspace will remain limited to those who can afford it and are willing to spend the time to learn how to use it—even though that access will become less expensive and simpler over time.

Suitability

Information is more valuable when it is suited to the needs of the consumer. The same information can be presented differently—with each presentation more suitable to a certain purpose than the other. One example familiar to all is the yellow pages vs. the white pages. The yellow pages are more suitable for the purpose of finding a vendor of a certain type, while the white pages are more suitable for finding a specific name. In the random rush to provide information in cyberspace, not all information will be suitable even for the purpose for which it is intended, much less suitable for everyone and every purpose. This presents a challenge to ensure that the gains derived from increased convenience and granularity are not offset completely by losses in quality and suitability. Early pioneers attempting to address this challenge of suitability are focused on various searching and filtering mechanisms. Yahoo, for example, is actually attempting to develop a hierarchy of all human knowledge—what they refer to as an "ontology."[18] They also provide a basic search engine that searches the titles for your word(s), helpfully offering links to other search engines such as AltaVista, Lycos, OpenText, and DejaNews after giving the word its best shot. AltaVista has perhaps the most comprehensive search engine based on a constantly updated context index of almost every Web site in existence. DejaNews maintains enormous indexed databases of newsgroup archives. The thought is almost frightening. Do you really want that classified ad containing every detail of your *Playboy* collection available to your children in 20 years? What about that long-forgotten but ill-advised flame taken out of the heated context of the moment and thrown back in your face when you run for President? The very thought prompts second thoughts about posting in newsgroups. Nothing might encourage self-restraint quite so readily as the indexed immortality of ones own words.

What is still largely missing (but which will, I predict, emerge in greater strength) are good, well-known, reputable card catalogs, critics, commentary, and best-seller lists for cyberspace. Such services might even constitute enhancements to the roles of editor, publisher, and reporter. What is clear is that reputations established in the mass media will play a critical role in this process, which will be just as chaotic in cyberspace as it has been in the real world of bookstores. Microsoft has already hired the well-known political commentator Michael Kinsley away from the mainstream media to head the development of *Slate*, an online editorial and commentary. So although there will be significant changes to the mass media (with cyberspace as a component), they will not involve the disappearance of traditional forms of information—only the evolution of those forms.

Cyberspace itself is well suited to some applications and needs but not others. For example, I would hardly expect cyberspace to replace or even revolutionize the very human aspects of such "meatspace" (the human dimension outside cyberspace) activities as dating, partying, going to a dentist or doctor, taking a vacation, churchgoing, engaging in team sports, socializing, gardening, offering charitable service, dining out, farming, sharing the holiday season with family, shopping at malls, and so on. Cyberspace is, instead, suitable for communicating, finding information, learning, sharing, purchasing, researching, reading, writing, publishing, and so on. Anyone, including me, who says that cyberspace will change and reshape our world certainly doesn't mean that every aspect of life will, or even should, change. Instead, the suitability of information in cyberspace can often simply make the difference between moments of mild disappointment and moments of delight. Two contrasting examples: I recently visited the home page of a well-known company because I had seen in a press release that a friend had recently been appointed chief financial officer and I wanted to see if perhaps there was mention of the appointment or even a directory of employee Internet IDs so I could send an informal note of congratulations. There wasn't. The information provided was elegantly done but unsuitable for my purposes. In contrast, I recently visited the Team OS/2 home page and found a pointer to a page entitled "OS/2 Must-Have Utilities." Needless to say, for someone who uses OS/2 as much as I do, the title piqued my interest. This page represented someone's excellent effort to sort through the thousands of OS/2 shareware programs available and list, by category, the several dozen judged to be most useful—the very best of breed. By clicking on the program name, I could get a detailed description of the program, and by clicking on the filename, I could download the file on the spot. What's more, in subsequent visits, I found that those that were new were marked as such and listed in their own category—making this page a once-a-month stop for me, so that I can quickly and efficiently stay up to date on the latest of the inexpensive software available for OS/2. Delightfully suitable!

Finding the information that is best suited for you can sometimes be a challenge—but once you've found a good source of information, just like a favorite TV show, you can return again and again if the information is of recurring value. Savvy information providers would be wise to nurture such relationships by seeking feedback regarding the suitability of the information provided. Then, enhancements and adjustments can be continuously made to improve the suitability and hence the quality of the information provided.

Scarcity

Scarcity affects the economic value of information. When I was a financial analyst at IBM in Boca Raton in the years when the IBM AT dominated the market, IBM carefully controlled information about unannounced systems under development. Because my job made it necessary for me to know IBM's plans, I was able to compare the realities of scarce information with the speculations and "facts" reported in the trade press concerning the next-generation PC. Journalists were so anxious for a story they concocted one from what few bits and pieces of information they could elicit from IBM suppliers, business partners, or employees. The value of the information was so great and so scarce that even spurious information and speculation was considered valuable enough to print. Much industrial espionage has its roots in the competitive value of scarce information. Trade secrets, such as the recipes for Coca Cola and Kentucky Fried Chicken, are valuable because they cannot be duplicated.

On the other hand, the more widely disseminated the valuable information is, the greater its value to society as a whole. Educated citizens are of great value in any society. Market forces will inexorably make more and more information available at lower and lower cost—including information about your bank accounts, purchasing decisions, your friends and associates and their contact information, civic and social opportunities, sporting events, theater, public policy, taxes, the law, education, career opportunities, investments, and much more. Most information will simply be free, and it will be more abundantly available than ever before. Since the value of such information itself is inherent and not based on its price, the decreases in the price and increases in the supply of most information could trigger growth in our economy as a whole as information and knowledge increase productivity and the effective use of other forms of capital.

Information and Infrastructure

By traditional models, multinational corporations are big. Global corporations are synonymous, in fact, with "big business." Small companies traditonally have served local markets, and as businesses expanded, they extended their reach first to the national marketplace and later to the global marketplace. Now, however, the information revolution, particularly the Internet, changes everything. The WWW levels the playing field. The Web site of a small business fills just as much of an individual's screen as the Web site of a multinational conglomerate. Small businesses can extend their global reach as easily as large businesses. Large businesses will be forced to think small to remain nimble and competitive. Cottage industries have access to information resources formerly available only to companies with big research budgets and market intelligence staffs. As better information about goods, services, and information is made available on the nets in easily accessible formats, the global market, accessible through the global networks, will reward excellence and focus—with much less regard to size than in the past.

Big Business

In the modern parlance of American culture, "big business" has become almost synonymous with power—the global reach of many companies exceeds the global reach of most governments. Large companies have been able to leverage their size to accomplish things that are completely out of reach of well-funded entrepreneurs and even small governments, such as launching communication satellites and laying communication cables across oceans. Large companies nurtured an entire generation of diligent employees and their families, with good salaries, good benefits, and job security.

Yet lately, big business, when faced with hundreds of thousands of layoffs, upheaval, takeovers, and foreign competition, has often seemed remarkably powerless and incompetent in the face of the dynamics of our modern market economy. Even in the face of high growth in the computer and telecommunications industries, IBM is down almost 200,000 people in the last decade while AT&T is down almost 40,000 in the last few years. For all its commercial power and technical research, big business has *not* been the primary driving creative force behind cyberspace. Although IBM, AT&T, MCI, Sprint, and others laid a groundwork for the business use of worldwide global networks, and often employed many of the cyberspace pioneers, the real advances in bulletin boards, online services, the Internet, and conferencing communications have come from those who were motivated and inspired by reasons other than the corporate imperative to survive and generate profits for shareholders. Vincent Cerf, Ward Christensen, Mike Cowlishaw, Bob Metcalfe, Tim Berners-Lee, Marc Andreessen, and other pioneers have generally been more intent on creative activity and creating value for themselves and others, as I've exemplified throughout this book, than on generating profits for a large company and its shareholders. Dynamic growth and energetic, living markets are less likely to arise when there are bureaucratic or technological barriers to entry; and systems like the Internet that trust and value the individual will almost invariably out-thrive more structured and bureaucratic systems such as a commercial on-line service. For every significant achievement by a large company, such as Lotus Notes, there are hundreds of individuals working alone or in small teams on ideas and products, such as bulletin boards, TCP/IP, HTML, Mosaic, or Yahoo!, that revolutionize cyberspace with stunning advances in simplicity, capability, or economy.

Big companies have, nonetheless, embraced this laissez-faire reality, how-ever slowly. IBM changed its entire corporate strategy from a monstrous, software-centric strategy called Systems Application Architecture (SAA) to today's "network-centric" strategy. Microsoft changed its corporate strategy from a focus on controlling proprietary programming interfaces and the proprietary Microsoft Network to the embrace of the Internet's more open standards.[19]

For most big companies, telecommuting is becoming recognized as a more viable option, in spite of the reluctance of management to agree to work arrangements that remove employees from sight and management control. IBM, for example, has dramatically cut expenses and increased morale by moving most of its sales force out of the office, giving them a laptop and telephone line connections back to the office. Many companies, including IBM, provide employees with access to the Internet, accompa-nied with strict company policies against using such access for unapproved or personal use.

For those companies whose business is based on information, the land-scape is changing rapidly and dramatically. The Telecommunications Act of 1996 removed many of the former restrictions on companies that have heretofore kept long distance companies, local phone service, cable compa-nies, and entertainment companies from competing with one another or even from engaging in much cooperation. Now, we can expect a free-for-all of choices and service options as the newly unleashed phone companies and cable companies vie to provide Internet access, long-distance services, local calling and connectivity services, entertainment, satellite services, hundreds of broadcast channels, digital music and video, and even informa-tion and services no one has thought of yet.

As compelling and attractive an option as the World Wide Web is today, it might conceivably be a dress rehearsal for the technologies of tomor-row—IF big business can forge new alliances and make the necessary investments to provide information and service direct to homes via systems similar in simplicity and function to high-definition television and Nintendo-like computers or set-top boxes. I'm not holding my breath, however—the track record of big business cooperation and alliance is more dismal than the track record for big business itself when it comes to creating new technological standards that make sense and are so appealing that they are widely and quickly accepted. Besides, no matter how powerful big business is, it can't force consumers to accept a proprietary, limited network in lieu of the open, unlimited network that is already available. At least that's what Microsoft learned when it created the proprietary Microsoft Network and put a sign-up icon on the opening screen of Windows 95. Consumers still ignored it in droves.

What I believe will happen, therefore, is that companies will simply provide simplified access to the Internet and the World Wide Web as the means of delivery for their content and services. Big business will probably provide the hardware and software necessary to enable consumers to access the Web, while the Web itself and the infrastructure of the Internet will continue to be the open standard that will enable all of us to be both consumers and providers at the same time. New, independent networks that are more reliable and responsive will also emerge but will probably serve specialized purposes at higher cost.

Big business will not go away, but its nature may change. Even though IBM would have liked to have retained leadership in the personal computer market, it simply couldn't compete with smaller, hungrier companies like Microsoft and Intel. Smaller companies without large bureaucracies can turn on a dime and seize the low-hanging fruit of obvious opportunities far more quickly and nimbly than big business. IBM is already learning to pull in its horns and focus on those things it can do best: ambitious projects requiring patient, steady management, prodigious research, and the best thinking of dozens of minds poring over every detail and possibility until it's just right.

Small Businesses and Cottage Industries

The opportunities for home-based and small businesses have never been greater. An entrepreneurial subculture has exploded upon the scene in the last decade. Many of those laid off by one industry after another and one large company after another and many of those who retired early with the time and money required to start a business of their own, have become entrepreneurs and joined the ranks of small business, many to great success. Small companies are already finding enormous success in tapping the potential of cyberspace. Even from the early 1980s, thousands of bulletin board operators, communications software companies, sysops providing specialized forums and services for the online services, and shareware authors have done very well. In less than a few short years, there has been an explosion in the growth of local Internet Service Providers and World Wide Web page creators and consultants. I'm confident that we will soon see an explosion of online retailing and online applications that could shake the foundation of some big companies—just as the PC industry, Intel, and Microsoft have shaken IBM.

A sole proprietorship suddenly has the same access to customers in cyberspace that a huge conglomerate has, and anyone in the world has the same access to information that someone in the nerve centers of the world, such as New York or Tokyo, might have. On the Web, small companies that provide valuable services have just as respected a presence as large companies. CDnow, at www.cdnow.com, opened its virtual doors in 1994 and has been a smash hit, offering extensive databases of music CDs and selling thousands of CDs per month.[20] Amazon Books, at www.amazon.com, did over $5 million worth of business last year not through discount pricing so much as outstanding service, in addition to providing a searchable database of over one million titles. If you are the author of one of those million books, you can write a comment (sales pitch?) on any of your books that becomes part of the database and answer some online questions, which become available to readers as an "author interview." Avid readers can write a review of any book listed, and others can read it online. That sort of interactivity and fostering of community is good business. Contrast the Amazon approach with that of most big publishers and big businesses, which tend to create pages that are more like works of art behind glass. So far, on the Web, small and lively would appear to be far more popular than big and aloof. I'm certain that small, specialized vendors will continue to increase in number and importance, because someone who has invested of themselves in starting a commercial Web site is more likely to be focused on the customer than a Web-page designer focused on pleasing the boss with art and fancy.

Cyberspace is making it possible for small companies to take advantage of some opportunities traditionally affordable only to big companies. Although starting any small business these days is as much headache as adventure, setting up a Web site and opening for business can be simpler and less expensive, with the right professional help, than setting up an equivalent retail store. Once established, your customers do much of the work for you—they have done the product research on their own, they provide you with fully completed orders, and they provide payment through your site with credit card or other payment information that is usually processed by the time you fill the order. And if you are selling information itself, all you need do is keep it current—a process that can often be automated. Even in a more complex small business environment, such as a consulting firm, information is easily obtainable without the maintenance of large staffs dedicated to its gathering and presentation. Critically important contacts can be made in cyberspace without expensive travel. Access to millions of customers is possible without risking tens or hundreds of thousands of dollars on advertising. Small businesses can enhance their access to the advantages of economies of scale by association. As John Naisbitt points out, "Small is powerful—and small is getting more powerful—but appropriate scale is what is beautiful."[21]

PITFALLS IN A WIRED ECONOMY

There are important economic barriers and pitfalls that remain to be addressed before cyberspace will be either the "friction-free" market envisioned by Gates or the economic engine of prosperity apparently envisioned by Wall Street. Everywhere we turn, there is talk of our wired future. When I began working on this book, I was concerned that the title *Cyberspace* would be too esoteric and unrecognizable to the average person. Now I'm concerned that it's too generic, given all the attention being paid to the Internet and cyberspace issues. Obviously, I'm not concerned that cyberspace is receiving so much attention; my concern is that there may be a frantic, frenzied, foolhardy edge to the attention—a herd instinct and mad rush to judgment that distorts the important and necessarily deliberate processes of resource allocation in the markets and of laying a firm foundation of consensus for publicly accepted standards.

No Greater Fools

Although information and innovation are driving the information revolution, capital from the stock market, venture capitalists, entrepreneurs, and other investors is providing the fuel. A potential danger occurs when markets become overheated and too much money chases too few good opportunities too soon. The resulting backlash can later deprive many innovative companies of the fuel required for the effective launch of good ideas.

One well-known market phenomenon is the "greater fool" theory. Although this is a fairly rare phenomenon, precedents do exist, and the possibility of a repeat showing should never be ignored. In Holland centuries ago, rare varieties of tulips were so highly prized by the upper classes that the resulting increase in prices attracted increasing amounts of attention from connoisseurs, scholars, professional growers, speculators, and eventually ordinary people. The apparently expansive strength of the market deceived many who believed that the tulip market would continue to show increasing strength. Ultimately, a bandwagon mentality overcame common sense as many paid much more for tulip bulbs than they could possibly be worth in relative terms, apparently on the basis of the "greater fool" theory—that no matter how foolish a price seems, since that is the market price there must be another greater fool who will pay even more later. In other words, at some point, people weren't buying tulip bulbs—they were buying a lottery ticket rooted in self-fulfilling assumptions about human nature. At that point, however, rumors of regulatory intervention had a powerful and swift downward effect on prices as all of the greater fools begin acting rationally, selling every tulip bulb possible. Since there were suddenly so few greater fools left, the artificially inflated prices plummeted, leaving the money in the hands of those who had sold while there were still plenty of fools looking for greater fools.

This "greater fool" theory drives chain letters, pyramid schemes, and, unfortunately often, markets. In the rush to stake a claim in cyberspace, the cost of some Web sites and the stock price of some companies have probably escalated beyond reason—judging by the failure of some sites to meet expectations and the volatility of some stock prices, at least. Some companies are privately grumbling about the lack of measurable return on their Web site investment. Investors are shaking their heads at the market volatility. Many companies have built web sites based on the "field of dreams" assumption: If you build it, they will come. It would seem that either the market truly understands the momentous economic implications of cyberspace or that there are indeed no greater fools than those who invest in cyberspace stocks and Web sites without thoroughly researching the underlying potential and risks of each venture.

Even more ominous is the potential impact of cyberspace discussions on markets. For example, the stock of a small Utah company named Iomega increased in value by a factor of about twenty times during 1995. Iomega has long produced high-density removable media for personal computers and has enjoyed tremendous success producing high capacity removable disk drives, including the Zip and Jaz drives, but the talk on Wall Street was how discussion on an America Online forum for investors called "The Motley Fools" might have triggered a dramatic run-up of the stock price for Iomega. In a *Wall Street Journal* article, Roger Lowenstein quotes Kenneth Israel, Jr., the SEC's district administrator in Salt Lake City, as saying:

"Obviously there is some concern with what is going on over the Internet generally — not to say there is anything illegal going on. This is a new world for everybody." Lowenstein then goes on to ask, "Is aggressive and possibly manipulative promotion—an activity rightly regulated in traditional 'public' forums—getting a free ride on the info highway?"[22]

It would appear that it is, since almost all manner of speculation concerning publicly held companies can be found on all the major online services, as well as in numerous Internet newsgroups. Yet it might just as easily be argued that laws preventing the spread of information about such companies work against the public interest. It's a genuine conundrum. Obviously, genuine insider trading needs to be prevented, and information must be carefully controlled by companies—but how can speculation, discussion, research, and commentary be separated from market manipulation?

Before IBM acquired Lotus, for example, there were numerous cyberspace discussions of the possibilities, apparently generated not by leaks but by savvy individuals who noted the financial and technological trends that made Lotus attractive to IBM. As soon as the announcement was made of the takeover, the discussion turned to the fate of Jim Manzi, the Lotus CEO. Even though it was announced that Manzi would be made a senior IBM vice president, several astute observers agreed with the prediction that Manzi would make a play to head all software efforts within IBM, would be rebuffed, and would resign within a matter of months. If IBM had been a smaller company, the stock price might have been affected, and anyone who knew to rely on the predictions found on the forum might have benefited. That's a legitimate market risk that should not be regulated. The problem with rumors, however, is that no matter how compelling the reasoning, not everything predicted comes true. Whether discussing publicly traded companies or a multilevel marketing scheme or some other opportunity, the reliability of the sources of information (even rumor) is critical and will, therefore, continue to be important. We should ask ourselves the same questions about information in cyberspace that we ask about any information we receive: Where is it coming from? Do I trust that source? How accurate has the source been in the past? Might that source have personal interests or hidden agendas to protect or promote? Unsophisticated investors are those most at risk of succumbing to this particular pitfall—including many of the instant millionaires created by the cyberspace markets.

Individuals making investment decisions must decide whom to believe and how to act on their beliefs. Then, if those decisions are made wisely, we will all enjoy the benefit of proper judgments and prudent risk-taking and avoid the pitfalls of rampant speculation and being caught on the wrong side of the greater fool theory. The allocation of resource in our economy will be more efficient and effective if there are no "greater fools."

Desperately Seeking Standards

We face a crisis in cyberspace: whether we will have public or private standards. Standards are those conventions by which we are able to cooperate more easily to improve our mutual welfare. Standards should not be confused with preferences or styles. Standards involve the interfaces that enable and ensure cooperation but not the diversity that enables and ensures innovation. For example, whereas standards involve those conventions that enable us to quickly adjust to and drive a new car, preference might be the factors determining the comfort and appearance of the car. Standards would include the location and function of the steering wheel, instrument panel, brake, and gas pedal, the location of the speedometer and the units of measurement it uses, and the type of fuel used by the car. Preferences involve the choices we have that benefit rather than seriously inconvenience us, such as color of the car and interior, whether the speedometer is analog or digital, the size of the steering wheel, and whether the transmission is automatic or manual.

Standards surround us and include such conventions as weights and measures, the form of electric plugs and light bulbs, the means of connecting electronic appliances to one another or television sets to signals, the sizes of paper, the sizes and shape of mattresses and sheets, and the frequencies at which you receive radio and television stations. One important aspect of a standard is that the more people adopt it, the greater the value it has to those who adopt it.

For example, let's use a familiar example of a universal standard—the format by which digital music is stored and played on a compact disc (CD). In this case, the consumer electronics industry united with the music industry to produce and adopt a common standard that everyone adheres to, to the benefit of all. The companies making CD players can differentiate their products based on features and cost; yet they will sell more of their players because they need support only one format. The music companies need produce only one form of each new CD released—knowing that it doesn't make any difference what kind of player you have. And you benefit because the costs are much lower—you need buy only one type of player, the distribution costs are lower, and the economies of scale are greater. Most importantly, you can choose your music from a broader range of choices based on your preferences rather than the availability of music in some specific format.

Using the same example, let's look at an alternate scenario that might have occurred if the standard had developed under a less cooperative, more competitive set of assumptions. Suppose every consumer electronics company had rushed to market to produce digital music players in its own format, claiming that its format was somehow superior to the formats of the other companies. In order to listen to music, you would need to buy CDs in the format of the player you chose to buy. Music companies would need to produce each title in multiple formats, but because of the economics of the situation, only the most popular titles of each album would be available for all players. Most of the less popular titles would be available only for the most popular players. Faced with such a situation, consumers buying early in the cycle would have probably tried to guess which player would be the most popular player in order to maximize their chances of getting the best music and the most choices. So consumers in such a position would try to be keenly aware of the choices and reasoning of everyone else also making the same decision. They might pay close attention to the reputation of the companies producing players and carefully consider the recommendations of gurus and columnists and friends. Most consumers would simply delay their decision until it's more obvious which choice most everyone will make. When that does become obvious, then a "tipping effect" would occur as more and more consumers felt comfortable buying the newly selected market "standard." The company that produced the selected standard would then enjoy the power to direct the course of that standard in the future, should any changes ever be desired or necessary, since the millions of consumers who invested in the standard would not want to repurchase their CD collections in a different format without a compelling reason to do so.

This scenario occurred with IBM, Apple, Radio Shack, Commodore, and Atari in the early days of personal computers. Each had its own format for running software, largely determined by the microprocessor (such as those made by Intel, Motorola, or Zilog) and other considerations such as the means of accessing memory, inputs, and outputs (including peripherals). IBM was the latecomer to the market, but because of its reputation, it was chosen as a market standard within two years of its first appearance. Even IBM was caught off guard when the market tipped in its favor and IBM-compatible became the dominant standard. Eventually, when IBM tried to innovate and change certain standards with its PS/2 series, the market simply rebelled when it appeared that IBM was trying to make the standards more proprietary. As a result, the hardware standards for personal computers is splintered. The concept of "IBM-compatibility" or an "IBM standard" has lost a great deal of its meaning as consumers are forced to be systems integrators to accomplish tasks that should be simple—such as upgrading memory or installing a new device. Quite simply, the personal computer industry is plagued by a lack of standards. Incompatibilities, monolithic designs, and proprietary schemes are now simply taken for granted.

Now let's look at another possible scenario in relation to the example of a CD. Suppose every music company decided to compete for your music dollar by producing its albums on compact discs using its own size and technical format. The companies making CD-players and boom boxes would need to produce each variety of player in multiple formats. In order to listen to their music, consumers would need to buy players that recognize the format of whatever music companies produced the music they wanted. Rather than purchase every player required to listen to the albums from every company, consumers would probably try to judge which company would have most of the desirable music and purchase players for that company's music and thereafter limit music purchases to that one standard. The cumulative effect of consumers making such choices would probably eventually lead to a very few dominant music companies and numerous small niche companies.

This is similar to what happened with the operating system standard. Many software companies have been producing software for a number of operating systems, including DOS, Windows, Windows 95 and Windows NT (Win32), Apple's Macintosh, OS/2 Warp, and Unix—but Microsoft has been able to "tip" the market in favor of Windows. Because Microsoft's DOS was necessary to the operation of every IBM-compatible system sold, Microsoft was able to leverage their control of DOS into market dominance for Windows as well. Besides Microsoft, nobody but IBM could sell DOS or Windows, and even IBM was subject to serious limitations governed by the "Joint Development Agreement" between the two companies. On July 15, 1994, the government filed a complaint charging Microsoft with violating Sections 1 and 2 of the Sherman Anti-Trust Act, 15 U.S.C. @ 1-7 (1973), but on the same day the parties filed a proposed consent judgment. The Justice Department's investigation of Microsoft's business practices revealed that Microsoft had violated antitrust law in securing Windows as the standard, but the remedy was little more than an agreement between the Justice Department and Microsoft that Microsoft would cease doing those things in violation. The market damage was already done, however. It had tipped in favor of Windows, giving Microsoft control in important standards. According to James Gleick, author of *Chaos* and *New York Times* writer,

> the operating system has become, from the consumer's point of view, a useful package of software. From a different point of view, however — the point of view of the essential underlying structure of modern computing—the operating system Microsoft owns has become something else altogether: a collection of standards.[23]

The importance of elegant standards simply cannot be overstated. When such standards are chosen carefully through public processes, everyone benefits. They simply work for us and we don't need to think about them much. When private interests gain the power necessary to dictate standards, however, innovation suffers. According to Gleick,

> Ultimately, only one kind of company can play the standards game risk-free: a company with a monopoly. The risk for everyone else is that the company that owns the standard can change it without warning, can give its own programmers special advantage and can freeze innovation elsewhere.
>
> "We've lost this notion of a public standard as good," says Alex Morrow, general manager of architecture and technology at Lotus. "Instead we have this new thing, a quasi-open private standard that's controlled by one company. That's where innovation is going to suffer."[24]

Microsoft is not the issue—perhaps we owe Microsoft a debt of gratitude for being so effective in controlling standards that the issues are being raised. The real issue is the public interest in public standards. I believe it is axiomatic that no private business should own or control public standards—yet, to the best of my knowledge, we have no clear, effective public policy on the control or definition of public standards, especially technological standards. That deficiency allows private interests to control publicly important standards, thus limiting the progress in those standards to those innovations that originate with or can be acquired by the controlling private interest. We are, as a society, ambivalent—caught between our desire to serve private economic interests as well as the public welfare. Yet both can be better served if the determination and control of standards is an open, public process. The best ideas and thinking of a wider variety of experts can then be brought to bear on the problems, resulting in more elegant and enduring standards. Without the need to compete with proprietary standards, private interests can serve customers through innovations in service and product rather than standards, resulting in increased abundance for public *and* private interests.

There are numerous standards-setting organizations that have long demonstrated the value and efficacy of open standards.[25] The primary U.S. standards organization is ANSI, or American National Standards Institute. Worldwide, other such standards organizations include DIN (Germany), BSI (United Kingdom), AFNOR (France), UNI (Italy), NNI (Netherlands), SAA (Australia), SANZ (New Zealand), NSF (Norway), and DS (Denmark). The parent organization is the International Organization for Standardization, or ISO, in Geneva. Ironically, the ISO standards produced and published by these organizations are not available on the Internet, because they are copyrighted and expensive. Naturally, this at least partially defeats the purpose of having open standards. Even more troubling, however, is the fact that these standards bodies are largely dependent on corporate customers worldwide who purchase the standards and provide the time and travel for those attending the committees to define the standards. Thus, ISO standards generally lag market realities rather than leading the way.

The Internet, however, has been different. The Internet Engineering Task Force (IETF) is the primary Internet standards body. Over the years, the Internet has evolved as necessary based on the ideas of Internet users—not executives, professional planners, or formal committee members. Anyone could volunteer to be on the task force and work on areas of interest. Anyone could submit ideas as a "request for comments" (RFC). Many did, and many were adopted. Tim Berners-Lee, for example, created the World Wide Web that way. The guiding policy of the IETF was clearly articulated by Dave Clark, one of the group's leaders, in 1992: "We reject kings, presidents, and voting. We believe in rough consensus and running code." The philosophy has worked rather well and delivered to us the Internet as it exists today. Now, however, both the IETF and the World Wide Web Consortium (W3C) are threatened by the serious invasion of commercial interests. It remains to be seen whether either can survive as an independent standards-setting body for the Internet, or whether they will be rendered into a rubber-stamp status by aggressive commercial interests seeking to set market standards based on market dominance rather than consensus.

There is a government agency in Gaithersburg, Maryland, called the National Institute of Standards and Technology. I once visited its drowsy campus and found, in the lobby, pictures, quotations, and exhibits that lent justification to its existence as a useful government agency to assist industry in the development of technology . . . needed to improve product quality, to modernize manufacturing processes, to ensure product reliability . . . and to facilitate rapid commercialization . . . of products based on new scientific discoveries.[26]

The NIST, unfortunately, is a bureaucracy. It is largely failing to fulfill its critical mission at a time when we, the people, are desperately needing cyberspace standards. While NIST focuses on scientific measurements, promoting the metric system, and furthering the Malcolm Baldridge Quality Awards, it has not been as effective in representing the public in the process of establishing the public technical standards that are making and will make such an enormous difference in our future. Even though we, the people, get to choose between the competing standards offered by competing companies, we aren't offered the third (and best) alternative: agreement and cooperation between the competing companies in terms of the underlying standards. In spite of the protestations of Bill Gates that he's helpless to do anything that the market doesn't want, I know from personal experience that we are indeed often at the mercy of powerful business interests with far less concern for our welfare or the common good than any of us would probably be likely to believe. What should be a matter of paramount public welfare in the information revolution has been abdicated to the private sector. The answer isn't necessarily to give more money to the NIST—it's for the NIST to exercise leadership in cooperation with the executive and legislative branches of government to represent the people in the critical process of establishing public standards, and to keep us informed about the decisions being made today that will affect our lives tomorrow. It's time for more accountability—and that starts with our demanding it.

I believe the failure of publicly accountable bodies to establish a leadership in the role of setting critical standards through an open, accountable public process involving business, government, academia, and the people results in harm to business and public interests in at least three ways: (1) privatized standards are inherently weak as technological foundations because they serve private corporate purposes that are usually contrary to public purposes, (2) there are too many overlapping standards, and (3) standards can be (and have been) manipulated (churned) for private purposes.

Weak Foundations

Privatized standards are like foundations of sand—they are built upon the ever-shifting base of competitive advantage rather than the more durable foundation of public welfare. Even as the public and markets tend strongly towards the adoption of standards whenever shared standards are important, as demonstrated in the CD examples, there is enormous market advantage to be found in establishing proprietary technology as a standard. For every company, such as Sun, that have sought and gained market advantage in open standards, there are several other companies, such as Microsoft, Novell, Creative Labs, and Apple that have gained significant advantage in the successful establishment of proprietary technologies as standards. Many companies have tried, through alliances, to unseat existing standards with superior technology, but such efforts rarely succeed. In my opinion, such alliances are usually doomed because they are formed to unseat the market leader and replace existing standards rather than to serve the public interest in strong, durable standards.

Unfortunately, political philosophy plays such a significant role in these decisions that it is often difficult to maintain rational dialogue on the subject. On the one hand, many Republicans seem to believe and act as if the market will work social miracles so long as government is out of the picture, and on the other hand, many Democrats seem to believe that the cure for most social ills is government intervention. Further complicating the picture, however, is the possibility that companies also have ideological agendas that serve their market position. IBM, for example, is more conservative, reserved, careful, and business-oriented than is Netscape, whose leadership is younger, more daring, and more likely to provide open systems and standards, relying on constant innovation. These ideological differences are rather obvious in the following statement by Marc Andreessen: "And Notes [the Lotus product IBM acquired with Lotus and is now using to tie corporate systems to the Internet] is so expensive to deploy, it's so complex and monolithic. It's a very IBM-like product. It will be interesting to see if there is a future for it in these open network environments, where people are looking for more flexible systems."[27] Netscape and Notes are two very different approaches to the same problem—it can actually be said that Notes is the more elegant of the two approaches, providing many more tools for teamwork, security, and end-user function. Yet Andreessen is right about it being monolithic and less flexible—there are tradeoffs that were made to obtain the other advantages sought by IBM, which are more important to businesses than to individuals. The differences are rooted deep in the product—but stem from the ideological differences between the two companies. Those ideological differences will, in the long run, touch us all depending on which products we choose to use.

Similar ideological differences were also a constant in the marketing struggles I faced with Microsoft—even though I was more inclined to see the environment as Microsoft did (as a series of individual decisions rather than as fewer corporate decisions), I could also understand IBM's perspective. OS/2 was more reliable, more efficient, and better crafted—yet it still couldn't unseat the snazzier, snappier Windows. At least some of that must be attributed to Microsoft's predatory behaviors which leveraged Microsoft's position with DOS and illegally cemented Windows as the standard on almost every new system which shipped between 1990 and 1994, when Microsoft reached an agreement with the Justice Department. Nonetheless, the fact that IBM was simply too slow to respond to Microsoft's actions during those years simply further cements the importance of understanding that the world of business is just as political and ideological as the world of government and politics. It's just that the debates are more esoteric and are generally conducted in closed environments where "free speech" is not always respected and protected with quite the same zeal as in our public life.

The foundation of standards upon which we build cyberspace should be as ideologically neutral as possible, providing a broad range of choices, and thus promoting common interests. Optimally, those foundational standards will be a matter of public discussion, where free speech can influence decisions still being made. Businesses are generally very responsive to customers—if the issues are discussed openly and fairly; but it is usually not in the best interest of any business in a leadership position to see such discussions ensue. Profits are seen to come from maximizing the amount of money one can get from customers; and the less customers know about the decisions being made by the companies, the more likely they are to happily comply with the interests of business. The tobacco companies are but one obvious example of this dynamic; the split and struggles between IBM and Microsoft is another. Sometimes, memos from such decisions are made public, through leaks or legal battles, but the vast majority of such discussions and decision-making is never committed to paper. Worse, those "in the know" have been committed both by law and their word to uphold the confidentiality of what they've learned in such discussions. Absent changes in the political and social structure surrounding the standard setting processes, the important decisions about the public standards of cyberspace will be made without the assistance or approval of the people by companies exercising market power to optimize their profits. The result could be a foundation of sand upon which we build a cyberspace future fraught with instability and further conflict.

A Plethora of Standards

One result of our failure to ensure that the public interest is represented in the setting of public standards is in the existence of multiple, overlapping standards that dilute the effectiveness of any one standard and defeat the purpose of having standards in the first place. For example, in the late 1960s and early 1970s, the industry was struggling over standards for recording tape. Consumers faced the choice between reel-to-reel, 8-track, and cassette tapes. In hindsight, we can see that the benefits of having the choice weren't as significant as the benefits of standardization, and the money many wasted on 8-track tapes has become a cultural joke. Obviously, we would have been better off if the industry had cooperated in an attempt to establish a single standard—perhaps even a blend of the advantages of each format.

Similarly, in the PC arena, there are multiple operating system "standards"—DOS, Windows 95, Windows 3.1, Windows NT, OS/2, Unix, Mac, and Linux. As someone who once analyzed and debated in great detail every possible difference among the operating systems, I can say with some assurance that most of the operating systems do essentially the same thing at the core, but have been enhanced and differentiated for competitive advantage. Certainly, the public interest is served by having so many choices—but I believe that the public interest would be served even better if there were one primary operating system standard, with only essential function. Even if we were to adopt as our standard the least intuitive and most bloated of the alternatives, it would probably be much better for us all than having so many slightly different alternatives that dilute application development resources and discourage innovation.

The same potential for too many variations applies to other standards and to cyberspace. We are beginning to see indications that competition will result in a splintering of the standards for Web page interactivity, connectivity, security, exchange, encryption, and so on. We need public standards, but we can expect suboptimal, overlapping standards if private companies remain in control of those standards. We sometimes wrongly consider such things as the choice of a WWW browser to be "preferences" rather than standards, and because we rightly want to avoid mandating common preferences, we too frequently avoid enjoining important standards. The result is usually a splintered standard that offers the illusion of choice at the expense of slowed progress in those arenas of innovation that are subordinate to or dependent on the standard.

So far, because of the IETF process, the Internet has been remarkably free from the problems derived from multiple conflicting standards in hardware, software, connectivity, and interfaces. Many Internet standards overlap (such as Gopher and the WWW), but they also interoperate. Because the IETF operates on a voluntary, ad hoc basis, the standards defined through the process have generally been necessary, important standards. Important innovations, such as the WWW, have been frequent, but without overturning existing standards. Because the standards have been open, they have been more readily adopted universally. WWW creator Tim Berners-Lee, for example, asserts that if he had tried to patent and control the technological standards upon which the WWW is built, its development might have stalled as other companies came up with their own solutions to avoid paying him a licensing fee. Under such a scenario, the Web may not have become worldwide, according to Steve Higgins in an *Investors Business Daily* profile of Berners-Lee.

The World Wide Web Consortium under the direction of Berners-Lee, was established to ensure open standards for the Web and is sponsored by over 120 companies but, unfortunately, the competitive struggles between industry powerhouses is beginning to color the standards landscape with more proprietary shades. For example, Netscape released its proposed extensions to HTML standards in its products before their acceptance by the W3C, which triggered debates about whether Netscape was truly committed to open standards. Microsoft has clearly stated and demonstrated their strategy of including open Internet standards in their proprietary operating systems—which could easily result in the privatization by Microsoft of those standards. Netscape and Microsoft are trading salvos over proposed style sheet specifications, prompting *WebWeek* to report that the specifications for style sheets, along with several other proposed standards, were stalled while the W3C sorted out how to best define the meaning of "supporting a standard."[28] The threat to open standards from competitive pressures is real—as is the possibility that the processes by which open standards are derived might be ignored whenever any company feels that it can gain competitive advantage by doing so, thus leading to splintered, overlapping standards. We must resist such possibilities.

Abuse of Standards

In areas where technological change is constant and competitive pressures are high, succumbing to the temptation for those who control proprietary standards to abuse the public trust is far too common. Many technology companies that control certain standards deliver less than ideal products to their customers, often in order to motivate future upgrades and reap additional revenue. Sometimes they deliberately ship with bugs and limitations; sometimes they introduce elements of incompatibility or future obsolescence into their products; and sometimes they simply ship prematurely. When IBM shipped the 6Mhz IBM AT in 1984, savvy engineers discovered that the system could be easily upgraded to an 8MHz system by adding a crystal costing only a few dollars to the system. IBM had apparently designed the system around the 8MHz speed but had deliberately limited the speed. I remember my surprise when I learned that an IBM executive had issued an engineering change to eliminate the "free upgradability."

Similarly, Microsoft shipped a minor modification to Windows 3.1 (Windows 3.11), ostensibly to fix a minor bug and add support for a few new devices. Many were puzzled that Microsoft would go to such trouble to ship such a minor upgrade and suspicions were raised within IBM, on forums, and in the trade press when it became obvious that the upgrade had been modified just before release such that it also rendered Windows 3.11 incompatible with IBM's successful upgrade to Windows 3.1, OS/2 for Windows. Considering that Microsoft enjoyed a near monopoly with Windows and DOS on new systems shipped, the move effectively eliminated OS/2 for Windows as a potential purchase for anyone purchasing a new computer or installing the Windows upgrade. Microsoft had introduced a slight (and unnecessary) modification to its Windows standard, adding one more minor variation to that standard for consumers to be concerned with.

Those are just two of many examples I could offer of the abuse of the proprietary control of standards.[29] The competitive nature of business often results in a similar churning of standards and abuse of standard-setting power. In cyberspace, we will face the same abuses if any company succeeds in gaining control of standards there. The Department of Justice has reopened its investigation of Microsoft, presumably to investigate the possibility that Microsoft is attempting to leverage their dominance of operating systems standards to the eventual control of Internet standards. Microsoft has announced their intention to give away their Web browser, Internet Explorer, and include HTML in the operating system—leaving fewer reasons for anyone using a Microsoft operating system to install Netscape's browser or any plug-ins not supporting Microsoft's standards.

If history is any indication of the future, once any company gains control of a cyberspace standard, we will face the manipulation of that standard for competitive and other private purposes. Standards are too important to be left in the hands of private interests.

POSSIBILITIES FOR THE WIRED ENTERPRISE

The Internet is indeed ripe with opportunity, across a broad range of disciplines. Big companies or small, the impact of cyberspace will likely range from earth shaking to insignificant. Although it is impossible to predict every important aspect of the Internet's future, there are some possibilities and probabilities that are already clear, and there are others we can and should address now. I'll share some of the highlights of those possibilities by the major functional disciplines of business—namely marketing, human resources, research and development, and finance—in the following sections.

Marketing

Marketing is all about closing the gaps between companies—and their products and services—and their customers. Traditional definitions of marketing included all activities involved in the transfer of goods from the producer or seller to the consumer or buyer, including advertising, shipping, storing or selling—but the term as it is used today is even broader. It includes the transfer of services and information in addition to goods as well as determining customer needs, defining solutions to address those needs, and communicating those solutions to customers and potential customers. Companies have traditionally relied on such activities as marketing research, product definition, advertising, public relations, distribution, and sales to market products and close the gaps between supplier and consumer. The ever-increasing reach of cyberspace has and will continue to transform marketing by providing a more effective means of reducing those gaps. Already, toll-free numbers, telemarketing, and home shopping networks have brought companies nearer consumers by eliminating the "middleman," but the surface of potential has barely been scratched. Companies can hear the voice of customers more quickly, with greater clarity, than ever before *if* convenient cyberspace conduits for interactivity between customers and company employees are available. IBM's market development organization was astounded by the power of Team OS/2 and the willingness of volunteers to promote OS/2 on their own time and at their own expense. Traditionally, they were wholly dependent on IBM's sales force and retail channels—and struggled to grab the attention of either. But with Team OS/2, new possibilities surfaced and before the phenomenon was over, the benefits derived from Team OS/2's cyberspace enthusiasm included hundreds of column-inches of additional media coverage for OS/2, increased exposure for OS/2 software vendors and IBM business partners, thousands of hours of demonstrations, dealer training, and persuasion, thousands of e-mail messages and posts defending OS/2 against ignorance and attack, thousands of dollars of donations to charity raised at Team OS/2 events, more books on OS/2 than would have otherwise been published, and significantly improved morale for OS/2 developers. Team OS/2 helped IBM close gaps to customers that IBM didn't know existed. Steve Mastrianni, consultant and author, noted:

Team OS/2 members traveled to trade shows, computer fairs, schools, church meetings, computer clubs and department stores, all at their own expense and without pay to plug their favorite operating system. I am absolutely sure that without Team OS/2, OS/2 would not even be on the radar screen today.[30]

Other companies such as Dell Computers are using information available at their Web site (http://www.dell.com) to close the gaps between company and customers while also reducing support costs. At Dell's Web site, you can learn about Dell products, download software and updates, troubleshoot problems, search press releases, find information about the company, study investor information, obtain technical support, apply for a job, learn about the latest in research and development, and, of course, buy a Dell. Everything, it seems, that affects a customer's experience with a company is of concern to marketing—and in cyberspace, that can include almost everything publicly known about a company. Those companies that can help customers be more productive, avoid frustration, and feel good will benefit.

Even though the potential customers who are online now are likely to be highly educated with higher incomes—desirable customers in their own right—we still haven't seen the dramatically simple access device that could bring the rest of the country (indeed the world) onto the Internet within a few short years. If or when the World Wide Web is brought into homes via a simpler interface than phone lines, modems and computers, we can expect to see dramatic changes in the nature of sales in America. Although many love the physical aspects of shopping, even they might rather forego a traditional shopping trip that would require looking in many stores for the best price when a quick trip to cyberspace might gather all the information necessary to do a comprehensive comparison of price, features, and existing customer satisfaction. Home shopping via TV doesn't even come close in terms of function and convenience offered—and yet has been remarkably successful, nonetheless. Cyberspace shopping is certain to be a smashing success.

Let's examine the potential of those elements of marketing that are most likely to benefit from cyberspace.

Product Definition and Quality

In the process of listening to one's customers or even other companies' customers online, products can be defined and enhanced early in the definition process. One of the most significant tensions in most businesses is the inherent conflict between time-to-market and product quality. The markets are littered with products that were released too soon or too late. OS/2 1.2—too soon, Lotus 1-2-3 for Windows—too late. Timing can be everything.

The sooner accurate information from customers and market research can be gathered and processed, the sooner product definitions can be established and corrections to products and strategies can be made. Windows 95 went through some of the most extensive beta testing ever, most of which was managed using cyberspace communications. As an ambitious first release, the results are impressive—to this skeptic, at least.

Even if cyberspace beta-testing fails, cyberspace feedback can prevent an escalating product-quality fiasco. In the month before the PS/2 was scheduled to ship, I experienced significant problems with the interoperability of the new 720K and 1.44MB diskette drives. The engineers refused to believe that my problems were real or serious until I used the internal forums to identify several others having identical problems. The engineers flew out to examine my systems and the problem was identified and manufacturing corrected much sooner than it otherwise would have been. When OS/2 Warp was first released, online feedback from early reviewers identified an installation bug so quickly that IBM recalled the boxes already shipped and was able to correct the bug without seriously impacting the original shipping schedules. When Netscape Navigator 2.0 was released, creative hackers quickly found and publicized flaws in its security. The fixes were made available the following week, and the downloadable versions of Navigator were corrected quickly. Because cyberspace compresses the time required for iterative communications, problem identification and solution can happen within a shorter time period than ever before. We are thus all the more likely to have quality products—which benefits consumers and providers alike.

Advertising

Advertising is an accepted fixture in our culture, so it is only natural that it would penetrate cyberspace in forms suited to the medium. Initially, online ads were viewed with disdain by those who frequented bulletin boards, the Internet, and even some commercial services. Prodigy's early use of banner ads in the mid 1980s to keep monthly rates low was greeted with widespread derision and scorn by many cybernauts at the time; but when Yahoo began to accept advertisements in 1995, scarcely a whimper of protest was evident. The culture change in cyberspace seems to have coincided with the commercialization of the Internet. Prodigy had charged subscription fees, but Yahoo was freely provided. Individuals recognized that without advertising revenues, Yahoo could only stay in business by charging individuals for its services directly.

Advertising is used to increase consumer awareness and positive impressions of a given offering, invite or incite a customer to take a particular action, or to create a perceived need or image that resonates with potential customers. Advertising is most useful when it targets specific audiences. For example, manufacturers of high performance auto parts would find a receptive target audience in *Car and Driver.*

Cyberspace is ideal for targeted advertising because it is a random access medium, meaning that consumers have an almost infinite number of choices every time they access it and, therefore, select their consumption according to their interests each time. Thus, advertisers can better match their offerings with an audience most likely to buy. This is true to some degree of television and radio as well, although both are a hybrid of random access and serial access—meaning that although consumers have a choice between as many as fifty to one hundred or more channels, they are limited by the schedule within each of the channels. As radio and TV become available digitally on the Web or online services, however, the nature of their advertising will be transformed as well. Technologies that allow consumers to request specific types of information, filter other types, and transparently share information about themselves with potential advertisers will further facilitate the kinds of focused, targeted ads that benefit vendors and customers alike. There may even be "ad-free" pricing and "ad-full" pricing for a variety of content, with gradations in between. Advertisers will almost certainly be able to target their audiences with far greater precision than ever before, and consumers will likely face fewer totally irrelevant ads in cyberspace than on less-targeted media.

Consumers can also simply choose to search for information about offerings directly. The World Wide Web is full of advertising. The home pages of most companies are advertising, in effect, arguably aiming to achieve the same objectives as traditional advertising: building image, enhancing awareness, and creating a sense of need while inviting action and offering positive information and even assistance. Some ads and sites are so interesting that consumers seek out the ads. Imagine multiplayer video games and virtual reality simulations available for free from an advertiser over the Net. The game would be thematically focused on a company's product just as today's video games are often focused on characters from cartoons and animations. Entertainment, education, and commercial propaganda—all in one package.

There is little question that advertising will change in form and content as it moves online. Although it's too soon to predict every nuance of these changes or just how prevalent and pervasive advertising will be online and how this will affect the advertising industry in general, I believe that there is one trend that strongly indicates the shape of things to come for advertising. That change is the blending of information and advertising.

Whether information is becoming more like advertising hype or advertising is becoming more like informative is moot—what is clear is that the lines are blurring. The forces that are leading in this direction are quite strong, as evidenced by the following excerpt from an online interview I had with Paul Gillin, executive editor of *ComputerWorld*:

> The beauty of online services, from the reader's perspective, is that they can see only what they want to see. And a lot of people would rather not see advertising. It's incumbent upon the advertisers to figure out a way to make their messages attractive enough that users will stop to look at them, and I have a lot of confidence that they will do that. It will be a completely different paradigm, however. Display advertising like you see in *Newsweek* will not work on a computer screen.
>
> The role of the publishers will be to help the advertisers find a technique that works in the new media. They'll be working hard at this as well, because there's a lot of money at stake. Between the two forces, I think there will be some solutions. The very survival of print publishers and advertising agencies depends on it.[31]

One of the most significant of these new solutions will be the increased use of endorsement, both direct and oblique. There is ample cultural precedent for this shift outside cyberspace. For example, when Reese's Pieces played a significant role in the movie *E.T.*, sales jumped. Now, companies routinely pay movie producers to include products in movies and even television shows. Rush Limbaugh sometimes endorses products he likes on his radio show even if they aren't advertisers—perhaps knowing that the makers of such products often become advertisers when sales jump following the endorsement. In the computer industry, many companies have long supplied anyone with press or consultant credentials with complementary "evaluation" copies of their software, knowing that a single endorsement from a credible influencer can trigger an avalanche of sales.

Because individuals often look to cyberspace for honest opinions and experience and answers to questions, we can expect to see a lot of endorsements, and we shouldn't expect such endorsements to be labeled as paid advertising, even if they are. On the other hand, most of those who are offering such evaluations are more mindful of their own reputation and credibility, and even if they have received the product at no charge for evaluation, I would not expect such a person to be swayed one way or the other by the fact that they received a free copy of the product. Thus, since there are no controls online against hidden agendas, the adage "let the buyer beware" should not be forgotten. Take recommendations from strangers with a grain of salt, even if several strangers offer the same advice. The reasons the opinions of PC columnists such as John C. Dvorak, Jerry Pournelle, Jim Seymour, and Bill Machrone are so highly valued is because they have been providing good advice and making quality judgments for years. In cyberspace, credibility will be more valuable than ever—with most consumers relying less and less on traditional advertising and more and more on credible endorsements.

Those of us who have been online for some time now have been witnessing this blurring between the lines that separate advertising, information, entertainment, commentary, and news. This blurring is occurring outside cyberspace as well, but it is perhaps most notable online. For example, two companies were featured in a *Wall Street Journal* story as having gotten their start using cyberspace as a springboard. Both companies were in the mail order OS/2 software business. Both of these companies (The Corner Store and Indelible Blue) were successful at increasing sales with remarkably little advertising overhead. How?

- by posting the "news" that they were open for business, including the nature of their offerings, in forums such as OS2USER, where such information would be welcomed
- by following those forums most frequented by OS/2 users and building goodwill by offering help and answering questions, with their company name and toll-free number in their taglines
- by building relationships with potential customers, suppliers, and influencers through online interaction

Interestingly, these companies were remarkably successful in building positive images in cyberspace, even when overt advertising and self-promotion were disdained by the online communities they served. Because both companies were providing useful information in response to customer questions and concerns, their presence was usually welcomed by their online audiences.

We will, no doubt, see plenty of infomercials online—many Web sites today could probably be classified as interactive infomercials. Infomercials don't necessarily need to be one half-hour long and run in the middle of the night on an obscure cable channel—the specifications sheet for a personal computer is an infomercial, for example. The Web will be full of those product details that sellers believe might attract buyers or serve existing customers. Unfortunately, during 1996, a number of conversations on

CompuServe forums have centered on the almost alarming rise in the amount of junk e-mail being sent out indiscriminately over the Internet. One such junk e-mail I received on October 18, 1996, from InfoLink Communications (auto@ilcom.com) evangelized "the e-mail distribution business" and offered to sell 10,000 e-mail addresses for $4.95 or 500,000 for $49.95. No wonder that America Online (AOL) announced in September 1996 that it had blocked incoming e-mail to subscribers from five Internet sites sending large volumes of unsolicited commercial e-mail. AOL claimed that customers had been complaining "vociferously" about the deluge of junk mail from Cyber Promotions, Inc.—owner of three of the five sites. A week later, United States District Judge Charles R. Weiner ordered AOL to stop blocking the sites until the courts address the legality of junk e-mail and the efforts of commercial online services to protect members from such mailings. Whatever the outcome, junk e-mail could be less of a problem than junk physical mail, since junk e-mail can be controlled technically with filters or other features of e-mail reader software. Junk e-mail may simply prove to be less effective than the alternatives.

Don Peppers and Martha Rogers point out that the "formerly implicit bargain between advertiser and consumer is likely to become decidedly explicit."[32] In other words, an advertiser might offer to pay for your pay-per-view movie if you watch a two-minute video and then answer a two-question pop quiz correctly. You could even eventually face a menu of ads from which to choose during each time-out in high-profile sports activities.[33] You choose the Sara Lee ad from the half dozen choices, watch the commercial, and a coupon worth $1 off on a cheesecake prints out on one of the special-purpose printers connected to your household network (along with the interactive television and all of the other cyberspace access devices).

Another evident trend is advertising via press release. Many companies have for years carefully crafted press releases containing selected facts designed to convey messages consistent with advertising and image-making efforts. Although journalists in the traditional sense of the word might skip over such press releases as hype, the press releases are on the wire and are often treated by many customers and publications just as if they had been written by a journalist and not by a company or their public relations firm. Online, there are no editors or censors—so people read (or skip) such releases based on whether the headline or material is of interest, not whether the content is "advertising" and hype or not. Thus, companies can simply purchase their way onto one of the wire services and send out their enhanced advertising and marketing messages as press releases. Subscriptions to online clipping services yield a significant number of press releases that announce products and corporate promotions. Since those press releases often contain valuable information for customers and even competitors, they are generally not as unwelcome as a typical ad might be.

Someday, we may sit down to read a personal communications device with a "soft display" that resembles a printed page in color and resolution with even better durability than paper or glass and have information (including advertising) delivered in accordance with a finely tuned personal profile. Because most of the information will be less intrusive than it is today, we may be less able to distinguish between advertising and interesting content. The lines may never completely disintegrate among advertising agencies, public relations firms, opinion makers, and credible journalists—but those lines are already blurring. Savvy companies will take note and take advantage of the new opportunities to advertise in creative and informative ways to bring additional value to customers.

Customer and Vendor Relations

In the decade I have spent in marketing, what is most evident to me is that the success of any company depends upon its relationships with its customers. Few enterprises can long survive without positive word of mouth or repeat customers. These relationships are built over time in any number of creative ways, but building them is difficult and wrecking them can be remarkably easy. One of the easiest ways to destroy relationships with customers is to neglect relationships with suppliers. It is far more difficult to fulfill commitments, real or implied, to customers if a supplier fails to deliver. Only good relationships in both directions can ensure the continuation of a thriving, healthy business. Cyberspace offers a wide variety of creative new ways for businesses to create and solidify these relationships.

Companies can be closer to their customers through cyberspace—and those companies who learn to use cyberspace to listen carefully to customers will enjoy a competitive advantage. Alan Ashton, cofounder of WordPerfect, told me over lunch in 1988 that the secret of WordPerfect's success had been its toll-free product support. Ashton saw it not as an expensive form of customer support, as it was generally viewed by competitors, but as a cost-saving means of serving multiple purposes, such as quality control, gathering marketing research and intelligence, finding ideas for research and development, training programmers to understand the customer perspective, tracking (and increasing) customer satisfaction, building brand image and loyalty, and simply building positive relationships with customers. I believe that companies will always be able to differentiate themselves by a customer-responsive presence in cyberspace, which encourages positive word of mouth. This presence can take numerous forms, including virtual teams of product enthusiasts, cyberspace public relations, interactive Web pages such as Dell's, gathering competive information, and capturing public demographic information about customers.

In addition to the previously described phenomenon of Team OS/2, IBM's customer support bulletin board, accessible by telephone, was an early model of what is possible to provide significant value to customers in a cost-effective manner. Developed by Wyn Easton, Dave Both, Mark Chapman, and others, it stood for years as a pre-WWW example of the support leverage and reach that could be offered by a small, dedicated team to thousands of customers. It offered new and old product and marketing information, technical details and specifications, end-user discussions, system files and updates, shareware, and bulletins. Like most other companies in the personal computer business that have maintained similar bulletin boards, IBM's bulletin board is being replaced by or transformed into Web pages that, unlike bulletin boards, don't require a long-distance call to access. Customers or potential customers will eventually be able to access a company's Web page and there do all the things mentioned previously as well as search company databases for employee contacts, purchase company stock, participate in research studies, vote on product features, and take advantage of special promotions and contests.

Increasingly, my experience with live customer support reps is that they end up referring me to the bulletin board to download a file that will solve my problem—so now I go to the support bulletin board first. Companies that don't have such a facility are more likely to lose customers. As more customers come online, an increasing number of companies will almost certainly find such "cyberspace consumer centers" of at least as much value as toll-free numbers dedicated to the same purposes.

There will be a wide variety of information available in cyberspace that will be used to facilitate relationships with suppliers, vendors, customers, and competitors, including including market segmentation data, demographics, ideas for business planning and opportunities, salary comparisons, forecasts, prices, policy, etc. Customers are often remarkably willing to share valuable personal and demographic information if they are confident that it will be used to improve personal service. Peppers and Rogers, authors of *The One-to-One Future: Building Relationships One Customer at a Time,* argue that "success in the new environment" will require "producing a high-quality product and service," "developing long-term relationships with customers," "differentiating among customers," and "initiating, maintaining, and improving dialogues with individual customers."[34] I agree without reservation. Those who succeed in cyberspace commerce will be those who learn to apply cyberspace technologies, at the right price, to the worthwhile pursuit of serving and delighting people.

Distribution

Vendors, suppliers, and consumers are bound by symbiotic ties. One aspect of keeping close to customers via cyberspace that has already seen wide acceptance and use is Electronic Delivery Interchange (EDI). This decade-old set of definitions for the exchange of formal business information has become a standard serving to enable "just-in-time" production, facilitate electronic invoicing and payment, improve inventory management, expedite electronic communications, enhance record-keeping efficiency, and more. It is already used by many companies doing business on the Internet and the World Wide Web, and should certainly be imbedded in most popular software supporting commercial transactions in cyberspace. When coupled with bar-coding technology, even dramatic improvements in tracking and distribution of physical objects can be improved using cyberspace. Federal Express, for example, can tell you at its Web site exactly where your package is at any given moment. The delivery personnel pass a bar-code wand over the package at key checkpoints in the delivery process, so you can know the moment it's delivered. Businesses can similarly find a variety of means to improve important relationships through the creative application of cyberspace technologies to increase efficiency, reduce errors, increase responsiveness, and attain new levels of service.

Public and Media Relations

One of the most rewarding of my cyberspace efforts with IBM in communications and marketing was to use cyberspace as a public relations medium. By traveling cyberspace, answering questions, monitoring discussions involving IBM, and helping journalists, consultants, customers, and others online, I was able to not only build goodwill for IBM (at least with some of my cyberspace constituents), but also provide valuable market feedback to IBM executives about programs, possibilities, and customer suggestions. Customers, after all, are the experts on how companies can best meet their requirements; and there is no better way to stay close to the customer than in cyberspace, where customers are generally well informed and can tell you precisely how you compare with the competition.

Even small companies can catch some degree of public attention in cyberspace. Celebrity publicist Michael Levine, in *Guerrilla P.R.*, advises readers to "computerize yourself," going online to exploit the "electronic media."[35] Online, any business can publish, posting its press releases. Information that has been crafted and well targeted for its intended audience is almost always well received. Furthermore, developing valuable media contacts in cyberspace is possible for those with interesting stories to tell or for those who possess access to information valuable to journalists. Paul Gillin of *ComputerWorld* once observed that cyberspace is a haven for journalists and writers because, by and large, they are "information junkies."[36] Certainly, companies that relate to journalists via e-mail in addition to telephone and mail contact have an advantage in telling their stories. E-mail has the marvelous advantage (to a writer at least) of being noninterrupting, easily deleted, and, within the bounds of e-mail etiquette, requiring no response. Hence, it seems to be a preferred form of interaction for most writers and reporters who use it.

The media themselves will probably be more responsible in all reporting, not only because news of errors or ways in which a writer might be out of touch spread quickly online but also because they can get better information closer to the source. *PC Magazine* has an entire discussion section for each of its major writers and columnists on ZiffNet, where readers can interact with and hold writers accountable for what they have written. Writers can gain valuable feedback concerning their work. Bill Machrone of Ziff Davis has actually made such interactions the topic of numerous columns, which not only makes for interesting reading, but also, arguably, increases readership and Machrone's credibility. The *Time* cover story on cyberporn may have drawn a firestorm of criticism; but, to his credit, author Philip Elmer-Dewitt went toe-to-toe with critics online, admitting mistakes as appropriate and defending his work against unjustified attack. *PC Week*'s Peter Coffee has often engaged critics of *PC Week* online, consequently gaining a reputation for fairness and accuracy. Many writers, including James Gleick (*Chaos*), Gloria Brame (*Different Loving*), Jerry Pournelle (*The Mote in God's Eye*), James Fallows (*Breaking the News*), and Orson Scott Card (*Enders Game*), have been online for years, offering and gaining insights. I could go on and on with lists of respected media figures who are online interacting with readers. Such writers are obviously not only convinced of the value of online interaction in staying in touch and building or defending credibility but also in learning and reporting with the insight that can often be gained from direct interaction with proponents and opponents alike.

The possibilities for companies and the media are obvious. The media can gain valuable information, perspective, sources, and credibility through their online interaction; company representatives don't need a degree and ten years' experience in media relations to influence what appears in the media.

Corporate Communications

Corporate communications have changed remarkably in just the last 10 years. For example, when I joined IBM, I (and most peers) would stop each day at the cork-backed bulletin board to read the IBM news and bulletins posted daily. If the local site communications group didn't think an item was worth posting, I had no way of knowing it. In many ways, ignorance was bliss. I usually had no idea what was going on in the other divisions of the company and trusted that all would continue to go well. Today, however, IBM employees can choose to read as many or as few bulletins online as they wish. The corkboards haven't gone away, but you rarely see anyone reading them. An online mainframe program, named INEWS, makes it possible for IBMers worldwide to have timely access to bulletins selected according to customized rules and global categories. Any IBMer can stay fairly well informed and take a greater interest in corporate decisions and actions.

Internal company communications are being transformed. Where once such communications were often filtered and the opportunities for exchange with other employees were limited by necessity and opportunity, now communications are open and almost unlimited. Employees regularly discuss the meaning of executive decisions. Rumors relating to company decisions are spread with remarkable rapidity and, in my experience at least, can be remarkably accurate. Employees who are wired learn the art of reading between the lines of corporate announcements by following the internal and external discussions surrounding such announcements. Cross-functional and even transcontinental communications are not only more easily and transparently facilitated now but also more often necessary.

Sales

Although sales of goods and services online were a quarter of a billion dollars in 1995, by the year 2000 they are expected to be at least $10 billion. To put that in perspective, however, total retail sales in the United States alone are currently about five hundred times higher, at $5 trillion. Mail order sales are already ten times as high, at $50 billion.[37] Nonetheless, it's safe to say that a healthy share of the growth in retail sales will eventually be diverted to cyberspace sales. Wal-Mart has already declared its intention to be a leading cyberspace retailer. Sales at Sharper Image (online) are growing fast. Shopper's Advantage and the CompuServe Mall have been doing well in cyberspace for years. 1-800-FLOWERS has been so successful in its cyberspace marketing on Prodigy and the Web that FTD florists might have cause for concern.

Yet secure, convenient digital checking and cash systems are just beginning to arrive. CyberCash has already debuted its CyberCoin electronic cash system, which requires "wallet software" that works with various financial institutions and online merchants. Christmas crowds in 1997 might be more evident in the delays on the Internet than in the lines at the stores. It is not likely that all of the billions of dollars in online spending will be in addition to current retail spending—it would seem that retail sales through traditional channels will be negatively affected at least to some degree, even if it's only a slowdown in sales growth. Most likely, the physical world shopping experience will change in order to complement cyberspace, just as the moviegoing experience has changed to complement home viewing of movies via cable, video tape, and pay-per-view. Barnes and Noble has already successfully pioneered the concept of providing physical comforts to browsers; I look for similar changes in a variety of other physical space shopping areas as well. The competition between cyberspace shopping and physical retailing will be healthy—encouraging each to focus on its own strengths. Theoretically, physical shopping offers the advantages of immediacy, sociality, and tangibility; whereas cyberspace shopping offers greater choice, comparisons, convenience, and savings.

Human Resources

The last decade has witnessed a major change in the role of the human resource departments of most large companies. Where once they were concerned with attracting and retaining top talent by providing excellent but cost-effective benefits and maintaining fair and equal treatment of all employees, they are now also concerned with the effects of downsizing and restructuring, avoiding lawsuits, encouraging retirement and redeployment, outsourcing, telecommuting, and managing transitions.

The same social forces that are leading us towards a worldwide information infrastructure are leading us towards new corporate infrastructures. Whether by overcoming barriers to communication and commerce or by moving towards a better informed, more egalitarian populace, the changes that are underway ask us to reexamine the relationships between people and the structure of the organizations to which they belong. These changes—from the authoritarian to the egalitarian, from the hierarchical to the networked, and from management to leadership—will be driven by cyberspace.

Attracting and Retaining Talent

Although at times it may seem like there's not enough of the "best" to go around, at least where talent is concerned, the real problem is probably inefficient matching mechanisms. Cyberspace can play several key roles in the human resource role of attracting and retaining talented personnel.

The most obvious way is to use cyberspace to recruit employees for available positions, whether from within the company or without. Job offerings can be posted online in special repositories, many of which are already in place. Many companies, including IBM and Hewlett Packard, have job posting resources in place, providing new and existing employees with details of opportunities. When standardized, centralized nationwide and regional repositories of easily searched job opportunities and resumes are available, the Internet might even allow companies to avoid the costly and often ineffective classified ads placed in local newspapers nationwide. Anyone who has been through the process of preparing resumes, interviewing, and recruiting knows that the process of matching talent with opportunity has enormous room for improvement. Because cyberspace offers the prospect of universally accessible, centralized, indexed repositories of resumes and opportunities, it is an ideal means of improving the career courtship process. Even better, if subsequent interactive communications are properly used, they can further ensure that the on-site interview time is spent most effectively on qualified, interested, well-informed candidates. This alone could improve overall economic productivity and growth.

There is no way to measure how much inefficiency and waste result from preparing resumes that will never be read and reading resumes that were sent out indiscriminately, but there is little doubt that it's significant. Similarly, no one knows exactly how much productive time is spent by management searching for the ideal candidate, and then settling for a less-than-ideal match in order to prevent further wasted time in broadening the search. We might also ask, rhetorically, how much talent is wasted when those millions who are underemployed keep working at jobs that utilize only a small portion of their training and abilities because they simply aren't aware of the other options available to them. Matching tools, as sophisticated or more than those found at www.careerpath.com or www.career-builder.com, combined with better means of helping potential employees articulate experience, talent, and interest will almost certainly improve the cumbersome process of matching productive work with a productive employee.

One attraction for many of those who grew accustomed to Internet access in college will be excellent access and regular usage at work. I would be reluctant to underestimate the importance of this consideration to students just entering the work force who take e-mail and World Wide Web access for granted and can't imagine working for a company that doesn't aggressively exploit cyberspace. Many companies, however, are concerned that employees will abuse access to cyberspace by surfing the net at random, downloading pornography on company time, playing games, and engaging in a variety of nonproductive or even subversive communications with coworkers. Consequently, many companies have implemented firewalls—secure systems that restrict employee access to selected portions of the Internet at the same time they prevent outsiders from accessing the company's computers. Indeed, there will inevitably be some abuse by employees even if companies adopt strict guidelines. Ultimately, however, the case is not much different from providing employees with a telephone. Most simply need it to do their jobs effectively, and the best form of management control is hiring people with proven character, communicating expectations, building the business on beliefs and values, and then trusting employees to exercise good and appropriate judgment—taking action only when patterns of abuse are evident.

Telecommuting

Telecommuting, or working from home via cyberspace, is attracting increased attention as an important element in human resource management. According to a survey released by Telecommute America!, 92 percent of the executives of companies with telecommuting programs agree that telecommuting benefits employers as well as employees. The survey, conducted in September 1995, also reported that telecommuting programs are in place at two-thirds of Fortune 1000 companies and that half of those programs had been instituted since 1993. A majority of those companies expect such programs to continue to grow, while almost 60 percent of the companies without telecommuting programs expected to institute one before 1998.[38]

Almost 7 million Americans are involved in telecommuting, working either from home or from some other off-site facility, at least part of their work week.[39] One Minnesota Department of Transportation survey indicates that more people in Minnesota telecommute to work, without any public investment, than use public transit, which has an annual public cost of $250,000,000.[40]

The implications are significant. Telecommuting promises increased flexibility in location and relocation for businesses and reductions in traffic congestion and pollution for cities. Telecommuting benefits employers with improved morale, lower costs, increased productivity, and the ability to recruit from a larger pool of talent, including mothers, the handicapped, and older workers. Employees benefit by being able to tailor work hours in noncontinuous blocks, work when they are most productive, avoid spending time on commuting, face fewer interruptions, and work in a more familiar, comfortable environment.

The key to an effective telecommuting program for any business include clarification of expectations on both sides. Employees company-wide should understand the qualifying factors that make telecommuting a win for the company as well as the employee, including such factors as the degree of face-to-face contact with coworkers required, whether the employee's inputs and outputs can be handled remotely, the degree to which employee and management objectives, goals, and schedules can be clearly defined, the possibility of complications from unions or other legal or environmental factors, and the amount of the financial responsibility assumed by the employee for expenses such as equipment, software, utilities, and supplies used.

Outsourcing

As technology has grown more sophisticated, it has contributed to the importance of automation managed by highly specialized knowledge workers. This trend has led to significant increases in outsourcing—turning to outside contractors to handle work previously handled by company employees. Traditionally, companies have tried to control every aspect of managing their business. Computer companies had accounting departments and accounting firms had computing departments. Law firms had couriers and large courier companies had lawyers. Large companies had a wide variety of employees who addressed every functional need of the company, and turning outside the company for temporary help was considered a sign of weakness. No more. As the levels of sophistication and specialization required in each functional discipline have increased, at least some downsizing in the last decade has occurred because it is now more economical to outsource specialized functions not directly related to the core competency of the company than it is to retain control of such functions within the company.

Many complex functions such as programming, payroll services, tax compliance, internal auditing, employee benefits, claims administration, equipment maintenance, office administration, manufacturing, transportation, sales and marketing representation, legal advice, public relations, merchandising, and even design engineering and strategic planning are being outsourced.

The benefits of outsourcing are many. Costs decline as the work is handled by more efficient specialists working with lower overhead, capital is freed, partnering with world-class experts makes available resources and expertise not available internally, roadblocks disappear as the responsiveness and effectiveness of functional areas increases, strategic benefits emerge when businesses are free to refocus on their core competencies, and the sphere of management concern is reduced. The disadvantages are that employees must be redeployed, retrained, or laid off and that a business loses some degree of control over those functional areas outsourced.[41]

Cyberspace not only facilitates outsourcing, but may further drive it because cyberspace encourages the specialized exchange of information that is one of the factors making outsourcing economically feasible. The trend towards outsourcing provides evidence that some of the market efficiencies that come with the application of specialized knowledge are leading us to new organizational structures such as the virtual corporation, where each company identifies its core competencies and outsources everything else.

Structural Changes

As more individuals adopt the use of e-mail and other cyberspace communications technologies, they will become more adept at handling the challenges of the age. This will, in turn, mandate changes to organizational structure, practice, and policy.

As I noted previously, Tom Peters argues effectively in *Thriving on Chaos* that the world around us is now undergoing such frequent and radical change that it has changed most of the rules about how businesses should operate. He points out that only thirty years ago companies were comfortable projecting the price of oil or the interest rate thirty years into the future; now they cannot comfortably predict such variables thirty days into the future. He demonstrates that most American companies are based upon a set of assumptions that no longer apply—namely that the world is a stable, predictable place.

That paradigm of stability with its assumptions of stability, hierarchy, and order led to bureaucracies that provided for consensus decision-making in order to minimize corporate mistakes. The stability of the environment contributed to the success of painstaking analyses and deliberate responsiveness to aggregated customer needs.

In effect, we're witnessing a struggle between two worlds: the hierarchical and the networked. The hierarchical paradigm is tightly structured and controlled. In computing terms, the mainframe is the ultimate model—centralized control over the vast power of the single system serves the coordinated goals of those umbilically attached, from the top down. Clearly defined management disciplines contribute to order and predictability. Every person sitting in front of a terminal is a servant, in a clearly defined role, to a stable organization with a clear mission and purpose.

The networked paradigm, on the other hand, is loosely defined, chaotic, and responsive. The client-server relationship is the ultimate model—decentralized, empowered individual clients seek to find creative expression and fulfillment, drawing on and adding to the resources of the server and thus the network. Every person views the network as an extension of self, contributing to the welfare of the whole according to his or her own unique abilities, knowledge, and skills.

Vastly different organizational structures and lines of communication are required by the two models. Under the hierarchical model, represented by the pyramid below, decision-making, responsibility, and authority are centralized at the top and delegated from the top to the bottom. Each person in the hierarchy is accountable only for himself and subordinates. In this environment, critical communications must not flow directly across the organization bypassing the chain of command, but must move up and down the chain as appropriate to ensure that awareness, responsibility and accountability are maintained.

Under the networked model, represented by the overlapping circles below, decision-making is local to coincide with the owner of each specific responsibility. Authority is tied to responsibility by mutual agreement at the time that responsibility is assumed. Everyone is accountable for everything

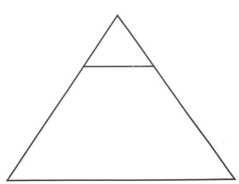

Hierarchical organizational structure

Networked organizational structure

and everyone, since ownership is shared. Communications occur directly between all involved parties without regard to hierarchy, since no hierarchy exists in a strictly networked organization. The communications themselves are networked.

Large, hierarchical, military-style organizations may still be the standard, but they are rapidly losing ground to smaller, flatter, more nimble organization structures. Peter Drucker, perhaps the world's most respected authority on management, noted in an August 1996 interview with *Wired Magazine* that "big companies have no future" and that "if you adjust for inflation there are very few of the Fortune 1,000 companies that have grown. But the medium-sized companies have grown very, very fast in the last 20 years."[42] Drucker notes three advantages that big companies once had, but that are now "all gone." First was that "they could get transnational or international money that a medium-sized company could not. Now everyone can." Second was the ability to obtain information. Now everyone has access to it. The third and most important advantage was the ability of large companies to attract talent. Now, "young, educated people do not want to work in the big institutions."[43]

Drucker compares the current structural model of management to the opera, where the conductor "has a very large number of different groups that have to pull together. The soloists, the chorus, the ballet, the orchestra, all have to come together—but they have a common score." Significantly, he says that nobody has found a way to actually implement such a system structurally in a large company.[44]

One model, facilitated by cyberspace, holds significant promise—the virtual company. Formed to address immediate opportunity, such an organization draws on the needed resources that cross the boundaries of function, expertise, company, and country. These organizations come together as needed and then simply disband following the accomplishment of the specific purpose for which they were created. In contrast to the traditional pyramid model of most large corporations, a virtual corporation is best described using a model of dynamic overlapping circles.

I believe that the most effective structures will be multiple teams of fewer than twelve people that act consistent with open communications directed by central authority, a compelling vision, and coordinated missions. Creative small businesses have the advantage of being able to build their structure to match the environment, but large businesses have the advantage of power, depth of resource, and experience. Significant opportunity and competitive advantage awaits those companies willing to aggressively reexamine the assumptions underlying their organizational structure and to adjust as necessary.

Leadership issues

Consistent with the changes in organizational structure, changes in leadership style are required to address the challenges presented by freely flowing information and individual commentary. Management alone is no longer adequate.

In a classic *Harvard Business Review* article titled "Managers and Leaders: Are They Different?," Abraham Zaleznik articulates the difference between a manager and a leader and identifies a possible reason for the differences.

> A managerial culture emphasizes rationality and control. Whether his or her energies are directed toward goals, resources, organization structures, or people, a manager is a problem solver. . . . It takes neither genius nor heroism to be a manager, but rather persistence, tough-mindedness, hard work, intelligence, analytical ability, and perhaps most important, tolerance and goodwill.

Leaders, on the other hand, are

> active instead of reactive, shaping ideas instead of responding to them. Leaders adopt a personal and active attitude towards goals. The influence a leader exerts in altering moods, evoking images and expectations, and in establishing specific desires and objectives determines the direction a business takes. The net result of this influence changes the way people think about what is desirable, possible, and necessary.[45]

In my experience, there are more managers than leaders in bureaucracies and more leaders than managers in cyberspace—at least according to Zaleznik's descriptions. This should not be surprising, since the pioneers of any frontier are most likely to be leaders. Astute managers, however, also stand to gain from cyberspace. This gain can be realized not necessarily because cyberspace can transform managers into leaders, but because cyberspace can be used to facilitate the task of discovering and benefiting from the ideas of leaders.

In a cyberspace community, one quickly comes to recognize and value those who are most helpful and insightful. Such individuals emerge as natural leaders in virtual teams. I have seen entire teams made up of such individuals engage in chaotic discussion, out of which eventually emerges a consensus—solutions that are stunning in their power, creativity, and elegance. The process may have been less than efficient, including outrageous ideas and trivial chatter—and therefore one that managers would typically have never encouraged or even allowed—but the results speak for themselves and emphasize the value of this type of leadership to management. I have also seen wise managers recognize the value of such leaders and nurture and motivate them by spending the time necessary to gain their loyalty by sharing those things managers often have which leaders often need—resource, contacts, and ability to shelter the leader from the corporate politics which so often alienate and irritate leaders.

Outside large companies, however, even leaders and entrepreneurs with low tolerance levels for the style and mind-set of traditional managers are using cyberspace to great advantage. There, they find and develop contacts, learn of market opportunities, identify competitive threats, brainstorm, gather information, and otherwise seek competitive advantage and cooperative leverage.

In examining some of the implications of this management/leadership dichotomy for cyberspace, we should examine the underlying reason for the difference. Is it learned or innate? Zaleznik presents his case rather convincingly that it is, at least to some degree, an inherent part of individual personality. He points out that managers work to narrow possible outcomes in order to simplify and reduce risk, while leaders work to expand them, trusting that positive outcomes and having additional choices will outweigh the negatives of the ensuing chaos. According to Zaleznik, these fundamental perspectives correlate well with another dichotomy: "once-born" and "twice-born," as described in William James's *The Varieties of Religious Experience*. Zaleznik equates managers with the "once-born," or those "for whom adjustments to life have been straightforward and whose lives have been more or less a peaceful flow since birth." Leaders and "twice-borns," however, "have not had an easy time of it. Their lives are marked by a continual struggle to attain some sense of order."[46]

Perhaps this explains "Generation X," a term coined by Doug Coupland, author of the book by the same name and of *Microserfs*. Are there more leaders in this latest generation than there were in previous generations? In my experience, there are. If Zaleznik's assertions about the roots of a leadership world view hold, then perhaps the significant increases in divorce rates and broken families, latch-key children, and television have yielded at least one positive consequence—more "twice-born" personalities and therefore more leaders to fuel the growth and progress of the cyberspace generation. If so, that offers insights into the diversity and chaos of the "cyberspace culture," or at least that portion evident in *Wired*.

Assuming everyone is either a manager or a leader, the implications for large companies and small companies alike are profound. Large companies must find ways to reorganize and decentralize wherever possible to take advantage of the innate leadership potential of employees and business partners, without giving up the economic advantages of being big, such as economies of scale. Medium-sized and small companies should exploit their natural advantage of flexibility, unity, and focus to identify and hire the right mix of leaders and managers to populate effective functional teams.

What's more, today's managers can learn leadership skills from employees by looking in on the public conferencing of collaborating employees— lurking. Executives can thus access a wealth of raw data about the impact of such things as company policy, products, strategies, and technologies— direct from the employees themselves in unfiltered, collaborative, problem-solving exchanges. Even controlled flames can be valuable in an environment where leaders are willing to accept and learn from subordinates in an amicable environment. Those executives with the courage, confidence, and ability to interact directly with employees in cyberspace can probably gain buy-in and employee loyalty at unprecedented rates. Such leaders are truly rare; Bill Gates is one. Imagine what might be possible in a company where collaborative communications are part of the fabric of the company—fewer meetings, more consensus, better decision-making, and more understanding would be the likely results when the executives of such companies are truly leaders. To date, the collaborative communications of most companies have been centered around Lotus Notes, e-mail, Group Decision Support Systems (GDSS), and home-grown conferencing systems. The successes of even those piloting ventures have convinced many participants that some of the problems of highly political organizations can be overcome by a top-down emphasis on open, many-to-many communications. Wise management will facilitate the use of such communications to free natural leaders from the constraints imposed by traditional hierarchical organizations and communications. The payoff can be enormous.

Research and Development

Engineers, programmers, scientists, and researchers have been using cyberspace to coordinate and accelerate research and discovery for over two decades. In fact, online communication was created to facilitate discussions of technical issues. Collaborative communications are the ideal means for the sharing of knowledge quickly and easily, which is such a critical part of the discovery process.

Under the able direction of Nicholas Negroponte, the MIT Media Laboratory has been enormously successful in developing creative concepts and prototypes which fuel the imaginations of executives, researchers, inventors, politicians, engineers, and academicians worldwide. The Media Lab acts as a giant nerve center for creative ideas where cyberspace and the real world meet. Visiting executives can see demonstrations that range from the transfer of information from one person's shoes to another's via the low-voltage electrical current of a handshake, to computerized Lego blocks. Researchers explore the human-machine interface in all directions, pushing the frontiers of virtual reality, artificial intelligence, interactive cinema, holography, video compression, gaze recognition, face recognition, and speech recognition. Negroponte has carved out a niche demonstrating the power of cooperation between industry and academia worldwide, and between disciplines as varied as science and engineering and art and communications.[47]

IBM's Research Facilities in Yorktown, New York; Zurich, Switzerland; LaGaude, France; Hursley, England; and Almaden, California, are connected to one another for collaborative research. While at IBM, I was occasionally able to witness intense discussions surrounding rapidly unfolding and highly charged areas of research such as superconductivity and cold fusion. Our mental image of scientists as solitary researchers making dramatic discoveries published in carefully reviewed journals may very well give way to a new image of collaborative teams making dramatic announcements online.

As has been noted, the body of the world's knowledge and its technological application has been growing at such a dramatic rate that some say that we have lost our individual and collective ability to cope with this upheaval productively—that technology is overpowering our humanity. Given the potential for exploration, cooperation, and archiving made possible by cyberspace, however, I'm optimistic that the technological advances derived from cooperative, team-based research and development efforts will contribute to our humanity.

Exploration

The joys of Net surfing could lead to a creative explosion and a renewed interest in the creative sciences that will provide business with the innovative engineers, researchers, and creative product champions that will drive the economy and improve our prosperity.

My 12-year-old son, Jared, for example, has been pestering me to give him full access to the World Wide Web. Why? Because there are "cool" things to do there, according to his science teacher. This is the same boy who has been trading the details of *Star Trek* research and development possibilities with strangers on Prodigy for the past year. If we can make cyberspace safe for the explorations of youth, then the very young today can have free access to hyper-linked information that would have probably brought gasps of astonishment and delight from the likes of geniuses such as daVinci, Newton, and Einstein. There is simply no telling what extraordinary outcomes will result as the very young explore the collected knowledge of the ages available in cyberspace, with mentoring teachers and parents at their side, and willing tutors available on every forum. This next generation could witness the most significant leap in educational attainments of any in history, and the consequences of that leap could be an ever-increasing acceleration of innovation and consequent prosperity.

Joint Ventures

Even though the results to date have been less than spectacular, cooperation between researchers who were once competitors is increasing, enabled by cyberspace communications. Throughout the industrial world, there is more cooperation than ever before; and whenever there is cooperation over distances, you will find cyberspace communications making a difference—enabling cooperation and collaboration never before possible in a cost-effective manner.

In many cases, it is the engineers themselves who are forging the e-mail and collaborative links that enable them to achieve so much in less and less time—but management and executives also stand to benefit significantly, as noted in the section on leadership. Cyberspace communications will not only facilitate communication between teams and key individuals to make existing alliances work, but will also aid in the generation of creative ideas and contacts leading to new alliances and joint ventures. Virtual corporations should increase in importance as specific researchers combine their efforts to produce economically valuable and patentable ideas and technologies to benefit the joint creators.

New opportunities also await those companies that form to nurture the creation and management of intellectual property. In fact, many companies are transforming themselves into what some are calling the "media companies of the 21st century." Disney merged with ABC and hired Michael Ovitz, one of the most powerful agents in Hollywood, as president. Microsoft is recreating itself more in the image of a digital, interactive media company than a software company. According to industry analyst Denise Caruso, Microsoft has invested between $0.8 and $1.5 billion in media-related ventures. She quotes Nathan Myhrvold, Microsoft Group Vice

President of Applications and Content, as saying, "Yes, we are becoming a media company."[48] Bill Gates, through a company he owns named Corbis, has been buying the digital rights to images for years and now owns the rights to over one million such images.[49] AT&T recently divested itself of its computer division and Bell Labs, forming a new company. Nynex and Bell Atlantic have agreed to merge.

The confluence of cable, television, telephone, the Internet, and software will, quite simply, reconfigure the structure of power in the entertainment and information industries. Joint ventures and restructuring supported by and addressing cyberspace will fundamentally change the landscape of business—possibly requiring a redefinition of the related industries.

Finance

When financial and other information about investment opportunities is immediately and broadly accessible, markets are, theoretically, more efficient. There are a number of markets that operate through a real-time auction process, including stock markets, commodities exchanges, and currency exchanges. As news enters the market, it may motivate buyers and sellers to take action, thus affecting prices. The sooner everyone has access to the same information and the sooner those decisions are able to hit the market, the better the markets work to ensure equality for all buyers and sellers. In other words, cyberspace can enable more efficient financial markets by reducing or eliminating the frictions of differences in information, distance and time. This cyberspace-enabled efficiency has long been with us in the form of the tickertape, news wires, broadcast news, and the immediacy of telephone communications—but there is still room for improvement. Trading stocks without brokers directly online, for example, would even further reduce those frictions.

However, cyberspace communications also introduces a wild card into the equation: not everyone will be able to tap into the same information in cyberspace at the same time or in the same places. Thus, we will probably see even more volatility introduced into such markets as a result of the availability of better (or worse) information in cyberspace than in the real world. The Iomega example introduced earlier, where a variety of information introduced on a forum first clearly drove the market price of the stock, is one example. Another is the rapid ascent and volatility of Netscape.

Think back to where you were in January of 1993—that's when Marc Andreessen released the first version of Mosaic on the Internet. A year later, Jim Clark formed Mosaic Communications and lured Andreessen and other key Mosaic developers to the new company. In rapid succession, the company changed its name to Netscape, released its first Netscape browser which quickly wrested the market from Mosaic, and decided to go public—all within its first year and a half. The wired community buzzed with information about the strategic prospects of a company that might be able to wrest industry control from Microsoft. In August 1995, the Netscape Communications initial public offering was met with a frenzy of purchasing that drove the price from its $13 initial estimated offering price to $28 actual offering price (for those fortunate enough to actually line up a source for the shares) to $75 in the first few hours of trading, before finally closing the day at $58. In the last quarter of 1995, Netscape's stock price jumped from below $25 to higher than $80, only to fall back to $35 during the first quarter of 1996. The second quarter of 1996 saw the price then jump back up to $75 before falling to $35 in the third quarter of 1996. Whatever the cause, that's volatility. I expect it will become even more pronounced in markets that depend on fast-breaking information to determine prices.

Investing

Institutional investors and individuals both can enjoy the information advantages of cyberspace. There is a wealth of financial and corporate information available online—from both the commercial services and from the Net. The Securities and Exchange Commission filings for publicly-held companies, such as the 10K reports, can be had at no charge at http://town.hall.org/edgar/edgar.html. Stock quotes are available on all of the commercial services and even from the World Wide Web—at least on a 15-minute delay basis. Company histories, current news, economic data, forecasts, demographics, and financial reports can all be found online. Peter Lynch, the spectacularly successful former manager of the Fidelity Magellan Mutual Fund, has long championed the idea that investors can beat the market by carefully selecting companies based on personal experiences with quality and a common sense approach to analyzing the company's prospects. Such information will be more easily obtained in cyberspace, where ones own experience and opinion can be compared with the experiences and opinions of others. Most useful and revealing of all, however, may often be the information provided by the company itself on its own Web pages—especially the information that is targeted at potential and existing customers. In cyberspace, gathering additional information about companies often results in a broader perspective—even if one shies away from the potentially distorted online discussions of a company's prospects, although I would argue that those discussions, accurate or not, influence the stock price, and therefore became part of what must be known about a company.

Many investment firms, including Charles Schwab, offer online trading and account management—enabling customers to manage portfolios, IRAs and pension funds using a computer and a modem. According to William M. Bluestein, codirector of Forrester Research, there will be 1.3 million online shareholder accounts by 1998, up from 600,000 today.[50]

Financial newsletters have traditionally been an unbiased source of valuable information, but now at least one newsletter and its corresponding Web site carry a disclaimer noting that at least some of the companies analyzed have paid a "research and promotional fee." In spite of the obvious conflict of interest, the newsletter and Web site seem to be doing very well. In any case, investment decisions should only rarely be made solely on the basis of online tips, and all information received from cyberspace should be scrutinized carefully before relying on it to make investment decisions.

On the flip side of growing one's investments, there are plenty of opportunities to be fleeced. Besides the speculations of the forums, one newsgroup (biz.misc) is well known as a paradise for get-rich-quick offers and pyramid schemes and scams. Whether on the Internet or on the online services, some posters are simply well-disguised pitch men, while others are outright con artists. Although some such posts are immediately recognizable as lacking credibility, the only way to cull many posts is to follow the discussion groups for long enough to gain a sixth sense, often referred to online by the crude term of "bs detector," or rely on the collective opinions of others as garnered from the discussions. Thus, if we choose to draw information from cyberspace discussions, the number of choices we must make and the stakes in knowing the difference between truth and error increase.

I trust that appropriate cultural and legal steps will be taken to ensure equity in the markets. Eventually, I foresee market forces bringing many additional investors into cyberspace, which will fuel demand for stocks, increase the value of information about investment opportunities and increase the efficiencies of the market in providing capital to those companies best able to use it effectively.

Stock Markets and Exchanges

NASDAQ is perhaps the first cyberspace stock exchange. Unlike the New York and American Stock Exchanges or the Chicago Futures and Options Exchange, NASDAQ has no physical home. It exists instead in the network of participating companies, who buy and sell based on bids and offers gathered and distributed in cyberspace. Although NASDAQ is not yet perfectly efficient, probably because a perfectly efficient exchange would leave less commission in the pockets of the market makers and exchange members, it is nonetheless a prototype of the future of trading.

Consumer-friendly laws are already being sought that could easily challenge the near monopoly of the existing exchanges. The advantages are so significant to investors that such a development could rock the foundations of Wall Street. Currently, billions of dollars in commissions annually are pocketed by traders, stock brokers, and commissioned salespersons. The value added by these middlemen? Regulation, information, and centralized facilitation of exchange. The latter two can conceivably be assumed by a highly secure online exchange; however, the former presents the most significant barrier for the moment to the movement to eliminate the broker and leave more capital in the pockets of investors.

Capital Formation

Speculate with me for a moment. If information, opportunity, and, consequently, wealth are distributed more evenly as a result of cyberspace, then might the traditional concentration of investment capital in the hands of Wall Street investment bankers and venture capitalists become more decentralized? Middlemen (including stock brokers and traders) are rendered unnecessary by friction-free markets. If corporate downsizing continues, small businesses prosper, energized by new opportunities in cyberspace. Could the middle class, at least, then begin to enjoy greater wealth and power, resulting in a resurgence of the American dream for anyone willing to work and exercise creative discipline in cyberspace? Even if it's too soon for the answers, the time is right to ask the questions.

In Seattle, Washington, the emergence of thousands of "Microsoft millionaires" and several billionaires has fundamentally altered the economic dynamics of capital formation there. In Washington and even nationwide, numerous other companies have been formed deploying the wealth created by Microsoft's success, including Egghead Software (Spokane, Washington), Corbis (Bellevue, Washington), America Online (Vienna, Virginia), SureFind Corp. (Seattle), Darwin Molecular Technologies (Bothell, Washington), Telescan (Houston, Texas), Virtual Vision (Seattle), Asymetrix (Redmond, Washington), Metricom (Los Gatos, California), StarWave (Bellevue), Cardinal Technologies (Lancaster, Pennsylvania), Real Audio (Seattle), and hundreds more. The same dynamics will extend to cyberspace. Cyberspace will create at least as much liquid wealth; much of which will be available to fund other companies. Given the investment capital already flowing into cyberspace, it is likely that cyberspace will continue to be a place where innovative ideas and proven management, when combined, will find ready funding from venture capital firms and an ever-increasing number of millionaire "angels" alike.

NETTING IT OUT

Cyberspace provides new opportunities for anyone willing to explore the elimination of some of the traditional barriers to commerce. Time, distance, ignorance, and other boundaries, can all be mitigated as obstacles to exchange by the appropriate use of cyberspace technologies. As the Internet, particularly the World Wide Web, continues to grow, other barriers will fall as well. Difficulties in the pricing of knowledge and information, the lack of an online currency standard, cultural resistance to paying for information except as a product or service, resistance to insecure transmissions and foregoing privacy, and technological and other usability barriers will be addressed and resolved—just as we have always overcome obstacles to our progress and technological evolution.

Although the individual and social benefits of cyberspace are important, they can't hold a candle to economics as a driver for its development. Thus, it is almost inevitable that business will be a primary defining force behind the standards that will shape the very nature of cyberspace in our generation. Even so, consumers can make their voices heard during the formative periods of those standards and again when choosing to adopt them as their own. If the standards-setting process is commandeered by private interest, government intervention may be necessary in order to prevent the market damage that is likely to result from privatized monopoly standards that give single companies inordinate power to set prices high, stifle innovation, and limit choices.

As the barriers fall, new opportunities for existing and new businesses will be found in rich abundance. Consumers will discover wants and needs they didn't know they had as the energies of a free market quickly move to match available technology against those desires and requirements. Every functional area of business, including marketing, sales, finance, human resources, law, and communications will be affected. If the typically human pitfalls of greed and raw ambition can be identified and avoided, it may not be too great a stretch to imagine that the "trickle-down" theory may finally become real, as all benefit from decades of unprecedented growth. On the other hand, we may find that the application of technology for its own sake or our own sake without an offsetting willingness to consider the well-being of all might introduce further economic polarization as the rich to get richer while the poor get poorer. Only time will tell.

CHAPTER SEVEN

GOVERNMENT AND POLITICS

Harnessing the Power of Revolutionary Change

Incessant change, everlasting innovation, seem to be dictated by the true interests of mankind. But government is the perpetual enemy of change.

—William Godwin

Nowhere has rapid, constant, beneficial change been more evident than in the information industry. Moore's law (which is named after Intel founder and Chairman, Gordon E. Moore, and states that microprocessor power grows exponentially, doubling every eighteen months or so) will almost certainly hold true for many microprocessor generations yet to come. For the last two decades, this power has touched every aspect of our lives, even for those who have never touched a personal computer. The machines that surround us—cars, phones, televisions, computers, VCRs, and even kitchen appliances—are smarter than ever. The role and pace of technological change in daily life, community life, and politics cannot be overlooked, because technology now shapes our daily lives perhaps even more than government does. The old saw that conservatives resist change and liberals embrace it is no longer reality. Both political orientations must not only embrace change but also must position themselves as agents of change to have any hope of regaining power or staying in power. Change has become a political constant. The forms of communication that engender change—pagers, cellular phones, calling cards, fax machines, toll-free numbers, e-mail, videoconferencing, and online forums—have never been so propitiously available. We are more aware of our world than ever before—the good, the bad, and the ugly confront us in unprecedented daily doses through television, radio, magazines, books, and now, computer-mediated communications. Yet the communications revolution is still in its infancy.

The pace of change in the information industry has created, worldwide, reasonable expectations for more global change, at an ever-accelerating pace—yet government has unwittingly positioned itself as both an agent of the changes to come and a target. In less than a decade, the view of the online world has been transformed from a sometimes weird, wired, underground embryonic subculture into an infant mainstream culture to be kissed by politicians of every stripe, dirty diapers and all. Al Gore and Newt Gingrich may be the two politicians most in tune with the wired constituency, but even Ted Kennedy has a Web page. The January 1996 passage of the Telecommunications Act ensures that the coming changes will present fresh challenges, pitfalls, and possibilities; yet it also clearly demonstrates the extraordinary ideological gap that exists between politicians in our existing systems of government and theoreticians in the cyberspace dominion. Government, like any bureaucracy, jealously guards its own power to manage change and shape change to serve the will of its constituency. Yet the Communications Decency Act (CDA), the federal government's attempt to balance free speech and decency in cyberspace, demonstrates a sobering eagerness to initiate change rooted in a woeful lack of understanding and a gross failure to appreciate the dynamic quality of cyberspace communications. The federal government's prolonged failure to relax export controls over encryption technology demonstrated a distressing resistance to necessary change. Government has plainly demonstrated that it is Godwin's "enemy of change"—thus inviting conflict and rendering itself less relevant in the task of shaping the future.

We are caught in a dilemma: even though we can't agree on the appropriate role of government in coping with or initiating change, most of us can still agree that the world and cyberspace are facing unprecedented change and stands in need of additional unifying standards. Anarchy seems preferable to a witless governing bureaucracy; yet we desperately need the societal agreement and cohesion we seek from government, now more than ever before. We need agreement on the critical importance of information and cyberspace; we need common means of information exchange; we need larger (higher bandwidth) shared conduits for information transfer, we need electronic money; we need privacy standards; we need simplified access methods and standardized interfaces; we need increased security and protection; we need standards for labeling content; we need differentiation of public and private spaces; and we need just enough regulation to ensure that the Information Superhighway serves individuals and the public good more than it serves greedy robbers, information barons, terrorists, hostile countries, ambitious dictators, or anyone else who would selfishly exploit others in the virtual world.

Picture a superhighway with no consensus about which lanes to use, no agreement on maximum or minimum speed limits, nothing to prevent pedestrians, equestrians, or picnickers from camping in and using the fast lane, few traffic signs, a thousand exits per mile (many of which are unlabeled or falsely labeled to attract curious visitors), rest stops that might or might not have restrooms, and so on. Imagine that every state in cyberspace has its own rules of the road, with no traffic signs. That is not far from being analogous to cyberspace as it exists today. There are a few well-established but primitive norms for such things as "netiquette" and basic technical standards, but there is much less agreement on most important technological or social standards.

Unfortunately, no one seems willing or able to create standards that serve the public and communities more than private economic interests. Our public standards are being set by private interests, perhaps because big business seems to be less threatening than big government. Our sense of community is changing; our loyalty is shifting. We no longer seem to view our nation, or state, or even our city as our binding, primary community. The government is no longer seen as the unifying voice of the people. Government is often seen as the enemy of the people rather than the manifestation of the will of the people. Governments are more often seen as dumb, senseless bureaucracies than as organizations of individuals bound by a common cause.

We may be seeing the early manifestations of a struggle, in both cyberspace and the real world, for freedom from impersonal bureaucracy run amok, whether that bureaucracy takes the form of government or big business. Frustrations are bubbling to the surface with increasing frequency. A career consultant working for a respected nationwide executive search firm told me that he would not be surprised to see "violent uprisings" of salaried workers at blue-chip companies if current trends in exorbitant executive compensation accompanying insensitive downsizing continue. Although that view may be a bit extreme, what is clear is that these yearnings for empowerment rooted in security may very well be triggered by the social, economic, and political conditions of distrust that accrue when law-abiding citizens are increasingly the victims of crime, loyalty to company is often rewarded with layoffs, morality suffers from ardent existentialism, and leadership is stifled under the weight of bureaucracy. Those who have access to the Information Superhighway in one form or another have probably

tasted of the revolutionary empowerment and access that come from be-
longing to this world without limits or boundaries; yet only a few of those
who populate the governments of the world seem to have any real idea of
the dynamic they face. The potential for revolution, which is already underway in cyberspace, is ripe.

There is a specter haunting the political universe—the specter of a
revolution that will inexorably transform our sense of community. MIT
sociologist Sherry Turkel says we are in a transition period she calls "the
liminal moment, . . . a moment when things are betwixt and between,
when old structures have broken down and new ones have not yet been
created. Historically, these times of change are the times of greatest cultural
creativity; everything is infused with new meanings."[1] David Gergen has
said that "the communications revolution . . . has become the greatest
friend of individual liberty in the world. It is empowering people all over
the world. The communications revolution is supplanting the Communist
revolution."[2]

Today, the leaders and élites of this revolution are those who are learning
and using empowering new technologies. As Stewart Brand says, "fundamentally, élites drive civilization."[3] This revolution began with the advent of
personal computers and is gaining momentum as those computers link in
powerful networks. *Wired Magazine*, perhaps the most important new
magazine in a generation, is full of the angry voices of revolutionaries.
Simon Davies, addressing *Wired* readers, says: "We must seize every tool
at our disposal to bash Congress and make our voices heard. . . . If Net users
want to preserve what remains of their rights, they must learn to play
political hardball. . . . We must wage a battle for the future using sticks and
stones, because those are the only weapons that seem credible to our Nean-
drethal opponents."[4] There is much talk of overthrow and the evils of
big government, including one column in which Brock Meeks lists "The
Rogues Gallery" (James Exon, Dianne Feinstein, Patricia Schroeder, John
Conyers, and Barbara Boxer) who "helped make censorship a reality on the
Internet."[5] John Perry Barlow wrote a "Declaration of the Independence of
Cyberspace" the day the CDA was signed into law, stating: "Governments of
the Industrial World, you weary giants of flesh and steel, I come from
Cyberspace, the new home of Mind. On behalf of the future, I ask you of
the past to leave us alone. You are not welcome among us. You have no sov-
ereignty where we gather. . . . We will create a civilization of the Mind in
Cyberspace. May it be more humane and fair than the world your governments have made before."[6]

Just because you don't read it reported clearly in the press doesn't mean
it can be discounted as insignificant. The press underestimated the "revolu-

tion" behind the 1994 elections. The "mainstream media" seemed to ignore Rush Limbaugh until he became part of that "mainstream media" from which people draw their perspectives. Although the press reports at length on cyberspace and new developments there, I find that the flavor of the revolutionary fervor can be gained only by actual participation in cyberspace forums coupled with readings of magazines dedicated to online phenomena, such as *Wired* or *Boardwatch*. There is something important happening that hasn't been captured—something I don't think anyone can possibly grasp.

Yet what is certain is that before long, the tools of today's revolutionary élite will be in the hands of Everyman. George Gilder notes that "the linked PCs of today and the teleputer a combination of television and computer] networks of tomorrow seem formidable—difficult to get in and drive. At times they appear to be the tools of a new élite. But teleputers feed on the most rapid learning curves in the world economy and in proportion to their powers are the cheapest technologies in history. Just as the TV, once an exotic tool of the élites, became even more ubiquitous in America than the telephone or the automobile, the teleputer will end the decade not as a luxury but as an indispensable appliance."[7] As Nicholas Negroponte points out, "the existing élites are often those who have the least impact on civilization. But once you do have an impact, you become part of a new élite."[8]

Whichever élite we may choose to resist or embrace, we the people now have an opportunity perhaps unlike any since the American Revolution to choose our destiny for the next century as we shape the standards, structure, culture, society, and governance of cyberspace. We can embrace this wave of change in order to harness its power to fulfill our cultural and societal ideals, as did the founding fathers. Or, in fear and trepidation, we can continue to cling to the status quo and build on foundations of sand in attempting to manage and control change by political rather than principled means as we watch it crash on the shores around us and drag us out to the sea of ever more unmanageable and unpredictable transformation and polarization. The strategy of hope is to embrace change, with faith in the excellence of each individual and a passion for those rights that constitute our common welfare.

HARBINGERS

What has happened in the computer industry over the past decade could very well presage some of what will happen to government and other influential political forces during the next. The computer industry is well down the road to understanding the dynamics of incessant change, offering a fascinating glimpse into the implications of these transformations on the fortunes of individuals and organizations, as a harbinger of the tumultuous changes we might predict for citizens, politicians, governments, and observers.

The parallels are striking: IBM, like the federal government, was a benevolent bureaucracy that stood as the provider of industry standards, an umbrella for prices, economic protection of employees, and an example of the kinds of near-monopoly profits that accrue to any company that can control information processing standards relatively free from government intervention. The personal computer was as revolutionary a stimulus to American business in the 1980s as cyberspace communications technologies will be to society and government in the 1990s and beyond.

The themes that have played out in commerce are also being played out in government, with a seemingly beneficial lag that offers opportunity to learn and benefit. These themes are familiar politically: centralization vs. decentralization, rapid response vs. responding conservatively with caution, distribution of power vs. consolidation of power, cradle-to-grave entitlement vs. fiscal responsibility, egalitarian democracy vs. representative republicanism, and proactively managing change vs. reactively responding to change.

In 1984, the year I joined IBM as a financial analyst, IBM was riding the waves of technological change as masterfully as a champion surfer. IBM was so successful in managing change and controlling an industry that Apple found a ready audience with ads that evoked images of IBM as Big Brother from George Orwell's *1984*. IBM executives spoke of reaching $100 billion in revenues by the end of the 1980s. The media fawned over IBM, and the friendship of an IBM executive or two was often a ticket to influence and power for journalists, columnists, and consultants. Even Big Government lost its battle to reduce the size and power of Big Blue.

IBM was routinely considered to have the best management in the world, and IBM management believed that changes in technology could be carefully managed to provide optimum value to customers and stockholders. Their view of the future of computing, shared by most large businesses, rested on a master–slave (a term that was often used) vision of centralized power and intelligence, with millions of dumb terminals attached to a mainframe. IBM management saw personal computers not as distributed processing peers in global networks; but rather as more intelligent dependent terminals. IBM's organizational structure was remarkably consistent with this master-slave vision. IBM headquarters in Armonk, New York, was the White House, Congress, and Supreme Court rolled into one, with hierarchical, dependent subsidiary organizations with less independence than any

U.S. state. In spite of IBM's founding belief in "respect for the individual," IBM structure was an imbalance of centralized power and privilege at the top and ambitious expectations and a sense of entitlement at the bottom. In between could be found the "big gray cloud" of too many ambitious career bureaucrats, many of whom had more experience in managing the political processes of IBM than in running a viable business. IBM exercised control over almost every aspect of employee behavior, through its mandatory "Business Conduct Guidelines." When IBM began to realize that things were going wrong, senior executives began to emphasize the importance of empowerment, customer satisfaction, personal initiative, and accountability. Yet they were seemingly bound by the bureaucracy and layers of vested interests, unable to fully address the root problem: the hierarchical command structure that rewarded heads-down focus on one's own performance plan, even without regard to the welfare of the company as a whole.

The trade press and certain customers and analysts first turned on IBM in the late 1980s following IBM's attempts to establish new IBM standards in the PC industry. By the early 1990s, respect for IBM in the industry was fading fast. Many of the more humanistic elements of IBM policy were abandoned one by one in favor of bottom-line, big-business-as-usual personnel practices. IBM's once-potent weapon for employees, the Opinion Survey, came to be little more than a meaningless bureaucratic exercise. Similarly, many in management viewed the handling of anonymous complaints named "Speak Ups" as a bureaucratic demand rather than as an opportunity to improve. The "Open Door" policy no longer meant that you would actually get to see the person you wanted to see, but, rather, some other subordinate designated to investigate and whitewash as necessary. Documented proof of management dishonesty no longer meant automatic and immediate termination for the offending executive or manager. Employee morale at IBM fell precipitately; few employees still speak of IBM as the "special company" with the "family atmosphere" it once was. IBM is just another big company in America. So what led to these changes, even as IBM frantically tried to respond with a "market-driven" strategy?

Simple: nimbler competitors offered change, ready or not, to the market before IBM could because of its rigidly hierarchical structure that devalued individual initiative. IBM neglected the basics—the Basic Beliefs, the basics of management, the basics of running a business prudently, and the basics of valuing customers and employees, and, most important, the basics of change. In spite of IBM's enormous technological prowess and resources, IBM management believed that change could be managed on its own terms by its own timetable rather than on customer terms and by customer timetables. Dramatic advances in technology were not brought to market as quickly as they should have been, and IBM watched competitor after competitor " borrow" IBM technology and make it more successful than IBM did. Technologies such as Reduced Instruction Set Computing (RISC) chips, Winchester disk drives (still the most common type of hard disk type sold), relational database technology, Structured Query Language (SQL), Query By Example (QBE), the personal computer architecture, and Video Graphics Array (VGA) were borrowed and copied and popularized by others.

IBM's insular assumptions about the importance of "account control" and "market leadership" were utterly discredited and destroyed in less than a decade by the pell-mell customer rush to embrace personalized computing power. IBM had literally created its own undoing—Microsoft, Intel, and other companies wrested control of standards and market power from IBM as they out-negotiated, outsmarted, and out-hustled the lumbering giant.

With management that had neglected the basics of business, IBM and its "big-is-beautiful" management style had no more chance against Bill Gates and his "lean and mean" Microsoft machine than today's "unwired" politicians will have against the growing numbers of cyberspace-savvy companies and constituents. IBM had no idea that the public hunger for standards would grant such legitimacy and power to Microsoft and Intel that both companies would turn into a thorn in IBM's side. IBM's arrogance was so great that it turned down opportunities to invest heavily in Microsoft, offered by Bill Gates, and sold a 15 percent stake in Intel. IBM had no idea that its first entry into personal computing would establish standards that would not only last for decades to come, but would also hinder IBM's efforts to establish new, more elegant standards later. Small companies leveraged those standards to harm IBM far beyond IBM's ability to imagine in 1981, when those standards were chosen to create a machine that IBM expected would sell 250,000 units and enable IBM to compete with Apple in the "hobbyist" market.

In particular, Microsoft ripped the mantle of industry leadership away from IBM using tactics that continue to have serious implications for cyberspace and government. Until recently, neither the government nor the trade press could be seen as eager to argue with, much less fully expose, the aggressive practices of those in power at Microsoft. With a few rather notable exceptions, such as James Gleick, Wendy Goldman Rolm and Nicholas Petreley, members of the media have treated Gates and Microsoft with kid gloves. No wonder—even the government seems helpless in the face of Microsoft's overwhelming financial success. Even though the Justice Department, in the lawsuit it was prepared to file in July of 1994, stated that "Microsoft's monopoly power allows it to induce [PC] manufacturers to enter into anticompetitive, long-term licenses," the consent decree Microsoft signed was a mild rebuke.[9] The government had even less of a chance against Microsoft than IBM did. Gates, who had outnegotiated IBM's lawyers, negotiated with Anne Bingaman, antitrust chief at the Justice Department, and staff. Speaking to reporters soon after the negotiated terms of a consent decree had been signed, Gates shrugged it off as unimportant, telling reporters that he didn't anticipate any "adverse financial impact on Microsoft."[10] In hindsight, Gates was right. Without retroactive sanctions or penalties, even IBM's technically elegant alternative—the award-winning OS/2—couldn't shake the Windows hold on the market.

Microsoft was years ahead of the government. Nothing in the decree would undo the establishment of Windows as a key standard that Microsoft controls to its advantage over rivals. Four attorneys with the Palo Alto law firm of Wilson, Sonsini, Goodrich & Rosatti, including Gary Reback, wrote a white paper for the Department of Justice detailing "Why Microsoft Must Be Stopped." The article is a startling portrait of how Microsoft "targets particular markets, establishes marketing and, in particular, technological links to those markets from established monopolies, and then leverages its power to monopolize the target markets."[11] In other words, Microsoft uses its proprietary standards coupled with the perception that it creates and controls market standards to extend its control over new market standards too.

For example, in the late 1980s, Microsoft trailed the leaders (WordPerfect, Lotus, dBase, Harvard Graphics, Corel, and PageMaker) in every key applications area. For years, Microsoft urged these developers and others to develop new applications for OS/2. In a move later declared a violation of United States antitrust law by the Department of Justice, Microsoft offered computer manufacturers discounts on DOS and Windows both if they paid a royalty for every system shipped, whether or not the customer actually wanted DOS and Windows, thus establishing Windows as the standard instead of OS/2. Microsoft began shipping its primary Windows applications in a low-priced suite named "Microsoft Office for Windows," which put competitors shipping specialized products on multiple platforms, such as WordPerfect and Borland, at a serious competitive disadvantage. Most Microsoft competitors had committed to OS/2 development and were not only behind in the development of Windows products, but claimed that Microsoft didn't readily share the technical details of allowing Windows products to work together. What's more, few of the companies had the product line breadth to match Microsoft's strategy without banding together. As sales of Windows increased, the sales of Microsoft's applications soon passed the sales of the leading DOS applications, and Microsoft found itself firmly in control of the desktop applications market as well as the desktop operating system market.

In early August 1996, the tactics used by Microsoft to attack Netscape's lead in the Internet WWW browser and server software market attracted the attention once again of the Justice Department. According to John Markoff in a *New York Times* article, Netscape accused Microsoft of antitrust violations for placing limits on the number of Internet connections that can be made to a single copy of Microsoft's NT Workstation operating system software.[12] Although the details are esoteric and technical, Netscape's complaint is, in my opinion, wholly justified. Netscape's product, which requires an operating system product, costs $295. Microsoft offers its equivalent product bundled with the Microsoft Windows Server NT operating system for $699. It also offers the Microsoft Windows NT operating system alone, in what Microsoft calls a "Workstation" version, for $319. Netscape's product works with either of the two versions of Windows NT, except that Microsoft included a licensing provision in the lower-priced product that restricts to ten the number of Internet connections it can make, thus forcing customers who need the Internet server capability to purchase the more expensive server version of Windows NT. Since that version includes the Microsoft equivalent of Netscape's software, its purchase, in turn, renders the purchase of the Netscape software unnecessary. The most troubling aspect of this abuse of Microsoft's market clout and control of standards is that there are only a few very minor technical tuning differences between the two versions of the Windows NT software—the license provisions is thus clearly a competitive artifact without a reasonable technical justification. In my experience with Microsoft, this is not an isolated example of their business practices and competitive tactics. It is, rather, fairly common: using its market clout and control unfairly without consideration for either customers or competitors.

In my opinion, the real world consequences of Microsoft's control over a very important personal computer standard include

■ software titles that cost more than they need to
■ incompatibilities between various versions of the operating system and applications
■ fewer application choices

- poor integration between software and hardware
- increased costs of hardware components and peripherals—since they must deal with multiple operating systems originating from the same company (i.e. DOS, Windows 3.1, Windows 95, Windows NT, and OS/2) and incompatibilities between them

Microsoft has also included Internet connectivity and browser software with Windows 95 and has announced plans to imbed the browser seamlessly into Windows 95 file and network access. While Microsoft licensed Java from its developer, Sun Microsystems, it appears that Microsoft intends to encourage the use of its own variation, tightly integrated with its ActiveX controls. With its seemingly unlimited marketing muscle and standard-setting clout, Microsoft appears poised to wrest the market leadership and standard-setting capability away from open standards bodies such as the IETF and W3C. Reback et al. point out in their report, speaking of American "software and on-line information services," that "without government intervention, Microsoft will in short order crush this competition."[13]

RAMIFICATIONS

So what does this all mean to cyberspace and our future? Plenty. We face the most significant task of this century—that of building an elegant information infrastructure, including technological standards that will serve the diverse purposes of education, communications, entertainment, commerce, and government for generations to come. We face the possible reconstruction of government as we know it. We face wrenching change, ready or not. We may not be able to predict exactly what is coming or when; but that shouldn't stop us from preparing as best we can.

If we examine the parallels between the PC revolution, IBM, and the information industry and cyberspace revolution, government, and society, then we might find value in examining the trends and changes that have affected IBM over the last decade. Such a comparison suggests that big, centralized government will continue to suffer loss of power as voters demand decentralization, empowerment, and freedom from centralized control and bureaucratic delays and waste. This is hardly news to anyone with half an eye to voting trends. Yet it comes at a time when leadership and the binding ties of societal cooperation may be more important than at any time since the last world war. Politicians may misinterpret demands for less bureaucratic government as a demand for no government and leave the nation vulnerable to selfish business interests.

Over the next few years, the American people will face significant changes in technical standards brought on by a new worldwide information infrastructure that is forming even with minimum government assistance with breathtaking speed. These changes will affect such everyday acts as watching television, making a telephone call, listening to the radio, computing, reading newspapers and magazines, and daily communications with coworkers, friends, and loved ones. The principles by which we guide policy and set critical standards should weigh heavily in favor of humanity over technology—with an emphasis on respect for the individual, interdependent distribution of power, and individual and social responsibility and accountability. Unfortunately, those are not the values or principles that are likely to drive the establishment of those standards. Instead, from government, we get laws that may aim for the noble goal of protecting our children but instead ride roughshod over cyberspace culture and the civil rights of cyberspace residents. From industry, we get a plethora of standards, standards churn, and proprietary, inconsistent "standards" with inaccessible features and quick and dirty, inelegant "first-to-market" kludges (poorly engineered fixes). The good laws and good standards that do emerge often seem accidental.

There is much debate about what should be done, and by whom. Newt Gingrich argues that "we ought to just liberate the market and let the technologies sort themselves out over the next 10 or 15 years. Then, maybe, we revisit the question of whether you need regulation. In the near future, though, we should be driving for as little regulation as possible."[14] Gingrich has also called Bill Gates "the most important entrepreneur of his era, on a par with Henry Ford in his."[15]

On the other hand, Vice President Al Gore believes that government does have a role to play. Gore and Clinton have been vocal proponents of government support for high technology initiatives and have proposed spending $2 billion over five years to give teachers and students access to the Internet.[16] Speaking to technology managers at a government technology conference in 1994, Gore described the need for government involvement: "If we do not move decisively to ensure that America has the information infrastructure we need, every business and consumer in America will suffer. . . . To understand what new systems we must create, though, we must first understand how the information marketplace of the future will operate."[17] Speaking of the Telecommunications Act, which essentially liberated big business while imposing few new standards, except the much-maligned Communications Decency Act, Gore said, "The highest bidders, not the highest principles, have set the bar. . . . America's technological future is under attack by shortsighted ideologues, who pretend to understand history, but in fact have no understanding whatsoever."[18]

Both positions have merit. But judging from the past, particularly the experience of IBM and Microsoft, neither position alone holds the answer. Can we pay too much attention to recent history as the standards that constitute that infrastructure are determined? If we ignore the selfish and competitive forces that would shape those standards to serve their own ends, won't we be saddled with a system that serves a wide variety of special interests and the public good only insofar as is necessary to ensure acceptance? Those in positions of power and influence have a fundamental obligation to study, recognize, and understand the trends, the pitfalls, the existing phenomena, and the representative possibilities.

The recognition that a number of important standards must be public property and must not be left at the mercy of narrow economic interests is a critical first step toward a National Information Policy, which should rightfully proceed the construction of a National Information Infrastructure. Those who understand the technological issues best almost unanimously prefer open standards. As *InfoWorld* columnist and technical expert Brett Glass stated in conversation with me in June 1996, "We need open, not proprietary, standards. When patented or proprietary technologies are adopted as standards, it is like giving the company a license to print money at the expense of the public."

Let me offer just one of many possible scenarios that might highlight some of the potential consequences of allowing the market, rather than some form of government accountable to the people, free rein to determine the standards that will govern our daily experiences. Assume that the market continues to be the source of most relevant standards, as it is today. A foreign company develops an access device that costs $250, includes a remote control pointing device and a keyboard, connects to your television, VCR, your PC, and/or your phone or cable wires, offers video-on-demand capability and free, integrated access to the Internet—including long distance service over the Internet to anyone else with such a box at a penny a minute. The market would adopt a standard like that virtually overnight. After all, it's an offer we can't refuse.

Now assume that such a company had sold one hundred million of such devices and American companies had fully adjusted to market demands by providing programming and support for those boxes. Then, some of those who have bought and are using the boxes notice an extra phone call or two each month charged to their phone bill, or a duplicate charge on a credit card here and there. An ingenious hacker gets curious and discovers a "back door" into the box's sophisticated encryption systems which allows the foreign company to monitor and collect every piece of information about its customers and their cyberspace activity right over the Internet. Every purchase made, every video ordered, every e-mail sent and received could be interpreted, indexed, and stored in your personal marketing profile on the foreign company's enormous database. An investigation ensues and it is discovered that the recent boom in the foreign county's economy has come because this company that "set the standard" has used the information secretly gathered about its customers worldwide (with full support from the foreign government) to seed new foreign businesses that manipulate the information gathered (including competitive information gathered from employees of competitors) to dominate other markets. Some of these companies might be less than reputable, engaging in credit card fraud, telephone fraud, theft of computer time and resource, information redirection, industrial espionage, and other such relatively unnoticeable or untraceable electronic crimes. Billions, perhaps trillions, of dollars could be diverted, and there would be little that anyone could do to recover it. Even worse, the market standard would be thrown into disarray, and we would once again be at the mercy of some other company willing to set our standards for us.

If we allow the market alone to define the standards that will influence our lives for years to come, I am confident that we cheat ourselves and our children by so doing. We simply cannot allow any company, no matter how well-meaning, to control critical standards. Nothing proprietary should ever be considered a standard; no standard should ever be permitted to remain proprietary. Standards should be developed by those disinterested in the economic rewards derived from the adoption of a standard—the bulk of those rewards should accrue to those who use the standard, since its value is primarily derived from its widespread use. Legal doctrines such as "increasing returns" and "essential facility" are only beginning to recognize the economic reality of public standards as a natural societal and economic resource that should not be considered intellectual property.

Yet the ultimate purpose of markets and businesses—to maximize the return on the investment of the owners—cannot be ignored, either, since it is clearly the most potent source of innovation and ever-improving products, services, and information. Free markets have clearly blessed our lives with innovations that government never would have conceived or produced.

We are already familiar with the results when government, following the familiar process of "legislate and regulate," attempts to micromanage the process instead of the results—nitpicking, burdensome regulations that dictate to businesses how they should run their business in ridiculous detail. For example, the FCC regulation order to cable companies following the passage of legislation governing the cable TV industry dictated pricing at multiple levels, customer service details such as how long companies could take to answer the phones, and even the return on investment. Even the well-intentioned but poorly conceived Communications Decency Act is an example of what can go wrong when government attempts to regulate standards without industry and public involvement.

Yet such absurdities and abuses should not tempt us to take our eye off the ultimate purpose of government—to promote the common welfare of the people. The best examples of government involvement are those that force industry to set goals consistent with the public welfare but leave industry free to invent the means to achieve the goals mandated by government. Examples include the establishment of automobile safety, gasoline usage, and antipollution standards, all of which have been remarkably effective in preventing "the tragedy of the commons"—a term derived from the title of a well-known economic work by Garrett Hardin demonstrating that enterprises and individuals acting in free markets, left alone, are motivated to overuse and exploit shared resources.[19]

So are we stuck in an unresolvable dilemma? Only if we embrace the fallacy of bifurcation and assume that either industry or government alone must possess the power to define and set standards. What is required now, as never before, is an ambitious, concerted, cooperative effort by government (the people) and industry. Our apparent distrust of cooperation need not extend to concerted efforts where our national welfare is at stake. In cooperation, the inherent interests of the respective parties need not be neglected—especially when the cooperation is open. Thus, there should be a place for media, academia, and the public in the cooperative effort to define and establish public standards and policy for cyberspace as well. Anything less will leave us fighting for years to come. Standards are too basic and too important to trust to any single segment of society.

In the process, I believe that recent history has shown that any standard, existing or adopted, that attempts to lean too strongly toward the preservation of the existing centralization of power will probably be replaced by a far more radical and revolutionary standard than might otherwise have been adopted by more prudent thinkers. Just as surely as IBM failed to preserve its power, so will the federal government, big business, and the mass media find it difficult to preserve their power unless they radically reshape their own exercise of that power. It will be difficult enough to tame the existing anarchy on the Net, but the attempted exercise of raw power that ignores the existing cyberspace culture will be undermined and defeated just as surely as was IBM's 1987 attempt to establish proprietary PC standards.

Those standards that are adopted must rely heavily on those same principles of interdependent decentralization that first empowered the United States as a young nation or they will be overthrown by more radical, but not necessarily superior, standards. Superior standards are not automatic. They are usually established by rare visionary leaders acting in concert with others. Surely government can find ways to make working partners of such visionaries and savvy observers as John Perry Barlow, Tim Berners-Lee, Stewart Brand, Stephen Covey, Peter Drucker, Esther Dyson, James Fallows, Mitch Kapor, George Gilder, James Gleick, Tom Peters, Paul Romer, and Alvin and Heidi Toffler. Never mind that their visions often diverge and their politics often seem to conflict. If we are to truly respect diversity, then we must look to that diversity for the saving graces of compromise and synergy.

Perhaps even more significantly, the truth will set us free only if the truth is made available to us. Traditionally, journalists and writers belonged to a noble profession devoted to reporting the facts and enlightening the electorate—often at great personal risk and cost. Yet something seems out of order. Even the free press is failing us, as documented by James Fallows in *Breaking the News*. Fallows details the many roots of the failure, including the lack of ethical discipline, the media bias for superficial political commentary over in-depth analysis, the view that conflict equals news, while consensus-finding and problem-solving do not, and the tendency for TV panels and the lecture circuit to corrupt the process by which we gain our information about what is happening in government and politics.[20] Although I am obviously unable to do Fallows and his arguments justice in a single paragraph, I trust that most of us can agree that the news is indeed broken, and that informed choices simply cannot be made in the absence of high-quality information.

The media should pay even more attention to reporting the upsides and downsides of emerging technologies, addressing the concerns of ordinary people, consumers, and technologists, while paying appropriately less attention to political and commercial issues. Reporters should dig and discover what the industry leaders, Internet committees, and think tanks are doing to unite and seize the opportunity to define standards and contrast those approaches with those underway (often secretly) within companies and government. If we expect an information infrastructure that will support us well into the future, we cannot rely on special interests to provide it or the supposedly free press to describe it until our society undergoes the kind of dramatic change that perhaps only a revolution can provoke.

The media themselves will certainly not escape the effects of the revolution. Cyberspace offers individuals an unprecedented opportunity to bypass the media and go directly to others with their messages. Bob Beckel, Democratic analyst and public relations expert who ran Walter Mondale's Presidential campaign in 1984, says:

> [The Internet] is providing an opportunity for people to sit out there in their homes and express this view and collectively find others who want to engage in debate over those views. We're looking at the single biggest revolution in American politics as an organizing tool, because it does take away a lot of the interpersonal barriers that have been there before.[21]

In January of 1776, Thomas Paine published *Common Sense*. Within three months 120,000 copies had been sold, and it had been published for countless other readings in newspapers. It was a sensation. It may not have reached quite as large an audience as the O. J. Simpson verdict or a Super Bowl game, but it changed the course of history by inspiring in the colonists a passion for the ideals of freedom and justice, combined with a heightened sense that such ideas were realistically achievable. Six months later, Paine's friend and intellectual soul-mate, Thomas Jefferson, had penned the Declaration of Independence, borrowing heavily from Paine,[22] and the American Revolution had begun. As the citizenry in cyberspace increase in number and access to the same alternate sources of information, the chances increase that compelling ideas such as Paine's might trigger a new revolution.

It might be said that a revolution is the manner by which passionate elements of a society attempt (and even succeed) in overturning a political process supposedly gone far astray in favor of its sudden replacement with supposed common sense, reason, and truth. It is entirely possible that this revolution could take an abstract form never before seen: a revolution of the mind and spirit—a new declaration of independence by the citizens of cyberspace demanding recognition of cyberspace as a borderless new state which is not and cannot be governed by traditional jurisdictions of law and government. When I first wrote the preceding sentence, it hadn't yet happened. On the day the Communications Decency Act passed, however, John Perry Barlow wrote his "Declaration of the Independence of Cyberspace" and posted it online. If you want to understand the revolutionary free spirit of cyberspace and the "in-your-face-but-get-out-of-mine" culture of cyberspace—then Barlow's declaration is must reading. See http://numedia.tddc.net/scott/declaration.html.

Such a revolution could indeed create a new world order. Government and the media would see their power decrease significantly. These institutions are already viewed with increasing disfavor by the populace, who see them as top-heavy with power, influence, and corruption. They are quite vulnerable as higher-quality information sources become available to those who have previously been relatively dependent on centralized authority for information. Both government and the media have been magnets for those who seek power, including the ambitious and arrogant. Given the American propensity to challenge the arrogant and entrenched, the balance of power has always tended to favor the individual and compelling ideas. With the advent of the possibility of collective, connected communications, the prospect that ideas might trigger hundreds of thousands to take action and ignite the grassroots like a wildfire becomes every bit as real as the possibility in 1986 that the personal computer would inspire a revolution that would topple IBM and centralized processing as king of the information industry hill.

PITFALLS FOR A WIRED ELECTORATE

Whether we face revolution or evolution, there are a number of trends and challenges that we would do well to understand and face.

The very territorial authority and jurisdiction of government is challenged by the abstract, borderless nature of cyberspace. Even as cyberspace brings us together in ways never before possible, so it reveals our differences—leading to an increased splintering effect that might turn the melting pot into a boiling cauldron of tribes and special interests. Politicians without a moral rudder might find themselves whipped about by a plethora of such interests. Ultimately, those new technologies that provide such compelling instant feedback and polling may lead us into the dangerous temptations of a "majority rule superdemocracy," which is only a provoking emotion or two away from "mob rule" and over the brink into riot, violence, and destruction. The borderless nature of cyberspace coupled with the splintering effects leaves us vulnerable to new forms of electronic and economic warfare initiated by domestic and international lust for power and wealth.

Jurisdiction

Cyberspace doesn't recognize political borders. Although there are new boundaries in the sense that you can't get "into" certain places (such as online services or certain Web sites) in cyberspace without an account and a password, to date no government has been able to effectively superimpose external political boundaries on cyberspace. Indeed, it is exceedingly difficult to do so, as Singapore is discovering in its frustrated attempts to become a world information center by linking thousands of households to date to the Internet without sacrificing Singapore's restrictive controls over undesirable content such as pornography. Yet law and geographical boundaries are so closely intertwined that it is difficult to conceive of a law that is independent of territory. Thus, many legal scholars argue that new laws, which apply to cyberspace as its own distinct territory, are necessary.

David G. Post, of the Georgetown University Law Center, points out that the ties between territory and law can be attributed to power (sovereign control over physical space and people and things located in that space), effects (the impact of a behavior on inhabitants), legitimacy ("consent of the governed"), and notice (signposts signifying differences in law).

> Cyberspace radically undermines the relationship between legally significant (online) phenomena and physical location. The rise of the global computer network is destroying the link between geographical location and: (1) the *power* of local governments to assert control over online behavior; (2) the *effects* of online behavior on individuals or things; (3) the *legitimacy* of the efforts of a local sovereign to enforce rules applicable to global phenomenon; and (4) the ability of physical location to give *notice* of which sets of rules apply. The Net thus radically subverts a system of rule-making based on borders between physical spaces.[23]

Thus, cyberspace by its very nature presents revolutionary challenges not just to the United States of America, but to every government whose residents have access to cyberspace. The power of any government to enforce its laws on cyberspace is threatened by the basic structure of the Internet. Although governments can take action against physical servers located within its jurisdiction, the servers are only half of the equation. If a server in Hong Kong is providing pirated software for download at reduced prices, supported by the policy of the Chinese government, what power does the United States have to prevent U.S. citizens from accessing that site? The decentralized structure of the Internet makes it extremely difficult, if not impossible, to enforce restrictions, bans, and censorship.

Similarly, if a trademark is registered for use by one company within the United States and by another company in Japan, which government's authority to grant trademark protection takes priority in cyberspace? To date, there is no good way to distinguish between a Japanese site and an American site. In theory, domains (site addresses) could be assigned names that distinguish jurisdiction, but that would essentially require a dismantling of a healthy share of the Internet's naming structure—an extraordinarily large undertaking. Also in theory, each site could be required to serve notice of which jurisdiction's laws apply to the site—but that would probably be a meaningless exercise, since most users can't be expected to know all the applicable laws of every jurisdiction.

Taxation is another issue with close ties to jurisdiction—and perhaps the most important such jurisdictional issue to any government. Nexus, in this case the link between the taxing jurisdiction and the legal entity or activity being taxed, is of critical importance. Cyberspace might render certain taxes, such as sales taxes, impossible to assess or collect (even assuming that all taxpayers abide by the laws) because it renders the question of nexus problematic. Suppose it is determined that the physical location of the server that collects the money provides the nexus. In that case, companies providing servers (which can be accessed from anywhere worldwide for maintenance) would spring up in locations with no sales taxes. Suppose the nexus is derived from the physical location of the person selling the goods, who receives the revenue. In that case, corporations (virtual persons legally) would spring up in states or countries with no sales tax, owned and managed by individuals in other states. Suppose the nexus comes from the original physical location of the goods to be shipped. Then we would see more sales fulfillment warehouses in states with no sales tax, with the revenue flowing to individuals living in other states managing the site and receive the order from afar. It could easily become a game of cat and mouse between taxing authorities and cyberspace commercial concerns.

Countries, states, and even communities are already grappling with a host of thorny issues involving jurisdiction. Communities have traditionally been able to define and enforce local moral standards, and people gravitated to those communities that fit their preferences. If you thought the laws were too restrictive in Tennessee, you could move to California. If you thought the crime was out of control in New York, you could move to Utah. When cyberspace is available universally in every community, then communities are potentially no longer able to control or enforce local standards.

For example, one pornographer who ran a bulletin board in Milpitas, California, was convicted of trafficking in obscenity by a jury in Tennessee.

Whose "community standards" should apply in such a case? If the laws of any jurisdiction whose individuals have access to cyberspace apply to everyone in cyberspace, then we face a fundamental systemic imbalance—because laws are often in conflict. Gambling, for example, is legal in Nevada but illegal in Minnesota. Anyone who visits Nevada may also gamble. Thus, can someone who, for the purpose of gambling, accesses an Internet site whose server provides gambling and is physically located in Nevada be said to be "visiting" Nevada (in cyberspace), even though the person accessing the gambling site is still physically located in Minnesota? Minnesota and Nevada would probably have differing opinions about jurisdiction in such a case. In fact, the Minnesota Attorney General's office has issued a "Warning to All Internet Users and Providers" asserting that persons "outside of Minnesota who transmit information via the Internet knowing that information will be disseminated in Minnesota are subject to jurisdiction in Minnesota courts for violations of state criminal and civil laws" and has brought a civil action against Wagernet, a Nevada gambling service with a presence on the Internet.[24]

Many of these jurisdiction issues can be settled if we consider cyberspace a virtual place requiring its own virtual laws, such as those forbidding appropriation of intellectual property, theft or abuse of private data, unauthorized use of computer resources, and fraud. Within the overarching global jurisdiction of cyberspace, individual jurisdictions should also be granted authority to establish "law" within relevant guidelines, including appropriate consequences for violators. Obviously, the legal penalties for violation of cyberspace norms should be restricted to cyberspace consequences, such as loss of cyberspace privileges or the cancellation of an account, with physical penalties reserved for those who commit physical crimes. Online services, for example, should be largely free to set and enforce their own norms and rules, including those involving defamation, profanity, adult content, or anonymity. Commercial services could then differentiate themselves more precisely, and consumers would have a broader range of choices—including choices consistent with their own values.

Traditionally, laws have treated cyberspace as a mode of transmission rather than as its own jurisdiction. In determining the rules and laws for cyberspace jurisdictions, however, it is important to remember that, although the wires and connections and access devices and servers are located in physical space, cyberspace itself is a purely abstract space, existing in our minds. Thus, the laws that govern such a space must necessarily afford greater freedom and even license because the line between thought and speech and behaviors are much thinner than in the physical world. The nature of cyberspace demands that it be governed as its own jurisdiction, by laws that take into account the unique characteristics of cyberspace. We are far from that ideal, however, and until the competing powers with an interest in cyberspace recognize and accede to that ideal, we face one conflict after another in determining who governs what in cyberspace.

Feedback Overload and Attention Span Bandwidth

In theory, cyberspace should enable state and federal legislators and representatives to have a better sense for the mood of the people. In practical terms, however, this is a two-edged sword. The whole idea of having a republic is to be above the tyranny of majority rule and more dependent on the careful reasoning of elected representatives with the necessary wisdom and experience in public service to be working full-time on a variety of interdependent issues of importance to those represented.

Although cyberspace so easily enables feedback to one's representatives, such feedback is in constant danger of being devalued because of the sheer quantity and the difficulty in processing it all. Great ideas and clear thinking stand even less of a chance in getting through an avalanche of cut-and-paste-and-add-your-name e-mail feedback. Even large amounts of e-mail could be handled using various forms of artificial intelligence, including filters, word counters, vote counting mechanisms, and even cross-referencing to perform demographic analyses based on the source of the notes received. Nonetheless, all such mechanisms only serve to place additional barriers between representatives and those represented, eliminating one of the most important reasons for such communications: the flow of creative new ideas to address problems faced by society. What's more, if voluminous feedback replaces the judgment and character of representatives, then we have all of the disadvantages of a tyrannical democracy.

Wayne Rash, a columnist for *Communications Week* and author of a book on the impact of cyberspace communications on the 1996 elections, points to several other problems with feedback via e-mail. First, he says, it's too easy—the cost of writing and sending an e-mail message is so low that it is understandably devalued by representatives and their staff. Second, there are generally few clues regarding source in e-mail: no physical address, no phone number, nothing to tie the e-mail to a given constituency. Thus, those sending e-mail should always include and address or phone number with an area code in order to impart at least a modicum of credibility. Also, since there is a notable lack of security relating to e-mail, there is often no way to know who is actually sending the e-mail—whether it's coming from a constituent, a lobbyist, or just someone with an ax to grind. Spoofing messages is notoriously easy—one could send a message that looks as if it's coming from anyone. Finally, most e-mail simply prompts a tally on one side of a question or another before it is stored and ignored.

On the individual side, we face a glut of information—much of which is low quality. The number of issues demanding our time and attention far exceeds our time and attention. How much time should we devote to researching the issues that matter to us, and how do we choose which battles to fight? When feeding from a fire-hose of information, reactive consumption can become stressful indigestion unless we take a proactive role in seeking accurate, stimulating sources and amounts of information consistent with our values. If we value the sanctity of our home as a shelter from the world, for example, it doesn't make sense to leave the television on and tuned to CNN blaring the news around the clock. On the other hand, if we value an up-to-date knowledge of the issues and events that may shape our future, then it might make sense. In choosing the amount of information we need, however, I would suggest that most of us consume far more information than is ever useful to us. At IBM, one of the cultural mandates born of wisdom is "we can't boil the ocean." In other words, overestimating our ability to effect change is an ineffective strategy that leads to frustration. Understanding the limitations of our spheres of influence is more likely to yield gratifying and satisfying results. "Think globally, act locally" has become another cyberspace truism. Although we should be aware of the impact of our choices on the larger issues, we shouldn't presume to take responsibility for the problems of all the world. Doing what we can within our own sphere of influence is enough—we needn't adopt the stress of concern about those things we can't influence, even in cyberspace.

We should also "pick our battles." Thus, another way to cut back on our own consumption of irrelevant information, political or otherwise, is to seek only information that will aid us in decisions with a direct impact in our own personal lives. Picking our battles based on personal relevance will yield a higher level of personal satisfaction than in trying to influence laws that really won't make much of a difference to us personally.

Thus, the primary danger in information overload is our possible inability to apply a filter based on our values to the onslaught of information we face. More than ever before, knowing what we value and how to apply those values may be of critical importance in our pursuit of happiness.

Instant Democracy

The technological ability of citizens to vote instantly and directly on any issue at any time will have important implications, reopening the centuries-old debate regarding a pure democracy versus a republic. Obviously, the temptation to revert to instantaneous majority rule will be great—thus bypassing representatives, lobbyists, and the evils of campaign financing all in one fell swoop. There is talk of a "Democracy Channel" that would allow interested citizens to monitor debates and then vote on various issues, providing round-the-clock feedback to representatives.

It seems to me that such direct democracy is a dangerous course to choose. The vagaries of public opinion are notorious. Opinion polls can differ dramatically based on how the questions are asked, when the questions are asked, and who is asking the questions. Uninformed or misinformed opinions can make terrible law, and yet the opinion of the majority is often exactly that. In early trials of electronic forums, opinions have been shown to be easily and significantly influenced by even a one-hour documentary. Referendums often result in laws that discriminate against minorities—such as the 1992 Colorado initiative prohibiting laws granting equal rights based on sexual orientation, which was ruled unconstitutional by the Supreme Court.

Evan I. Schwartz, a former *Business Week* editor, raises some interesting questions about living in an electronic democracy:

> Won't it be harder than ever for Congress and the President to stand up for what's right, rather than what's popular? Can voter privacy be maintained, or will marketers get hold of everyone's voting records? Will everyone have access to the latest technology? Will the people really be getting their say, or will the whole process be controlled by moguls?[25]

Perhaps the Federalist Papers, in which James Madison, Alexander Hamilton, and John Jay present and argue the case for the Constitution and a republican form of government, may be reintroduced to a nation still struggling to balance majority rule against minority rights, divided in many of the same ways the nation was divided in 1787 when the Federalist Papers were written. The principles by which our Constitutional republic was established have not changed—a move to a centralized government where majority rules could be a disaster.

Even today, those politicians who are without a moral compass any more stable than the winds of public opinion can face a tough time as it becomes more difficult to deceive or satisfy a more informed electorate that is better able to unite with like-minded people nationwide. Philip Anderson, associate professor of business administration at Dartmouth College, points out that any group or candidate would be well served to "develop a reputation for being forthright as a matter of policy so they can respond to rumors."[26] Forward-looking politicians will recognize that firm personal convictions and character clearly articulated should ultimately win more votes than catering to special interest groups, even in cyberspace. With any luck, "the content of one's character" will increase in importance and carry the day in an environment where information is freely available, while those representatives lacking a moral compass, willing to tell the electorate whatever the electorate wants to hear, will be easily revealed and booted from office. Representatives voting their conscience after long and studied debates should never be considered obsolete, no matter how sophisticated the mechanisms by which those representatives are able to know the will of the people.

Special Interests, Tribes, and Political Parties

In the 1992 election, H. Ross Perot launched one of the most significant third-party campaigns since Teddy Roosevelt ran with the Bull Moose party in the early part of the 20th century. Colin Powell's flirtation, however brief, with a new party is also indicative of the general trend toward a more diverse electorate than perhaps can be truly represented by a two-party system. John Heilemann comments, "Perhaps what lies in store for our politics is a period of structural disarray, with as [political theoretician Kevin] Phillips puts it, 'the major parties fading and splinter groups growing . . . leaving the GOP and the Democrats as untrusted, partly burnt-out' institutional leftovers."[27]

Even if all popular alternate candidates were to vacate the scene or join one of the existing two parties, the splintering culture and the influence of online constituencies will probably ensure that the two-party political system will become a bit of an artifact, now that, according to the Wirthlin Group, between 20 percent and 30 percent of the electorate classify themselves as "Independent." It remains to be seen whether the two-party system can maintain its hold on the political processes.

Because it can be so easy to find like minds in cyberspace, special interest groups thrive there. *Newsweek* calls these online special interest groups "cybertribes," quoting polltaker Mike McKeon: "Forget geography. Forget race, gender. In cyberspace, you are what you care about."[28] What folks care about in cyberspace has proven to be remarkably diverse—and doesn't necessarily mirror the media's notion of what Americans care about. Whatever the mix of passions that trigger the formation of specialized forums and sites, the thought of special interest groups and tribes banding together online is not altogether an encouraging one. Although these cybertribes are just learning their political clout and are only beginning to flex their political muscles, the notion that there is some sort of "silent majority" going unrepresented in American politics may yet reappear in the form of those who don't have access to cyberspace. The threat of more divisiveness, more lobbyists, more shrillness in the national discourse, and less unity and cooperation may not be considered a positive prospect by many. The splintering of cyberspace could be a polarizing pitfall rather than an opportunity to find creative new possibilities.

Provocation

The most serious cause for pause comes from the thought that technologies used for good can also produce almost unimaginable evil. Radio, an early cyberspace communications technology so ubiquitous that it no longer commands our fascination, has long been at the center of bitter conflicts in troubled areas of the world. Consider the following from a story by John Balzar:

> Reporters Without Borders, the French-based media watchdog organization, concluded that Radio Mille Collines, a one-time radical station here in the Rwandan capital, has been the principal vehicle for incitements to the crime of genocide. The station was an arm of the Hutu extremists and its broadcasts urged listeners to "take your spears, clubs, guns, swords, stones, everything, sharpen them, hack them, those enemies, those cockroaches." Rwanda is far from alone in stirring trouble over the airwaves. The International Center Against Censorship documented that in South Africa, neo-Nazi Radio Pretoria was used in March 1994 to organize paramilitary opposition to democratic change. And government radio in Zaire was blamed for stirring ethnic violence in 1992–93 that displaced 500,000 people.[29]

Although it may be difficult to imagine computer-mediated communication being used to foment criminal genocide or even extensive crime, we should remember that in 1924, Herbert Hoover said, speaking of radio:

> Let us not forget that the value of this great system does not lie primarily in its extent or even in its efficiency. Its worth depends on the use that is made of it. . . . For the first time in human history we have avail-

able to us the ability to communicate simultaneously with millions of our fellowmen, to furnish entertainment, instruction, widening vision of national problems and national events. An obligation rests on us to see that it is devoted to real service and to develop the material that is transmitted into that which is really worthwhile.[30]

It is entirely likely that cyberspace communications will indeed be used to perpetuate violence, support crime, and prey upon the weak and unprotected—if not in the United States, then certainly in countries where morality is measured by degrees of power.

A variety of so-called "hate groups" are advancing their respective agendas online. A "Hate Watch" Web page, formerly sponsored by the Harvard University Library where the page editor works, monitors the proliferation, defining "hate group" as "an organization or individual that advocates violence against or unreasonable hostility towards those persons or organizations identified by their race, religion, ethnic origin, sexual orientation or gender also including organizations or individuals that disseminate revisioned or historically inaccurate information with regards to these persons or organizations."[31] The page also refers to the March 13, 1995, *New York Times* quote of Don Black, ex-Grand Dragon of the Ku Klux Klan and owner of the white supremacist home page "Stormfront," as saying that the "Internet has had a pretty profound influence on a movement [white supremacy] whose resources are limited. The access is anonymous and there is unlimited ability to communicate with others of a like mind."

One wonders about the tenuous, thin lines between hate, crime, civil strife, and outright civil wars and genocidal slaughters such as have occurred in Rwanda, Cambodia, and Bosnia. It seems that an informed and educated populace makes all the difference, which highlights the importance of developing a twofold public policy that will (1) establish and clarify the limits of free speech in cyberspace based on the same principles by which the limits of free speech in other media have been established and (2) find ways to extend the educational fruits of the Information Superhighway to all, just as we have found ways to extend public education to all.

Electronic Warfare

Winn Schwartau has long been a leader in raising a studied voice of warning concerning the consequences of an unfettered, insecure cyberspace. His book, *Information Warfare,* is must reading for anyone who might be tempted to take a rosy view of unlimited license in cyberspace. Schwartau asks us to imagine a world made up of companies that compete and settle disputes by regularly blitzkrieging each other's information infrastructure. A world where electronic and competitive espionage are the expected manner of conducting business. Or imagine a world in which personal revenge, retribution, getting even is only a keystroke away. What kind of world is this? This is the world of Information Warfare. And we, as individuals and as a country, are not prepared for the future we are creating.[32]

As money and power flow into cyberspace, conflict and warfare will follow. We are already seeing the early skirmishes in this electronic warfare. Software piracy flourishes in China to such an extent that the United States government feels compelled to crack down. The German government threatens to bring action against CompuServe, an American company, for enabling the flow of obscenity into Germany. Some of the best minds of Russian computer science, attracted by western wealth, have made their programming and hacking services available to the highest bidder. According to an Associated Press story dated June 5, 1996, the Pentagon has estimated that 250,000 attempts may have been made to infiltrate military computer networks in 1995—and, far more seriously, over 65 percent of those attempts were successful. In response, according to the story, the Clinton administration reportedly planned to form a team of computer experts called the Cyber Security Assurance Group to help protect computer systems from terrorists, respond to system emergencies, and investigate attacks in cyberspace.

The means of attack in waging cyberspace wars are many and varied. The threats include the theft and abuse of passwords, account numbers, data, software, trade secrets, competitive strategies, access methods, and other such information. Network signals can be tapped and stolen— enabling such theft. Viruses and worms can be released into networks with malevolent intent to destroy the data of enemies or competitors. "Backdoor" access can be coded into software and silicone chips (even by a single employee) and used surreptitiously or sold for purposes of information theft, redirection, or destruction. Of course, the most effective means have probably not yet been detected. Unlike physical assets, information is such that it can often be stolen and used without anyone knowing it.

Whether the electronic warfare of tomorrow is waged by countries, companies, organized crime, cartels, or individuals, we can't afford to ignore the probability that the more valuable cyberspace becomes, the more likely it is that enemies will be motivated to interfere with those benefits. This merely highlights the importance of a National Information Policy and of secure encryption available to everyone, not just governments and criminals.

POSSIBILITIES FOR A WIRED ELECTORATE

Although cyberspace is like an unruly youngster still testing its strength, we are already seeing some of its long-term potential, which could shake the foundations of our political institutions.

Users are beginning to recognize their power online. Jim Warren, a widely recognized champion of cyberspace democracy, was awarded the Dvorak Lifetime Achievement Award at a ONE BBS CON banquet I attended in Tampa Bay in August 1995. In his acceptance speech, he spoke about how the change of only a few percentage points in any direction can swing elections—thus making the number of minds that need to be changed or decided on any given issue surprisingly small. For example, in the 1995 referendum on Quebec independence, the vote was decided by only 53,498 votes of 4,756,229 votes cast. In other words, if 26,750 individuals had voted differently (less than 1 person out of 200), the election would have gone the other way.[33] This means that the power to change the outcome of elections is often held by a surprisingly small percentage of the people in many elections. Thus, it is obvious that if cyberspace provides the means to reach and influence even a relatively small number of people, it could easily swing the balance of power in any democratic republic. Cyberspace will therefore almost certainly play an increasingly import role in the future of politics, since some indeterminate number (well over 10 percent) of the United States population is now online, with no slowdown in growth projected.[34]

It should be clear that the potential for increased activism, participation, and influence in the future is great as technology enables previously futuristic possibilities. Here are some of those possibilities most worth watching.

Cyberspace Constituencies

The online world of cyberspace is as a tidal pool for special interest groups. Already, the World Wide Web contains resources on pages serving a wide variety of interests and affiliations. For example, two searches of the Yahoo index of Web site titles performed at different times yielded the number of sites for these sundry words shown in the table on page 394.

In the digital age, it is likely that many individuals can learn as much or more about a single issue as any representative, if they devote the time to such research, and that such individuals will establish public forums as a foundation for lobbying efforts. It is entirely likely that enterprising representatives might tap into such public forums to tap into the interest and energy of such civic-minded citizens. Although none of the three leading 1996 Presidential candidates responded to Jim Warren's public and written

WORD	NUMBER OF WEB PAGES FOUND 1/18/96	NUMBER OF WEB PAGES FOUND 10/23/96
television	760	913
computers	1021	731
gay/lesbian	330	663
environment	1041	658
Democrat	213	545
Republican	125	536
Catholic	198	517
Jewish	290	509
liberal	99	435
conservative	90	331
gun	51	199
abortion	46	167
blacks	42	144
Hispanic	29	120
Limbaugh	47	78
Mormon	28	76
senior citizen	17	52
terrorist	12	33
religious right	15	25
Ku Klux Klan	1	1

invitations to participate in a week-long, online debate,[35] similar forums will eventually allow our elected representatives and candidates to actually interact with constituents in cyberspace.

The CommerceNet/Nielsen Internet Demographics Survey (November 1995) found that 66% of Internet users are males and that WWW users are upscale (25% with incomes over $80K), professionals (50% professional or managerial), and educated (64% have college degrees)—which is not surprising given the existing "barriers to entry" to cyberspace, especially cost and technical expertise. Thus, any new political power derived from cyberspace in the near future could have important implications.

The potential for change rests not just in the ease by which online constituencies can make their wishes known but also in the ability to carry on a dialogue among themselves to plan political strategies and desired outcomes. If the smoke-filled rooms of traditional lobbyists were to move to the more open and visible forums of cyberspace where personal influence is reduced and the importance of reasonable discussion is increased, it is hard to imagine that such discussions wouldn't yield more effective strategies for political change.

Power to the People: Grass-Roots Phenomena

Americans usually have been willing to listen to those who make sense, without regard to their status or credentials. Although we have a propensity to heed those who tell us what we want to hear, it seems that anyone articulate enough and willing to climb up on a soapbox can often draw a crowd of interested and curious listeners. In the past half century, however, it would seem that the nature of the political participation of the citizenry has changed. Today, it is more likely that they draw their opinions from television and other sound-bite media. The dynamics of computer-mediated communications, however, could reverse that trend.

For example, Dave Hughes told me in a June 1996 phone conversation of a discussion where he and other residents of Old Colorado Springs were having a minor discussion of a local bond issue to fund a police operations center on "Roger's Bar BBS"—an early prototype for a civic-minded conferencing system. When a deputy police chief appeared on the BBS, arguing the case for the approval of the bond initiative, Hughes and others had the opportunity to ask questions and discuss the matter with someone who understood the importance of the issue. According to Hughes, this exchange led him and several others to change their minds and their votes about the initiative.

Hughes points out that there are several political phenomena online that could influence grass-roots politics. First, strictly as a matter of convenience, many individuals would never bother to attend a hearing on a matter, but are nonetheless willing to devote a few minutes to read about and discuss it online. Second, cyberspace technologies support all three parts of the political process: gathering information, public discussion and debate to consensus, and taking action. A sustained dialogue is possible online that is simply impossible at a meeting or hearing, where there is less time to ponder and digest the words that literally dissipate into thin air unless minutes or notes are maintained. The information and points generated by an online discussion can remain available for all to review long after the discussion actually takes place. The quality of discussion is at a higher level, because people think more about what they're going to say. Many assertions that are factually wrong that might slide by at a meeting get nailed online, where readers have the time and resources to check facts. Everyone can have a say before all is said and done, whereas at a meeting or a hearing, time and place impose constraints on discussion and require rationing of the time allocated to each person. Finally, Hughes points to the "ganging up" effect as a dynamic political force that Hughes says, on the balance, "is healthy as hell." I understand this "ganging up" effect as the process of coming to a consensus after an intelligent discussion and debate, rather than the rush-to-judgment character of the herd instinct. Hughes believes that "the online group dialogue, whether conferencing, mail-lists, online services, or newsgroups, matches the American political character."[36]

According to my conversations with Wayne Rash about his research into the 1996 political processes online, there are a number of groups outside the mainstream political organizations that are seeing dramatic returns on their Web site efforts. These organizations include grass-roots, nontraditional, ad hoc, and formal organizations that exist only on the Net and other groups devoted to single-issue politics. Rash believes that because politicians tend to be inherently conservative (whatever worked last time will be tried this time), politicians will probably increase their personal presence in cyberspace only when there is compelling evidence that such a presence has made a positive difference for some enterprising politician.

I expect that to happen. Articulate leaders could emerge from the ranks of the concerned online citizenry to assume elected office. Political parties can provide information to the curious, and use cyberspace for organizing, registration, and inexpensive communications with party faithful. Those who would simply like to serve and be more involved in local, state, or national politics will probably soon be able to find all the necessary information through indexed online searches.

In response, consistent with existing trends, it is likely that government will be forced to continue to accommodate the electorate by decentralizing government control, as citizens continue to demonstrate their willingness and newfound ability to influence decisions at whatever level of decentralization makes the most sense, from homeowners associations on up through state and federal governments.

Candidate Shopping Online

In the 1996 Presidential campaigns, the only major candidate in either party without an official Web page as of March, ironically, was President Clinton—Information Superhighway proponent and 1992 candidate of choice of many high-technology executives. It might be argued, however, that President Clinton already had his campaign Web site in place: namely www.whitehouse.gov. There were also several unofficial Web pages (positive and negative) devoted to Clinton, and most of the other Democratic candidates (including comedian Pat Paulsen) were also represented by official or unofficial Web pages.

My March visit to the respective official Web pages of each of the Republican primary candidates in 1996 proved quite revealing. Each provided information about the lives and beliefs of the candidate. Each also contained substantive discussion of the issues, but each was also differentiated in presentation and content. Bob Dole's page was the most graphically appealing and sophisticated—but lacked interactivity. There wasn't even an e-mail address designated for feedback. Pat Buchanan's site was the richest in content in spite of being managed by only one (apparently very productive) woman in the characteristic open and honest style that defines Net culture. Interestingly, Buchanan's site was also the only one that demonstrated an appreciation for grass-roots organizing using the Internet, with an open plea for volunteers for the "Buchanan Internet Brigade." Steve Forbes's site looked surprisingly cheap, but included a "Flat Tax Calculator," which allowed you to input your earned income, filing status, and number of dependents and receive in return the exact tax you would pay under Forbes's tax plan. Lamar Alexander's site was distinguished only by its lack of distinguishing characteristics.

My late-October visit to the Presidential candidates' official Web sites was also revealing. I should preface my observations by stating that my opinions of the Web sites is independent of my opinions of the candidates. All of the candidates offered common elements, such as position statements and papers, personal histories and biographies of the candidates, audio clips of speeches, downloadable files such as computer background images, registration pages to volunteer to help with the campaigns, and information about the campaign stops in each state.

President Clinton's site (http://www.cg96.org/new/index.html) was the most polished and appealing of any I've seen for a political candidate.

Although the domain name is apparently the result of waiting too long to implement the site (the obvious domain names, such as www.clinton.org, www.clinton96.org or www.clintongore96.org, were all in use by others), the site was otherwise well done. It didn't ask anything of visitors, offering instead a wide variety of choices for instant access to the items of interest. It was consistently positive, focused, warm, and upbeat throughout. It offered a variety of information, including a state-by-state recitation of improvements in statistical measures since 1992, several animated charts showing dramatic improvements in selected economic categories, a page honoring the campaign "volunteer of the week," and pictures and testimonials of supporters. Whatever one thinks of the President and Vice-President, one would be hard pressed to find fault with the marketing savvy evidenced at their Web page.

Ross Perot's official Web site (www.perot.org) was less interesting, but more direct and relevant. Perot's site contained information about his campaign by state, clearly articulated principles of reform, news relevant to the campaign, an interactive section including a chat room, forums, and a photo album, and a link to Perot's campaign headquarters.

Dole's site was technically sophisticated but unrefined from a marketing perspective. The domain name (www.dolekemp96.org), although more intuitive than the Clinton site's name, was difficult to guess, even though www.dole.org was apparently unused and available. The only items available from the main page were a section on the Presidential debates (hardly Dole's strong suit), an unsophisticated tax cut calculator, and a means to "customize your personal Web site"—that required visitors to fill in a survey asking for a variety of personal information, including name, address, and phone number, installed plug-ins, "issues you're interested in," and "coalitions you're interested in joining." Once crossing that hurdle, users faced a site that hardly seemed customized at all—my supposedly customized page contained sections titled "About the Team," "Dole Interactive," "The Dole Agenda," "Get Involved," "On the Campaign Trail," and "News Room." Even though I had given my name and state for registration, the page didn't seem to use either piece of information to customize my visit. State by state, the site offered a recitation of the negative impact of Clinton's record. The site did have some creative elements, including a trivia quiz on facts from Bob Dole's life, a crossword puzzle, and an opportunity to send a Dole postcard to a friend.

There is little doubt that spending several hours exploring the Web sites of each candidate in an election provides a much better view of the respective candidates than the same amount of time spent reading about the candidates in the general media, where one is most likely to be exposed to the reporter's opinion of the candidate's political abilities than a real perspective of the differences between the candidates.

However, an even better approach may be that taken by the Vote Smart project, a nonprofit, nonpartisan initiative backed by former Presidents Ford and Carter and many others, funded by member donations and grants from a variety of foundations, including the Ford Foundation and the Carnegie Corporation.[37] Their Web site at http://www.vote-smart.org lets voters and interested parties compare the backgrounds, records, and positions of a surprising number of cooperating political candidates. If you enter your Zip+4 zip code, the site presents you with a list of candidates for national office in your district with links to their responses to a standard question-naire on the issues, voting records, campaign donations, and Web pages. Personally, I found this site invaluable in deciding which candidates best matched my own positions on the issues.

Although as of October neither the Dole/Kemp site nor the Clinton/Gore site was reporting the number of visitors, Bob Dole's site claimed three million "hits," or file accesses, as of mid-February, 1996. Naturally, those hits include repeated accesses and multiple files per visit, but it is also a number from very early in the campaign. Assuming that by the November election, three million voters had actually accessed the Web sites of the candidates and were influenced by those sites to the extent that each of those voters voted for the same candidate, that would be more than enough votes to swing the national election in November. It is entirely possible, given the explosion of interest in cyberspace and the millions of individuals who have access to the Internet, that we had one of the best-informed electorates, if not the highest turnout, in history in November 1996—in spite of the rel-atively modest effort of the candidates themselves to explore or exploit cyberspace as a powerful new campaign tool.

Political Humor

Anyone willing to speak his or her mind and bare convictions risks ridicule in cyberspace. As Rush Limbaugh has demonstrated rather con-vincingly, the power of humor and satire is potent and can be potentially devastating in the political arena. Such political humor can change minds and sway opinions; however, the potential for abuse is as real as it has ever been for political humor. For example, in spite of all of the abuse directed at Dan Quayle as Vice President, I had reserved judgment—until a visit to a World Wide Web humor site featuring what were alleged to be direct quotes from Quayle speeches helped me see why Quayle was receiving such attention from late-night talk show hosts. Dozens of collections of supposed excerpts from Quayle's speeches[38] included the following:

> Republicans understand the importance of bondage between a mother and child.
>
> —Vice President Dan Quayle

> I was recently on a tour of Latin America, and the only regret I have was that I didn't study Latin harder in school so I could converse with those people.
>
> —J. Danforth Quayle

> What a terrible thing to have lost one's mind. Or not to have a mind at all. How true that is.
>
> —Vice President Dan Quayle, winning friends while speaking to the United Negro College Fund

> If we don't succeed, we run the risk of failure.
>
> —J. Danforth Quayle

> I believe we are on an irreversible trend toward more freedom and democracy--but that could change.
>
> —Vice President Dan Quayle

Few of these Quayle "quotes" are accurate. None are legitimately documented on the Web, and yet there are literally dozens of pages containing the quotes with the attribution to Dan Quayle. Until Jerry Pournelle pointed out to me during a review of this chapter that the quotes were inaccurate, I had unconsciously (and wrongly) dismissed Dan Quayle as a serious candidate for my future votes. We can bemoan the unfairness of inaccurate political humor, but I believe the political effect of such humor is, unfortunately, much the same as if it were accurate. As noted at one site (http://www.webhippie.com/danquayle.html), "In all fairness, some political commentators have raised doubts about the authenticity of some of these Dan Quayle quotes. This, however, makes them no less funny:-" Fortunately, politicians can refuse to take themselves too seriously and use self-deprecating humor, in much the same way Ronald Reagan did and Al Gore has. Gores's opening lines in a visit to the David Letterman show was to ask Letterman, "How can you tell the difference between secret service agents and Al Gore?" Answer: "Gore is the stiff one."

For balance, consider these excerpts from the "Politically Correct Primer":[39]

> Q: HOW DO I KNOW WHEN AN ANIMAL HAS RIGHTS?
>
> A: The general rule is as follows:

> IF AN ANIMAL IS RARE, PRETTY, BIG, CUTE, FURRY, HUGGABLE, OR LOV-ABLE, THEN IT HAS RIGHTS.

Examine the following chart:

RIGHTS	NO RIGHTS
cow	cockroaches
cute bunnies	flies
dolpins in tuna nets	tuna in tuna nets
whales	sharks
red squirrels	red squirrels
owls	loggers
harbor seals	barnacles

It's not difficult to find just about every opinion imaginable in cyber-space, and someone who will argue for it—often with devastating humor or even with relentlessly irrefutable sophistry. One example is a well-done parody of campaign Web pages entitled "Fidel in '96" and subtitled "Send the Ultimate Outsider to Washington." Such humor has always been a key part of the political process; but now, indexed and accessible by topic or name in cyberspace, it could be more influential than ever in changing perceptions and thus the landscape of politics.

Online Oversight

As we learned in school, the United States federal government consists of legislative, executive, and judicial branches to pass, enforce, and interpret the laws under which we, as citizens, are obliged to live by virtue of the benefits we receive from society. Government "of the people, by the people, and for the people" (to use Lincoln's inspired phrasing from the Gettysburg Address) can remain true to that charter only through oversight by the people and accountability to the people. In theory, that's how our government has always operated. The legislature publishes, at taxpayer expense, the *Congressional Record* in the belief that citizens should have access to all of the official words and actions of their elected representatives. Any citizen can use the Library of Congress or can sit in on the public debates of the legislatures or have access to most of the records regarding the activities of their federal, state, and local governments. This process by which government is held accountable is often called oversight, in the sense of "watchful care."

Still, the bulk of government does not reside in the elected legislatures, elected executive offices or judicial branches themselves. Most of our actual government can be found in the unelected administrative agencies, bureaus, and services such as the CIA, FBI, IRS, ATF, DOT, and so on. Because the bureaucrats of these agencies are only indirectly accountable to elected officials and to the "people," they are often able to operate in relative obscurity and without as much review or disclosure as do elected officials and judges. Even when the opportunity exists for the public to review draft decisions, regulations, codes, and amendments, the timing, availability, and awareness of such opportunities are often out of sight and out of mind for most individuals, leaving the door open for special interest groups and lobbyists to have disproportionate influence on matters of importance.

Although it can be argued that such influence by those most interested in any given piece of legislation means that things are working as they should, it can also be argued that easier access might give ordinary citizens a greater say in the workings of government and reduce the power and influence of special interest groups and lobbyists. Some citizens might be required to work during the times designated for public discussion or debate of a given issue, and others may simply not live near the capital where the hearings are physically held. Most are simply not aware that they have the option to participate in the process, much less of when specific matters are scheduled for discussion.

The effective use of interactive, computer-mediated communications can effectively reduce the impact of timing, proximity, and ignorance as barriers to the increased participation of the citizenry in the oversight and advice functions of government. The legislative and policy-making functions of government can and should make drafts of proposed changes to existing codes and law available online, enable feedback via e-mail, and/or provide for public discussion online. By so doing, we could easily see significant improvements in the process whereby government actually serves the people. Cyberspace can facilitate oversight not only of pending legislation, executive orders, and judicial decisions, but also of administrative matters. Now, drafts of decisions and tentative decisions can be submitted on the Net for easier access to anyone interested than previously possible. The means for interested citizens to collaboratively discuss and suggest improvements and changes can be enabled. With the appropriate search and indexing tools, each person can then track and represent his or her own special interests. Ultimately, the quality of the laws, rules, and regulations we live by should improve through these legitimate cooperative processes enabled by new forms of collaborative communications.

Goodbye 1040

Tax law will almost certainly evolve significantly as cyberspace becomes more prevalent and the jurisdiction issues provide ever-increasing challenges to governments. Obviously, real estate and property taxes will not be much affected; however, sales taxes and income taxes could be significantly affected, since both forms of tax are dependent on a paper trail and upon nexus—either of which can be problematic for authorities in cyberspace. My best guess is that when we have electronic money with low-overhead tracking, there eventually will be a tax built into the transfer of money itself, whether it is a value-added tax or a tax on transactions. Such a tax could be based on convoluted schemes that computers and banks can calculate for us, much as cash registers calculate sales tax today—and would therefore have the singular advantage of providing automatic, computerized tracking that would all but eliminate the hidden tax of time spent complying with IRS filing and payment requirements. Such a tax would have other advantages as well, including spreading the taxable events so thin that it would not likely discourage the exchange of all but the largest financial transactions. It would also have an inherently progressive nature that would tax luxuries more than necessities. Of course, any new tax is considered a bad tax; however, I believe that most Americans would be delighted to trade in the current burdensome income tax system for some sort of financial exchange tax or value-added tax that would result in overall lower taxes for the bulk of the populace and the elimination of the annual April 15 nightmare.

Electronic Registration and Voting

Just as "motor voter" registration has become a reality over the objections of many, so could online registration and voting. There may be resistance to this prospect so long as those with access to cyberspace tend to be those who can easily afford computers and modems; but at some point, I expect voting to be handled digitally, by providing computers of some sort at polling places as well as enabling those with access to the Internet to register and vote as well. Voter registration is already computerized, so allowing registration and voting online can not only provide increased convenience to citizens but also save the government money currently used to enter data from voter registration cards into the computer as well as reduce the burden of volunteer work required to track and monitor voting.

Electronic Town Meetings

Although there is little doubt that the concept of electronic town meetings has validity as an agent of change, such meetings have been overhyped in spite of the fact that few people know precisely what one is. Almost every network and CNN have introduced programs following such a format designed to draw opinion and feedback from everyday people. Unfortunately, there is no way to avoid staging, scripting, and prearranging any such event meant to reach out to millions of people—a million voices simply cannot be heard, unless those voices are responding in real time to binary or multiple-choice questions already prepared by moderators, effectively defeating the purpose of such a large forum.

Instead, greater value for an electronic town meeting could be derived from increasing levels of citizen representation, similar to the National Forum on Issues held in Austin, Texas in January 1996, exploiting the new possibilities enabled by conferencing communications. Such representation would not replace existing government but would serve as a resource for ideas and solutions in a way that polls and elections cannot. Neighborhoods might have their own meetings to discuss the relevant issues and ideas facing the individuals in their neighborhood, drafting proposals and resolutions based on a rough consensus, and appoint one representative who would present the neighborhood proposals and resolutions at the city level with other neighborhood representatives. They in turn could discuss and debate and vote on each proposal, electing one representative to carry the ideas forward to the state level. Those representatives would repeat the process until one person from each state moves to the national level for an electronic town meeting from which would emerge only the best ideas from the nation's neighborhoods. Each issue would be categorized as local, city, state, or national for debate and resolution at the appropriate level.

Delegates could "attend" the meetings in cyberspace over a period of weeks or even months until all representatives had a chance to review, debate, and vote on each resolution. These virtual meetings would allow considered discussion rather than heated debate, because the dynamics of online communications are such that there is less pressure to respond immediately and more time to mull over possibilities and consider alternate points of view. If the participants understand that they are tasked to find mutually acceptable proposals within limited periods of time, they will be less likely to engage in endlessly pointless debate and more likely to attempt to forge a consensus of ideas and creative solutions.

Full participation could be enabled at a very low cost, since public libraries near the homes of representatives could be funded with a terminal and software to provide access to the necessary "grass-roots" forums for any county or state representative who lacked access to his or her own terminal. Such electronic town meetings, enabled by technology but spurred by a revitalized sense of possibility, might return a sense of ownership of government to the people far more effectively than instantaneous digital voting or even interactive opinion polls posing as electronic town meetings.

I suspect, based on my experience with the impact of conferencing communications on the political processes within IBM, that we would be surprised by the efficacy of such a process—even though the proposals would not carry the weight of law and would still require action from the legislatures to become law. Obviously, only a very small percentage of the proposals that originate at the neighborhood level would ever be made law, but that is consistent with the desires of the Founding Fathers that government be kept at a minimum.

Unlikely Agreement

The media analysis of the debate between President Clinton and Speaker of the House Newt Gingrich in the spring of 1995 seemed to have missed the most significant aspect of the story. Steeped in the Washington assumptions regarding win/lose political struggle, the media focused on who won the debate, whether Clinton wasn't giving more credence to Gingrich than was warranted and whether Gingrich was exploiting the opportunity to debate the president as a prelude to his bid for the Presidency. What went unnoticed, or at least largely unreported in relation to the debate, was that both Gingrich and Clinton have sought advice from Stephen Covey, proponent of the *Seven Habits of Highly Effective People*, which includes the following comment on seeking unlikely agreement:

> When you see only two alternatives—yours and the "wrong" one—you can look for a synergistic third alternative. There's almost always a third alternative, and if you work with a Win/Win philosophy and really seek to understand, you usually can find a solution that will be better for everyone concerned.

Newt Gingrich uses a reading in his college course cowritten by Covey on "personal strength in American culture," and Bill Clinton has spent a day or two with Covey at Camp David.[40] So here was a case where two of the most powerful men in America were trying to put principle ahead of politics to sit down together and discuss the issues in front of America, and the cynical media missed the real story in their divisive focus on newsworthy disagreement rather than on noteworthy agreement.

Another surprising example of unexpected cooperation leading to synergy can be found on Capitol Hill, where Ted Kennedy, a Roman Catholic liberal from Massachusetts, and Orrin Hatch, a conservative Mormon from Utah, have not only cooperated on the passage of numerous bills, including the Kennedy-Hatch bill that authorized $600 million in anti-AIDS funding in 1990, but are also good friends. As described in Lee Roderick's engrossing biography of Hatch, *Leading the Charge*, Hatch and Kennedy bridged their ideological differences and found common solutions to problems as diverse as labor, religious, and health issues. Kennedy even referred reporters to the agreeable Hatch following the 1991 Palm Beach fiasco at the Kennedy compound, in spite of (or perhaps because of) Hatch's squeaky-clean lifestyle.[41]

Too often, in politics, disagreement and contention serve more hidden agendas than accord and understanding. Yet history holds many examples of those who have overcome significant differences and found inspiring agreement. A Pharaoh believed a slave named Joseph and made him a minister following the interpretation of a dream—thus avoiding serious famine for Egypt. The Founding Fathers were able to forge, even from the raw materials of differences, passion, and commitment, a Constitution that has changed the world perhaps unlike any other agreement ever reached. Mahatma Gandhi forged an extraordinary alliance within India, long separated by cultural and religious differences, in working with the British toward a peaceful independence and separation from Great Britain. South Africa's F.W. deKlerk and Nelson Mandela were able to overcome challenging, long-standing differences of enormous complexity to eliminate apartheid and hold the first fully democratic elections in their country's history.

Cyberspace offers new means by which committed parties can wrest understanding and consensus from the jaws of misunderstanding and dispute when those parties are committed to seek alternative resolutions to their disparate interests. Finding common ground, although an uncommon occurrence between supposed opponents, can become common—it's our choice.

National Information Policy

Cyberspace may be the impetus for a new look at the issue of standards and who should set and own them. Markets are notoriously quick to adopt standards that may be the best available at the time, but which quickly prove to be inadequate for the future. We live with such standards anyway because they're already the standard. Microsoft's DOS is but one example. Consumers are seemingly willing to endure almost any substandard technology in chasing after the siren song of "compatibility," which is a rational thing to do on the individual level, since widely adopted standards have such enormous value. On a societal level, however, it can be a disaster. The market is often a poor judge of the elegance and long-term benefits of standards, especially when the choice is between a dollar today and two dollars tomorrow.

The denizens of cyberspace, government, business, and the media are now engaged in a self-defeating struggle to preserve the existing bases of power that will probably instead, ironically, challenge the very essence of influence and power worldwide. The government of the United States of America created the Internet; and then when intervention was most important, in a monumentally short-sighted decision, abandoned it to commercial interests—virtually ensuring the wealth of those best positioned to make a grab for power and access.

One early result of these competing interests is the 1996 Telecommunications Act, which laudably frees a variety of companies to serve our interests better through open opportunity. Unfortunately, it probably doesn't go far enough to ensure compatibility between the products of the competing companies, which virtually ensures that we will face divisive differences in the products we use in the future. For example, an advanced technology called Integrated Services Digital Network (ISDN), which promises to use existing phone lines to provide two digital phone numbers and lines in only one twisted-pair wire (with enough bandwidth for real-time video interaction), is currently seriously hampered by major differences in implementation technology between the various phone companies. Anyone who wishes to install and use such a phone system must navigate and deal with a hideous tangle of technical jargon and acronyms, including NT-1, switch type, line speed, DTE, protocol, SPID, POTS, DNR, V.25, and more. If you move or travel from an area served by, for example, Bell Atlantic to an area served by Southwestern Bell, you can't just plug in your ISDN equipment and expect it to work. You'd need to reconfigure all your hardware and software from scratch—a tedious process. Without some form of government or public intervention or leadership, however, this kind of reverse technological servitude where humans serve technology and bureaucracy will only get worse, because business is inherently founded on the cultural assumptions of competition and differentiation, not on standardization and cooperation. Fortunately, in this particular case, we may have another chance with a superior technology (compatible with ISDN) named ASDL—but unless we get our act together soon, it will become one more of the all-too-common variety of standards that, unfortunately, are standards in name only, since every company's implementation differs in many of the important details.

We can, and should, harness the power of government to ensure the necessary cooperation to address these issues. Winn Schwartau argues persuasively for a national convention or initiative to establish such standards, in the form of a "National Information Policy:"

> Not all fifty-five of the men who came to Philadelphia in 1787 signed the Constitution. Of the thirty-nine who did, some signed it reluctantly. Everybody made compromises—some more than others—but in the end, they created a work that has endured for thirteen generations. They knew that unless they found answers, there could be no country, certainly not the one they envisioned. Despite seemingly endless conflict, despite professional, political, and personal discord, they found strength in what united them, not what made them different. . . .
>
> Today, our challenge is similar: to set up housekeeping in Cyberspace before the guests arrive. We have to define our future role in the global village, not let those stronger and better prepared dictate our limitations or cause us to be victimized. Building a National Information Infrastructure without a National Information Policy is like trying to build a skyscraper without an architect, without blueprints, without engineers, without a foundation. That is clearly a backwards approach.
>
> A National Information Policy shouldn't be thrown together piecemeal or be allowed to evolve from political, technical, or special-interest whims. It must be comprehensive and as all-inclusive as possible. . . .The opportunity is to define our destiny.[42]

Schwartau is right on target—but it will probably take the leadership of a bold president to make it happen. Few others could marshal the national will that will be required, and it is such a nebulous concept that it would require savvy presentation. The importance of a National Information Policy derived from the best thinking of our generation, that provides a vision for the future of cyberspace and outlines the path toward unifying standards, cannot be overstated.

NETTING IT OUT

While government has already seen the effects of many of the changes stimulated by the rush to cyberspace, the most far-reaching changes are certainly yet to come. As technology continues to move information and thus power into the hands of individuals with the concurrent decentralization of economic and political centers of power, we must face the prospect of further shifts of power. Where we once had our choice of three, maybe four, networks, there are now dozens of cable channels competing for attention—with more to come. Where we once gathered our news from the same limited choice of sources, we now draw our perspectives from a bewildering array of sources ranging from CNN to zines—specialized magazines addressed to small but avid audiences. The same demands for choice and variety that has given us 50 channels and more will lead us to programming on demand. Those same forces leading to decentralization, which have prospered newsletters and zines with specialized, highly focused content, will encourage cyberspace forums, newsletters, sites, and videos of great specificity. Just as our relationship with television once united us for a few decades of relative cultural unity, so will the decline of network television as we know it, as described by George Gilder in *Life After Television*, lead us into new possibilities to recreate our political arena and the operation of government. A new power structure could very well be forming as free thinkers begin to coalesce around compelling discussions and leaders in cyberspace. The political rank and file has changed. Those who wink at the phenomenal developments surrounding cyberspace as a passing fad are likely to be among the first victims of these waves of change and revolutions.

Politicians would be wise to pair with respected analysts and the leaders of commerce, education, and government to ensure that the changes are founded in enduring principle, abandoning the politics of division and all-consuming self-interest in favor of a more enlightened willingness to seek synergy instead of simply compromising. Leaders in government and commerce would do well to heed the lessons of the past decade in the personal computer industry—and exploit rather than fear the power of the change that will occur, no matter how revolutionary. Change or die is the watchword in technology, as it will be in politics. Standards must be developed and adopted soon, in a joint effort between government and commerce, lest the marketplace splinter so badly in a plethora of competing standards that the end users of technology are required to become part-time telecommunications engineers in order to use the technologies that are supposed to serve instead of demand. The media need to be more concerned with substance and less concerned with image and politics as a matter of survival in the face of cyberspace communications. Citizens and consumers need to be certain to stay informed and put their money and their votes where their values are.

It will behoove us all to remember, though, that all politics are ultimately local. In cyberspace, the dynamics of communications are such that you can either reach agreement through high-quality dialogue, or you can argue endlessly in low-quality contests leading nowhere. After years of debate and dialogue, I've learned that the agreements we should seek most often are those agreements that can make a difference to us personally. Why spend hours and hours debating the intricacies of national tax policy with someone who has as little clout in the matter as you have? Of course it can be entertaining, but surely we have better things to do than argue with one another to no purpose better than ego-feeding one-upmanship. Even assuming two people come to a revolutionary agreement after much intellectual toil, they have accomplished little to improve anyone's life if no one takes it one step further and actually communicates the idea or agreement reached to someone in a position to make a difference.

Too many providers of information or participants in the discussions that occur in cyberspace seem to be operating under the assumption that the information and dialogue will make a difference somehow just because it's there for everyone to read, as if someone important in a position of power were always lurking. Obviously, votes can be influenced—which may be enough of a difference to justify the time spent on the discussion; but more often than not, the discussions are just a form of entertainment with combatants already firmly entrenched in their respective positions. In my opinion, this siren song of promising possibilities is luring many an intellectual boat into a whirlpool of lost ideas and onto the shoals of wasted time. So empower yourself—discuss matters that are within your own sphere of influence and simultaneously work to expand that sphere of influence by reaching agreement with those who can make a difference. By so doing, we can cooperate to create the affirmative virtual political communities of the future.

Cyberspace may or may not trigger the violent overthrow of repressive regimes, or even the establishment of a new abstract and borderless free state, but it can enable daily revolutions in our individual lives. Communities form, debates rage, information is exchanged, people react, and groups take action to solve problems. There are argumentative and bitter flame wars that accomplish nothing; but there are also ideas, dialogue, and actions that make all the difference. Few who enter cyberspace remain untouched; yet there is currently little cohesion in this technological revolution. The voices of the revolutionaries in cyberspace are but one force among many that seeks to change society and the shape of the future. No hopes need rest in some future global revolution—the revolutions that matter most will be those that are local.

Every time I log on to cyberspace, it seems I learn something new, or deepen a relationship, or meet someone new, or encounter a new idea. Revolutions can indeed be a matter of individual change on a small scale. If a family changes in a certain way that brings greater peace and harmony to the family, isn't that more momentous in the life of that family as any law likely to be passed by Congress and signed by the President? Not that government is irrelevant, but shouldn't we focus the bulk of our efforts on improving those things nearest and dearest to us? As a political decision, that is one that indeed makes eminent good sense: "Think globally; act locally." The shift away from a reliance on centralized federal solutions and towards local solutions for individuals, families, and neighborhoods will do more to improve our personal lives than any amount of the national politics, which seems to be our primary political concern, judging from the content of most media reports. Seeking local solutions is the wave of change most readily enabled by cyberspace-interdependent progress that will serve us well in our personal lives. While we as individuals work vigorously to establish firm localized foundations, groups such as big government, big business, state and local governments, small business, mass media, and the local media must indeed work together to ensure a foundation of viable standards that will serve us well into the future—but no one should lose sight of why we are building that foundation. It is individuals and families who must be targeted as the special interests that matter most and who will ultimately be most affected by the waves of change wrought by cyberspace.

CHAPTER EIGHT

THE NET OF IT ALL

Facing the Future Today

We have a choice: to plow new ground or let the weeds grow.

> —Attributed to Jonathan Westover, a fictitious person,
> in the Virginia Department of Agriculture report
> entitled "Plowed Ground" for fiscal year 1958–1959

Cyberspace is an extraordinary garden of human experience. I have come to know and appreciate in cyberspace a wide variety of individuals—cynics and the idealists, the kind-hearted and mean-spirited, movers and shakers, lurkers and observers, arrogant and meek, old and young, religious and profane, professionals and lay people, corporate executives and blue-collar workers, the trustworthy and charlatans, rich and poor, wise and foolish, contentious and peacemaking, writers and readers, students and teachers—people, of course, like you and me. I've been angry at them. I've laughed *with* them, and I've laughed *at* them. I've wanted to throttle them, and I've wanted to hug them. The compelling theme of my experience in cyberspace is that even though it may seem to a casual onlooker to be a dull technological experience, it is instead an intensely human experience. The transfer of bits across wires or waves is merely the technological means to the ultimate end of cyberspace communication— the sharing of human concerns, human ideas, human ideals, and human passions. That is the cyberspace I know—a human dimension of unlimited potential to bless or curse our lives. Whether cyberspace becomes a blessing or a curse depends upon the quality of the ideas we sow and nurture in its garden. The garden of cyberspace will be rich in natural beauty if that's what we nurture, or beggared for grace if we insist on letting the weeds grow.

IDEAS HAVE IMPACT

Ideas change the world, for better or worse. The eighteenth-century idea that "all men are created equal and that they are endowed by their Creator with certain unalienable rights," including "life, liberty, and the pursuit of happiness," has changed the course of history and the face of the world and its political landscape unlike many ideas before or since. The idea that slavery could be justified led to generations of cruelty, civil wars, and generation after generation of courage and struggle in the face of prejudice and bigotry. The idea that a savior, messiah, or deliverer might rescue tribes or nations or even all humankind from death and evil has inspired much of humankind throughout recorded history. The idea that vengeance is justified by a jealous god when visited upon his enemies has led to crusades, inquisitions, jihads, terrorism, and religious wars throughout history. The idea that our lives are improved by beauty and inspiration has led to nurturing and protecting nature, great art, poetry, literature, and music. The idea that humankind is united by common hopes and desires and should thus live in peace and work together towards noble ideals has prompted enormous strides in civilization and society. The idea that competition, greed, and selfishness are inherently good is probably at least partially responsible for the privatization of public standards, which is rooted in a business culture that is seemingly just as senseless and insensitive as society's failure to properly care for the poor and less fortunate among us. This is descriptive of a culture that can often be as suspicious and afraid of cooperation as it is of conspiracy.

The sheer quantity of ideas, ideals, and beliefs that bind us as a culture is staggering. Ideas come at us in a constant stream—most of which we accept uncritically, thus forming our culture and shaping our destinies. Yet not all of those ideas are of equal value. Some are of enormous value; others are of dubious value; and still others do great harm. The measure of an idea's worth cannot be measured in its popularity but only by the results and fruits yielded from its embrace and practice.

There has been no shortage of creativity to date in cyberspace—it has been built on creative ideas. The Internet was constructed upon the contributions of thousands of individuals giving freely to create "rough consensus and working code." Text-oriented computerized bulletin boards have given way to the many-splendored multimedia World Wide Web. The idea behind shareware—that consumers should be the judge and arbiter of the value of software following a trial use—could very well become a successful economic model for the sharing of many kinds of information that can't be valued accurately any other way. Computer-mediated conferencing has facilitated the creation of virtual communities that stand to redefine our notion of self and community. Creative ideas have created new means to secure information and our privacy.

Individual cyberspace visionaries and explorers have blazed the trails and mapped the territory before and after William Gibson gave it a name. Their ideas already benefit many of us significantly. Vinton Cerf, Ron Rivest, Adi Shamir, and Len Adleman, Dennis Hayes, Ward Christensen, Bob Metcalfe, Mike Cowlishaw, Ray Ozzie, Stewart Brand, Tom Jennings, Mitch Kapor and John Perry Barlow, Tim Berners-Lee, Marc Andreessen, David Chaum, and, of course, many others have defined the essence of the nature of cyberspace with their distinctive individual creativity and contributions. Vinton Cerf and his team created the software and protocol standards for a decentralized network that is the foundation of the Internet. Rivest, Shamir, and Adleman developed the public key encryption technology that has revolutionized the security of private communications and exchange and promises to provide increased security and privacy in cyberspace. Dennis Hayes created the Model T of microcomputer modems—allowing personal computers to connect via ordinary phone lines. Ward Christensen worked with his friend Randy Seuss to transform a computer system into a bulletin board system that allows people to transcend time and space to access the benefits of computer networks. Bob Metcalfe helped create Ethernet, allowing fast, low-cost, direct connections between computers. Mike Cowlishaw, an IBM Fellow, created and refined many of the tools and commands used for conferencing systems and software repositories, which concepts have influenced other systems within and without IBM. Ray Ozzie developed Lotus Notes, a trailblazing "groupware" application. Stewart Brand and friends created the structure and support for The WELL, a prototype virtual community. Tom Jennings developed the first worldwide network of cooperating bulletin board systems, demonstrating the incredible power of grass-roots networks of systems and people. Mitch Kapor and John Perry Barlow created the Electronic Frontier Foundation to preserve individual liberties in cyberspace. Tim Berners-Lee created HTML, a protocol that facilitates the cooperation between networked computers for displaying and maintaining a wide variety of data, which, in turn, laid the foundation for the World Wide Web. Mark Andreessen authored Mosaic, an ease-to-use browser for accessing documents written in HTML. By making the browser freely available on the Internet, Andressen unleashed the power of the WWW. David Chaum has created the technical and theoretical foundation that enables electronic cash. Many more will yet emerge to shape the cyberspace experience.

These individuals may not be household names, but I'm confident that history will remember them kindly as the inventors and architects of cyberspace. Every one of them created a tool for cooperation and exchange. Cyberspace, as we know it today, wasn't born as the product of any single genius but rather from the cooperative spirit of many brilliant men and women working together, even indirectly or unknowingly, to improve our ability to work together. Cyberspace represents a triumph of cooperative genius, demonstrating the power of creative individuals who "stand on the shoulders of giants."

This complementarity of individual excellence, which is also the basis of civil society and economic prosperity, is one of the primary defining principles of cyberspace. The world of personal computers and, by extension, cyberspace has always been characterized by an excellence of youthful talent that serves us all. Even as the exuberance and idealism of youth have forged the technological foundations of cyberspace from the raw materials of personal computers, digital bits, and networks, so are the stability and wisdom of age and experience required to refine and temper the ethical norms and culture of cyberspace. The dynamic quality of youthful excellence can complement the static quality of ageless, enduring principles and values to produce the excellence in talent and potential yet required as we quite literally redefine and reinvent society, both online and off. There can be little doubt that new ideas are yet to emerge that will also have the power to transform our world, our lives, and civilization—for better and worse. From the chaos of this threshold, this "liminal moment," will emerge the basis of a new world order that includes cyberspace. Ready or not, it will come. As the denizens of cyberspace frame its culture and establish its communities, standards, and ideals, we have new opportunities to empower one another with respect, trust, and cooperation, reflecting the best of all human endeavors.

Even today, cyberspace enables us to share ideas, information, and conversation with those we would otherwise never meet. The attributes that make computer-mediated communications (conferencing) different from previous means of brainstorming or idea generation include the following:

▪ Individuals do not need to be linked in time or in space in order to interactively exchange ideas and critiques of ideas because there is a convenient, accessible time and space buffer introduced by the ability to store messages in cyberspace.

■ The nature of conferencing encourages more reflective, thoughtful participation by those who have a stake in the dialogue—the time buffer can be used to reconsider initial, emotional reactions.

■ Everyone can have a say—rationing of linear time amongst participants is unnecessary.

These simple innovations in communication can make an enormous difference not only in the quality of ideas exchanged and information available to us but also in our ability to analyze more ideas and consume more information in less time and with less effort—depending on the quality of the participation.

What's more, cyberspace commerce, trade, and exchange are creating and will continue to create unpredictable forces that will transform our world economy, law, governments, and social order. Cyberspace will become an enormous free market of goods, services, and information. Cyberspace will be our most significant education and information resource—a breeding ground for new ideas and the means by which those ideas are conveyed. We have only begun to dabble with this aspect of its potential. Many companies, journalists, writers, politicians, and analysts are already using cyberspace to gather feedback and information from customers, clients, competitors, and potential audiences. Unfortunately, most of the gathering is done by individual initiative and is mostly one way. As companies and civic institutions begin to discover the power of interactive brainstorming in cyberspace by interested parties to solve real problems, it will become a common means of generating dialogue to transform organizations, nurture change, and benefit lives.

Yet it seems that many have yet come to terms with the need for change or the negative directions that change might take without more proactive intervention and cooperation. Many are horrified at the thought that terrorists, drug dealers, and pornographers can exploit this new medium with impunity. Others are equally horrified that our civil rights, particularly freedom of speech, could be restricted by government. Many in the government seem "scared bitless" at the thought that ordinary people worldwide will have at their disposal the means to correspond with anyone on the planet without fear of incrimination through interception, while many others recoil at the thought that privacy might become little more than a fond memory after big business and government exploit our personal data without authorization and with increasingly ruthless precision.

It seems at times as if wisdom and common sense have been abandoned where cyberspace is concerned. Selfish opportunism often seems the order of the day. Applying the laws of every jurisdiction worldwide to cyberspace (as if borders had meaning in cyberspace) seems to be a narrow attempt, destined to fail, to establish localized control over a global phenomenon. The notion that any national government can exercise effective control over content on the Internet is simply misguided and defies common sense. Thus, such actions as the passage of the Communications Decency Act are not solutions—they only exacerbate the problems and raise questions about government ignorance of cyberspace and irresponsibility toward it. Attempts to apply ineffective, cumbersome client-side filters to shield our children from obscenity is not much better on the solution scale than the CDA. Abandoning the public interest in elegant standards to single companies and "market mechanisms" is the equivalent of granting large tracts of public land (including national parks) to private companies or individuals for the purpose of maximizing profits from their exploitation. Maintaining export restrictions on encryption technology that is already available worldwide is another example of a knee-jerk attempted remedy that is neither a solution nor an answer.

Far more appealing are visionary measures which recognize that change is inevitable and therefore innovation (technical and social) is required. As a borderless, abstract world, cyberspace needs its own governance. It even needs its own constitution—one that recognizes the absolute importance of freedom of conscience without denying the existing sovereign powers of states and nations to limit the physical acts of subjects to secure the common good. Rather than adopting censorious laws to control content in cyberspace, we need to cooperate to distinguish between fit and unfit content for children. In particular, the Platform for Internet Content Selection (PICS) deserves universal support. PICS would allow individuals to control their own environment in cyberspace, empowering parents to make cyberspace a suitably public space for their children by filtering sites with undesirable content. Even if compliance with PICS by sites and browsers alike were to be mandated by law, such a law would probably be just as constitutional as consumer protection laws, mandating only appropriate labeling rather than prohibiting the speech itself or requiring government censorship. Such a system would protect freedom of speech while also making cyberspace a safe place for the general public by restricting private content to spaces inaccessible to children.

We also need the innovation of constructive public dialogue in cyberspace that transcends typically competitive, winner-take-all political debate and the cynical reporting surrounding such debate. We need new processes of open cooperation to set important public standards that prevent government bureaucracies, businesses, or even "the market" from defining them for us. "The market" is not synonymous with the people—a market can only reactively choose from the choices provided by business; the people can proactively define for businesses the choices they demand. The people—each individual with an interest in the impact of any public standard—should be free to contribute requirements, ideas, technology, and programming to the standard-setting process—but the resulting standards should be elegant and open—rooted in proven technology acclaimed by a rough consensus, with nonproprietary ownership. In the process of establishing such a process, we may also need to rethink intellectual property law as it applies to public standards. We can find ways to reward contributors without giving anyone an unfairly predominant proprietary interest in public standards, which derive more of their value from their widespread use than from their originality or creativity.

Unfortunately, our idealism and trust in the unlimited potential of cyberspace must be tempered by the realistic expectation that not everyone is ready for the liberty and freedom offered by cyberspace. No one who would attempt to harrass, intimidate, and harm others in cyberspace should remain free to so exploit the empowering capacity of cyberspace communications indefinitely. Those who flame, rage, profane, defame, and spew hatred harm us all and test our love and tolerance for free speech. As we struggle to reconcile individuality and liberty with democratic equality and social harmony, we must remember that responsible action must accompany liberty. As the British philosopher Edmund Burke said,

> Men qualify for civil liberty in exact proportion to their disposition to put moral chains on their own appetites. Society cannot exist unless a controlling power is put somewhere on will and appetite, and the less of it there is within, the more there must be without.[1]

Our laws provide that those convicted of theft, murder, fraud, rape, assault, and libel forfeit their right to move freely in society. Similarly, spammers, harrassers, defamers, liars and others who prove themselves unable or unwilling to respect others in cyberspace should forfeit their right to move freely in cyberspace—yet at the moment there are few effective mechanisms to enforce such restrictions. In real space, identity is characterized by names, appearance, addresses, and numbers. The apprehension of criminals depends on identity. In cyberspace, however, identity can be more easily disguised, using identification numbers, pseudonyms, anonymous remailers, or e-mail addresses bearing little or no relationship to physical identity. Most commercial services allow pseudonyms and make obtaining a new user identification name or number so easy that even cancellation of one's account is not much of a deterrent—but at least users must establish a billing identity to use the service. The Internet is even more notoriously lax in security—anonymity is the most compelling form of privacy available. This failure to differentiate between those conditions and purposes requiring meaningful accountability and those that are best served by anonymity has its roots in the technological structure of cyberspace as much as in its youthful idealism; but it has had and will continue to have far-reaching consequences. Cyberspace culture is prone to permissiveness. Even criminal behaviors are difficult to apprehend or prosecute because the perpetrators are often difficult to identify with certainty. At some point, we will need more effective methods to certify identity in cyberspace, in conjunction with appropriate avenues for guaranteed anonymity as discussed in Chapter 3. Otherwise, accountability will be limited to those willing to be held accountable.

Fortunately, cyberspace is young. We still have a golden opportunity to forge a technological infrastructure that addresses a wide variety of concerns, which will, in turn, determine the nature of cyberspace. There is an increasing recognition of the need for universal cooperation toward this end. Deputy Attorney General Jamie Gorelick, according to a July 16, 1996, Reuters report, told a Senate panel, "What we need, then, is the equivalent of the "Manhattan Project" for infrastructure protection, a cooperative venture between the government and private sector to put our best minds together to come up with workable solutions to one of our most difficult challenges."[2] German Minister Claudia Nolte, in a United Nations discussion of ways to protect women and children from violence and sexual exploitation, said, "Because the Internet knows no national borders, we will be able to protect youth only through international standards."[3]

We do indeed need to cooperate to define workable international standards. Cyberspace needs creative solutions to facilitate the encryption and increased security necessary to protect our privacy and monetary currency without compromising national security interests. We need standards for exchange, such as e-mail, e-conferencing, and e-money. We need a means of differentiating between public and private spheres in cyberspace, enabling individuals to start their own conferencing spaces and to administer them according to their own rules as either public or private spaces. Perhaps most importantly, we need norms and new laws that protect intellectual property in cyberspace specifically, to stimulate economic growth without encroaching on legitimate free speech or hindering the spread of ideas. After all, the foundation purpose of intellectual property law, in the United States at least, is not primarily to enrich individuals or encourage the hoarding of ideas for profit—it is to facilitate the spread of ideas that can change the world.

My hope for cyberspace is that it will become a constructive forum for sharing and distributing ideas that will benefit individuals, family, and society. We have an opportunity to once again seek the answers to the ageless questions of humankind, this time with more hope than ever before of finding satisfying answers. What is truth? What is good? Where is the balance between individual liberty and excellence and our societal need for mutual respect and harmony? Variations of those questions and the issue of freedom have been discussed in cyberspace for years now and are boiling over into the mass media. Within a decade, cyberspace will *be* the mass medium. Each of us will have the opportunity to differentiate ourselves by the quality of our ideas, and if we cooperate, we can benefit not only from our own creative ideas but also from the creative ideas of others.

The pioneers, settlers, and squatters of the virgin territories of cyberspace have divided some of that land into plats of social order and plowed it into furrows of discipline—for the simple reason that its natural resources can only be found in the mind and have greater value if shared. Yet the vast bulk of the territory is naturally untamed. If there is gold in cyberspace, it is not a treasure that can be touched. If there is timber there, it cannot be possessed or felled by any one person. The natural resources of cyberspace are found in the embrace of minds, namely understanding, knowledge, synergy, shared vision, and productive, cooperative action—civic virtue. Without visitors, any given space in cyberspace cannot exist. Without sharing and cooperation, the natural resources of cyberspace are squandered and destroyed.

If we wish those intellectual resources of cyberspace to become more abundant, we must value and secure them. We must find ways to assign appropriate economic value to the abstract resources of cyberspace just as we have found ways to assign monetary value to physical resources. We must find the means to inexpensively share cyberspace resources through appropriate degrees of protection of intellectual property. If we succeed, we could see a worldwide explosion of economic activity, where scarce physical natural resources are conserved but more abundant abstract intellectual resources produce unprecedented progress, economic stimulation, and well-being. If we fail, we could witness destructive, endlessly brutal competition and electronic warfare, where wit, words and cunning are the weapons of choice and those who wield them well will be the strong who survive and dominate cyberspace.

If the potential of cyberspace is to be realized, its natural resources must be available to everyone. The embrace of minds that is the heart of cyberspace will be an incestuous one indeed if those minds are exclusively wealthy, technically inclined, and politically powerful. Cyberspace must be even more expansively embracing than society as a whole and should not be allowed, through plan or neglect, to become the domain of a new elite. We must encourage and nurture a culture of inclusion and cooperation. We must mandate equal access for all. We must ensure that public resources, such as airwaves and standards, benefit all as greatly and equally as possible, and are efficiently maintained as public rather than private property.

Any number of ideas might emerge to solve the compelling problems we face in cyberspace; however, many will probably be rejected out of hand too quickly. The best answers are not always the obvious answers. Constitutions are not forged in a day. Now, more than ever, we need a fresh appreciation for the power of ideas. Even thought we don't always understand the origins of new ideas, we do know that compelling ideas can now be transmitted and communicated quickly and powerfully, even across cultures and national boundaries. Even though we may not quickly reach agreement, we know that there is value in working towards agreements that may not be contained in either side of the initial arguments.

DICHOTOMIES AND EASY ANSWERS

Too often, we make choices before we've even considered the alternatives, much less the consequences. We often identify only two of the most obvious alternatives and move on to the process of selecting one or the other. We often look for an easy answer—seemingly unaware that the quality answer is often found only after we have explored a whole range of choices, thus increasing our knowledge and understanding of the issues while simultaneously increasing the likelihood that a superior solution will emerge.

Too many of the choices we face in cyberspace and society seem to be framed erroneously as mutually exclusive alternatives, such as pornography vs. free speech; pro choice vs. pro life; evolution vs. deity, more prisons vs. more crime; deficits vs. taxes; less government vs. more civic virtue; anonymity vs. accountability; church vs. state; security vs. protection; open standards vs. useful standards; relaxed intellectual property laws vs. more intellectual property; and so on. In business and politics, we too often invest in our own ideas as if they were property, and the best ideas of both sides—which might be combined to enormous synergistic advantage—languish individually as either/or alternatives. Rather than focus on common interests and seek to build consensus solutions, adversaries often highlight differences and seek to thoroughly discredit adversaries. We therefore drown in false dichotomies, plagued by bifurcation.

There is a crying need for ideas to advance the potential of cyberspace that transcend the obvious. For example, rather than battle over censorship vs. pornography, we can focus on creating technological labeling and filtering and other solutions (such as PICS) to keep pornography out of the reach of children and children out of the reach of pornographers. Rather than bemoan the intrusion of advertising in cyberspace, we can focus on means that direct nonintrusive advertising to those who can benefit from it or want it in exchange for content. Rather than debate whether anonymity should be protected in cyberspace, we should explore means to prevent or allow anonymity in the various spaces within cyberspace as appropriate, fully disclosing the nature of each space. Likewise, instead of debating various proposed standards from different companies and wasting time and money on dead-end standards, we should be working together to ensure that the standard we adopt is a public asset that includes the best of all proposed standards and related ideas. Many other issues in cyberspace also require utilitarian solutions. Such solutions are easily within our reach and could be included within the technical infrastructure of cyberspace. Unselfish cooperation will engender more utilitarian ideas than will brutal competition—the Internet itself is a product of such open cooperation.

It is easy to feel trapped and become cynical in the face of polarization and false dichotomies; nonetheless, I trust that common sense and mutual respect can ultimately emerge as cultural characteristics in cyberspace, creating a rainbow of choice where once there was only the storm of struggle. The beauty of this awakening to a wired world is that the false dichotomies that polarize us as a society can be reexamined, one by one, in the cooperative process of identifying bipartisan alternatives and constructive, utilitarian solutions. In questioning our choices, we might recall the words of Robert Kennedy: "Some men see things that are, and ask, 'Why'? I see things that never were, and ask, 'Why not'?"

FORGING THE FUTURE FRONTIER

So here we are, standing on the edge of a frontier, bursting with untrammeled intellectual beauty. The territory, however abstract, is real. To pioneers who are rushing to stake a claim, it might seem that the whole world has already beaten them there. Social institutions, business, and government are rushing to stake their claims and possess it. The reality, however, is that we are still tramping along a wide-open, virgin territory that is unlimited and infinite in nature. This frontier is not the last frontier—it is the future frontier. There, we can choose to plow new ground or let the weeds grow. Plowing new ground is difficult; it demands of us a commitment to shared values and rule of law, a love of capital-Q Quality, and a devotion to action. Letting the weeds grow is easy—it's the default condition. We need think nothing, commit to nothing, and do nothing. Anyone who has gardened knows that weeds grow freely, often choke out the desirable plants, and are difficult to eradicate. Their proliferation, however, can be minimized, so that the wide variety of plants we nurture and value can thrive.

The unplowed ground in the garden of cyberspace is the anarchic space where minimal standards, technical or moral, have been instituted or enforced. Its weeds are words and acts that lack quality and good and cheapen the cyberspace experience. The fundamental questions we must ask ourselves as we embark on our separate explorations and adventures in cyberspace are not so much questions of survival and subsistence but of fulfillment and realization. As Sherry Turkle asks,

> What is the connection between my physical and virtual bodies? . . . What is the nature of our social ties? What kind of accountability do we have for our actions in real life and in cyberspace? What kind of society or societies are we creating, both on and off the screen?[4]

As free individuals, we choose what to believe about cyberspace as we face these and other fundamental questions about this new frontier. Can we as individuals affect the reality of cyberspace? What kind of life will cyberspace bring us? Who are we in cyberspace? How do we relate to one another there?

Whatever the future holds, we would be well served to learn the basics of going online, working to expand our horizons in cyberspace. We can focus on our sphere of influence, beginning with that over which we have absolute control—our own beliefs and our online objectives. We can learn to share ideas online, finding increased freedom as we learn more about ourselves and others and the roles we play—using careful reasoning and respect for others as a prerequisite for serious dialogue. We can seek to minimize the impact of wrongdoing in our explorations of cyberspace by avoiding those areas there that are likely to be inconsistent with our own personal values, and teach our children to do the same. We can use e-mail and other cyberspace communications technologies to our advantage in extending the range of our relationships and improving their quality. We can participate in online dialogue and discussion carefully, choosing our communities with an eye to maximizing the value of the time we spend there. We can proactively choose those values that matter most to us, and band together with others of like minds in order to seek social and government policy and change consistent with those values. We can lobby companies for products and features consistent with our needs. We can band together with others who demand open standards to avoid the products of companies that attempt to establish proprietary standards. We can participate in online commerce by purchasing or making available goods, services, and information.

I believe that we can shape cyberspace to our own liking, without forcing others to accept our preferences. The territory is big enough for all of us. In the face of the enormous potential for destruction, harm, and disintegration posed by cyberspace technology, the infinite amount of psychic space in cyberspace offers countering hope. Cyberspace will challenge us individually in ways we have never before faced. It will remain a place of polar extremes, where every aspect of life, positive and negative, is as near to us as we choose. It will present us with the opportunity to choose and test our beliefs and assumptions and challenge us to choose beliefs and assumptions that enhance the quality of our life.

Therein is the challenge and potential of cyberspace: to shape it to serve us well. There is much that remains to be further shaped and molded about cyberspace: its popular meaning, its culture, its norms of behavior, principles of acceptable discourse and exchange, its modes of communication, its technological structure by which we are empowered or limited, and its standards, which define the effectiveness and efficiency of our experience there. Still to be defined and embraced in this fertile frontier are standards and principles for security, exchange, privacy, commerce, intellectual property, ownership, governance, enforcement, and jurisdiction.

I foresee a changed world—one that ultimately offers us more personal, social, commercial, and political choices than ever before. If we are given choices, we can choose wisely. That belief implicit in the Constitution. If enough individuals choose to cooperate in harmony rather than to fight and war, society flourishes. If we choose good for others, we choose good for ourselves—and vice versa. As the statesman Cecil said, "Every year of my life I grow more convinced that it is wisest and best to fix our attention on the beautiful and the good, and dwell as little as possible on the evil and the false."[5] Note that technology is neutral, but that the standards and choices imbedded in technology may not be so neutral. Those choices (policy, law, norms, and structure) form the bedrock and soil of society and have an impact on daily life that simply cannot be ignored. In the final analysis, however, the choices we make personally about the seeds we plant in that soil—the ideas we embrace and the ideals we seek—will do even more to color the gardens of our lives with beauty than the nature of the environment within which we live and move. As stated by Henry David Thoreau, "The perception of beauty is a moral test."[6]

FREE TO CHOOSE

We constantly face choices. Even when we feel trapped, we have more choices than we realize. Haven't we all had the experience of fretting over whatever new stew we're in or whatever tough trial we face, only to be inspired when we see someone else in a similar predicament extricate himself or herself by force of choice, using wits and the creative application of imagination? In the movies, it seems that our heroes—larger-than-life characters such as Jean-Luc Picard, Indiana Jones, James Bond, Luke Skywalker, or Will Smith—overcome insurmountable odds because no matter how dire the predicament, their creativity and insight enable them to make the right choices every time. Picard, in one episode, faces a clone of himself from the future who was found drifting in space in a solitary shuttlepod. In a moment of challenging introspection, Picard realizes that the clone had made a choice that resulted in the destruction of his ship, the *Enterprise*, and its crew. He knows that he will soon face that choice, so he reexamines every decision and is able to overcome his normal best judgment and choose an alternate course that saves his ship and crew. Indiana Jones and his instincts are always one quick step and one instantaneous choice ahead of danger. James Bond, with the help of ingenious devices created by an anticipatory genius, manages to regain control of his destiny no matter how often he is captured or how dismal his prospects or limited his choices. Luke Skywalker, in the film *Star Wars*, flies a single craft through a hail of enemy fire and, by being in tune with "the force," succeeds in firing on the only spot on the entire Death Star so vulnerable. Will Smith, the heroic fighter pilot in the movie *Independence Day*, makes one right choice after another to destroy the mother ship of the alien invaders, following his instincts while nonetheless carrying out his orders. Our modern heroes are those who act on principle, choose wisely, and face enormous odds with courage and hope.

There is something that these and other heroes in our culture share. It is a spiritual quality—the willingness to act consistent with one's best self, with great assurance, and with the confidence that springs from fulfilling one's passion. Instinctively, we recognize this fully alive quality of fictional heroes that enables them to face every new situation with grace and courage; yet we are prone to dismiss that same quality from our own lives as unrealistic, fantastic, fanatical, or fictional, in spite of the fact that there are so many real-life heroes who possess or possessed the same inspiring qualities—George Washington, Abraham Lincoln, Helen Keller, Martin Luther, Mahatma Ghandi, Eleanor Roosevelt, Martin Luther King, Jr., Michael Jordan, and Nelson Mandela, to name but a few. Whomever you choose as your heroes, you will probably find that it is their essential personal integrity and devotion to ideals that is so appealing and inspiring, even if you disagree with their ideals, ideas, or politics. The fact that the real-life heroes face real-life problems with inspired solutions only adds to our sense of respect.

So why discuss heroes and self-knowledge and personal integrity at the end of a book on cyberspace? Because I believe the choices we make, individually, over the next decade will mean more than the choices made in any other generation since the one that began in 1776. We live in the generation that is defining and will define the nature of cyberspace for ourselves and our children and their children and their children's children, in the same way that the signers of the Declaration of Independence and the framers of the Constitution defined the essential nature of America, even to this day. We need heroes now more than ever; if there are to be any such heroes of the cyberspace revolution, they are living today. We should not only seek them out and support their efforts and follow their leadership in cooperative efforts, but also work personally to define cyberspace by the choices we make daily. Our choices define our life experience, and even though some of us may indeed live lives "of quiet desperation," even that, in the final analysis, is a choice we make. We can choose otherwise—to follow our passions, our hearts, and our best selves. We can indeed choose quality and excellence for ourselves. As Ralph Waldo Emerson said of the natural world, long before cyberspace was considered, "Beauty is the mark God sets on virtue. Every natural action is graceful; every heroic act is also decent, and causes the place and the bystanders to shine."[7]

Let us make cyberspace such a place. We owe it to ourselves and to our posterity.

CHAPTER 1 Cyberspace, an Introduction

1. John Heilemann, "The Making of the President 2000," *Wired* 3.12 (December 1995): 218.
2. James Y. Bryce, *Using ISDN* (Indianapolis: Que, 1995), p. 466.
3. *Webster's Tenth New Collegiate Dictionary.*
4. Stephen R. Covey, *Seven Habits of Highly Effective People* (New York: Simon & Schuster, 1989), p. 219. Covey says, "Most people are deeply scripted in what I call the Scarcity Mentality. They see life as having only so much, as though there were only one pie out there. And if someone were to get a big piece of the pie, it would mean less for everybody else. The Scarcity Mentality is the zero-sum paradigm of life."
5. Garry Trudeau, *Doonesbury* (Universal Press Syndicate, March 10, 1996).
6. Clifford Stoll, *Silicon Snake Oil* (New York: Doubleday, 1995), pp. 3–4.

CHAPTER 3 Cyberspace Culture, Ethics, and Law

1. Pirsig refers to the Swedish word "kulturbärer" in his discussion of the unexpected success of *Zen and the Art of Motorcycle Maintenance* in the Afterword of of the Bantam Books edition, saying that "Culture-bearing books challenge cultural value assumptions and often do so at a time when the culture is changing in favor of their challenge." He mentions *Uncle Tom's Cabin* as one such book.
2. Robert M. Pirsig, *Lila* (New York: Bantam Books, 1991), p.121.
3. Ibid, p. 159.
4. Ibid.
5. Ibid, pp. 162–163.
6. Ibid, p. 164.
7. Viktor E. Frankl, *Man's Search For Meaning* (New York: Washington Square Press, 1963), pp. 58-59.
8. John Perry Barlow, "Crime and Puzzlement: Desperados of the DataSphere," http://www.uci.agh.edu.pl/pub/security/big.brother.txt (June 8, 1990).
9. Ibid.
10. Katie Hafner and John Markoff, *Cyberpunk* (New York: Simon & Schuster, 1991).
11. Hafner and Markoff.
12. Molly O'Neill, "The Lure and Addiction of Life Online," *The New York Times*, March 8, 1995, p. B1.
13. Bill Waterson, *Calvin and Hobbes*, Universal Press Syndicate, November 26, 1995.

14. James Thurber, quoted from the "Concise Columbia Dictionary of Quotations," in the *Complete Writer's Toolkit*, Version 1.0.

15. Frankl, pp. 58-59.

16. Robert Bolt, *A Man For All Seasons* (New York: Scholastic Book Services, 1967), p. 88.

17. Philip Zimmerman, "PGP™ Users Guide, Volume I: Essential Topics" from the documentation accompanying PGP version 2.6.2 (October 11, 1994).

18. Jim Warren, "The Persecution of Phil Zimmerman, American" (January 8, 1996), http://www.contra.org/pgp/PhilZimmerman.html (September 6, 1996).

19. Jon Lebkowsky, "The Internet Code Ring! An Interview with Phil Zimmerman, Creator of PGP," http://www.well.com/user/jonl/works/pgp.html (March 1993).

20. Bruce A. Lehman, Assistant Secretary of Commerce and Commissioner of Patents and Trademarks, Chair, "Intellectual Property and the National Information Infrastructure: A Preliminary Draft of the Report of the WorkingGroup on Intellectual Property Rights," http://www.uspto.gov/text/pto/nii/ipwg.html (July 1994).

21. Pamela Samuelson, "The Copyright Grab," *Wired* 4.01 (January 1996): 134.

22. CompuServe Online Service, "CompuServe's Operating Rules," Go Rules. (September 10, 1996).

23. My personal favorite is *Netiquette* (San Francisco: Albion Books, 1994) by Virginia Shea.

24. All exchanges are from personal archives of author. The incident occurred in March 1994.

25. Lance Rose, "Anonymity Online: Its Value, and Its Social Costs," *Boardwatch Magazine*, 9.06 (June 1995): 100.

26. Ibid, p. 102.

27. 18 USCS 2510.

28. From marketing literature for the Internet Law Symposium 95 held in Seattle.

29. See http://www.america.net/com/liberty/commonsense.html.

30. At http://jg.cso.uiuc.edu/pg/welcome.html.

31. Lance Rose, *Netlaw* (Berkeley: Osborne McGraw-Hill, 1995), p. 96.

32. *Sony Corporation of America v. Universal Studios, Inc.*, 464 U.S. 417 (1984).

33. Rose, *Netlaw*, p. 104.

34. See http://lcweb.loc.gov/copyright as a starting point.

35. Dan L. Burk, "Trademarks Along the Infobahn: A First Look at the Emerging Law of Cybermarks" (1995), http://www.urich.edu /~jolt/v1i1/burk.html (September 14, 1995).

36. Thomas Jefferson, "A Bill for Establishing Religious Freedom," known as "The Virginia Statute for Religious Freedom" (1779), quoted by George Seldes in *The Great Thoughts* (New York: Ballantine Books, 1996), p. 229.

37. Bolt, p. 91.

38. United States Constitution, Amendment I.

39. See full text of decision at http://www.eff.org/Alerts/HTML/960612_aclu_v _reno_decision.html (September 14, 1996).

40. Harvard Classics, *American Historical Documents* (New York: P.F. Collier & Son Corporation, 1938), "The Articles of Confederation," Article V, p. 160. "Freedom of speech and debate in Congress shall not be impeached or questioned in any court, or place out of Congress, and the members of Congress shall be protected in their persons from arrests and imprisonments, during the time of their going to and from, and attendance on Congress, except for treason, felony, or breach of the peace."

41. *Schenck* v. *United States*, 249 U.S. 47 (1919).

42. Jake Baker Information Page (November 11, 1995) http://www.mit.edu: 8001/activities/safe/safe/cases/umich-baker-story/Baker/Jake_Baker.html (September 14, 1996).

43. Jonathan Wallace and Mark Mangan, *Sex, Laws, and Cyberspace* (New York: Henry Holt and Company, Inc., 1996), p. 65.

44. Brock N. Meeks, "Same Old Shit," *Wired* 3.11 (November 1995): 88. Meeks says that a government representative "proceeded to blow smoke up the ass of more than 100 crypto wonks" and that the key escrow system was "cooked up by the nation's top spooks at the National Security Agency." He refers to "several of the more nefarious aspects of Clipper" and presumes time and again to know the motives of civil servants. He calls the government's attempts at compromise "nothing more than an elaborate shell game" and asserts (without supporting evidence) that it is "just another step toward satisfying the FBI's real jones: outlawing the use of private-encryption schemes" and that "government would love to squash this last outpost of privacy—your ability to choose your own "non-government certified" encryption technology.

45. Evan I. Schwartz, "Wanna Bet?" *Wired* 3.10 (October 1995): 134.

46. 74 F.3d 701, 704-05 (6th Cir. 1995).

47. 96 C.D.O.S. 609. *United States of America, Plaintiff-Appellee*, v. *Robert Alan Thomas and Carleen Thomas, Defendants-Appellants*. No. 94-6648 (January 29, 1996), http://www.callaw.com/tommy.html (September 14, 1996).

48. Rose, *Netlaw*, pp. 222–223.

49. Telecommunications Act of 1996 (February 1, 1996), http://thomas.loc.gov/ cgibin/query/z?c104:s.652.enr: (September 14, 1996).

50. Ibid.

51. Ibid.

52. Ibid.

53. Ibid.

54. Ibid.

55. Ibid.

56. Ibid.

57. Ibid.

58. Ibid.

59. *ACLU* v. *Reno* (June 12, 1996), http://www.access.digex.net/~epic/cda/cda_opinion.html (September 9, 1996)

60. Ibid.

61. Ibid.

62. Ibid.

63. Ibid.

64. Ibid.

CHAPTER 4 The Individual and Excellence:

1. Thomas J. Peters and Robert H. Waterman, Jr., *In Search of Excellence: Lessons from America's Best-Run Companies* (New York: Harper & Row, Publishers, 1982).

2. Thomas J. Watson, Jr., *A Business and its Beliefs: The Ideas That Helped Build IBM*, McKinsey Foundation Lecture Series, Graduate School of Business, Columbia University (New York: McGraw-Hill Book Company, Inc., 1963).

3. Joy Wolfram, "Suggestion Award Winners Score Unexpected Windfalls," *Mid-Atlantic Area News*, 2.04 (1990): 4.

4. "Ideas that fetched more than a million," *Think,* 51.04 (1985): 31.

5. Carla Lazzareschi, "Under the Big Gray Cloud at IBM," *Los Angeles Times Magazine,* February 2, 1992, p. 24.

6. Paul B. Carroll, "IBM Wants Its Managers to Encourage Certain Workers to Leave the Company," *The Wall Street Journal*, May 23, 1991, p. A4.

7. *The Wall Street Journal,* August 7, 1991.

8. *Business Week,* editorial, June 17, 1991, p. 120.

9. Laura Brennan, "Scathing Words from Akers Spark Uproar at IBM," *PC Week*, June 3, 1991, pp. 129–130.

10. Evelyn Richards, "Turning IBM Around," *The Washington Post,* November 24, 1991, p. H1.

11. "Time for 'The John Akers Gang' To Go!" *Resistor: A Newsletter of Information and Solidarity*, no. 33 (November 1991), IBM Workers United.

12. Beth Freedman, "IBM Creates Post to Push OS/2 2.0 into Mass Market," *PC Week*, February 17, 1992, p. 113.

13. John F. Akers, "Key to Growth and Progress: 'A Healthy Level of Tension,'" editorial, *Think,* 57.3 (1991).

14. Ibid.

15. Wayne Rash, Jr., "The Ethical Revolution," *OS/2 Professional*, 1.5 (August 1993): 75.

16. Charles Bradlaugh, as quoted in *The Great Thoughts*, compiled by George Seldes (New York: Ballentine Books, 1996), p. 54.

17. "Browne Demonstrates Support for Internet Freedom," http://www.rahul.net/browne/news-internet-freedom-1.html (May 6, 1996).

18. Tom Potter, tdp@ix.netcom.com, "Re: What's wrong with child labor?" *alt.politics.libertarian* (May 6, 1996).

19. Tom Ender, 73511,3611@compuserve.com, #: 632043, Sb: Corporate Welfare, CANOPUS FORUM, *CompuServe* (April 10, 1996).

20. Craig Goodrich, craig@airnet.net, "Re: A Rude Awakening—Dunblane Massacre," *alt.politics.libertarian* (April 3, 1996).

21. silveroak@chaos.connect-bbs.com, "Re: Evil, Completely Evil," *alt.flame.abortion* (April 15, 1996).

22. Steven Meece, smeece@chat.carleton.ca, "Re: Marijuana vs. Hockey," *carleton.general*, (April 17, 1996).

23. From *Famous Quotes*, a collection on CD-ROM © 1995 by Infobases Incorporated.

24. *Webster's Tenth New Collegiate Dictionary.*

25. "Quotable Quotes," *Readers Digest* (April 1996), p. 177.

26. James Madison, quoted in, Seldes, *The Great Thoughts*, p. 288.

27. "In Memoriam. . . ," http://www.goodstuff.prodigy.com/okc/ okcmemr.htm (September 19, 1996).

28. Joseph Stalin, from "Conrad's Collection of Famous Quotes," 1995, http://www.cyberus.ca/~clabonte/quotes.htm, Conrad E. Labonte, ed., (September 19, 1996).

29. David L. Norton, *Personal Destinies* (Princeton, NJ: Princeton University Press, 1976), p. 10.

30. See http://www2.dgsys.com/~tgolden/honor.html.

31. I am indebted to Terry Warner at Brigham Young University for the concepts of self-betrayal and collusion, or mutual betrayal.

32. Gibson, *Neuromancer*, p. 5.

33. Sherry Turkle, *Life on the Screen: Identity in the Age of the Internet* (New York: Simon & Schuster, 1995), p. 268.

34. Ibid, p. 260.

35. Phyllis Phlegar, "A Psychologist's Look at Cyberspace," *Boardwatch Magazine* 9.10 (October 1995): 82.

36. Graham Lea, 100137,655@compuserve.com, #:619478, Sb: BARKTO REVEALED?, CANOPUS FORUM, *CompuServe* (March 21, 1996). Lea refers also to his BillWatch column in *Computing* dated March 21, 1996, and to two articles in *The New Yorker* that appeared just before the Barkto incident—"An Anthropologist on Mars" (December 27, 1993), which mentions Barkto and discusses autism, and "E-mail from Bill" (January 10, 1994), which refers to the author's interesting interactions with Gates. An article in *Time* entitled "Diagnosing Bill Gates" (January 24, 1994), which speculates about the "interesting" parallels between the two articles, preceded the "Barkto" posts by a matter of days.

37. David Shaw, "Is the Messenger to Blame? Journalist's Cynicism Cited as a Reason for the Nation's Unease," byline referencing the *Los Angeles Times*, *Austin American Statesman* (May 6, 1996), p. D1.

38. Howard Rheingold, *Virtual Communities* (New York: Harper Perennial, 1993), pp. 32–37.

39. Anthony Pratkanis and Elliot Aronson, *Age of Propaganda*, (New York: W. H. Freeman and Company, 1992), pp. 3–4.

40. Colin Gabriel Hatcher, angels@wavenet.com, "CyberAngels Code of Conduct, v.1.5," from e-mail to author dated September 22, 1996.

41. Avery Lackner, 71773,3642@compuserve.com, "#: 651862, Sb: #Ethics of THE book," CANOPUS FORUM, *CompuServe* (May 11, 1996).

42. "CyberAngels—Welcome!" http://proaxis.com/~safetyed/CYBERANGELS/cyberangels01.html (September 23, 1996).

43. Ezra Taft Benson, "Pride," *http://www.lasertone.com/~rc/pride. html* (April 12, 1996).

44. Adam Smith, *The Theory of Moral Sentiments* (New York: Liberty Classics, 1976), pp. 250–251.

45. Turkle, *Life on the Screen,* pp. 210–232.

46. Bill Gates, *The Road Ahead* (New York: Viking Penguin, 1995), p. 219.

47. Joan O'C. Hamilton, "Darwinism and the Internet," *Business Week,* June 26, 1995, p. 44.

48. "Utah System of Higher Education: Technology and Distance Education Initiative," "Mission Statement," http://www.utahsbr.edu/tech/intro.htm (September 24, 1996).

49. "Web66: A K12 World Wide Web Project," http://web66.coled.umn. edu (September 24, 1996).

50. "Web66 at Hillside Elementary School," http://hillside.coled.umn.edu (September 24, 1996).

51. "Speeches by William Gibson and Bruce Sterling," May 10, 1993, National Academy of Sciences Convocation on Technology and Education, Washington D. C., http://www.portnet.k12.ny.us/port2000 /future.htm (April 10, 1996).

52. Jerry Pournelle, private e-mail message to author, September 25, 1996.

53. George Gilder, *Life After Television: The Coming Transformation of Media and American Life,* Revised Edition (New York: W. W. Norton & Company, 1994), p. 49.

CHAPTER 5 Society and Community

1. Stephen Manes and Paul Andrews, *Gates—How Microsoft's Mogul Reinvented an Industry and Made Himself the Richest Man in America* (New York: Doubleday: 1993), p. 424.

2. Beth Freedman, "IBM Creates Post to Push OS/2 2.0 Into Mass Market," *PC Week*, February 17, 1992, pp. 114, 116.

3. Paul Sherer, "Team OS/2 is Preaching IBM Gospel," *PC Week*, March 30, 1992, p.131–132.

4. John C. Dvorak, "Microsoft Under Fierce Attack," *PC Magazine,* November 21, 1995, p. 89.

5. Bob Berger, "The Circuit Rider," *NetGuide*, September 1995, p. 30.

6. Ray Oldenburg, *The Great Good Place: Cafés, Coffee Shops, Community Centers, Beauty Parlors, General Stores, Bars, Hangouts and How They Got You Through the Day* (New York: Paragon House, 1989).

7. From *Famous Quotes,* an infobase distributed on CD-ROM by Infobases International Inc., Orem, Utah.

8. Robert D. Putnam, http://calliope.jhu.edu/journals/journal_of_democracy/v006/putnam.html, "Bowling Alone: America's Declining Social Capital," *Journal of Democracy* 6.01 (January 1995): 65–78.

9. From Nicholas Lemann, "Kicking in Groups," *Atlantic Monthly*, April 1996, p. 22, referencing Edward Banfield's *The Moral Basis of a Backward Society.*

10. Peter Steiner, from *The New Yorker*, 1993.

11. Mercer Harz, 70431,150@compuserve.com, #: 647064, Sb: #646889-SU-U-SU-me, CANOPUS FORUM, *CompuServe* (May 3, 1996). According to Harz, "In terms of copyright, a work is displayed publicly if it is displayed 'at a place open to the public or at any place where a substantial number of persons outside of a normal circle of a family and its social acquaintances is gathered.' That definition is contained in the Copyright Act, 17 U.S.C. 101."

12. United States Constitution, Article 1, Section 8.

13. *United States* v. *Paramount Pictures, Inc.*, 334 U.S. 131, 158 (1948).

14. H.R. Rep. No. 2222, 60th Congress, 2nd Session, 7 (1909) (report accompanying the Copyright Act of 1909).

15. George Washington, address to the officers of the army, Newburgh, New York, March 15, 1783. From *The Writings of George Washington*, ed. John C. Fitzpatrick, vol. 26 (1938), p. 225. From *Famous Quotes.*

16. Adlai E. Stevenson, speech to the state committee of the Liberal party, New York City, August 28, 1952. From *The Papers of Adlai E. Stevenson*, vol. 4 (1974), p. 63. From *Famous Quotes.*

17. Gary Wolf, "Who Owns the Law?" *Wired* 2.05 (May 1994): 98.

18. American Association of Law Libraries Task Force on Citation Formats, http://lawlib.wuacc.edu/aallnet/citeform.html (March 1, 1995), "Report, AALL Task Force on Citation Formats" (October 7, 1996).

19. Rick Georges, http://www.review.net/Lawyer/columnists/futurelaw.1.26.html, Jan. 26, 1995, "Law World Ready for new Public Domain Legal Citation System," *Future Lawyer* (October 7, 1996).

20. John Perry Barlow, "The Economy of Ideas: A Framework for Rethinking Patents and Copyrights in the Digital Age (Everything you know about intellectual property is **wrong**)," *Wired* 2.03 (March 1994), pp. 85–90, 126–129.

21. Thomas Jefferson, http://www.eff.org/pub/EFF/quotes.eff (October 2, 1996), "EFF Quotes Collection 14.5" (October 7, 1996).

22 Barlow, p. 86.

23. Esther Dyson, "Intellectual Value," *Wired* 3.07 (July 1995): p. 137.

24. From press release titled "MCI Statement on Pending Vote in the House Sub-committee on Courts and Intellectual Property on HR 2441," May 13,1996.

25. Jack Rickard, "An Obscenity in Oklahoma and Streetgangs Online," *Boardwatch Magazine,* June 1994, p. 9.

26. Steven Levy, "No Place for Kids? A Parents Guide to Sex on the Net," *Newsweek,* July 3, 1995, p. 48.

27. Philip Elmer-Dewitt, "On a Screen Near You: Cyberporn," *Time,* July 3, 1995, pp. 38–45.

28. Jonathan Wallace and Mark Mangan, *Sex, Laws, and Cyberspace* (New York: Henry Holt and Company, Inc.), pp. 125–152.

29. Ibid, p. 150.

30. Brock N. Meeks, "The Obscenity of Decency," *Wired* 3.06 (June 1995): 86.

31. Michael A. Norwick, "How Many Web Sites Went Dark: An Educated Guess (V.10)," *Boardwatch Magazine,* April 1996, pp. 117–118.

32. Lance Rose, "Legally Online: A Picture Is Only Worth 1,000 Words, but a Dirty Picture Can Bring In a Fortune," *Boardwatch Magazine,* November 1992, p. 26.

33. Catharine A. MacKinnon and Andrea Dworkin, "Pornography and Civil Rights: A New Day for Women's Equality," p. 73, from a review by David A. Orthmann at http://www.igc.apc.org/nemesis/ACLU/Porn/OrthPornCivil. html.

34. Steven Hill and Nina Silver, http://www.igc.apc.org/nemesis/ACLU/Porn/HillSilverOrd1.html, "Civil Rights Anti-Pornography Legislation: Addressing the Harm to Women."

35. Ibid.

36. *Schenck v. United States, Baer v. United States,* 249 U.S. 52 (1919).

37. John Underwood, "How Nasty Do We Wanna Be," *Executive Excellence,* April 1991, p. 20.

38. Bob Metcalfe, "Computer Laws Galore, but One Is Holding Back the Information Age," *InfoWorld,* May 6, 1996, p. 52. See http://www.infoworld.com.

39. Sue Halpern, "Winged Victories," *NetGuide,* February 1995, pp. 52–56.

40. Research by D.I. Hitchcock, as reported by *The Wirthlin Report,* 6.02 (March 1996), determined that there are at least 17 "universal values," including hard work, harmony, helping others, honesty, self-discipline, self-reliance, individual rights, accountability, orderly society, respect for learning, openness to new ideas, freedom of expression, respect for authority, personal freedom, personal achievement, thinking for oneself, and achieving financial success. According to the report, "Though these values are universal, societies differ in terms of the extent to which they adopt each."

41. Leonard J. Arrington and Davis Britton, *The Mormon Experience: A History of the Latter-day Saints* (New York: Vintage Books, 1979), p. 44. The order remained technically in effect for well over a century.

42. Lou Gerstner, http://www.ibm.com/IBM/IBMGives/k12ed/lvgngasp.htm, "Remarks of Louis V. Gerstner, Jr., Chairman and CEO IBM Corporation, at

the National Governors' Association Annual Meeting, Burlington, Vermont, July 30, 1995" (October 12, 1996).

43. John Perry Barlow, http://www.hotwired.com/club/special/transcripts/barlow.html (November 30, 1995), "It's a Poor Workman Who Blames His Tools" (May 2, 1996).

CHAPTER 6 Business and Economics

1. George Stalk, Jr., and Alan M. Webber, "Japan's Dark Side of Time," *Harvard Business Review*, July–August, 1993, pp. 93–94.
2. Bill Gates, *The Road Ahead* (New York: Viking Books, 1995).
3. Ibid, p.158.
4. Cambridge Work-Group Computing Report, "Microsoft Chooses Diversity Over Dominance," December 18, 1995.
5. Debora Spar and Jeffrey J. Bussgang, "Ruling the Net," *Harvard Business Review*, May–June 1996, p. 127.
6. Thomas J. Peters and Robert H. Waterman, *In Search of Excellence* (New York: Harper & Row, 1982), pp. 40–52.
7. Stephen R. Covey, *Principle-Centered Leadership* (New York: Summit Books, 1990), pp. 157–159.
8. Ibid.
9. Kevin Kelly, "The Economics of Ideas," *Wired* 4.06 (June 1996): 150.
10. *Business Week*, 21st-Century Capitalism, Special Issue, p.109.
11. Charles Miles, "The New Network Firm: A Spherical Structure Built on a Human Investment Philosophy," *Organizational Dynamics*, vol. 23 (April 1, 1995), p. 5.
12. According to my notes from the 9th Annual Computer Law Conference, "Communicating and Conducting Business Online," sponsored by the University of Texas School of Law, Austin, Texas, May 16–17, 1996.
13. One of the better papers on this subject can be found at http://www.law.miami.edu/~froomkin/ocean1-7.htm: Michael Froomkin, "Flood Control on the Information Ocean: Living with Anonymity, Digital Cash, and Distributed Databases."
14. Kelly Holland and Amy Cortese, "The Future of Money," *Business Week* (June 12, 1995), p. 69.
15. Esther Dyson, "Intellectual Value," *Wired* 3.07 (July 1995): 137.
16. John C. Dvorak, "Dvorak's Offbeat News Summary," *PC Magazine,* October 11, 1995.
17. Nicholas Negroponte, "The Next Billion Users," *Wired* 4.06 (June 1996): 220.
18. Steve G. Steinberg, "Seek and Ye Shall Find (Maybe)," *Wired* 4.05 (May 1996): 110.
19. Many analysts believe that Microsoft's embrace of open Internet standards will be temporary and that Microsoft will attempt to leverage their dominance in operating systems to gain proprietary control of popular Internet standards such as browser, programming, and interface standards. Gary Reback, an attorney with Wilson Sonsini Goodrich & Rosati in Palo Alto, California, has

brought many similar business practices of Microsoft to light in arguing for new views of antitrust law that recognize such concepts as the "tipping" effect towards market standards, "lock-in" of existing standards, and the "increasing returns" that can be derived from control of such standards through "bad acts." See "Why Microsoft Must be Stopped," *Upside*, 7.02 (February 1995): 52–67.

20. Vic Sussman with Kenan Pollack, "Gold Rush in Cyberspace," *U.S. News & World Report*, November 13, 1995, p. 74.

21. John Naisbitt, interviewed by John Kelly, "Mr. Big Trend," *Wired* 2.10 (October 1994): 115.

22. Roger Lowenstein, "Who's the Fool in Iomega's Skyrocket?" *The Wall Street Journal,* May 23, 1996.

23. James Gleick, http://www.around.com/microsoft.html, "Making Microsoft Safe for Capitalism." First published in *The New York Times Magazine,* November 5, 1995.

24. Ibid.

25. The "Standards FAQ" maintained by Markus Kuhn and available at http://www.cis.ohio-state.edu/hypertext/faq/usenet/standards-faq/faq.html is worth reading.

26. Quoted from the entry for NIST in Yahoo! on May 22, 1996.

27. Marc Andreessen, interviewed by Chip Bayers, "Why Bill Gates Wants to Be the Next Marc Andreessen," *Wired* 3.12 (December 1995): 236.

28. Whit Andrews, "Netscape Resists a Fait Accompli and Gets an Earful," *WebWeek*, 2.10 (July 22, 1996): 1, 58.

29. Others include modem-maker Hayes's attempts to distinguish its modems from clones, Microsoft's use of OLE in its software suite to wrest control of the applications software market, IBM's attempt to use Micro Channel Architecture to rein in the competitive threat of clones, and so on.

30. Steve Mastrianni, from an unpublished article titled "A Few Reasons Why OS/2 Failed (One Person's View)," June 17, 1996.

31. Paul Gillin, from a May 6, 1995, e-mail message to author.

32. Don Peppers and Martha Rogers, "Let's Make A Deal (If You Pay Attention, We'll Pay Your Way)," *Wired* 2.02 (February 1994): 74.

33. A similar scenario is posed by Robert D. Shapiro in a sidebar to "Is Advertising Finally Dead?" *Wired* 2.02 (February 1994): 71.

34. Peppers and Rogers, p. 126.

35. Michael Levine, *Guerrilla P.R.* (New York: HarperCollins, 1993), p. 141.

36. Gillin, from a May 3, 1995, e-mail message to author.

37. Mary Modahl, interviewed by Harvey Blume, "Touchstone," *Wired* 4.05 (May 1996): 127.

38. Cambridge Work-Group Computing Report, "Telecommuting: Popular With Employees, But What Does Management Think?" October 30, 1995, p. 1.

39. Mark Roger, "Communication is Key for Telecommuters," *Indianapolis Business Journal,* Vol. 16, November 27, 1995, p. 14A.

40. John Sanger, "Telecommuting Revolution Carries a Two-edged Sword," *Minneapolis-St. Paul CityBusiness,* Vol. 13, July 7, 1995, p. 8.

41. Dale Buss, "Growing More by Doing Less," *Nation's Business*, Vol. 83, December 1, 1995, p. 18.

42. Peter Drucker, interviewed by Peter Schwarz and Kevin Kelly, "The Relentless Contrarian," *Wired* 4.08 (August 1996): 119.

43. Ibid.

44. Ibid.

45. Abraham Zaleznik, "Managers and Leaders: Are They Different?" *Harvard Business Review*, March–April 1992, p. 127–128.

46. Ibid, p. 132.

47. Fred Hapgood, "The Media Lab at 10," *Wired* 3.11 (November 1995): 142–145.

48. Denise Caruso, "Microsoft Morphs Into a Media Company," *Wired* 4.06 (June 1996): 130.

49. Richard Rapaport, "In His Image," *Wired* 4.11 (November 1996): 172.

50. "Big Fund Companies: Some Funds Join Cyberspace Hype," *The Wall Street Journal*, May 22, 1996.

CHAPTER 7 Government and Politics

1. Sherry Turkle, from a profile by Pamela McCorduck in "Sex, Lies, and Avatars," *Wired* 4.04 (April 1996): 109.

2. Walter Truett Anderson, "Cyberism Becomes Ideology of the '90s," *Long Beach Press-Telegram*, April 3, 1996.

3. Thomas A. Bass, "Being Nicholas," *Wired* 3.11 (November 1995): 200.

4. Simon Davies, "Don't Mourn, Organize!" *Wired* 4.03 (March 1996): 86.

5. Brock Meeks, "The Rogues Gallery," *Wired* 4.04 (April 1996): 80.

6. Barlow, http://numedia.tddc.net/scott/declaration.html (February 8, 1996), "Declaration of the Independence of Cyberspace" (October 22, 1996).

7. George Gilder, *Life After Television*, Revised Edition (New York: W. W. Norton & Company, 1994), p. 216.

8. Thomas A. Bass, "Being Nicholas," *Wired* 3.11 (November 1995): 202.

9. Gilder, p. 202.

10. Wendy Goldman Rohm, "The Inside Story: *United States* v. *Microsoft*," *Information Week*, August 1, 1994, p. 13.

11. Ibid, p. 14.

12. Gary L. Reback and others, "Why Microsoft Must Be Stopped," *Upside*, February 1995, pp. 52–67.

13. John Markoff, "Netscape Notifies Justice Dept. of Its Microsoft Complaint," *The New York Times*, August 7, 1996, p. D4.

14. Ibid, p. 66.

15. John Heilemann, "The Making of the President 2000," *Wired* 3.12 (December 1995): 228.

16. Ibid, p. 222.

17. Andrew Lawler, "Clinton's R&D Achievements Tilt Towards Technology," *Science,* February 23, 1996, p. 1049.

18. Michael Sullivan-Trainor, *Detour: The Truth About the Information Superhighway,* (San Mateo, California: IDG Books Worldwide, Inc., 1994), p. 67.

19. Ibid, p. 153.

20. Garrett Hardin, "The Tragedy of the Commons," *Science,* December 1968, p. 1243.

21. James Fallows, *Breaking the News: How the Media Undermine American Democracy* (New York: Panthon Books, 1996).

22. Bob Beckel, quoted in "How to Influence Press Coverage," *U.S. News & World Report,* February 19, 1996, p. 55.

23. According to Seldes in *The Great Thoughts,* p. 353, a facsimile of the original draft Paine submitted to Thomas Jefferson, published in America by The Thomas Paine Foundation, indicates that Paine was the originator of many of the ideas and poetic prose of the Declaration of Independence, including the following text: "We hold these truths to be Self evident: that all Men are created equal and independent; that from that equal Creation they derive Rights inherent and unalienable; among which are the Preservation of Life, and Liberty, and the Pursuit of Happiness."

24. David G. Post, "Jurisdiction in Cyberspace: Who Makes the Law?" from the proceedings of the 9th Annual Computer Law Conference: Communicating and Conducting Business Online, May 16–17, 1996, Austin, Texas, Tab 1, pp. 3–5.

25. See http://www.state.mn.us/cbranch/ag/memo/txt.

26. Evan I. Schwartz, "Direct Democracy," *Wired* 2.01 (January 1994): 75.

27. Vic Slussman, "A New Precinct: Cyberspace," *U.S. News & World Report,* February 19, 1996, p. 62.

28. John Heilemann, "The GOP Big Tent is Full of Holes," *Wired* 4.04 (April 1996): 64.

29. Howard Fineman, "The Brave New World of Cybertribes," *Newsweek,* February 27, 1995, p. 30.

30. John Balzar, "Africans Get the Word by Radio; Continent's Masses Rely on Broadcasts—but Governments Rule the Waves," *The Los Angeles Times,* October 25, 1995.

31. Todd Lappin, "Déjà Vu All Over Again," *Wired* 3.05 (May 1995): 175.

32. The Editor of HateWatch, "A Guide to Hate Groups on the Internet," http://hatewatch.org (October 23, 1996).

33. Winn Schwartàu, *Information Warfare* (New York: Thunder's Mouth Press, 1994), pp. 14–15.

34. "Quebec Referendum Votes" (October 30, 1995), http://www.southam.com/edmontonjournal/archives/reftest.html, *The Edmonton Journal* (October 23, 1996).

35. The CommerceNet/Nielsen Internet Demographics Survey (November 1995) found that 17% of those surveyed have Internet access and 11% (24 million) have used the Internet in the 3 months prior to the survey.

36. Jim Warren, "Telecomm 'Deform' & Online Campaign Successes," *Boardwatch Magazine*, April 1996, p. 95.

37. From the author's contemporaneous notes of a June 4, 1996, telephone conversation with David Hughes.

38. "Project Vote Smart," http://www.vote-smart.org/about/about.html (October 24, 1996).

39. The Quayle quotes can be found on dozens of Web pages, including http://www.quayle96.org/qquotes.html and http://www.pncl.co.uk/~dienes /quayle.html. Some of the pages reference "The 776 Stupidest Things Ever Said," by Ross and Kathryn Petras.

40. Saul Jerushalmy and Rens Zbignieuw, 1992, "The PC Manifesto, V3.0, Featuring a PC Primer and Revised PC Lexicon," http://www.uib.no/ zoo/brage/ PC.html (October 25, 1996).

41. Edna Negron, "Clinton Consults Motivational Gurus," *Newsday*, January 4, 1995, p. A08. See also Bob Woodward, http://wp1.washingtonpost.com/wpsrv /national/longterm/choice/choice1.htm, "At a Difficult Time, Spiritual Adviser Aided First Lady's Search," *The Washington Post*, June 23, 1996, p. A01.

42. Lee Roderick, *Leading the Charge* (Salt Lake City: Gold Leaf Press, 1995).

43. Schwartàu, p. 352.

CHAPTER 8 The Net of It All

1. Edmund Burke, quoted by Jeffrey R. Holland in a speech attended by author titled "Key to Liberty in Human Heart" delivered June 30, 1996, at Brigham Young University, reported in a July 6, 1996, supplement to the *Deseret News* titled "Church News."

2. Jim Wolf, "U.S. Urges 'Manhattan Project' for Cyber Security," *Reuters News Wire*, July 16, 1996.

3. "German Official Says Internet Needs International Controls," *Dow Jones News Wire*, July 17, 1996,

4. Sherry Turkle, "Who Am We?" *Wired 4.01* (January 1996): 198.

5. From *Famous Quotes*.

6. Ralph Waldo Emerson, 1836, "Nature," http://divweb.harvard.edu/csvpl/ee/ em-1836.htm, (October 28, 1996).

INDEX

440